BISEXUALITY
AND THE
CHALLENGE
TO
LESBIAN
POLITICS

D1560198

THE CUTTING EDGE:
Lesbian Life and Literature

THE CUTTING EDGE:
Lesbian Life and Literature

•

Series Editor: Karla Jay

The Cook and the Carpenter: A Novel by the Carpenter
By June Arnold
With an Introduction by Bonnie Zimmerman

Ladies Almanack
By Djuna Barnes
With an Introduction by Susan Sniader Lanser

Adventures of the Mind:
The Memoirs of Natalie Clifford Barney
Translated by John Spalding Gatton
With an Introduction by Karla Jay

Sophia Parnok: The Life and Work of Russia's Sappho
By Diana Burgin

Paint It Today by H.D. (Hilda Doolittle)
Edited and with an Introduction by
Cassandra Laity

The Angel and the Perverts
By Lucie Delarue-Mardrus
Translated and with an Introduction by Anna Livia

Heterosexual Plots and Lesbian Narratives
By Marilyn R. Farwell

Diana: A Strange Autobiography
By Diana Frederics
With an Introduction by Julie L. Abraham

Lover
By Bertha Harris

Elizabeth Bowen: A Reputation in Writing
By renée c. hoogland

Lesbian Erotics
Edited by Karla Jay

Changing Our Minds: Lesbian Feminism and Psychology
By Celia Kitzinger and Rachel Perkins

(Sem)Erotics: Theorizing Lesbian : Writing
By Elizabeth A. Meese

*Bisexuality and the Challenge to Lesbian Politics:
Sex, Loyalty, and Revolution*
By Paula C. Rust

The Search for a Woman-Centered Spirituality
By Annette J. Van Dyke

*I Know My Own Heart: The Diaries of Anne Lister,
1791–1840*
Edited by Helena Whitbread

No Priest but Love: The Journals of Anne Lister, 1824–26
Edited by Helena Whitbread

THE CUTTING EDGE:
Lesbian Life and Literature

•

Series Editor: Karla Jay
Professor of English and Women's Studies
PACE UNIVERSITY

BISEXUALITY AND THE CHALLENGE TO LESBIAN POLITICS

•

Sex, Loyalty, and Revolution

•

Paula C. Rust

NEW YORK UNIVERSITY PRESS
New York and London

NEW YORK UNIVERSITY PRESS
New York and London

© 1995 by New York University

Library of Congress Cataloging-in-Publication Data
Rust, Paula Claire, 1959–
Bisexuality and the challenge to lesbian politics : sex, loyalty,
and revolution / Paula Claire Rust.
p.   cm. — (The cutting edge)
Includes bibliographical references and index.
ISBN 0-8147-7444-X (cloth).—ISBN 0-8147-7445-8 (pbk.)
1. Lesbians—United States—Attitudes.   2. Lesbians—United
States—Identity.   3. Lesbians—United States—Psychology.
4. Bisexual women—United States—Attitudes.   5. Bisexual women—
United States—Psychology.   6. Bisexuality—Political aspects—
United States.   7. Lesbianism—Political aspects—United States.
8. Sexual behavior surveys—United States.   I. Title.   II. Series:
Cutting edge (New York, N.Y.)
HQ75.6.U5R87   1995   95-31419
305.48'9664—dc20   CIP

New York University Press books are printed on acid-free paper, and
their binding materials are chosen for strength and durability.

Manufactured in the United States of America

10 9 8 7 6 5 4 3 2 1

Dedicated

to all the women who made this study possible
by taking the time to complete a very long questionnaire
in the hope that our lives would become a little less invisible

and

to the memory of
Martin P. Levine
whose encouragement and mentorship
made this book, and my career as I know it, possible.

• CONTENTS •

• FOREWORD •

Despite the efforts of lesbian and feminist publishing houses and a few university presses, the bulk of the most important lesbian works has traditionally been available only from rare-book dealers, in a few university libraries, or in gay and lesbian archives. This series intends, in the first place, to make representative examples of this neglected and insufficiently known literature available to a broader audience by reissuing selected classics and by putting into print for the first time lesbian novels, diaries, letters, and memoirs that are of special interest and significance, but which have moldered in libraries and private collections for decades or even for centuries, known only to the few scholars who had the courage and financial wherewithal to track them down.

Their names have been known for a long time—Sappho, the Amazons of North Africa, the Beguines, Aphra Behn, Queen Christina, Emily Dickinson, the Ladies of Llangollen, Radclyffe Hall, Natalie Clifford Barney, H.D., and so many others from every nation, race, and era. But government and religious officials burned their writings, historians and literary scholars denied they were lesbians, powerful men kept their books out of print, and influential archivists locked up their ideas far from sympathetic eyes. Yet some dedicated scholars and readers still knew who they were, made pilgrimages to the cities and villages where they had lived and to the graveyards where they rested. They passed around tattered volumes of letters, diaries, and biographies, in which they had underlined what seemed to be telltale hints of a secret or different kind of life. Where no hard facts existed, legends were invented. The few precious and often available pre-Stonewall lesbian classics, such as *The Well of Loneliness* by Radclyffe Hall, *The Price of Salt* by Claire Morgan (Patricia Highsmith), and *Desert of the Heart* by Jane Rule, were cherished. Lesbian pulp was devoured. One of the primary goals of this series is to give the more neglected works, which constitute the vast majority of lesbian writing, the attention they deserve.

A second but no less important aim of this series is to present the "cutting edge" of contemporary lesbian scholarship and theory across a wide range of disciplines. Practitioners of lesbian studies have not adopted a uniform approach to literary theory, history, sociology, or any other discipline, nor should they. This series intends to present an array of voices that truly reflects the diversity of the lesbian community. To help me in this task, I am lucky enough to be assisted by a distinguished editorial board that reflects various professional, class, racial, ethnic, and religious backgrounds as well as a spectrum of interests and sexual preferences.

At present the field of lesbian studies occupies a small, precarious, and somewhat contested pied-à-terre between gay studies and women's studies. The former is still in its infancy, especially if one compares it to other disciplines that have been part of the core curriculum of every child and adolescent for several decades or even centuries. However, although it is one of the newest disciplines, gay studies may also be the fastest-growing one—at least in North America. Lesbian, gay, and bisexual studies conferences are doubling and tripling their attendance. Although only a handful of degree-granting programs currently exists, that number is also apt to multiply quickly during the next decade.

In comparison, women's studies is a well-established and burgeoning discipline with hundreds of minors, majors, and graduate programs throughout the United States. Lesbian Studies occupies a peripheral place in the discourse in such programs, characteristically restricted to one lesbian-centered course, usually literary or historical in nature. In the many women's studies series that are now offered by university presses, generally only one or two books on a lesbian subject or issue are included, and lesbian voices are restricted to writing on those topics considered of special interest to gay people. We are not called upon to offer opinions on motherhood, war, education, or on the lives of women not publicly identified as lesbians. As a result, lesbian experience is too often marginalized and restricted.

In contrast, this series will prioritize, centralize, and celebrate lesbian visions of literature, art, philosophy, love, religion, ethics, history, and a myriad of other topics. In "The Cutting Edge," readers can find authoritative versions of important lesbian texts that have been carefully prepared and introduced by scholars. Readers can also find the work of academics and independent scholars who write about other aspects of life from a distinctly lesbian viewpoint. These visions are not only various but intentionally contradictory, for lesbians speak from differing class, racial, ethnic, and religious perspectives. Each author also speaks from and about a certain moment of time, and few would argue that being a lesbian today is the same as it was for Sappho or Anne Lister. Thus, no attempt has been made to homogenize that diversity, and no agenda exists to attempt to carve out a "politically correct" lesbian studies perspective at this juncture in history or to pinpoint the "real" lesbians in history. It seems more important for all the voices to be heard before those with the blessings of aftersight lay the mantle of authenticity on any one vision of the world, or on any particular set of women.

What each work in this series does share, however, is a common realization that gay women are the "Other" and that one's perception of culture and literature is filtered by sexual behaviors and preferences. Those perceptions are not the same as those of gay men or of nongay women, whether the writers speak of gay or feminist issues or whether the writers choose to look at nongay figures from a lesbian perspective. The role of this series is to create space and give a voice to those interested in lesbian studies. This series speaks to any person who is interested in gender studies, literary criticism, biography, or important literary works, whether she or he is a student, professor, or serious reader, for the series is neither for lesbians only nor even by lesbians only. Instead, "The Cutting Edge" attempts to share some of the best of lesbian literature and lesbian studies with anyone willing to look at the world through lesbians' eyes. The series is proactive in that it will help to formulate and foreground the very discipline on which it focuses. Finally, this series has answered the call to make lesbian theory, lesbian experience, lesbian lives, lesbian literature, and lesbian visions the heart and nucleus, the weighty planet around which, for once, other viewpoints will swirl as moons to our earth. We invite readers of all persuasions to join us by venturing into this and other books in the series.

We are pleased to include Paula C. Rust's *Bisexuality and the Challenge to Lesbian Politics: Sex, Loyalty, and Revolution* in The Cutting Edge series. Like *Changing Our Minds: Lesbian Feminism and Psychology* by Celia Kitzinger and Rachel Perkins, Rust tackles a controversial topic within the lesbian community. In a thoughtful study that is both enlightening and provocative, Rust analyzes the bisexual woman, a person who has often been marginalized or even scorned within the lesbian community. Bisexual women and men will find this book affirming, and those who are either firmly homosexual or heterosexual will find this book to be a treasure of useful knowledge.

KARLA JAY
Professor of English and Women's Studies
Pace University

• Acknowledgments •

First and foremost, I am deeply grateful to the 470 women who took the time to participate in this study during its many interview and questionnaire phases, from the "speed demon" who completed the questionnaire in a mere 45 minutes to everyone who gave five or six hours of their lives to help make this project happen. Special thanks go to the six women who assisted me by conducting the early phase interviews, giving me feedback on the questionnaire, and finally distributing questionnaires to several hundred women: Beth Masck, Beverly Santiago, Debbie Hillebrand, Elizabeth S., Lorna Rodríguez Rust, and Susan Gold.

I would also like to thank the members of my dissertation committee, who supported me in the research on which this book is based. When I decided to do research on lesbians' attitudes about issues that are important within the lesbian community instead of research on a "safe" topic with a "broader" appeal, I thought I was risking my career. Who would take me seriously, and how would I ever find a job? Mary Jackman, Mayer Zald, Beth Reed, and Mark Chesler enthusiastically supported me throughout the project. My most sincere thanks go to Mary Jackman, who spent many, many hours straining her eyes over the initial draft of my dissertation, patiently wading through pages of detailed digressions and writing over and over again the comment "cut drastically." The support I received from the University of Michigan extended beyond the efforts of individual faculty; the Horace H. Rackham School of Graduate Studies gave me the grant that made the research possible.

I am also grateful to those people who have supported me since, including the members of my department at Hamilton College who are my friends as well as my colleagues, Doug Raybeck who gave me the nudge I needed to start publishing the findings of my research, Niko Pfund of New York University Press who was interested enough in my work to inquire about it, Karla Jay who accepted it as part of her series "The Cutting Edge," all the editors and anonymous reviewers along the way who taught me the writing skills I thought I had, my mother Mildred Rust who eagerly reads everything I write, and both my parents for giving me a solid start in life and a love of knowledge. In addition, several undergraduate student assistants helped with various stages of data preparation and coding. My thanks to each of them, especially Jacqueline Vargas and Danielle LaGrange for doing the most tedious kinds of work carefully and cheerfully at all hours of the day and night. The book you hold in your hands is not a revised dissertation; it is a book written from the ground up with the help and support of many people.

Finally, my deepest gratitude and love go to my most enthusiastic supporter, Lorna Rodríguez Rust, who has been with me through everything for the last eleven years. I saw her through her board exams, and now she has seen me through the birth of my first book.

• INTRODUCTION •

—I feel people who think they are bisexual are confused about it, or in transition.

—It does not exist.

—Everyone is inherently bisexual.

—Bisexuals are indiscriminate—they just sleep with anybody.

—People who love people regardless of sex.

—In a more egalitarian society, I'd be much more supportive of women who choose to sleep with men, but now, I'd prefer them to unite with lesbian women and build the strength of our community and movement.

Bisexuality touches very sensitive personal and political nerves among lesbians. The very idea sparks heated debate. Does bisexuality really exist, or is it a phase one goes through while coming out as lesbian? Are bisexuals women who have succeeded in casting off the repressive strictures of our sex-phobic society in order to express the full range of their sexuality, or are they lesbians suffering from an internalized homophobia that prevents them from recognizing their true sexual nature? Is bisexuality a sign of political cowardice among those who are unwilling to give up heterosexual privilege, or is it the next step in sexual liberation?

Bisexuals are beginning to organize politically. Local bisexual organizations that began as support groups have become increasingly political and begun to network with each other. In June of 1990, the North American Multicultural Bisexual Network[1] was founded at the BiPOL conference in San Francisco; in October of 1991, the First International Bisexual Conference was held in Amsterdam; in April of 1993, bisexuals marched in the National March on Washington for Lesbian, Gay *and Bi*

Rights and Liberation; and in June of 1994, the Third International
Conference Celebrating Bisexuality was held in New York City. Lesbian
and gay organizations at colleges and universities are changing their
names to include the word Bisexual. Newly established newsletters provide a forum for political bisexual voices, and books by and for bisexuals, including *Bi Any Other Name: Bisexual People Speak Out* and
Closer to Home: Bisexuality & Feminism, have begun to appear.

This movement is still in the initial stages of building an ideological
and organizational foundation. It will remain invisible to the general
heterosexual population for quite some time, but the rumblings are
already heard within the political lesbian community. As these rumblings
grow louder, the debate over bisexuality in the lesbian community inten-
sifies. The question of whether the lesbian movement is approaching a
"crisis" is a matter of semantics that is best left to propagandists. Of
much greater interest is the question of why bisexuality is such a focal
point of attention among lesbians. What are the issues raised by bisexuality, and why are these issues of concern to lesbians? What does the
lesbian debate over bisexuality reveal about the political and cultural
ideology of lesbianism and the structure of the lesbian movement?

In order to understand the issues, it is necessary to listen to lesbian
voices. Some of these voices are found in the newsletters and magazines
produced by the lesbian movement, whereas others are not. The former
are more likely to be the voices of politically active lesbians with extreme
views and time to spend writing political statements. Are these voices
representative of lesbians in general, or are they merely the voices of the
few vocal lesbians who have opinions and the resources to express them?
Can the rank-and-file lesbian who conceals her identity for fear of losing
her child and her job be bothered about the issue of bisexuality, and if
so, does she share the opinions that are expressed in the newsletter that
arrives at her post office box in a plain brown envelope?

It is also useful to listen to the voices of social scientists, not as
"experts" but as social commentators whose opinions and analyses carry
the weight of authority. These voices are of particular consequence
because they are considered the voices of reason, objectivity, and truth.
As such, they define the neutral position from which other positions will
be judged as partisan, self-interested, or uninformed. Social scientists
are, however, as much products of their social environment as the people
they study. Their opinions serve as a particular kind of mirror for social

issues, a mirror that dissects and detects but that ultimately reflects light produced by other sources.

You, the reader of this book, will hear these voices through another voice. That voice is mine. Throughout the book, I defer whenever possible to the original voices of the women who wrote articles in the lesbian press and the women who participated in my study. However, short of publishing in raw form the approximately 15,000 pages of questionnaire responses and interview transcripts that form the basis of this study, I cannot help but superimpose my voice on theirs. Simply by choosing which quotes to include and then by organizing this material, I place my stamp upon it. You should, therefore, know who I am.

I am a white, able-bodied, lesbian-identified feminist sociologist. Allow me to elaborate. Lesbian feminist culture has been my "home" culture since I attended my first Daughters of Bilitis meeting in 1977 at the age of 18. That doesn't mean that I consider lesbian feminism above criticism or that I agree with everything that has ever been said in the name of lesbian feminism. On the contrary, because it is my culture I claim the moral right and obligation to criticize it as an outsider cannot. I was out and politically active as a lesbian in both college and graduate school. Now, as an associate professor, I am out to those who care to know as well as many who don't, but my political energy has been diverted toward the task of managing my career. I console myself by thinking that simply being out as a lesbian professor is a political act.

I have been studying lesbian cultures and communities since 1982, when I interviewed about two dozen lesbians ranging in age from their teens to their seventies. I talked to these women about several issues, and bisexuality was one of them. In the mid 1980s, I decided to do something I thought I would never do again—I became involved with a man for the first time in several years. I continued to identify as a lesbian, a fact that was known to all parties involved and eventually led to the end of the relationship a few months later. In the meantime, however, I became more deeply aware of my own attitudes toward bisexuality as well as the attitudes of the great monolithic Lesbian Community—you know, the one that sets the standards for political correctness and the one that nobody I know will admit belonging to.

That experience helped shape my next research project, which was a study of lesbian and bisexual women's attitudes toward, among other things, bisexuality. Over four hundred women took part in the study, which forms the basis of this book and is described in greater detail in chapter 3. As a result of this work I became fascinated by the concept of bisexuality. It would appear that I have done so at an opportune moment in history, because the beginning and growth of the bisexual movement is causing bisexuality to become a politically hot topic. By the same token, however, I have become interested in bisexuality at a very sensitive historical moment as well.

When I announce to my friends that I am studying bisexuality, I receive a variety of reactions, including expressions of all of the attitudes that I describe in this book. I am frequently asked "Are you bisexual?" or, more pointedly, "You're not bisexual, are you?" This is a very difficult question to answer. First, since I no longer conceptualize sexuality as essential, I don't see myself "as" anything. Second, the question of whether I am bisexual (or whether anyone else is) depends on how one defines bisexuality. Each definition makes internal sense; pick one and I'll answer the question. Finally, the answer depends on which of my many selves is being asked the question. My political self? My sexual self? My emotional self? My sociologist self? By the time I finish explaining why I find it difficult to answer the question, my inquirer has usually answered the question to her own satisfaction as you, the reader, also may have done by now. As I said above, I am a white, able-bodied, *lesbian-identified* feminist sociologist.

Having introduced myself, I will lay down my personal pen (or computer keyboard, as it were) and pick up my (ahem) objective social scientist's pen. This pen usually writes in the third person, as if I were not a lesbian myself and as if I did not share and sympathize with the feelings of the women who participated in my study, and it occasionally transforms inanimate objects and abstract ideas into the subjects of sentences, but it writes with my accent.

The first chapter looks at the debate on bisexuality as it appears in lesbian newsletters and magazines. What issues are raised and what opinions are expressed in this forum? Who is speaking and who is listening? How is the issue of bisexuality constructed by those who are speaking and for those who are listening? Chapter 2 examines the recent writings of social scientists on the subjects of sexuality, lesbianism, and bisexuality. What have researchers discovered about lesbians and the lesbian community? What have they discovered about bisexuals? How do social scientists conceptualize sexuality, and where do lesbianism and bisexuality fit into these models of sexuality?

Chapter 3 introduces the study of lesbian and bisexual women that forms the basis of most of the book. It describes the methods used and the sample obtained. The uninterested reader can easily skip this chapter, or read only the segment entitled "The Women Who Responded" for a description of the race, class, age, sexual, and other demographic characteristics of the women who took part in the study. Chapter 4 describes the attitudes of self-identified lesbian respondents toward sexuality in general and bisexuality in particular. Are the issues raised by these women similar to those raised in the lesbian press? How do these women feel about the issues? How do they think about sexuality, what does bisexuality mean to them, and how do they feel about bisexual women? Chapter 5 looks at whether lesbians of different races, ages, and so forth have different opinions about bisexuality, and whether or not lesbians' opinions depend on their own political orientations or personal experiences with sexuality. Chapter 6 analyzes the development of lesbian identity as a political identity through the turbulent feminist debates of the 1970s. In this chapter, I argue that bisexuality is a controversial issue for lesbians today because it touches sensitive nerves and uncovers disagreements that arose from these formative debates and were never resolved. The issue that excites us is not really bisexuality; the real issue is lesbianism. The so-called bisexual debate is really a debate over who we are and what we stand for as lesbians. In the last two chapters of the book, I turn my attention to bisexual women. In chapter 7, I describe their thoughts and feelings about bisexuality and sexuality in general, and in chapter 8, I take a brief look at the burgeoning literature written by and for bisexuals to see how bisexuals are beginning to develop an identity and a politics of their own. The development of a bisexual politic has the potential to radically alter sexual identity politics, and in this last chapter I examine the profound challenge it poses to the future of lesbian identity and lesbian politics.

1

DEBATE IN THE LESBIAN PRESS: INTRODUCING THE ISSUES

What does The Lesbian Community think about bisexuality? Before we can answer that question, we have to determine who The Lesbian Community is, and who speaks for It. The truth is that there is no single, monolithic Lesbian Community. At the very least, there are many different lesbian communities. Lesbian communities exist in many towns and cities. Even within a single town or city, there are often several lesbian communities. There might be communities of African-American lesbians, Euro-American lesbians, Asian-American lesbians, and Latina lesbians. Younger and older lesbians, lesbians who are politically active and lesbians who are closeted, working class, middle class, and upper class lesbians, temporarily able-bodied and physically challenged lesbians, softball players, lesbians in 12-step programs, and computer jocks might have separate communities of their own. Within our communities, each one of us experiences community differently, and many of us belong to more than one lesbian community. If you asked two of your lesbian friends to draw pictures of the lesbian community you share, they would probably draw pictures that were very different from each

7

other and different from the picture you would draw. We are all individuals. We have different needs, and we have different ideas about what lesbian community should be and what it is.

The Lesbian Community as a monolithic entity does not exist. But even if we recognize It as a fiction, most of us probably have a concept of The Lesbian Community and an image of what this Community is like. Intellectually, we know that lesbians have a variety of different opinions and experiences, but we still find ourselves saying, "the lesbian community thinks . . . " or "the lesbian community is. . . . " Intellectually, we know that there is no Lesbian Goddess of Political Correctness, but we still find ourselves engaged in a struggle over the rules She has set down. Intellectually, we know that lesbians who live in different parts of the country or whose skins are different colors might have different experiences as lesbians, but many of us feel a kinship across these differences because we are all lesbians. None of us can know every lesbian personally, and yet when we travel to a city we have never visited before, we feel at home. The women at the Center and the women at the bar look familiar, and we know how to talk to them.

Where do our images of The Lesbian Community come from? For most of us, our actual experience of lesbian community consists of our experiences within our local lesbian communities, which might be more or less homogeneous with regard to race, age, and class. But we don't need to have personal contact with other lesbians to know something about them. We read about them in lesbian and gay newsletters, newspapers, and magazines. The Lesbian and Gay Press tells us what lesbians in other places are doing and thinking, what is happening to them, and what their concerns are. This information has a profound effect on our images of The Lesbian Community, especially for those of us who live in rural areas or towns where there are few other lesbians and little local lesbian community. The Lesbian and Gay Press is our means of communication with each other.

The printed word also defines and creates reality. If an event is reported in lesbian and gay publications, then it is an important event and we can all find out about it. If it is not reported, then as far as The Lesbian Community is concerned, it might as well not have happened. If a lesbian publication runs an article about a particular issue, it sparks discussion among us. It might not have been more important than another issue that was not covered, but it soon becomes more important because it is the issue that "everyone is talking about." Soon, because we have been talking about this issue, we form opinions about it. Then we discover that we have different opinions. Then we discover that it *is* an issue because we are disagreeing with each other. We might even think to ourselves that before we read about it in our favorite lesbian magazine, we did not realize what a controversial issue it was. The Lesbian and Gay Press does not merely inform us about our Lesbian Community, it also plays an important role in creating our image of that Community, and in creating the Community itself.

But The Lesbian and Gay Press is not a monolithic entity any more than The Lesbian Community is a monolithic entity. We have a variety of different publications, each produced by a different group of people who have their own visions of The Lesbian Community. Each publication reaches a different audience, and each gives its audience the vision of its producers. If you were a rural lesbian whose only access to knowledge was a subscription to *The Advocate*, what would your impression of The Lesbian Community's attitude toward bisexuality be? Would you even think it was an issue at all? What if the nearest lesbian, ten miles away, subscribed to *Lesbian Contradiction* instead of *The Advocate?* How would her impression of The Lesbian Community's attitude toward bisexuality differ from yours?

To find out how The Lesbian Community is represented in The Lesbian and Gay Press on the issue of bisexuality, I selected a variety of different lesbian and gay publications. Because I wanted to find out how The Lesbian Community is portrayed in publications that reach a large number of lesbians and that appear to speak for all lesbians rather than for particular locales or constituencies, I favored national magazines but included a few newspapers and newsletters with large circulations. I chose to concentrate my attention on *The Advocate, Out/Look, 10 Percent,* and *Lesbian Contradiction.*[1] But before we examine the ways in which each of these publications portrays The Lesbian Community's opinions about bisexuality, we have to know something about the population each publication appears or claims to represent. Who reads each publication, and whose view of The Lesbian Community is portrayed by each publication?

THE PUBLICATIONS

The Advocate, Out/Look, 10 Percent, and *Lesbian Contradiction* claim national readerships. But each of these publications represents a particular segment of the lesbian and gay community and fulfills particular needs for its readers.

The cover of *The Advocate* proclaims the magazine to be "The National Gay and Lesbian Newsmagazine." "The" implies that *The Advocate* not only represents the gay and lesbian community, but that it is the only newsmagazine that does so. In short, it proclaims itself the quintessential representation of newsworthy happenings in the national gay and lesbian community. It is, in fact, a magazine with 58,000 paid subscribers[2], which celebrated its twenty-fifth anniversary in October 1992. The word "Lesbian" is a recent addition to the cover of *The Advocate,* which said "The National Gay Newsmagazine" until September 1990. As a Gay Newsmagazine, *The Advocate*'s focus was primarily gay male. Since 1990, coverage of lesbian issues has increased, and by the end of 1993, the editorial staff was one-third female, up from one-fifth a year earlier. To a large extent, the magazine fulfills its promise to represent both gay men and lesbians by focusing on news stories that are of interest to both sexes because they pertain to lesbian and gay rights in heterosexual society, and by including cover and feature stories on prominent lesbians and lesbian issues. Nevertheless, gay men and gay male issues still receive greater coverage. In 1994, seventy percent of the regular columnists and contributing writers were male. The magazine has a slick, supermarket checkout stand look; it is printed in color on glossy paper with photos or artwork on every two-page spread and commercial advertisements covering one-third of the page space.

The banner on the cover of *Out/Look* described the magazine as a "National Lesbian & Gay Quarterly." The first issue of the magazine was published in Spring 1988. In Spring 1992, Managing Editor Robin Stevens announced that the magazine was in financial trouble and needed contributions. In the following issue, Stevens announced that contributions had exceeded the amount necessary to bring the magazine back to financial health and that it was no longer in danger of folding. It was the last issue of *Out/Look* ever published. *Out/Look* focused on lesbian and gay male culture and ran cover and feature stories about political and cultural issues that arose *within* the lesbian and gay communities rather than news about our gains and losses vis-à-vis heterosexual society. The fact that *Out/Look* called itself a "Lesbian and Gay" magazine, whereas *The Advocate* calls itself a "Gay and Lesbian" magazine is symbolic; *Out/Look* achieved a greater balance in its coverage of lesbian and gay male topics. Gender balance had been a goal of the magazine since its inception, and this goal was reflected in the magazine's editorial staff, which ranged from forty to sixty percent female.[3] With a circulation of 17,000, *Out/Look* was not as glitzy as *The Advocate*. The front and back covers displayed color artwork, but the inside pages were printed in black and white on non-glossy paper and had far fewer commercial advertisements than *The Advocate*.

When *Out/Look* folded, subscribers received issues of the new magazine *10 Percent*. The masthead of the first anniversary issue described the magazine as "The magazine of people, arts, and culture for lesbians and gay men." The magazine is less narrowly focused on gayness than some other "lesbian and gay" magazines; although most articles concern specifically gay-related topics, others take gayness for granted as they focus primarily on topics of more "general" interest. For example, some articles in the "Environments" department would fit well in *Homes* magazine except for the respective genders of the people who own the gorgeous homes pictured in the large, full-color photographs. *10 Percent* caters to the reader who can afford to take ski vacations[4] and start small businesses.[5] It provides some political information, but *10 Percent* is most accurately described as overtly apolitical with a subtle leaning toward the conservative end of the gay spectrum. While other lesbian and gay magazines reported on the March on Washington, *10 Percent* gave readers tips about which gay historical sites to visit after the March.[6]

Lesbian Contradiction boldly proclaims itself "A Journal of Irreverent Feminism." The name says it all. Whereas *10 Percent* avoids controversy, *Lesbian Contradiction* has rushed headlong toward controversy since the very first issue, dated Winter 1982/83. Whereas *Out/Look* attempted to balance representation of women and men, *Lesbian Contradiction* is exclusively for women. Whereas *The Advocate* represents the gay mainstream, *Lesbian Contradiction* takes lesbian feminism as thesis and antithesis. *Lesbian Contradiction* is a forum for the debate of the "issues" that are so plentiful in lesbian feminism. Published on newsprint four times a year, *Lesbian Contradiction* does not accept commercial advertising and reports 1,000 paying subscribers.

COVERAGE OF BISEXUALITY IN THE LESBIAN AND GAY PRESS

The treatment of bisexuality in The Lesbian and Gay Press in the 1980s and 1990s shows several patterns. The most dramatic pattern is a historical one. In the 1980s, the issue was constructed in terms of lesbians or gay men having heterosex. Not until the late 1980s or early 1990s did bisexuality per se emerge as an issue. Some lesbian and gay publications made this transition earlier than others. Publications also differed from each other in the degree to which they presented the issue as important or controversial. Some portrayed bisexuality as an issue with important implications for lesbian and gay politics in general, devoting a great deal of space to articles about bisexuality and subsequent letters from readers. Other publications gave bisexuality little more than passing mention or treated it as an uncontroversial news item. Finally, once bisexuality per se became an issue, different publications identified the source of controversy differently and gave voice to different interest groups.

With its long publishing history, *The Advocate* provides a rare opportunity to observe the construction of bisexuality as an issue through the 1980s and early 1990s. In the 1980s, *The Advocate* published articles bearing titles like "Gay Men, Lesbians and Sex" by Pat Califia (July, 1983), "Yes, I'm Still a Lesbian—Even Though I Love a Man" by Harriet Laine (July, 1986), and "Unresolved Harmonies: The Ups and Downs of Not Quite Coming Out" by Mark Chaim Evans (November, 1989). None of these authors felt that the term "bisexual" described their experiences, although the theme of each article was the fact that the author had sexual desire or actual sex with members of both sexes. Califia acknowledged the possibility that her behavior might appear bisexual to others and explained why she could not identify herself as bisexual. In the same article, she offered an analysis of the social construction of sexuality and identity politics that placed bisexual identity on a par with other sexual identities. Laine did not mention bisexuality once. On the contrary, Laine considered herself no less a lesbian because she was having sex with a man and would "like to think that the definition of lesbian is not so constrained" that it excludes sex with men. Likewise, Evans referred to bisexuality only once, commenting that "I find it hard to believe in bisexuality."

The articles by Califia, Laine, and Evans represent the opinions of Califia, Laine, and Evans, but the letters to the editor that followed these articles represent the opinions of *The Advocate*'s readers. These letters indicate that, to the extent that *The Advocate*'s readers felt there was an issue at all in the 1980s, they accepted the authors' construction of the issue as one of heterosex among lesbians and gays; none reconstructed the issue in terms of bisexuality.

For example, subsequent to Califia's article, *The Advocate* printed one brief letter to the editor in which a male[7] reader expressed his appreciation of Califia's ability to "share bodies with other-gender partners without suffering identity crisis."[8] The letter did not use the term bisexual, but implicitly applauded Califia's ability to resist such a classification. Three years later, Laine's article generated a more lively response. Two male readers applauded Laine for her humanity and humanism and chastised those who would demand that she conform to narrow sexual scripts, and one female reader reproached Laine for presuming to call herself a lesbian and expending her energy on a man instead of using it to support womyn and the lesbian community[9]— exactly the attitude the male readers had condemned. None of these readers used the word "bisexual;" the male readers complimented Laine's "humanity," and the female reader informed Laine that she was "at least during the act, a heterosexual. Not a lesbian." Evans's article generated no controversy, possibly because as a man, Evans was not subject to lesbian identity rules and because, unlike Laine, he did not seek to defend his choices as informed and intentional. Instead, Evans invited readers to understand his story as an unfinished process of coming out, a familiar and politically unthreatening construction of his experience. Regardless of what accounts for the differences in the vigor of readers' responses to these three articles, one thing is clear: the issue for all three authors and their readers was not *bisexuality;* the issue was people who identify as lesbian/gay having sex with members of the other sex.

But some of *The Advocate*'s readers were beginning to think about bisexuality as an issue and to communicate this view to the magazine. In

1985, two letters to the editor criticized the magazine's previous year-in-review issue for missing opportunities to refer respectfully to bisexuality. One female reader asked why the word bisexual was put in quotation marks in a paragraph about Elton John and asked the magazine's gay readers not to trivialize bisexuality.[10] In a similar vein, a male reader pointed out that an article on Jacob Holdt referred to him as heterosexual and then quoted him talking about the experience of sex with a man. This reader challenged the magazine to tell the truth, which, in his opinion, is that Holdt must therefore be bisexual.[11] In 1989, Brian Miller wrote an article that bore a title similar to those published earlier in the decade, "Women Who Marry Gay Men."[12] Two issues later, a letter from reader William Wedin, Executive Director of the Bisexual Information and Counseling Service in New York City, criticized Miller for failing to acknowledge bisexuality as an authentic orientation. Wedin explained why this particular criticism came in 1989 but no earlier by commenting that Miller's "bi bashing" had come "at a time when bisexuals and their partners are just beginning to find a measure of self-respect." Miller defended himself by pointing out that the men he had interviewed were self-identified as gay, not bisexual. But apparently Wedin was not the only reader who perceived the men in Miller's article as unacknowledged bisexuals. In the next issue, a female reader offered her marriage to a bisexual man as an example that, contrary to the message given by Miller's article, such marriages can work.

Pat Califia was the first regular contributor to *The Advocate* to identify bisexuality as an issue and focus an article on it. In November 1990, she published a letter in her "Advisor" column from a reader married to a bisexual man, and although bisexuality was not the central issue in the letter, Califia took the opportunity to assert that there is such a thing as bisexuality. She gently dismissed the narrow definition of a bisexual as someone who "is always equally attracted to men and women and has exactly equal numbers of male and female sex partners" in favor of a broader definition of bisexuals as "men and women who have strong sexual or romantic feelings about members of both genders, who are capable of having sex or relationships with either men or women."[13]

Thereafter, bisexuality per se made infrequent appearances in *The Advocate*. In June 1991, the magazine printed a one-page article written by bisexual activists Lani Kaahumanu and Loraine Hutchins entitled

"Do bisexuals have a place in the gay movement?"[14] Kaahumanu and Hutchins, who had just published the anthology *Bi Any Other Name,* argued that bisexuals had always been involved in the "gay rights movement." They demanded the recognition of bisexual existence and the end of intolerance on the part of gays and lesbians in the movement. In July 1992, Lily Braindrop documented the growth of the bisexual movement and community and the push for explicit bisexual inclusion in the lesbian and gay movement, and challenged lesbian and gay attitudes about bisexuality in "Bi and Beyond." *The Advocate*'s letters to the editor column gave no indication that readers noticed the striking contrast between these articles' intentionally political approach to bisexuality and the approach that marked the 1980s, nor that readers had much of a reaction to the articles at all.

Meanwhile, *The Advocate* continued to publish articles about people who had sex with both sexes that referred tangentially if at all to bisexuality. For example, in 1990, Sandra Bernhard discussed her relationship with a straight man; the word "bisexual" did not appear in the article.[15] In 1992, Chunovic quoted Dack Rambo as saying, "I think a lot of people don't believe in a thing called bisexuality," implying that he believes that it exists but he doesn't apply that term—or any term— to himself.[16] In the next issue, Nona Hendryx's interviewer used the word "bisexual," and Hendryx did not reject the word but said, "I try to think of myself as asexual."[17] None of these articles gave any hint that bisexuality per se might be an issue in the lesbian and gay community, an impression that was reinforced by the lack of letters to the editor about these articles in subsequent issues of *The Advocate*.[18]

In the Lesbian and Gay Community represented by *The Advocate,* bisexuality is only one issue among many, and it is not a particularly controversial one at that. The issue of bisexuality did not supplant the issue of lesbians and gays having heterosex; instead, it simply joined an ongoing lesbian and gay discourse that was otherwise left unchanged. To the extent that bisexuality is an issue at all in *The Advocate,* the issue is whether bisexuals should be included in the lesbian and gay movement, and the weight of public opinion is in favor of inclusion. Lesbian feminists who object to bisexuality on political grounds are rarely heard from and marginalized as narrow-minded political extremists, whereas bisexuals themselves are applauded for their humanism and liberated thinking.

In contrast, *Out/Look* presented bisexuality as a controversial issue with important implications for lesbian and gay discourse. During its brief life, *Out/Look* published two articles relevant to the issue of bisexuality. In 1990, the cover announced an article by Jan Clausen entitled "My Interesting Condition" with the caption "When Lesbians Fall for Men" and a drawing of Cupid aiming an arrow into the breast of a woman wearing double women's symbol and "DYKE" buttons.[19] In Spring 1992, the cover of *Out/Look* asked "What do bisexuals want?" The headline graced a drawing of a woman in a short tight skirt holding the arm of a man and looking over her shoulder at a butch lesbian. She looked startled, and the thought bubble above her head was filled with exclamation points and question marks.

Similar to the approach used by 1980s *Advocate* articles, the issue in the autobiographical article "My Interesting Condition" was a lesbian-identified woman who became involved with a man, not bisexuality. But unlike the authors of *The Advocate* articles, Clausen dealt directly with the question of bisexuality. She explained that she did not identify as bisexual because she was reluctant to become invested in a new identity and because she did "not know what 'bisexual' desire would be, since my desire is always for a specifically sexed and gendered individual." Clausen characterized lesbian feminism as a way of life that is "very hard on women," and asked lesbian feminists to be more gentle with each other by relaxing their demands that the personal conform to narrow political prescripts.

Clausen's article was like a footstep in a minefield. The Spring issue included four letters from readers about Clausen's article. Two thanked Clausen for the article, one threatened to cancel her subscription to *Out/Look,* and the fourth blasted Clausen for claiming to be a lesbian.[20] All four letters were from women. But this was not the end of the furor. Reader response increased with the next issue of *Out/Look,* which included no less than seven letters: four applauding, three condemning. The four positive letters were from a bisexual activist woman, two men, and an anonymous reader, whereas the three negative letters were from two women and an anonymous reader.[21] The debate continued through the next two issues. In Fall 1990 and Winter 1991—a full year after the publication of the Clausen article—two female readers defended Clausen against the critical letters published the previous Spring and Summer.

The flurry of letters following Clausen's article clearly presented bisexuality as a controversial issue, particularly among women. But what *was* the issue, as reflected in these letters? On the positive side, Clausen was applauded for encouraging the acceptance of difference within the lesbian community, for speaking on behalf of those who feel alienated from the lesbian community because of their attractions to or relationships with men, for her courage in bucking the lesbian feminist paradigm, for her intelligence and freedom, and for writing honestly about a very human situation. On the negative side, she was criticized for writing about the wonders of heterosexual fucking in a magazine whose readers were looking for affirmation of their lesbianism and gayness, for using patriarchal arguments to attempt to excuse her "failures as a woman-identified-woman," for not having realized yet that only another woman can offer her true freedom, and for reaping "the benefits of the heterosexual world while homosexual women continue to struggle for legal and social advancement." She was also accused of posing a greater threat to the lesbian community than homophobes pose because women like her "dilute and pollute the very definition and essence of lesbianism" by calling themselves lesbians. One reader wrote, "I don't consider any woman a 'dyke' who sleeps with a man. Period." Clausen's Fall 1990 defender pointed out that some of the points made in readers' letters were not responsive to Clausen's article at all. She wrote that "the letters ignored what for me was the most significant point: that Clausen no longer feels she can attach a label to her sexuality. This point was made quite clearly, and I am confused by the letters condemning her for continuing to call herself lesbian." [22]

The fact that letters ostensibly written in response to Clausen's article were less than completely responsive to the article itself suggests that Clausen's article was only a trigger. Most of the women who wrote to the editor were obviously engaged in a much larger ongoing debate with a rather complicated history. The two men who wrote brief complimentary letters were apparently not party to the same discourse. Whether they were actually unaware of the heavy political debate within which Clausen's experiences took place, or whether, as men, they could not participate in this debate, their letters gave the impression that they were peacefully oblivious to the bullets flying past their ears.

Out/Look's Spring 1992 issue on bisexuality included fifteen pages of cartoons and a selection of articles titled "What do bisexuals want?"

"Just add water: Searching for the Bisexual politic," "Strangers at home: Bisexuals in the queer movement," and "Love and rockets." Under the titles, the authors explored the debate about bisexuality, analyzing the political sources of lesbians' concerns—and secondarily, the concerns of gays in general—about bisexuality and outlining the strategic and ideological difficulties facing the bisexual movement.

In the next issue, the editors wrote that they had "received a striking number of responses" to the issue on bisexuality, and that "Curiously enough, the last time we received this much mail was in response to Jan Clausen's 'My Interesting Condition'." "Tender spot?" they rhetorically questioned their readers. According to the editors, most of the letters they had received were from "bisexuals who felt uncomfortable with the constraints of a 'debate' around bisexuality as we had posited it." They included excerpts from these letters in a sidebar that spanned the length of a printed dialogue among three bisexual writer/activists who presented their views of what the issues really were. Amanda Udis-Kessler, Elizabeth Reba Weise, and Sarah Murray explained that bisexuals are diverse people with a variety of personal needs and political goals. Weise pinpointed the growth of the lesbian and gay movement during the 1970s and 1980s—especially the emergence of a political lesbian identity—as the source of the current antipathy toward bisexuality, and Udis-Kessler attributed the recent growth of a political bisexual identity to this antipathy. Weise also pointed out that some of the most active leaders in the lesbian movement were really bisexual women who either repressed part of themselves in the name of lesbian purity or remained quiet about their involvements with men, and who had recently begun to show "a little more of the reality of their lives." Bisexuals were not outsiders seeking to ride lesbian and gay coat-tails, but insiders who were finally being honest about themselves.

In the Lesbian and Gay Community represented by *Out/Look*, bisexuality is a very controversial issue with important implications for lesbian and gay discourse. In 1990, Clausen established a connection between "lesbians who sleep with men" and "bisexuality," thereby constructing bisexuality not as a new issue to be added to an existing repertoire, but as a challenge to ongoing lesbian and gay discourse. Lesbians' objections to bisexuality were aired generously and taken seriously, not marginalized and dismissed as they were in *The Advocate*. But by 1992, these objections were replaced by the voices of bisexuals themselves. The debate among lesbians about the place of bisexuals in the lesbian community had become a debate in which bisexuals themselves were an interested party and had an active voice. Bisexuality as an issue had been replaced by bisexual issues, for example, the development of a bisexual politic and the relationship between bisexual politics and lesbian and gay politics. Whereas *The Advocate*'s "Bi and Beyond" had framed the issue as one of bisexual inclusion in the lesbian and gay movement, *Out/Look* had gone one step farther to construct not only bisexuals, but a political bisexual voice.

Meanwhile, in the conservative world of *10 Percent*, the issue of bisexuality—let alone bisexual issues or the bisexual voice—barely exists at all. *10 Percent* came closest to tackling the issue of bisexuality in its second issue, published in Spring 1993. "My girlfriend is becoming the man of my dreams" was written by Kate Bornstein, a "bisexual heterosexual lesbian gay male transsexual woman who is in a committed relationship with a lesbian man named David."[23] She pointed out that bisexuals gained recognition by inclusion in the name of the 1993 March on Washington but transgendered people did not, thereby portraying bisexuals as members of the gay establishment that excluded transgendered people. Judging from the lack of letters to the editor in the next issue, readers had no opinion on the subject. The word "bisexual" appeared again a few issues later when Eric Marcus wrote, "I'm not even all that comfortable being grouped with bisexuals, let alone transsexuals, transvestites, and queer straights" because "we have different lives, face different challenges."[24] Two letters to the editor in the next issue disagreed, arguing that Marcus's attitude was divisive and phobic. Neither reader mentioned bisexuality except when quoting Marcus; the issue constructed was a general one concerning appreciation of diversity.

In lesbian and gay publications, the issue of bisexuality—which is primarily of interest to lesbians—competes for space with gay issues such as AIDS. In lesbian publications, more time and energy can be devoted to hashing out the details of lesbian ideology, including the political meaning of bisexuality. Dedicated to the discussion of issues that are relevant *within* lesbian feminism, *Lesbian Contradiction* provides a receptive audience for discussions of lesbians who have sex with men and bisexuality.

Like general lesbian and gay publications, *Lesbian Contradiction* initially constructed the issue as one of lesbians who have sex with men.

In issue number 2, "Many Lesbians Are Going Straight Now . . .—A Conversation" consisted of thirteen comments written on a wall in a women's bathroom, one in response to the other. The women had thirteen very different opinions and perspectives. Some discussed their feelings about lovers who leave them for men or offered opinions about whether lesbians who "go straight" are capitulating to compulsory heterosexuality or whether they were never lesbians to begin with. Others acknowledged their own attractions to men and wrote about the isolation they felt because they feared censure by lesbians. Voice #11 mentioned that she was just beginning to find support from other bisexuals and asked others not to judge her. Voice #12 agreed that "We should all be free to be who we are," but Voice #13 revealed that liberal views are not always accompanied by understanding, "[e]ven if some people can't make up their minds who they are!"[25] A year later, Gwen Fay expressed her exasperation over the fact that lesbians can be as prejudiced as anyone else, and deplored the fact that there are so few opportunities for us to air our differences that the conversation had had to take place on a bathroom wall.[26]

These opinions were echoed in 1989 after *Lesbian Contradiction* published "Desire and Consequences: Sleeping with a Strange Man" by Juana Maria Paz, "A Second Coming Out" by Stephanie Sugars, and "I'm Still a Lesbian" by Jane Dwinell.[27] One reader blasted the magazine for printing Paz's description of "women and men fucking each other." She did not "[condemn] Juana for having heterosexual sex" but she resented Juana's claim to lesbian identity and *Lesbian Contradiction*'s decision to give space to heterosexuality when space for lesbian expression was so limited already.[28] The editors defended their decision by reiterating the newspaper's mission to serve as a broad forum for discussion of feminism by all women, not only lesbians.[29] Dwinell wrote about her life as a lesbian-identified woman in a long-term committed relationship with a man. The response to Dwinell was even more vehement than the response to Paz had been. *Lesbian Contradiction* printed three letters from readers who denounced Dwinell for calling herself a lesbian, denying heterosexual privilege, trivializing the importance lesbians attach to the genders of women's sexual partners, and comparing lesbians' criticism of heterosexuality to society's condemnation of lesbianism.[30] The editors expressed their gratitude for a fourth letter, an "anonymous response from a woman whose way of relating to men and to lesbians reminds us how many more variations there are in these matters than we might think." The gratitude of the editors suggests that this was the only letter sympathetic to Dwinell received; this fact, and the anonymity of the letter's author, say as much as her letter itself does. Whereas the readers of *The Advocate* applauded humanism and characterized lesbian feminist objections to bisexuality as intolerant and outdated, the letter-writing readers of *Lesbian Contradiction* were almost universally antagonistic toward bisexuality. As much as the editors of *Lesbian Contradiction* wanted to present the other side of the debate, they could not because their readers apparently did not share the liberal humanist attitudes that dominated the pages of other lesbian and gay publications.

Although *Lesbian Contradiction*'s readers continued to debate "lesbians who sleep with men" through 1989, they also began discussing "bisexuality" in 1987, sooner than the more mainstream lesbian and gay publications. In "Thinking about Bisexuality" Marilyn Murphy and Irene Weiss argued that "non-lesbian" is a more appropriate term than "heterosexual" for women who live heterosexual lives, because "heterosexual" cannot be considered a sexual preference in a heterosexist society.[31] Lesbians are lesbians because they have chosen to live lesbian lives and identify as lesbians; most women who live heterosexual lives never chose to be heterosexual. The argument has interesting implications for bisexuals. The authors rejected the concept of bisexuality as a sexual/affectional preference. They argued that when a bisexual is with a man, she is heterosexual because she enjoys heterosexual privileges. But when she is with a woman, she is not lesbian because heterosexual privilege remains an option for her. She is, in fact, the only woman who consciously chooses heterosexuality because she is the only woman who ever lives a heterosexual life with full knowledge of the other option; the bisexual woman is, therefore, the only true "heterosexual."

The next issue of *Lesbian Contradiction* carried two letters from readers. One thanked Murphy and Weiss for giving her a good laugh by exemplifying the absurdity of the identity debates.[32] The other documented her own journey from political lesbian feminist dykedom, through her politically correct dismay as she realized she was attracted to men, to her current opinion that "[b]eing attracted to one sex or the other is not good or bad, it just is what it is. Political integrity is not based on whether we sleep with men or with women, but on how we

live our lives." Again, the fact that this reader chose to remain anonymous says as much as her letter does. [33] Although these two letters were
critical of lesbian feminist antagonism toward bisexuals, neither letter
conveyed a strong bisexual voice. The former dismissed the debate as
trivial; the latter was a plea for tolerance.

But a self-conscious and political bisexual voice did begin appearing
in *Lesbian Contradiction* in 1990, after Murphy's views were aired
once again in "The Gay-Straight Split Revisited." Dajenya deplored the
tendency of oppressed groups to argue over who's more oppressed,
rejected the accusation that as a bisexual she was "consorting with the
enemy," and presented her bisexuality as a source of political awareness
and action. [34] In the same issue, Jane Litwoman wrote that "gender is
just not what I care about," and analyzed the sources of her privilege
and oppression as a person who, in this "gender-fetishic culture," is
usually labeled "bisexual." [35] Three years later, Alena Smith wrote about
her ability to enjoy making love with both genders, and rejected the
stereotypes that as a bisexual woman she was "going through a phase"
or avoiding serious relationships. [36] Although self-consciously bisexual
voices appeared in *Lesbian Contradiction* two years earlier than they did
in *Out/Look,* they were individual voices that spoke of the personal,
sometimes in political terms but largely in reaction to lesbians' criticisms
of bisexuality; there was little evidence of the growing bisexual community with issues and interests of its own. In *Lesbian Contradiction,* the
"bisexual issue" is still a "lesbian controversy."

In summary, different lesbian and/or gay publications present the
issue of bisexuality differently, and some, like *10 Percent,* don't present
it as an issue at all. In the mainstream and traditionally male-dominated
pages of *The Advocate,* bisexuality is merely a topic for conversation.
Bisexuals came into existence when *The Advocate* wasn't looking and
when bisexuals wrote to *The Advocate* to announce themselves, *The
Advocate* duly reported their existence and then went on with business
as usual. Insofar as bisexuality is an issue, the issue is bisexual inclusion
and the predominant liberal humanist opinion favors inclusion. In contrast, in the Lesbian and Gay Community represented by *Out/Look,*
bisexuality is a controversial issue. Lesbian feminist concerns about
bisexuality were serious, but they belonged to an earlier era and their
merit is fading as the lesbian and gay mainstream returns to its humanist
origins. The bisexual movement is the wave of the future. Bisexuals not

only exist and belong in the lesbian and gay movement, but they have interests, issues, and a voice of their own. Bisexuals are no longer asking to be included in the lesbian and gay movement; they are in the lesbian and gay movement and they are also forming a separate community and movement. Finally, if one reads about The Lesbian Community in *Lesbian Contradiction,* one finds that lesbian feminist concerns about bisexuality are alive and well, and that they drown out the few anonymous humanists who dare dissent. There are a few political lesbians who ask not to be condemned for their heterosexual feelings, and a few bisexuals who reject lesbians' negative stereotypes about bisexuality and describe bisexuality in political terms, but there is little evidence of a collective bisexual voice or of a bisexual movement with issues defined by bisexuals.

Lesbians who read these different publications receive very different images of what The Lesbian Community thinks about bisexuality. Which image is accurate? Is bisexuality an issue, or not? If it is, what is the issue? Are objections to bisexuality limited to a few extremists whose politics are stuck in the 1970s as *Out/Look* suggested, or are they alive and well and dominating lesbians' opinions about bisexuality, as shown in *Lesbian Contradiction?* Are bisexuals visible, vocal, and independent political activists, or apologetic hangers-on? The truth is that none of these images are entirely accurate, because each reflects the opinions of only a segment of the Community. More importantly, however, articles and letters to the editor reflect only the opinions of those individuals who bother to express their opinions in writing and have the means to get them published. The vast majority of lesbians—and bisexual women—lack either the time or the inclination to write articles or letters to the editor. They might not even read the articles and letters written by others. What do they think?

To find out what lesbians and bisexual women think, we have to find the voices that are not represented in The Lesbian and Gay Press. This book represents those voices and demonstrates that both lesbians and bisexual women have strong and varied opinions on the subject. Most of this book focuses on the opinions of lesbians, among whom the issue of bisexuality is alive and well and very controversial. The intensity of lesbians' opinions about bisexuality suggests that the issue has very deep political implications. It is the argument of this book that these implications cut right to the heart of the meaning of lesbianism itself. As lesbians, we have fought long and hard for our lesbian identities and communities, and bisexuality constitutes a psychological, social, and political threat to these hard-won victories. It forces us to confront our own differences of opinion over what lesbianism is and what its political implications are; that is, who we are and what we stand for. In the early 1970s, we debated these issues openly as we laid the groundwork for the lesbian movement. Since then, the "who" and "what" debates have faded into the background, but the issues were never resolved. We still disagree about who we are and what we stand for. The topic of bisexuality uncovers these dormant issues and brings our differences to the surface. The energy with which we debate bisexuality today is none other than the energy with which we struggled to define ourselves two decades ago.

"Experts'" Voices: Lesbianism, Bisexuality, and the Social Sciences

We live in an age of science and technology. It is the era of computers, laser surgery, space travel, fax machines, and hydroponics. We look to science to answer our questions and solve our problems. We have learned that science is objective. According to my high school textbook, the scientific method involves asking a question, designing a study to answer the question, and then doing the study to find out the answer. Values, biases, and power do not enter the picture.

As a society, we are quickly finding out the hard way that this sterile image of science is false. Values shape the questions we ask and biases shape the way we ask them. The problems that are solved are often the problems of the most powerful in society, because the least powerful do not have the funding, training, or voice to put their problems on the agenda. Research on breast cancer has been dangerously underfunded in comparison to research on heart disease. Until 1993, the CDC definition of AIDS included opportunistic infections common among HIV infected men but not diseases common among HIV infected women, preventing women from receiving financial and medical opportunities available only to people with an AIDS diagnosis. We know almost nothing about lesbian health issues; we do not even know what the issues are.

Science does provide answers and solutions, but we cannot accept them at face value. We must study science with a critical eye, and select for ourselves that which is useful and that which is not. This is particularly true in an area as value-laden, controversial, and powerful as sexuality. This chapter will examine the contributions social scientists have made to our understanding of sexuality. In it, I will analyze the many different models of sexual orientation that are implicit or explicit in the sexological literature, and the ways in which these models have affected the questions that have been asked and the information we have gained about our sexuality. Readers who are familiar with the highlights of the history of sexology in the United States might want to skip to the subheading "New Models of Sexuality."

WHAT IS A MODEL?

A model, or paradigm, is a way of representing something. Usually, in the social sciences, models are used to make something that is intangible—for example, the economy—a bit more tangible. Nobody can *see* the economy, but economists have computerized models of the economy that allow them to understand the real economy and predict what it will do in the future. It is impossible to create a perfect model, because the process of modeling is the process of giving shape to something that does not have a particular shape of its own.

All models contain assumptions, and all models highlight some features while downplaying or concealing others. When I teach, I illustrate this point by pulling a chair to the front of the room, tilting it forward, and asking a student to tell me what color the top of the seat is. The student can see the top of the seat, so she gives me the answer. Then I ask her what color the bottom of the seat is. She hesitates, and then either says she can't tell or she guesses that it is the same color as the top of the seat. The fact is that, when viewing the chair from any given angle, she can see certain aspects of the chair but she cannot see others. If I were to turn the chair around, she would be able to see new aspects of the chair, but she would no longer be able to see the aspects she saw before. The chair looks different from each angle, and each angle displays some aspects while concealing others. Which view of the chair is the most accurate one? None. In order to fully know what the chair looks like, the student has to look at it from all different angles. Scientific models work the same way. We do not have to decide which model is the "best" or most "accurate." We need to try out all the models, learn something from each one, and then put all that knowledge together to form a more complete picture of the thing we are trying to understand.

THE GREAT DEBATE—ESSENTIALISM VERSUS CONSTRUCTIONISM

One of the most fundamental debates among social scientists who study sexuality is the question of whether sexual orientation is essential or constructed. In social and political discourse, we have become so used to referring to people as lesbians, gays, or heterosexuals, that we no longer question whether or not there might be another way to understand our sexual diversity. Many historians argue, however, that the concept of types of people who are defined by their sexual desires or behaviors is recent. The word "homosexual" was coined in 1869 by Benkert. Prior to the late 1800s, there were people who had sex with members of their own sex and people who were attracted to and fell in love with members of their own sex, but historians tell us that these people were not placed in a category and viewed as a certain type of person because of these behaviors or feelings.[1] They were simply engaging in some of the many forms of sexual behavior that are possible for humans, just as people today might have sex with brown-eyed or blue-eyed people, and might even have a preference for one eye color or the other, without being placed in categories and assumed to be particular types of people based on the eye colors of their sexual partners.

In other words, historical sexologists argue that the categories "lesbian/gay" and "heterosexual" are socially constructed. We have created these categories, and we place ourselves and each other in them on the basis of our behaviors and feelings. This does *not* mean that our desires are artificial or that we made them up; it means that we interpret our desires using the concepts and possibilities made available by our culture, and that we perceive our desires as indications of the types of people we are. It also does not mean that lesbian, gay, and heterosexual people do not exist. We certainly do exist, but we exist because we have come to understand ourselves this way. A house is no less real for the fact that it was built; we need shelter, and building a house is a fine way to give ourselves shelter. The longer we live in the house and the more comfortable we become in it, the more difficult it is to remember a time when the house did not exist. [2]

Essentialists, on the other hand, believe that sexual orientation or sexual desire is a characteristic that exists within a person. An "essence" is real in an absolute sense; it exists even in the absence of cultural interpretation. Essence is the thing that we would see if we could remove all our biases and cultural blinders. When we speak of "discovering" our sexualities, we are thinking in essentialist terms because we are assuming that there was something that existed within us even before we knew about it. When we say that we *are* lesbian/gay or heterosexual, we imply that we have a lesbian/gay or heterosexual essence, that is, that we are a particular type of person who has a particular type of sexual essence. In doing so, we create a bond between ourselves and other people who have the same essence because we put ourselves in a category together. At the same time, we emphasize our differences from people who have different essences by naming ourselves differently and putting them in an*other* category.

A Brief History of Sexology in the United States

The Interplay of Politics and Science and the Downfall of the Dichotomous Conflict Model of Sexuality

The word "heterosexual" was coined after the word "homosexual," and originally meant a person who was attracted to both sexes. [3] In the 1890s, it came to mean a person who is attracted to people of the other sex (Katz 1983), and thereafter, scientists and the public recognized two types of sexual people who are essentially distinct from each other. Zinik

(1985) called this dichotomous model of essential sexuality the "conflict model" of sexuality, because in it, heterosexuality and homosexuality are conceptualized as different and contradictory states of being. In other words, attraction toward people of the same sex and attraction toward people of the other sex are believed to be qualitatively different attractions, which either cannot coexist in a single person, or which conflict with each other when they do. In this model, the true bisexual person is either nonexistent or engaged in a constant struggle between conflicting desires for people of the same sex and people of the other sex.[4]

The first major challenge to the dichotomous conflict model of sexuality in the history of U.S. sexology came in 1948 and 1953 when Alfred Kinsey and his associates published two groundbreaking studies of sexual behavior, *Sexual Behavior in the Human Male* and *Sexual Behavior in the Human Female*. On the basis of national studies of women and men in the United States, Kinsey and his associates announced that 28% of women had experienced erotic responses to other women, 37% of men had had postadolescent sexual experience with another man to the point of orgasm, and an additional 13% of men had responded erotically to another man although they had never actually had sex with another man.[5] These findings shocked both scientists and the public, who had assumed that homosexuality was exceedingly rare. People who were attracted to members of their own sex found out that they were not alone at all. They began looking for each other, and organizations such as the Daughters of Bilitis and the Mattachine Society were founded shortly thereafter.

Perhaps even more surprising was the prevalence of bisexual behavior among Kinsey et al.'s respondents. Only 0.3 to 3% of women (between ages 20 and 35, and depending on marital status) and 4% of men (after the onset of adolescence) were exclusively homosexual, leading to the conclusion that 25 to 28% of women and 46% of men had been erotically responsive to or sexually active with both women and men. Among unmarried women, 4 to 8% reported more than incidental sexual experiences with or erotic responses to both women and men—more than the percentage who were exclusively homosexual. Kinsey and his associates developed the Kinsey scale to describe the variety they had found in their respondents' physical and psychic lives. On this seven-point scale, a "0" indicates a person whose erotic experiences and responses are entirely heterosexual, a "6" indicates a person whose erotic experiences and responses are entirely homosexual, and the scores "1" through "5" represent varying degrees of responsiveness to people of both sexes. This model of sexuality is considered an improvement over the conflict model of sexuality, because it is able to accommodate the variety in human sexual behavior and erotic response discovered by Kinsey and his associates.

A few years after the Kinsey studies, Evelyn Hooker demonstrated that trained clinicians could not differentiate the results of projective tests of heterosexuals from those of homosexuals, thus providing evidence that homosexuals display no more signs of psychopathology than heterosexuals (1957, 1958). Nevertheless, for the next fifteen years, psychiatrists continued to consider homosexuality a mental illness, and scientists motivated by the desire to prevent homosexuality tried to find out what causes it. Homosexual women and men remained hidden in a twilight world of bars and secretive homophile organizations.

The riots at the Stonewall bar in Greenwich Village, New York City, in June 1969, marked the symbolic beginning of a new lesbian and gay liberation consciousness. Lesbians and gay men were no longer willing to appease heterosexual society and avoid harassment by hiding themselves; they began openly demanding social acceptance and civil rights. Faced with vocal and visible lesbians and gay men, social scientists— some of whom were lesbian or gay themselves—rejected the pathological view of homosexuality and produced a virtual explosion of research on lesbians and gay men. Prior to 1969, the record number of articles listed under the topic heading "homosexuality" in any given year of the Sociological Abstracts was five. This number increased to thirteen in 1973, twenty-eight in 1977, thirty-nine in 1979, and topped forty in the 1980s. Most of these articles reported research on gay men, and those that included lesbians often did so as a comparison to gay men. The topic heading "lesbianism" did not appear until 1968,[6] and the number of articles under this heading did not reach thirteen until 1983.[7]

Researchers in the 1970s asked very different questions than researchers in earlier decades had asked. Instead of asking what causes homosexuality, social scientists began asking questions like "What is homophobia and what causes it?" "How does heterosexism affect the lives of gay and lesbian people?" "What is the process of coming out?"

and "What are the gay and lesbian communities like, how do people meet each other, and what kinds of social structures exist?" In other words, researchers shifted their attention away from lesbians and gay men as the "problem" and began defining homophobia and heterosexism as the problem. They began asking questions that lesbians and gay men themselves would ask, rather than questions that homophobes wanted answered. They began studying lesbians and gay men as people who live in social worlds, rather than as laboratory specimens. In the 1980s, many social scientists turned their attention toward AIDS.

Throughout the 1970s, 1980s, and early 1990s, it became increasingly evident that both the conventional conflict model of sexuality and the Kinsey scale were inadequate to describe the complexity of human sexuality. New research affirmed Kinsey et al.'s finding that bisexual behavior is more prevalent than homosexual behavior, especially when lifetime cumulative sexual behavior is considered (e.g., Diamond 1993; Hunt 1974; Janus and Janus 1993; Laumann et al. 1994; Rogers and Turner 1991; Smith 1991), and that bisexual erotic capacity is even more common than overt bisexual behavior (e.g., Bell and Weinberg 1978). Blumstein and Schwartz (1974, 1976a, 1976b, 1977a, 1977b) found that sexual behavior often does not correspond with sexual identity, and that individuals display considerable variation in their sexual behaviors and identities over their lifetimes, producing behavior that would be labeled bisexual when lifelong behavior or feelings are considered.

The need for a more sophisticated scientific model of sexuality was dramatically illustrated by the "blood supply scare" of the mid-1980s. The Centers for Disease Control, acting on early reports that most cases of AIDS were homosexual men, concluded that "gays" were at highest risk of contracting the disease and launched educational efforts aimed at gay men. What officials had failed to take into account, however, was the fact that behavior and identity do not always coincide, and it is one's behavior, not one's sexual identity, that determines one's risk for HIV infection. They also failed to take into account the prevalence of bisexual behavior. Many men who were having sex with other men were married and considered themselves heterosexual or bisexual, not gay. Messages about safe sex aimed at the gay male community failed to reach these men. This potentially fatal miscommunication occurred because scientists failed to question the simplistic model of sexuality in which there

are only two uncomplicated types of people, homosexuals and heterosexuals.

New Models of Sexuality

Social scientists worked to develop improved models of sexual orientation that would reflect their growing understanding of sexuality. Many
modified the seven-point Kinsey scale. For example, Bell and Weinberg
(1978) used two seven-point scales, one representing sexual feelings and
one representing sexual behaviors. The most complex modification to
the Kinsey scale is the Klein Sexual Orientation Grid (KSOG), on which
subjects rate themselves on 21 seven-point scales (Klein, Sepekoff, and
Wolf 1985). The scales measure the subjects' past, present, and ideal
ratings on seven components of sexual orientation: sexual attraction,
sexual behavior, sexual fantasies, emotional preference, social preference, self-identification, and lifestyle.

Other theorists proposed categorical models of sexual orientation in
which homosexuality and heterosexuality are joined by a third distinct
form of sexuality. An early categorical alternative to the simple dichotomous model was suggested by Feldman and MacCulloch (1971), who
distinguished between primary and secondary homosexual preference.
They defined primary homosexuals as people who have never experienced heterosexual arousal at any point in their lives, although they
might have engaged in heterosexual behavior for the sake of social
appearance. Secondary homosexuals, on the other hand, have experienced heterosexual arousal and activity. Traces of the concept of the
Kinsey scale are evident in this model with its implication that primary
homosexuals are "more homosexual" than secondary homosexuals.
Later, Feldman (1984) suggested that primary homosexuals and primary
heterosexuals correspond closely to Kinsey 6's and 0's, whereas secondary homosexuals are Kinsey 1 to 5's.

Other theorists, for example, MacDonald, referred to the third sexual orientation as bisexuality. MacDonald conceptualized bisexuality as
a combination of heterosexuality and homosexuality. He referred to
bisexuals as persons who "can enjoy and engage in sexual activity with
members of both sexes, or [recognize] a desire to do so" (1981:25). He
argued that bisexuality is a distinct form of sexual orientation and that
researchers should recognize it as such.

Brierley rejected the idea that bisexuality, heterosexuality, and homosexuality are distinct forms of sexuality. He suggested that individuals have numerous psychological and behavioral dimensions that form a system tending toward individualized homeostasis in the "well-integrated personality." Some elements of this system, such as gender identity, are core and therefore more resistant to change as the system adjusts to "maintain stability and to oppose external constraints" (1984:62). These systemic adjustments produce relationships between identity, behavior, and other personality dimensions that are unique for each individual. There is, therefore, no such thing as a "heterosexual" or a "homosexual" except insofar as some individuals happen to possess the characteristics that we associate with these categories of being.

Some theorists resurrected Freud's concept of "inherent bisexuality" (e.g., Freimuth and Hornstein 1982; Zinik 1985). Freud had argued that humans are born sexually undefined and that preferences for certain objects develop during childhood. He believed that "all human beings are bisexual by nature, in accordance with their phylogenetic and ontogenetic history" (Wolff 1971:20). If bisexuality is conceptualized as a universal human potential, then bisexuality is the original condition upon which heterosexuality and homosexuality are variations. This represents a significant departure from the concept of distinct heterosexual and homosexual essences, from which bisexuality emerges as a combination of or an unresolved conflict between these two states of being.

Drawing on the notion of a universal bisexual potential, Klein (1978) conceived of bisexuality in terms of a potential for "one hundred percent intimacy." Bisexuality in this sense is "the most complex state of sexual relatedness with people" and calls "for a wholeness of behavior" (Klein 1978:14) and a tolerance for ambiguity, in contrast to the limits on feelings and behavior implied by heterosexuality and homosexuality. Thus, rather than a combination of homosexuality and heterosexuality, bisexuality is, in Klein's eyes, a qualitatively different way of relating to people characterized by openness rather than limitations.

Some theorists questioned the century-old convention of defining sexual orientation in terms of the biological sex or gender of one's sex-object choice. DeCecco and Shively (1983/84), in an oft-cited article, proposed shifting scientific attention from its focus on the sexual individual to a focus on the sexual relationship as the unit of analysis. Ross (1984), Kaplan and Rogers (1984), and Freimuth and Hornstein (1982)

argued that social scientists should remove the emphasis on the biological sex characteristics of the partners in a relationship and step back to
ask which characteristics serve to define a sexual encounter for the
participants in the encounter. Kaplan and Rogers argued that while
biological sex is an important factor in choosing sexual partners, albeit
only because of the social emphasis placed on biological sex, other
gender-related characteristics are also influential because genitalia themselves are not immediately observable. Taking the argument a step further, Ross suggested that individuals might choose their sexual partners
on the basis of a number of characteristics, among which biological sex
might be more or less important. Ross and Paul (1992) suggested that
bisexuals could be conceptualized as individuals for whom biological
sex is a comparatively minor consideration in choosing sexual partners,
in contrast to heterosexuals and homosexuals who "have succumbed to
social pressures to adopt an exclusive and stable sexual orientation"
(Ross 1984:64).

Theorists who advocated abandoning biological sex-based or gender-based definitions of sexual orientation often suggested that research
on bisexuals would be particularly useful in developing a new model of
sexuality.[8] Among bisexuals, other characteristics that are important in
partner choice are not overshadowed by an exclusive choice on the basis
of gender. Therefore, these other characteristics should prove to be more
readily identified and studied among bisexuals than among homosexuals
or heterosexuals. In fact, Ross (1984:68) asserted that "[w]e can only
begin to understand the meaning of having a same-sex partner by looking at bisexuals . . . for whom gender is one of a number of determinants
in partner choice." The belief that bisexuals hold the key to understanding sexuality, including heterosexuality and homosexuality, is a far cry
from the attitudes of earlier theorists who ascribed to the conflict model
of sexuality and viewed bisexuals as either nonexistent or mere combinations of conflicting homosexual and heterosexual impulses.

Unfortunately, researchers have largely ignored the progress made
by theorists. A review of the research literature is outside the scope of
this book, but suffice it to say that most researchers continue to classify
people as either "lesbians/gays" or "heterosexuals." A few researchers
recognize a "bisexual" category, and some collect Kinsey scores that are
often used merely to place people into these categories. As MacDonald
(1983) pointed out, these practices lead not only to a lack of knowledge

about bisexuals, but also to poor quality knowledge about lesbians and gays, because people with varied sexual desires, behaviors, and identities are often lumped together within a single category. In my study, I refer to the women who participated as "lesbians" or "bisexuals" according to their own self-identities. These labels are not meant to imply that these women are "really" lesbian or bisexual in an essential sense, nor are they meant to gloss over the varied sexual experiences of the women collected under each label; on the contrary, I examine these differences and their implications. The labels are both a linguistic convenience and a way to show respect for the self-identities of the women who participated in this study.

3

BEHIND THE SCENES: HOW THE STUDY WAS DONE AND WHO PARTICIPATED IN IT

A BRIEF AND NONTECHNICAL LESSON IN SAMPLING THEORY FOR NONACADEMIC READERS

Chapters 4, 5, and 7 will present the findings of research in which I explored lesbian and bisexual women's opinions on the topic of bisexuality. But before I present the findings it is important for you to know something about the women who participated in the study. The odds are that you and your friends were not among the women who participated, so you might be wondering how the findings could possibly be relevant to you, much less reflect your own opinions. This chapter will answer that question, and it will give you information that you need in order to draw your own conclusions about the findings. Readers who are familiar with scientific sampling methods might want to skip to the subheading "How Lesbian and Bisexual Women Were Recruited to Participate in' the Study."

It would have been impossible, for many practical reasons, to survey all lesbians and bisexual women in the U.S. Instead of surveying an entire population, social scientists usually select particular members of the population as representatives of the population and survey these people. In other words, we take a sample of the population and then we use the information these people give us to draw informed conclusions about the population as a whole. In this way, scientists use limited financial resources to focus on getting the most accurate information possible from the people they have selected, instead of obtaining poor quality information from a larger number of people.

It may seem risky to draw conclusions about a whole population based on information from just a sample, and it can be if it is not done properly. How do scientists know that the people who are sampled really represent everyone else fairly? We do, if we have drawn the sample using methods that guarantee that each member of a population has an equal chance[1] of being selected for inclusion in the sample. When these methods are used, we can be reasonably certain that various segments of the population, and their opinions, are represented in the sample in the same proportion in which they appear in the population as a whole. Therefore, the sample should provide an accurate micropicture of the whole population. There is always a possibility that this will not be the case, but even the magnitude of this possibility is known if scientific sampling methods have been used. Social scientists generally do not report findings from a sample unless they are at least 95% certain that the findings are an accurate reflection of the whole population. Readers who are unfamiliar with scientific sampling procedures can consult any textbook on social scientific research methods.

But lesbian and bisexual women cannot be sampled using representative sampling methods. In order to draw a representative sample a researcher must begin with a complete listing of all members of the population. It would be impossible to make a list of all lesbian and bisexual women because many of us are isolated or closeted. Therefore, lesbian and bisexual women have to be sampled by methods that are designed to maximize the *diversity* of the sample, rather than its representativeness. In other words, participants need to be recruited in ways that guarantee that women of different socioeconomic classes, racial/ethnic groups, educational levels, incomes, ages, political orientations, etc., are included in the sample. Their number in the sample will probably not be proportionate to their number in the whole population, but they will be represented.

When samples are recruited by methods that emphasize diversity rather than representativeness, findings have to be interpreted with special care. For example, if I had been able to draw a representative sample of lesbians and I found that 15% had children, then I would be able to say, with a known degree of certainty, that 15% of all lesbians have children. But, since the lesbians who participated in my study are not a representative sample, I do not know how accurate it would be to conclude that 15% of all lesbians have children. I can, however, look at differences between groups of study participants with some confidence. For example, later in this chapter I will report that 15% of lesbian-identified women in the study had children, whereas 25% of bisexual-identified women in the study had children. On the basis of these results, I have reason to believe that in the population at large bisexual-identified women are indeed more likely to have children than lesbian-identified women. Neither the 15% nor the 25% might be accurate; both of these figures might be inflated or deflated. But, unless I have some reason to believe that there were factors in my sampling methods that affected lesbian-identified mothers' participation rate differently than bisexual-identified mothers' participation rate, I can cautiously assume that both figures are equally inflated or deflated and that the *difference* between them reflects a real difference between the rates of motherhood among bisexual and lesbian-identified women in general.

In chapters 5 and 7, the findings will sometimes be presented in terms of differences between lesbian and bisexual women, or between women of different ages, racial/ethnic groups, classes, etc. Most findings will not be presented in terms of percentages or other numbers; most will be anecdotal or narrative descriptions of the different opinions that were expressed by women who participated in the study. However, when findings are expressed in terms of numbers, they will sometimes be accompanied by a "test of statistical significance." There are many different kinds of statistical significance tests, and each is appropriate under particular circumstances, but all significance tests produce a "p-value." Above, I mentioned that social scientists do not usually report findings from samples unless they are at least 95% certain that the finding is an accurate reflection of the whole population. The degree of *un*certainty is measured by the p-value. The lower the p-value, the more certain the researcher can be that a finding in the sample is also true for the whole population. For example, if the p-value for a finding of difference between two groups in the sample is .05, then there is a 95% chance that these two groups really are different in the whole population. A p-value of .01 indicates 99% certainty, and so on. Significance tests were designed for use on representative samples, and they are accurate for these types of samples. Because the sample on which this study is based is not a representative sample, the significance tests are only guidelines to the certainty of the findings.

HOW LESBIAN AND BISEXUAL WOMEN WERE RECRUITED TO PARTICIPATE IN THE STUDY

In order to obtain as diverse a sample as possible, I used sampling methods designed to ensure the inclusion of women who were most likely to be undersampled. Women at risk of being undersampled included closeted women, geographically isolated women, and women who were not socially or politically active in lesbian or bisexual community organizations and events. Because of their social and physical isolation, these women would be less likely to hear about the survey and because of their closetedness or reclusiveness they would be less likely to participate even if they did hear about it. Older women, poor women, and nonstudents were also at risk of underrepresentation because they are less likely to be socially and politically active. Bisexual-identified women were more difficult to reach than lesbian-identified women because there are comparatively few organizations for bisexual women; most bisexual women had to be recruited through primarily lesbian networks. Finally, Women of Color have been underrepresented in previous research on lesbians. This is partly because most researchers are White Euro-Americans themselves, and therefore tend to focus on issues that are of interest to White Euro-Americans or fail to publicize their research in a way that welcomes participation from Women of Color as well as White women.

To overcome the bias against closeted women, geographically isolated women, and women who were not actively involved in lesbian/bisexual community events, I used a self-administered questionnaire[2] instead of the face-to-face interview or ethnographic methods that have usually been used to study lesbian and bisexual women. The questionnaire was distributed with postage-paid return envelopes so that respondents could return their completed questionnaires anonymously and at no financial cost to themselves. The goals of the survey were described on the cover of the questionnaire and the instructions inside the front cover and throughout the questionnaire were self-explanatory, thus eliminating the need for potential respondents to speak directly to a member of the survey staff before participating in the study. This enabled the questionnaire to be passed from one woman to another until it reached an eligible respondent, and allowed the questionnaire to reach socially peripheral lesbian and bisexual women and women whose fear of discovery might otherwise have prevented them from participating in the study. The success of these efforts to maximize the mobility of the questionnaire is evident in the fact that, although the target geographic area was a single midwestern state and 98% of the questionnaires were initially distributed in that state, completed questionnaires were returned from respondents in 24 states and Canada.

Six assistants who had conducted interviews in earlier stages of the study helped distribute the questionnaire. These assistants varied in age, political orientation, and sexual identity. They therefore had access to different segments of the lesbian and bisexual population, and were able to recruit a more diverse sample than I could have alone. Questionnaires were distributed by several methods, including booths at gay, lesbian, and women's conferences and through gay, bisexual, and lesbian social and political organizations, friendship networks, and newsletter advertisements. Particular efforts were made to contact bisexual organizations and organizations for lesbian and bisexual Women of Color, and to recruit Women of Color who belonged to predominantly White Euro-American organizations. Potential respondents were encouraged to take multiple copies of the questionnaire to distribute among their own friends and the members of other organizations to which they belonged. Calculation of an accurate response rate is impossible because some questionnaires probably never reached eligible respondents and some probably passed through the hands of eligible nonrespondents before reaching a respondent. However, 427 usable questionnaires were returned, representing a response rate of approximately 45% based on the number of questionnaires that left my hands.

THE WOMEN WHO PARTICIPATED—WHO WERE THEY?

The cover of the questionnaire explained to potential respondents that the following people were eligible to participate in the study: "women who consider themselves to be lesbian or bisexual, or who choose not to label their sexual orientation, or who are not sure what their sexual orientation is." This definition was intentionally broad, in order to encourage a wide range of women—including women who might not consider themselves members of The Lesbian Community—to participate. Inside the questionnaire, respondents were asked "When you think about your sexual orientation, what word do you use most often to describe yourself?" a question designed to elicit expressions of sexual self-identity rather than presented or perceived identity.[3] Respondents chose from among the following responses: lesbian; gay; dyke; homosexual; bisexual; mainly straight or heterosexual but with some bisexual tendencies; I am not sure what my orientation is (I do not know, I haven't decided, or I am still wondering); I prefer not to label myself. Respondents who answered that they preferred not to label themselves were directed to the follow-up question, "If you had to choose one term to describe your orientation, which would come closest to the way you feel?" and offered the following responses: lesbian/gay/homosexual, bisexual, I really can't choose. Each response to the initial and the follow-up questions was followed by instructions to skip certain subsequent questions. A small number of respondents failed to check a response to the questions about sexual self-identity; the sexual identities of these respondents were inferred from the instructions they chose to follow.

Seventy-eight percent, or 323, of the respondents unhesitatingly identified themselves as Lesbians, Dykes, or Gay or Homosexual women (figure 3.1).[4] An additional 9 respondents failed to answer the question about sexual self-identity but followed the instructions for lesbians throughout the rest of the questionnaire, and they were assumed to have lesbian identities also. Altogether, these 332 women will henceforth be referred to as "lesbians." Whenever these women are discussed as individuals, the terms they used to describe themselves will be capitalized. That is, if I refer to a respondent as a "lesbian," this means that she belongs to the lesbian subsample and might have called herself by any of the above terms. But if I refer to her as a Lesbian, then this is the specific term that she chose to describe herself. Likewise, if I refer to her as a Dyke, then this is the term she chose.

Ten percent, or 42, of the respondents identified themselves as Bisexual. Three women failed to answer the question about sexual self-identity but followed the instructions for bisexual women throughout the questionnaire and were assumed to identify themselves as bisexual. Altogether, these 45 women will be referred to as "bisexuals."

Finally, 7 women (2%) said that they were Heterosexual with Bisexual Tendencies, 14 women (3%) indicated that they were not sure what their sexual orientation was, and 25 women (6%) said that they preferred not to label themselves. In answer to the follow-up question, 8 of the women who preferred not to label themselves chose the label "bisexual," 14 chose "lesbian/gay/homosexual," and 3 refused to label themselves. Although some women did choose lesbian or bisexual identities when pressed, they preferred not to label themselves, and they are not considered part of the lesbian or bisexual subsamples in this study.

Most of the women who responded, regardless of their sexual self-identities, are well-educated Euro-American women. At the time of the study, three out of four were college graduates, and only 7% had no schooling beyond high school. Ninety-two percent are White, 3.4% are Black or African-American, 2% are Indian, and the rest belong to other racial groups. Although 24 states and Canada are represented in the sample, 93% of the women lived in the Midwestern United States. Since the population in the Midwestern states is 87.2% White,[5] if we assume that women of different racial groups are equally likely to be lesbian or bisexual, then the sample underrepresents Women of Color.

Most women were employed, as figure 3.2 shows. Despite their high levels of education and employment, however, participants in the study had low to moderate incomes. Almost a quarter lived in households with total annual incomes of less than $10,000 (figure 3.3). One-third lived in households with incomes of over $30,000, but only 19% of these women lived alone; the other 81% shared this income with at least one other person.

Participants ranged in age from 16 to 67. There were some differences among women of different ages in the terms they chose to describe their sexual self-identities (figure 3.4). At all ages, approximately three out of four women described themselves as lesbians. Among women who did not call themselves lesbians, however, older women were more likely to call themselves Bisexual than younger women. In fact, women aged 35 or older were eight times more likely than women in their teens or early twenties to call themselves Bisexual. Younger women, on the other hand, were more likely to say that they were "heterosexuals with bisexual tendencies" or to say that they did not know what their orientation was or that they preferred not to label themselves. Approximately one out of five women under 25 could not, would not, or preferred not to label her sexuality.

One out of five lesbian and bisexual women was not romantically involved with anyone at the time she participated in the study. Among lesbians, over half (55%) were involved in serious, committed relationships with other women, and 4 were involved with men. Bisexual women, on the other hand, were almost equally likely to be involved with women and men. But only 7 (16%) bisexual women were simultaneously involved with both women and men; 17 were involved in relationships with women only, and 12 were involved in relationships with men only. Most bisexual women described their relationships as serious relationships or marriages. Women who were unable or unwilling to label their sexuality were more likely than either lesbian or bisexual women to be single; one out of four was not involved with anyone. This was probably due to their young age. Those who were involved were twice as likely to be involved with women than with men, and just as likely as bisexuals to be involved in serious relationships with women.

Not surprisingly, bisexual women were more likely than lesbians to have been married to men in the past and they were more likely to have children. But a large number of lesbians had also had serious relationships with men. Four out of five bisexual women, and two out of five lesbians, had been seriously involved with or married to men (figure 3.5). Many lesbians who had not had serious heterosexual relationships had had casual heterosexual relationships or dated men; only 10% of lesbians had never had any type of heterosexual relationship at all. Twenty-five percent of bisexual women and 15% of lesbians had children.

Sexuality is not merely a matter of with whom a woman sleeps or with whom she slept in the past. Sexuality is also a matter of to whom she is sexually attracted and other factors. In general, one might expect that lesbians would be attracted to women and bisexual women would be attracted to both women and men. But feelings of sexual attraction are not that clear-cut, and neither are women's choices about how to identify themselves sexually. In fact, lesbian and bisexual women who participated in this study had almost as much in common as not with respect to their feelings of sexual attraction. Figure 3.6 illustrates the range of sexual feelings toward women and men that were reported by lesbian and bisexual women, and by women who could not, would not, or preferred not to label their sexuality.[6] Only one-third of lesbians (36%) said that their feelings of sexual attraction were exclusively toward women; two out of three reported that they had some heterosexual feelings. For most, these heterosexual feelings comprised only 10% of their total sexual feelings but some lesbians reported that up to 50% of their feelings of sexual attraction were toward men.[7] Bisexual women, on the other hand, reported feelings that ranged from 80% heterosexual to 90% homosexual. In other words, all bisexual women were attracted to both women and men, but so were most lesbians. Very few bisexual women reported that they were equally attracted to women and men (16%), and they were more likely to express a preference for women than a preference for men. Women who were not sure what their orientation was or who preferred not to label themselves covered as wide a range as bisexual women, from nearly exclusive heterosexual feelings to nearly exclusive homosexual feelings. For detailed information about the feelings of sexual attraction and relational histories of the women in this sample, see Rust (1992b).

As I explained above, I refer to the women who participated in this study as "lesbians," "bisexuals," etc., on the basis of their sexual self-identities at the time of the study. But many of these women have not had the same sexual identities throughout their lives. Some lesbians used to call themselves bisexual, some bisexuals used to call themselves lesbian, and some women who preferred not to label their sexuality had tried calling themselves both lesbian and bisexual in the past before they gave up labeling themselves. Among lesbians, 39% at one time called themselves bisexual.[8] Bisexual identity is often considered a stepping stone on the way to coming out as a lesbian. Slightly more than half of these lesbians called themselves bisexual before they came out as lesbians; in hindsight, these women might well see their earlier bisexual identity as a transitional stage. The other half, 17% of all lesbians, called themselves bisexual *after* they came out as lesbians. For these women, bisexual identity was not merely a stepping stone. Although they had returned to a lesbian identity by the time they participated in this study, they had considered themselves bisexual after, not before, coming out as lesbians.

Among bisexuals, 84% had called themselves lesbian in the past.

For these women also, bisexuality was not merely a stepping stone on the way to coming out as a lesbian; they had already tried to identify themselves as lesbian and decided to identify as bisexual instead at the time of the study. But bisexual identity had not been permanent for most of these women, either; three out of four had changed identities more than twice.

Likewise, most of the women who said that they were not sure what their sexual orientation was, or who preferred not to label themselves, were not merely in such an early stage of coming out that they had not yet taken on a sexual identity. Three-quarters of these women had identified as either lesbian or bisexual in the past, and most had identified both ways at different times in their lives.

In summary, the women who participated in this study overrepresent highly educated White Euro-American women, although women who did not attend college and Women of Color are represented. In terms of social class, income, age, sexual identity, sexual history, and sexual experiences, the participants are a diverse group. We can learn a great deal from the women who participated in this study, if we keep these facts in mind. Now, it's time to find out what they had to say.

4

LESBIANS' VOICES: WHAT DO LESBIANS THINK ABOUT BISEXUALITY AND ITS ROLE IN SEXUAL POLITICS?

A few of the women who participated in this study might have, on occasion, written a letter to *Out/Look* or an article for a regional lesbian newsletter, but most have not. The women who participated in this study are the women who read these letters and articles and respond to them privately. If they care about the issues raised, they might discuss them with personal friends; if they do not care, they might never finish reading the article. Whatever their thoughts and opinions, they do not appear in print and do not become a matter of public record. Yet, these are the thoughts and opinions of the lesbian community. Does this silent majority share the opinions expressed by the women whose voices appear in print? Do they consider the issues debated in the lesbian press to be important enough to have an opinion about? How do lesbians really feel about bisexuality, bisexual women, and social and political relations between lesbians and bisexual women? How do their feelings about bisexuality reflect their thoughts and feelings about who they are and what they stand for as lesbians?

Participants in this study answered several questions about their attitudes toward sexuality, bisexuality, and bisexual women. The most important question was a very simple open-ended one, "What is your opinion of bisexuality?" Although this question would seem to be a straightforward request for an opinion, the answers women gave revealed much more than that. The value of this question lies in the fact that it allowed women to define the issue of bisexuality themselves, in their own words, and then to respond to the issue as they saw it. Every lesbian respondent read the same question, but each transformed this question into her own before giving an answer. These answers therefore reveal what the issues are as well as how lesbians feel about them.

One of the most controversial issues is the question of whether bisexuality exists at all. This question was raised either explicitly or implicitly by more than half of the lesbians in the study, and the answers given covered the entire gamut from "it does not exist" to "everyone is inherently bisexual." Nearly as important is the issue of defining bisexuality; if bisexuality exists, what is it? Those lesbians who agree with each other that bisexuality exists disagree over what it is that they are talking about. Not only do lesbians have a variety of definitions of bisexuality, but these definitions of bisexuality reveal fundamental differences in the way lesbians think about sexuality in general and about the philosophical and political relationships between lesbianism and bisexuality.

Once the questions of existence and definition are answered, the question "What are bisexuals like?" arises. Lesbians hold a variety of beliefs about bisexual women, particularly about bisexuals' personal characteristics, sexual proclivities, and political allegiances. A few respondents not only described bisexual women, but compared lesbian and bisexual lifestyles in terms of their social and political implications or consequences. Finally, most respondents did answer the question that was asked, "What is your opinion of bisexuality?" by describing their own personal feelings about bisexuality and bisexual women.

In this chapter, I describe the variety in lesbians' images of and feelings about bisexual women; then, in chapters 5 and 6 I will analyze the individual and historical bases of these attitudes.

DOES BISEXUALITY EXIST?

This question is central to the debate about bisexuality. It is a fundamental issue over which there is considerable disagreement among lesbians, setting the stage for further disputes over the finer points of bisexuality. While some women answered this question with an unqualified "no" or "yes," others expressed more complex beliefs about the circumstances under which bisexuality might exist, the likelihood that people who appear to be bisexual are really true bisexuals, and the legitimacy of bisexuality as a sexual orientation. Figure 4.1 illustrates the proportion of lesbians in this study who hold certain opinions on the question of bisexual existence, but the great variety in their beliefs can only be appreciated by examining the actual comments of women who hold each opinion.

Lesbians Who Are Skeptical

There is widespread skepticism among lesbians about the existence of bisexuality. Very few lesbian respondents stated explicitly and unequivocally that there is no such thing as bisexuality, but many expressed serious doubts about whether it exists. In all, nearly one out of four lesbian respondents tends to believe that it does not exist (figure 4.1). Many of these women explained their opinions by providing descriptions of that which they do not believe exists. These definitions reveal that they base their opinions on a variety of different images of this nonexistent form of sexuality. For example,

> It does not exist. To be bisexual would mean that a person were simultaneously involved in an intimate sexual relationship with a man and a woman. It is possible but would be better described as schizophrenic. (Marlene)

> Bisexuality is a transition and exploration phase. Women may have sex with men and women but I think it's only possible to fall in love consistently with one sex or the other. (Stephanie)

> I don't believe it exists . . . I believe it's impossible to love men and women 50–50. One has to have stronger feelings one way or the other. (Naomi)

These three women have three very different definitions of what bisexuality would be if it existed. Marlene[1] defines bisexuality as simultaneous sexual involvement with both a man and a woman. Stephanie clearly rejects this definition, saying that it doesn't matter whom one has sex with; she defines sexuality in terms of "consistent" feelings of love.

Naomi is the most restrictive, defining a bisexual as someone who has exactly equal feelings of love for women and men. Arguing that such phenomena would be rare or impossible, these women conclude that bisexuality is nonexistent or, as in the case of Marlene, a form of mental illness.

Other women have broader definitions of bisexuality but still believe it does not exist. For example, Julia defines bisexuality as a simultaneous attraction to women and men, but because she believes that attraction to women and attraction to men are antithetical, she does not believe that simultaneous attraction would be possible:

> . . . it is very hard for me to conceive of a woman who is emotionally and physically attracted to women being also similarly attracted to men. I do not feel the two can co-exist. (Julia)

Many lesbians pointed out that some people claim to be bisexual, believe themselves to be bisexual, or behave bisexually, but argued that this bisexuality is illusory. Some fell short of actually saying explicitly that bisexuality does not exist, but the implication was unmistakable. For example, Karen believes that women who claim to be bisexual are really lesbians who either haven't realized it yet, or who are trying to preserve their heterosexual privilege or avoid stigma:

> My experience of women who define themselves as bisexual suggests that bisexual women are either really "lesbian" but using the bisexual label to preserve their heterosexual privilege in society or on their way to becoming a lesbian and using the bisexual label as a "safe" transition stage or experimenting with lesbianism but not in a serious way ("sexual tourists"). (Karen)

Other skeptics argued that claims of bisexuality are the result of confusion, youthful immaturity, lack of self-knowledge, indecisiveness, conformism, mental illness, or attempts to gain the acceptance of both the lesbian and heterosexual communities, to get the best of both worlds, to avoid stigma, or to avoid taking a political stand. Each of these beliefs about women who claim to be bisexual will be examined later in this chapter.

A number of lesbians were more circumspect about expressing their skepticism. They really don't believe that bisexuality exists, but they are willing to reserve their final judgment. For example, Jerri wrote, "I find it hard to believe that people can be bisexual since it is so removed from my experience." She left open the possibility that bisexuality really does exist and that her disbelief is a result of her inability to relate to it. Some lesbians' comments even contained a note of sympathy, as did Barbara's: "I am not convinced that it is a true entity but instead may represent a label attached to the group of people who are still struggling with their sexual identity and sexual preference."

Other women harbor clear-cut doubts about whether all bisexuality is illusory, leaving open the possibility that a few women who claim to be bisexual might in fact be true bisexuals or that they themselves might be wrong in assuming that bisexuality does not exist. Some of these women took pains to explain that their opinions about bisexuality are based on limited experience with bisexual women or on their own experience of identifying as bisexual when they were coming out, and apologetically acknowledged that their impressions of bisexuality might be inaccurate. For example, Donna admitted her ignorance,

> I don't think about it much. I don't think I'm well informed on the subject because I don't know one person who calls herself bisexual. My uninformed tendency is to believe that bisexuals don't know yet whether they are gay or straight and one day will decide. (Donna)

Sally apologetically drew conclusions based on her own experience and the experience of her friends,

> As I said before, I'd rather not label anyone—however, the bisexual people I know are rather confused—not sure where their "loyalty" lies. This is the way I felt pretty much during the two years I thought I might be bi. (Sally)

and Mona did not entirely rule out the possibility of bisexuality, although she is inclined to disbelieve people who say they are bisexual:

> Although I think many bisexual women are really lesbians who haven't reached the point of being able to say so (just a period of transition), I believe there are people who are truly bisexual. However, I know few bisexuals and am pretty ignorant of the subject. (Mona)

According to Mona, and several other lesbians who share her opinion, bisexuality is indeed a valid, albeit rare, orientation. Although they tend to be skeptical of other women's claims of bisexuality, they believe that among the many women who appear to be bisexual or who call themselves bisexual there are a few women who really are truly bisexual.

Liberal Opinions and Mixed Feelings

Several lesbian women in this study stated that sexuality is a private matter and that people have the right to do or be what they want (figure 4.1). This liberal opinion leaves the question of bisexual existence open; presumably, these respondents believe that a woman is bisexual if she says she is and that there is no universal definition of bisexuality on which to base an opinion as to whether bisexuality exists. Several of these women said simply, "to each her own," while others like Sue were only slightly more verbose: "Each of us has a right and a responsibility 'to thine own self be true.' Another person's sexual preference is not my business or concern."

Surprisingly few women expressed ambivalence or mixed thoughts about bisexuality. One of these women appears to be in a state of acute conflict over the question of bisexual existence,

> I believe in it and yet I don't. Which I guess means that while I know what it is (?) I don't understand it. But then I do. I wonder how can anyone know what gender they really are attracted to. And yet the men some bi women go with! (Amy)

but others seem to be quite content with their mixed feelings:

> My gut reaction is to think it's a cop-out for people who can't admit their homosexuality, but my intellectual reaction is much more positive. I have to think a lot to hold these negative feelings in check when dealing with bisexuals. (Sharon)

Bisexuality Exists

The question "What is your opinion of bisexuality?" which sparked all of the comments quoted above, is a very simple, direct question. But even simple questions contain assumptions. The assumption behind this question is that there is, in fact, something called bisexuality that one might have an opinion about. In other words, the question itself presupposes the answer to the question "Does bisexuality exist?" to be "yes." Respondents who believe that bisexuality does not exist could not answer the question as asked. Before they could answer the question, they had to challenge the assumption that bisexuality exists by stating that it does not exist. In contrast, respondents who believe that bisexuality does exist could passively accept the question's assumption and write an answer without giving a thought to the question of bisexual existence.

More than a third of the lesbian women who answered this question did exactly that (figure 4.1). They accepted the premise of the question that bisexuality exists and chose to discuss other issues relevant to bisexuality, referring to bisexuality as a real phenomenon. For example, Ruth commented that "this lifestyle could present problems," and Chris stated "I admire them and welcome them into our community." It is, therefore, reasonably safe to assume that these women, who comprised a plurality of the lesbians in the study, believe that bisexuality exists.

Given the ease with which lesbians who believe in bisexual existence could overlook the question of bisexual existence, however, it is surprising that nearly one out of five lesbians nevertheless stated explicitly that she believes that bisexuality exists (figure 4.1). Why would so many women have felt it necessary to state that which had already been assumed? Apparently, the question of bisexual existence is a salient one in lesbians' minds and they did not feel that the assumption could be taken for granted. The women's answers suggest that they were responding to an unspoken assertion that bisexuality does not exist, as if they had already read the answers of the women who do not believe that bisexuality exists and were responding to these answers instead of to the question that was written in the questionnaire. For example, Anne wrote, "I think many people are genuinely bisexual. I am often sad that the lesbian community can be so closed to bisexuality."

Many women described bisexuality as a valid, legitimate, or natural sexual orientation, or as one aspect of human sexual diversity. Comments by these women included "It is as valid a choice as any other," "A legitimate option," "It's one kind of sexual preference," "it is a state of being that some people exist in," "It's a valid orientation," "It is as natural as any other sexual orientation," and "It is one aspect of the wide spectrum of human sexual identity." One terse respondent said simply, "It exists."

Not every woman who believes bisexuality exists feels positively about it. Some women believe it exists, but are either indifferent to bisexuals or dislike them:

I feel it is a significant reality so I accept it. (Siana)

Some people are this way. They are set on both sexes (not undecided). I prefer not to socialize with them. When they do I feel intruded upon.

I have no interest in dating or having sex with bisexual women. They have men in their lives and I want nothing to do with them. (Keesha)

But most of the women who took time to defend the existence of bisexuality do feel positively about it and believe that it should be recognized as a sexual orientation on a par with lesbianism and hetero-sexuality.

Everyone Is Bisexual

Alongside the ever-present charge that bisexuality does not exist, there is also another idea about bisexuality that winds its way through the lesbian debate over bisexuality—the idea that everyone, or almost every-one, is really bisexual. This idea, expressed by one lesbian in six, recalls Freud's assertion that each individual is born with an unshaped sexual potential that becomes focused on particular objects as the individual matures psychologically and socially. Individuals whose sexual energies become focused on people of the other sex are heterosexuals and individ-uals whose sexual energies become focused on people of their own sex are homosexuals. It follows, therefore, that the unshaped sexual poten-tial is a *bi*sexual potential; everyone is born with the potential to relate sexually with either people of the other sex or people of their own sex. For example,

I think all of us are basically bisexual. We each have the potential to have sexual, affectional, emotional feelings for persons of either gender. (Ellen)

It's fine. I believe all people are capable of the gamut of sexual experi-ence. (Kim)

Bisexuality is the ability of an individual to be sexually and emotionally attracted to either sex. I believe the majority of people have this capa-bility if they were truly in tune with their feelings. (Renée)

These three comments reveal slight differences in the way these three respondents conceptualize bisexual potential. Ellen conceptualizes it as the capacity to have sexual and emotional feelings for both genders, whereas Kim conceptualizes it as the potential to have actual sexual experiences with both genders. Ellen and Kim made blanket statements that all people have bisexual potential, whereas Renée's comment is a bit less sweeping; she believes that a majority of people have this poten-tial. All three believe that bisexuality is no more than a potential and that many people might never realize this potential by having actual feelings or sexual experiences with both genders.

The idea that people are initially or potentially bisexual but then "sort themselves out" into lesbianism and heterosexuality is a recurrent theme in lesbians' comments. This argument allows lesbians to reconcile a belief in the prevalence of bisexuality with the scarcity of people who actually appear to be bisexual. Some respondents expressed this distinction between potential and actual sexuality as a distinction between being and doing,

> *In truth what we all are . . . what few can possibly practice. (Nancy)*

or as a distinction between potential feelings and actual behavior:

> *I believe that people have the possibility of falling in love with either gender but love and sexuality are not always equated. (Carol)*

Others argued that social and political factors cause the transformation of bisexual potential into monosexual reality. These factors include homophobia that prevents women from recognizing their attraction for other women,

> *It seems to be a natural development of most people, in terms of desire. Because of this country's homophobia, the practice of bisexuality seems less common. (Judith)*

rejection of bisexuals by both the lesbian and heterosexual communities,

> *Actually I think most people are bisexual. They just tend to identify with one sexuality because it's practically impossible to switch back and forth without being ostracized from your peers. (Maureen)*

the lack of a supportive bisexual community,

> *I think that it is very common, if not ubiquitous for women to be sexually attracted to both sexes at some times in their lives . . . I think it must be difficult to maintain a bisexual lifestyle because of the lack of a support community. I think people tend to sort themselves at one node or another. (Pamela)*

socialization,

> *I think it would be many people's choice if we were not taught to identify as either straight or gay. (Jane)*

or personal experiences:

*. . . by nature we are all bisexual . . . Our choices are based mostly on
social sex roles, somewhat on who's there for us when we're ready to
be sexual. (Alice)*

Many lesbians described an ideal society in which these social and
political factors would not operate, and in which everyone would be
able to express the full range of their sexual capacities without con-
straint. Some stated simply that in such a society, bisexuality would be
more common. For example, Cindy thinks that "it is a state of being
that some people exist in and that in a different society and time maybe
we would all have the capacity for." Others argued that bisexuality
itself would be a different phenomenon in an ideal society than it is in
contemporary society. In the ideal society, bisexuality itself would be
ideal, i.e., desirable and even beneficial. But under current political
circumstances, bisexuality takes on a very different meaning:

*In a perfect world perhaps it would be the norm . . . however, this is
not a perfect world . . . so . . . I think bisexuality is often a way of
keeping at bay the bad/negative aspects of homophobia while enjoying
a lot of the good parts of the lesbian community. (Rebecca)*

*. . . really I believe humans are "naturally" bisexual or multisexual.
But in contemporary culture, I think sexuality is so tied to emotional
and political issues that to be bisexual is to refuse to make a stand.
(Margaret)*

Among lesbians who believe that bisexuality would be the norm in an
ideal society but are unable to accept it in this society, some experience
their mixed feelings as ambivalence, or are confused by their own contradictory emotions:

*Part of me would like to believe that there can exist a perfect society,
truly spiritual, whole, undiscriminate (sic), where women, men have
become, have progressed to a sexless society—which then allows one
to call themselves bisexual (for want of a better term.) (Joan)*

*I think that ideally all people are born with the physical potential to
relate to both sexes . . . Today I feel as if society is so repressive that
our sexuality is less fluid. I have nothing against women or men who
are bisexual. I guess emotionally I feel some kind of resentment for
some unknown reason! (Laura)*

Not all lesbians who believe that most or all people are bisexual
used concepts like "potential" or "ideal" to explain this belief. Many

asserted that bisexuality is universal or widespread here and now. Among these lesbians, references to a continuum of sexuality or to "degrees" of sexuality/bisexuality were frequent. For example, June feels that "most people, women and men, are to a certain extent bisexual— but this constitutes a continuous scale, not clear distinctions between straight, bisexual, or gay." Although there are differences of opinion over whether and where to draw the lines that distinguish bisexuality from lesbianism and heterosexuality on this continuum, many of these women see bisexuality as overlapping lesbianism and heterosexuality. These respondents typically argued that although most or all people are "bisexual to a degree," most lean toward one direction or the other and are therefore "really" lesbian or heterosexual and should identify themselves as such. Apparently, on the sexual scale conceived by these lesbians, bisexuality encompasses the entire continuum with the presumed exception of the extreme endpoints, whereas lesbianism and heterosexuality encompass the entire continuum with the exception of the area immediately surrounding the midpoint. This conception of sexuality allowed these women to state that most or all people are bisexual while also asserting that women who call themselves bisexual are sometimes or frequently denying their own lesbianism. For example,

> I think everyone is bisexual to some degree. It is difficult for me to believe someone could be equally satisfied in a relationship with a man or woman. Some people hide behind this label because it's more acceptable than being gay. (Nel)

Thus, the concept of a sexual continuum, like the concepts of an ideal society or an unrealized sexual "potential," enables lesbians to reconcile beliefs about the universality of bisexuality with beliefs about the political undesirability of bisexuality or the suspicious quality of those who call themselves bisexual in this society.

Summary

The issue of whether or not bisexuality exists is a salient one among lesbians. Although the question "What is your opinion of bisexuality?" made no explicit reference to the issue of bisexual existence, more than half of lesbian respondents chose to address this issue more or less directly in their answers. This finding is all the more remarkable because many of those who addressed the issue believe that bisexuality exists. Within the context of a question that presumed bisexual existence, statements affirming bisexual existence were unnecessary. Apparently, the minority that does not believe in bisexuality is vocal enough to create a climate in which other lesbians feel compelled to assert their belief that bisexuality does exist.

In fact, the lesbians who participated in this study are as likely to believe that everyone or almost everyone is potentially bisexual as they are to believe that bisexuality does not exist. But the fact that no one except the proponents of the idea of a universal bisexual potential mentioned it indicates that this idea is less salient in discourse about bisexuality among lesbians. Apparently the idea of universal bisexuality, despite its popularity, has less impact on lesbian symbolic culture than the idea that bisexuality does not exist; the idea of universal bisexuality does not "hang in the air" as an idea to be reckoned with.

The finding that the question of bisexual existence is so important to lesbians is a bit surprising, given that the existence of bisexuality was not constructed as an issue in any of the lesbian and/or gay publications I examined in chapter 1. In The Lesbian and Gay Press, the issue is not whether bisexuality *does* exist, but whether bisexuality *should* exist, what its political implications are, and whether it belongs in The Lesbian and Gay Movement. The "issue of bisexuality" as it is presented in The Lesbian and Gay Press does not accurately reflect the issue as it is seen by the "lesbian-on-the-street." However, by overlooking the issue of bisexual existence and focusing on the implications of bisexuality, The Press accurately, albeit implicitly, reflects the fact that most lesbians believe that there is something called bisexuality.

What Is Bisexuality? Or, Will the Real Lesbian Please Stand Up?

If bisexuality does exist, then what is it? Is it a feeling or is it a lifestyle? Is it a preference or a choice? Is it sexual nondiscrimination or sexual indiscriminacy? Although most lesbian respondents believe bisexuality exists, for many this is the only point on which they agree; there are almost as many conceptions of bisexuality among lesbians as there are lesbians who believe it exists.

The question of what constitutes bisexuality is inextricably entwined with the question of what is lesbianism. By defining the boundaries of bisexuality, we define the boundaries of lesbianism, and vice versa. Sometimes the distinction between bisexuality and lesbianism is clear; a woman whose lovers have all been women and whose romantic and sexual feelings are exclusively same-sex is a lesbian, and a woman who has had equal numbers of female and male partners and feels equally attracted to women and men is a bisexual. But few of us fit either of these ideal images. Most of us have had some combination of female and male sexual partners, and many of us have some degree of sexual attraction toward men. Where, then, do we draw the line between lesbianism and bisexuality? How do we decide who is the real lesbian—indeed, whether we ourselves are real lesbians—and who is bisexual?

Nearly half of the lesbians who participated in this study provided definitions of bisexuality when they answered the question "What is your opinion of bisexuality?" Analysis of these definitions showed that there are a small number of criteria, which, like building blocks, are applied and combined in unique ways by each individual. The most commonly used criteria are behavior, used by nearly two-fifths of lesbian respondents, and feelings, used by one-quarter. Other criteria include identity, preferences, choices, and the importance of gender.

Bisexuality as a Matter of Behavior

Many lesbians define bisexuality in terms of behavior. In the opinions of these women, one is bisexual if one behaves bisexually. But what is bisexual behavior? Lesbians who define bisexuality in terms of behavior concur that the bisexual lifestyle involves some form of sexual contact with both women and men, but beyond this basic point, agreement breaks down. What kind of sexual contact is necessary to qualify one as bisexual? Is casual sexual contact sufficient, or must sexual contact occur within the framework of a serious romantic relationship? How much sexual contact with each sex is necessary—is a single experience with one or the other sex sufficient, or must a person have considerable sexual experience with both sexes in order to be considered bisexual? Must one enjoy these sexual contacts? Must one have exactly equal amounts of homosexual and heterosexual experience? Can homosexual and heterosexual experiences occur serially, or does bisexuality imply that homosexual and heterosexual relationships occur simultaneously? Differences of opinion exist on all these questions.

Compare, for example, the following two definitions of bisexuality:

A person who has sex with both women and men. (Jill)

To be bisexual would mean that a person were simultaneously involved in an intimate sexual relationship with a man and a woman. (Marlene)

Both of these women define a bisexual person as one who has sexual relations with both women and men, but they have very different ideas about the kinds of sexual relations that constitute bisexuality. In Jill's opinion, merely having both homosexual and heterosexual physical relations is sufficient to qualify one as bisexual. The context, quantity, and quality of these sexual relations are irrelevant. Marlene has a much narrower definition of bisexuality. According to her, to be bisexual one must not only engage in both homosexual and heterosexual physical relations; one must also be involved in intimate ongoing relationships with both sexes, and these relationships must be simultaneous. In other words, merely engaging in both homosexual and heterosexual physical activity does not constitute bisexuality; this activity must take place in sufficient quantity and within the right context in order to be defined as bisexuality.

Other lesbians are more concerned about the quality of homosexual and heterosexual relations than about their quantity, context, or simultaneity. Jamila and Greta define bisexuality as the ability to enjoy homosexual and heterosexual contact:

I think that there are times when anyone can enjoy sex be it with a man or woman. Bisexuality means you can enjoy it either way. The way I see it is if you enjoy it do it. (Jamila)

Many bisexuals have not realized or accepted that they are gay. Others may really be bisexual getting as much fulfillment from men as women. (Greta)

But despite their agreement on this point, these two women still have different conceptions of bisexuality. Jamila considers anyone who enjoys both types of sex to be bisexual, whereas Greta reserves the term for those people who enjoy the two sexes equally. Therefore, in the opinion of the first woman almost everyone is bisexual, whereas in the opinion of the second woman bisexuality is less common than it appears to be. Consequently, these two women have different attitudes toward bisexuality. Jamila takes a liberal "to each her own" stance, whereas Greta looks upon women who claim to be bisexual with suspicion.

Some women extrapolate the ability to enjoy both sexes into a need for both sexes, conceptualizing bisexuals as individuals who not only enjoy both heterosex and homosex but who need both heterosex and homosex. In this view, a bisexual person can never be completely satisfied with either a heterosexual or a homosexual relationship, since her need for the other type of relationship would be unfulfilled. Thus, bisexuals are doomed to a life of either alternating between homosexual and heterosexual relationships,

> Now, though, I am trying very hard to understand bisexuality. I feel that it must be a very difficult lifestyle . . . an emotional and sexual see-saw. (Kelly)

or juggling simultaneous homosexual and heterosexual relationships,

> I think that it would be a very hard way of life for me. I could not juggle the two. (Gina)

or indiscriminate sexual activity with anything that moves:

> [Bisexuality is a way] for highly sexed people who go either way to double their chances for sex. (Arlene)

Any of these three lifestyles would make a committed monogamous relationship difficult to maintain, if not impossible. Conceptualized in terms of coexistent homosexual and heterosexual needs or as the result of an overly active sex drive, bisexuality becomes incompatible with committed monogamy,

> If a person is settled with this identity I think it's great. I also believe that this lifestyle could present problems in needing both preferences met at same time—makes for a difficult monogamous relationship. (Ruth)

especially when homosexual and heterosexual needs are perceived as antithetical to each other:

> One who is attracted and enjoys a sexual relationship with both men and women. Sad that the inner conflict prevents the person to experi-

ence a complete commitment to one person in order to build a lasting relationship. (Cori)

The implication that bisexuals are incapable of committed relationships bothers many lesbians, who conclude that bisexuality is a symptom of an inability to commit oneself to a single partner. These lesbians often have moral objections to bisexuality as nonmonogamous by definition. Although they sometimes extend partial tolerance to bisexuality, they do so only under certain conditions and predict that problems will arise even under these conditions. For example, Bobbi feels that nonmonogamy would be OK if the participants were mature and honest: "I can accept bisexuality if . . . (1) the person is happy and can emotionally handle and accept their own sexual identity and lifestyle; and (2) they are honest and open with someone they are about to or are committed to in a relationship." Similarly, Jennifer's approval is contingent on the mutual consent of those involved, "Bisexuality is fine with me—as long as everyone is consenting." In contrast, Alison does not approve of nonmonogamy under any conditions; she would tolerate bisexuality only "If the person has a relationship with either sex and breaks it off totally, to start a relationship with the other sex."

Some lesbians who define bisexuality in terms of behavior disapprove of bisexuality for political as well as moral reasons. Many feel that bisexual women's associations with men disqualify them completely from political alliance or comradeship with lesbians. Others feel that bisexual women can and should align themselves with lesbians, but again, only if they follow certain rules. They have different opinions about what these rules are. Some don't care if bisexual women continue to sleep with men as long as they identify themselves as lesbians for political purposes. Other lesbians are angered by bisexual women who try to present themselves as lesbians because they feel that this is deceptive and disrespectful to lesbians. Still others feel that bisexual women should, for the time being, abstain from relationships with men and unite with lesbians until equality between the sexes has been achieved. Lesbians' political opinions about bisexuality will be explored in greater detail later in this chapter.

In summary, the most common criterion lesbians use to define bisexuality is behavior. That is, when most lesbian respondents were asked to discuss their opinions about "bisexual women," they pictured women who behave bisexually. But they have different opinions about what constitutes bisexual behavior. For some, it means simultaneous sexual relationships with both women and men, or an exactly equal amount of homosexual and heterosexual experience. Others have broader definitions, which include any woman who has had sexual relations with both women and men, or who could enjoy both homosexual and heterosexual relations. According to any of these definitions, bisexual women are nonmonogamous or at best serially monogamous by definition, and many lesbians who define bisexuality in terms of behavior are concerned about bisexual women's inability to commit themselves to a single partner. Others are concerned about the political implications of bisexuals' relations with men. For these reasons, bisexual women—defined as women who have sex with both women and men—meet with a great deal of disapproval and distrust from lesbians.

Bisexuality as a Matter of Feelings

Although the lesbians who participated in this study most commonly define bisexuality as a form of behavior, many are less concerned with actual behavior than with the feelings one has toward women and men. These lesbians define bisexuality as a matter of how one feels rather than how one behaves, and not surprisingly, they are more likely than lesbians who define bisexuality in terms of behavior to believe that bisexuality exists.[2] Although there are some differences of opinion among them over exactly which feelings should be defined as bisexual, these differences are fewer and more trivial than those that exist among lesbians who define bisexuality behaviorally. Like the latter, they are concerned about bisexuality, but their concerns have a markedly different character.

Most lesbians who define bisexuality in terms of feelings simply referred to bisexual women as having "attractions" to women and men. Some respondents specified that they were referring to both emotional and physical attraction, or to emotional, social, and sexual attraction. Dorothea described attraction as "the range of feelings allowing us to be sexually and romantically involved with women and men." Other respondents referred to "love," "affectional preference," or simply "feelings."

For the most part, these differences appear to be merely differences in wording rather than differences of opinion. The only issue over which these lesbians are substantially divided is the question of whether bisexuals are those rare individuals whose feelings for women and men are exactly equal in strength and quality, or whether everyone who has feelings for both women and men should be considered bisexual:

> *I feel we all have varying degrees of attraction to both sexes, and maybe bisexual people really are equally attracted to both sexes . . . (Juanita)*

> *I feel it is one aspect of the wide spectrum of human sexual identity. Just as there are women who are attracted to women, men to men, and women and men to each other to varying degrees, so there are also women and men who are attracted to both sexes to differing degrees. (Martha)*

Lesbians like Juanita who define bisexuality in terms of equal attractions for women and men generally hold more negative attitudes toward bisexuals than lesbians like Martha who define bisexuality as a broader range of feelings toward both women and men. The former typically believe that while most people experience attractions toward both women and men, everyone or almost everyone has a preference one way or the other. They feel that people should identify themselves as lesbian or heterosexual according to their preferences, and many expressed antagonism or impatience with people who do not. In contrast, the latter are generally very tolerant or accepting of bisexuality. Those who define bisexuality as encompassing a broad range of varying feelings of attraction toward women and men disagree, however, on the issue of whether people with bisexual feelings should act on these feelings. Some believe that they should,

> *I don't have any problems with it. If someone is attracted to both men and women, I think they should act upon it—it's not healthy to hide feelings like that. (Frances)*

whereas others believe that they should not.

Lesbians who define bisexuality in terms of a broad range of feelings toward women and men expressed concerns about bisexuality, but their concerns are very different from those expressed by lesbians who define bisexuality behaviorally. Instead of being concerned about bisexual women's heterosexuality and integrity, they are concerned about the difficulties that bisexual women must face. These difficulties include personal problems, such as combining two very different types of love, and social hardships, such as a lack of acceptance by both the lesbian and heterosexual societies:

> *It must be very difficult to be a bisexual because of the tremendous difference between loving women and loving men. I have trouble understanding/relating to "bi's." (Georgia)*

> *For persons attracted to both genders, I feel both envy and pity. They, in theory, could have the best of two worlds, but in reality, I fear usually neither gays or non-gays trust and accept them. (Abigail)*

Many, like Georgia, confessed that they have difficulty understanding bisexuality, usually explaining that it is so removed from their own experience that they cannot relate to it. Some have trouble understanding attractions to men because they have never felt attracted to men themselves, whereas others have trouble understanding how people could be attracted to both sexes. Nevertheless, their comments convey a note of tolerance and even warmth that is generally lacking from the comments of those who define bisexuality in terms of behavior or in terms of equal attractions to women and men. For example, Thelma accepts what she cannot understand:

> *I feel accepting of my friends who identify themselves as bisexual. I don't understand their ability to feel sexually attracted to and satisfied by both men and women. (Thelma)*

In summary, lesbians who define bisexuality in terms of feelings of attraction toward women and men are divided over the question of whether bisexuality should be defined as an equal attraction toward women and men, or as a combination of attractions toward women and men of varying degrees. Lesbians who define bisexuality in terms of equal attractions generally take a dim view of people who call themselves bisexual because they believe that most people have a preference for either women or men and that most bisexual-identified people use the bisexual label to avoid admitting their true preference. Lesbians who define bisexuality in terms of a broader range of feelings are generally tolerant and accepting of bisexuality, however. They are concerned about the difficulties bisexuals face in a society that validates heterosexual and lesbian identities and lifestyles but condemns bisexuality, even though many admit that they cannot relate personally because they are not bisexual themselves.

Bisexuality as a Matter of Identity—
Or a Denial of Identity

In an early phase of this research, 26 pre-test subjects were asked to rate the importance of various criteria in defining sexual orientation. Forty-six percent rated bisexual identity as "very important" or "essential" in defining bisexuality. Apparently, the women who participated in the pre-test felt that they accorded a great deal of respect to others' bisexual identities. When lesbian respondents in the main phase of the research were asked "What is your opinion of bisexuality?" many of them spontaneously mentioned bisexual identity. In this open-ended format, however, they usually mentioned it not to tout it as an important criterion of bisexuality, but to raise questions about its validity as a criterion. Of the 82 lesbians who mentioned bisexual identity, 57 did so to cast doubt on it. It would appear that when asked directly, lesbians generally say that they give serious consideration to other women's bisexual identities, but when they are allowed to express their thoughts in a less structured context their comments reveal that many do not in fact accord bisexual identity much credibility.

Most lesbians who are suspicious of bisexual identity believe that women who call themselves bisexual are really lesbians. They explained that bisexual identity is used by people who can't or won't acknowledge their true sexuality, i.e., lesbianism, usually because of homophobia. Other lesbian respondents do not necessary think that bisexuals *are* lesbians, but they do expect that bisexuals are women on their way to *becoming* lesbians. Both of these beliefs cast doubt on the authenticity of bisexual identity, and by implication, on bisexuality itself. I call these beliefs "existentially invalidating" beliefs, and I will discuss them in detail along with lesbians' other images of bisexual women later in this chapter.

A few respondents took pains to point out that their doubts about the authenticity of bisexual identity arose from their personal experiences with bisexual women, thus softening their criticism of bisexual identity. Marla, for example, sounded apologetic for her skepticism about other women's bisexual identities. She wrote, "I feel that sometimes women who claim to be bisexual are simply denying their homosexuality. This is based on only the people I know that say they are bisexual." Others commented that their impressions of bisexuality came

primarily from their own experiences. They recalled that they identified
themselves as bisexual before they came out as lesbians, and tentatively
drew on this experience to wonder if other bisexual-identified women
were also in the process of coming out as lesbians. For example, Doris
explained, "I think many women think in terms of bisexuality when they
are initially coming out—a transitional period—when I first fell in love
with a womyn my internalized homophobia was so great I couldn't
comprehend me being a lesbian."

Like Doris, Rhonda identified herself as bisexual before she came
out as lesbian, but in hindsight she interprets her experience in a very
different way:

> When I first entered the lesbian community I thought of myself as
> bisexual—and referred to myself as such. A very large group of women
> (friends) that identified themselves as "lesbian" said I was confused.
> Within six months of coming out, I started referring to myself as
> "lesbian." Found a much stronger sense of acceptance in the gay com-
> munity . . . bisexual people are not accepted and have a harder time
> than gay men and women. (Rhonda)

Rhonda believes that lesbians' suspicions about bisexual identity
pressure bisexual women into identifying as lesbian. If she were to
meet Doris, she might disagree with her that her period of bisexual
identification was a transitional phase. Rhonda might argue that Doris
is not a lesbian at all, but a bisexual woman who was pressured into
identifying as a lesbian and who, in order to authenticate her current
lesbian identity, now perceives her bisexual identity as inauthentic in
hindsight.

Such a process would tend to be self-reproducing; each generation
of women who are convinced to identify themselves as lesbians learns to
inauthenticate their own previous bisexual identities by explaining them
as transitional phases. These women, like Doris, then assume that other
women who identify themselves as bisexual are likewise "going through
a phase"; they expect these women to eventually come out as lesbians
just as they themselves did. Bisexual-identified women become aware of
lesbians' expectations, and this awareness creates the pressure to identify
as lesbian that Rhonda described. Those who are convinced by this
pressure to identify as lesbians become invested in authenticating their
own lesbian identities by inauthenticating their own and others' bisexual
identities, and the cycle continues.

But not all lesbian respondents who mentioned bisexual identity did so to cast doubt on its authenticity. Of the 82 lesbian respondents who referred to identity in their answers to the question "What is your opinion of bisexuality?" 25 referred to it for other reasons. Nine lesbians stated or implied that they accept other women's bisexual identities at face value, i.e., that they assume other women's identities are authentic reflections of their sexual essences. For example, Thelma expressed no suspicion whatsoever that bisexual-identified women might not be bisexual, which, according to her own definition, means that they are attracted to both women and men,

I feel accepting of my friends who identify themselves as bisexual. I don't understand their ability to feel sexually attracted to and satisfied by both men and women. (Thelma)

and Samantha believes that a woman's sexual identity should be respected and taken as the primary indicator of her sexuality:

It seems to be a viable lifestyle for some individuals. I support individual choice in defining ourselves. I, therefore, support individuals who choose bisexuality. (Samantha)

Five other lesbians went one step farther in authenticating bisexuality; so far, in fact, that they questioned the authenticity of lesbian identity. In contrast to the 57 lesbians who cast doubt on bisexual identity by stating or inferring that women who call themselves bisexual are sometimes or always really lesbians, Mae cast doubt on *non-bisexual* identity by implying not only that women who call themselves bisexual are authentically bisexual, but that many women who don't call themselves bisexual are also bisexual. She thinks that bisexuality is "the most common sexual orientation, if only people would admit it."

Despite their disagreements over the authenticity of various sexual identities, all 71 of the women discussed above—those who doubt the authenticity of bisexual identity, those who doubt the authenticity of non-bisexual identity, and those who believe in the authenticity of all identities—do agree on one point. They share the underlying opinion that sexual identity *should* reflect sexual essence. There are also lesbians who believe that sexual identity *should not* necessarily reflect sexual essence, especially when that essence is bisexual. In fact, some believe that essence should not be the determining factor in identity at all.

Loretta, for example, believes that although women might be essentially bisexual, they make choices regarding which sex or sexes they will become sexually involved with, and their identities reflect, or should reflect, these behavioral choices:

> *I think that almost everyone is bisexual but some choose to place their emphasis on one end of the scale . . . I think that many lesbians could be involved with a man and straight women with other women if they allowed themselves to. I see people who call themselves bisexuals as those who do not wish to choose. (Loretta)*

Other lesbians believe that identity reflects, or should reflect, a woman's political commitments. Gilda, for example, believes that it is woman-identification, not sexual behavior, that distinguishes lesbians from bisexual women. In other words, lesbians and bisexual women might have identical sexual behaviors and feelings; the difference lies in their political orientation, not their sexuality:

> *I know many lesbians (including myself) who relate romantically/sexually with men and women yet identify strongly as lesbians. To me a bisexual is someone who goes either way sexually but is not particularly woman identified. (Gilda)*

Rebecca would approve of Gilda's decision to identify herself as a lesbian:

> *I think bisexual women while they may practice bisexuality ought to identify as lesbians to strengthen the lesbian movement. I believe the old line about identify with the oppressed group and not the more privileged one. (Rebecca)*

In summary, the majority of lesbians who mentioned bisexual identity did so to discredit it. In general, lesbians tend not to accept other women's bisexual identities at face value; usually, they suspect that women who call themselves bisexual are really lesbians. Very few lesbians spoke up to defend the authenticity of bisexual identity and express their respect for women who choose to identify as bisexual, but a few of those who did went so far as to cast doubt on lesbian identity instead. Finally, some lesbians do not believe that identity should reflect essence at all; they feel that identity should reflect a woman's political convictions, not her sexual behaviors or feelings. To them, the issue is not authenticity, but politics.

Bisexuality as a Matter of Preferences or Choices

Some lesbians simply referred to bisexuality, or sexuality in general, as a matter of "preference" or "choice" without specifying what is preferred or chosen. Among those who referred to unspecified preferences, eleven consider bisexuality a sexual preference, whereas four conceptualize it as a *lack* of preference. For example, SueAnne called bisexuality "one kind of sexual preference," and Helen thinks it "must be difficult not to have a definite preference one way or the other." The ten lesbians who referred to sexuality as a matter of choice were evenly divided between those who consider bisexuality a choice and those who consider bisexuality to be the absence of choice, or a failure to choose.

Lesbians who consider bisexuality to be a positive sexual preference or choice generally expressed empathic and tolerant attitudes toward bisexuality. Many took the liberal stance, "if that's what a person is happy being, go for it," or explicitly stated that the bisexual preference is as valid or legitimate as the homosexual and heterosexual preferences are. In contrast, lesbians who define bisexuality as a lack of preference or choice are inclined to accuse women who call themselves bisexual of cowardice. At the very least, they are uneasy around women whose loyalties are not clear. Madeline, for example, is "more comfortable with people who have made definite choices for one sex over the other."

Bisexuality as a Matter of Gender Blindness

The foregoing discussion demonstrates one point very clearly. Lesbians define bisexuality in a variety of different ways. Despite this great variety, however, all of the definitions examined so far have one thing in common. They all describe bisexuality in terms of the gender(s) of one's sexual partner(s) or potential partner(s). Defined by behavior, bisexuals are people who engage in sex with both women and men. Defined by feelings, bisexuals are people who are attracted to or capable of loving both women and men. Defined by preferences, bisexuals are either people who have preferences for both women and men or people who lack a preference for one over the other. These definitions of bisexuality retain the emphasis on the gender(s) of one's partner(s), an emphasis derived from the gender-specific definitions of homosexuality and heterosexuality.

A very small number of lesbian respondents—fewer than one in twenty—have a very different type of definition of bisexuality. Rather than conceptualizing bisexuality as a combination of homosexuality and heterosexuality, thus emphasizing gender, these women choose to deemphasize gender by conceptualizing bisexuality as the ability to love people *regardless* of their gender. Bisexuals are, by this definition, people who love people rather than people who love women and men. For example, Prudence defines bisexuals as "people who love people regardless of sex."

These women harbor some of the same reservations about bisexuality that other lesbians do:

> I don't understand it because I can't relate to men the way I do to women (any more than I can understand heterosexuality). It's possible that it is the ideal—relating to people regardless of gender, but I tend to think (perhaps wrongly) of the bisexual as sexually oriented instead of emotionally oriented. (Willa)

Most, however, believe that bisexuality is the most natural or ideal form of sexuality, arguing that it reflects an openness toward people and experiences or a more humanist way of relating to people. This ideal is achieved by a few healthy and untraumatized people in this world and could be achieved by all people in a less sexist, more humane world. In effect, bisexuality is the sexual equivalent of equal opportunity; as Esther put it, "One way to look at it is they give all people equal footing." Once gender discrimination is eradicated, perhaps we will all be able to look past each others' genitals and genders to the human beings inside.

Summary

Lesbians define bisexuality in different ways. Many define it in terms of behavior, whereas others define it in terms of feelings of emotional or sexual attraction that might or might not be expressed through behavior. A few lesbians think of bisexuality as a positive sexual preference or choice and, conversely, a few think of it as a lack of preference or a failure to choose. Even among lesbians who use the same criterion to define bisexuality, there is considerable variation in the way they apply this criterion to distinguish bisexuality from homosexuality and hetero-sexuality. But whether defined in terms of behavior, feelings, preferences, or choices, bisexuality is usually defined in terms of gender; for example, as sexual behavior with both women and men, or as a choice between women and men. A very small handful of lesbians define bisexuality as the ability to love or be attracted to people regardless of their gender.

Lesbians who use different definitions of bisexuality tend to have different attitudes toward it. For example, lesbians who define bisexuality in terms of behavior tend to be skeptical about its existence and reluctant to become too closely involved with bisexual women, whereas lesbians who define bisexuality in terms of feelings are more tolerant and concerned about the difficulties they think bisexuals must face. It is not surprising that lesbians who define bisexuality differently have different opinions; after all, they are talking about entirely different things.

WHAT ARE BISEXUALS LIKE?

The question "How do lesbians picture bisexual women?" bears a disquieting resemblance to questions like "How do whites picture blacks?" and "What is the male ideal of womanhood?" In the past few decades, we as a society have become increasingly sensitive to the dynamics of stereotypy and oppression. One after the other, oppressed groups among us have begun to resist the economic, social, and political structures that cause their disadvantage, fighting to change not only these structures but also the prejudicial attitudes of the powerful members of society who benefit from the same structures. As a result, those of us who are oppressed ourselves or who are sincere in our hatred of oppression have become sensitized not only to sexism, racism, heterosexism, ableism, and age-ism in particular, but also to the form of prejudicial thinking in general. We are suspicious of any statement that sounds like a generalization or that refers to people as members of groups instead of individuals.

Making generalizations about the objects in our environments, including other people, is a natural and necessary human skill. Generalization involves overlooking individual differences in the effort to find similarities. Without this skill, we would be unable to learn from our

experiences, unable to plan future activity, largely unable to communicate with each other, and unable to empathize with the experiences of
other people. So when does this natural and necessary capacity for
generalization become objectionable? It becomes problematic when the
objects we generalize are other human beings, and when our capacity to
perceive similarities impedes our ability to perceive individual differences
as well. At that point, we begin to see other people as no more than
group representatives and we begin to treat them as members of categories instead of individuals. We then look at Black people and see nothing
but black; we look at White people and see nothing but white. Instead
of facilitating social interaction, our ability to generalize becomes an
obstacle to social interaction that robs others of their individuality by
replacing it with stereotypes.

    Failure to perceive the individual differences among members of
other social groups is only one side of the coin of stereotypy. The other
side is failure to recognize the similarities between members of other
groups and members of one's own group, including oneself. It is difficult
to identify or empathize with someone who bears no similarity to oneself; those who appear entirely foreign to us often appear subhuman
because we are unable to recognize their human qualities. In short, we
objectify them; by denying their similarity to ourselves, we deny their
humanity. Such is the psychology that makes killing an enemy during
wartime a moral act.

    How does all of this relate to the discussion of lesbians' views of
bisexual women? Is it a simple exploration of the necessary human
capacity for generalization, or is it an indictment of lesbians for stereotyping bisexual women even as they condemn the ignorance of homophobic heterosexuals? This depends more on the answer to the question
"How do lesbians picture bisexual women?" than it does on the question itself. It depends on whether lesbians' images of bisexual women
leave room for individual differences among bisexual women. It also
depends on whether these images leave room for the perception of
similarities as well as differences between lesbians and bisexual women.
To find out, we cannot examine lesbians' attitudes toward bisexuals in a
vacuum; we must compare them to lesbians' images of themselves. The
question is no longer "How do lesbians picture bisexual women?" as it
was originally phrased, but rather "To what degree do lesbians picture
bisexual women as different from lesbians and as more homogeneous
than lesbians?" It is not very useful to know that some lesbians believe

that bisexual women are confused, for example, unless we also know whether or not they believe that lesbians are more or less confused than bisexual women and unless we know whether they believe confusion is universal or merely common among bisexual women.

The lesbians who participated in this study answered several specific questions about their images of both bisexual women and other lesbians. These questions are described below under the subheading "A Note about Method," which may be skipped by the uninterested reader. Respondents' answers to the question "What is your opinion of bisexuality?" which have formed the basis of the foregoing segments of this chapter, were also used as sources of information about lesbians' images of bisexual women.

For the purpose of discussion, lesbians' images of bisexual women fall roughly into four categories. Unflattering images are those that might not be clearly negative, but that are not images most people would desire to project themselves. Positive images, in contrast, ascribe an exalted moral, social, or existential status to bisexuality. Existentially invalidating images challenge the authenticity of bisexual identity by calling into question the existence of bisexuality, and political images concern the social and political advantages or disadvantages that bisexuals face vis-à-vis lesbians.

A Note about Method

In addition to the open-ended question "What is your opinion of bisexuality?" respondents were asked several closed-ended questions about specific beliefs that they might have about bisexuality. Whereas women's responses to the open-ended question provide rich information about the subtleties and varieties of their beliefs, this information is neither systematic nor comprehensive because each woman answered the question in her own way. Closed-ended questions, on the other hand, do not reflect subtle differences in the thinking of women with similar beliefs, but they do provide systematic information about the strength and popularity of certain key beliefs. Taken together, the two sources of information provide a more complete picture of lesbians' images of bisexual women and of how bisexual women differ from lesbians than either would provide alone.

The closed-ended questions included questions about the beliefs that bisexuals are really lesbians, that bisexuals are in transition to lesbianism, that bisexuals are less committed to their female friends than lesbians are, that bisexuals are less politically trustworthy than lesbians, and that bisexuals are more likely to pass as heterosexual. Each of these beliefs was mentioned in some form by pre-test respondents in the current study, and all have been reported in previous research by other social scientists. However, the evidence from previous research is entirely qualitative and anecdotal. Quantitative data, which would provide an indication of the popularity and strength of these beliefs among lesbians, as well as a means of assessing the demographic and social correlates of these beliefs, did not exist until the current study. Other closed-ended questions asked about lesbians' beliefs about bisexual women's political interests and experiences of prejudice and discrimination, an area that has received very little attention in previous research.

The closed-ended questions used a variety of different formats to measure lesbians' beliefs and the wording of all these questions can be found in the tables at the end of this book and in the appendix of Rust (1993b). Some beliefs were measured with a single question that asked respondents to make a direct comparison between lesbian and bisexual women. For example, beliefs about personal commitment were measured by asking respondents to indicate on a seven-point scale how strongly they agreed or disagreed with the following statement:

> Bisexuals are not as committed to other women as lesbians are; they are more likely to desert their female friends.

The single-question/direct-comparison format was also used to measure beliefs about bisexuals' trustworthiness and differences between lesbians' and bisexual women's political interests.

Other beliefs were measured by asking respondents separately about their images of lesbian and bisexual women, and then comparing these two images to determine the degree of difference respondents perceived between lesbian and bisexual women. For example, the following pair of questions asked respondents to assess the degree of prejudice experienced by lesbians and by bisexual women:

> How much prejudice do you feel there is in the general U.S. population against lesbians/gay women?

> How much prejudice do you feel there is in the general U.S. population against bisexual women?

Each question was followed by a seven-point response scale that ranged from "No prejudice at all" (1) to "More than against any other single group" (7). Because these two questions used identical wording, they are comparable to each other and subtracting one answer from the other produces a measure of the degree to which a respondent believes that either group experiences more prejudice than the other.[3] The paired-question/identical-wording format was also used to measure lesbians' perceptions of the degree of discrimination faced by lesbian and bisexual women, and the ability and desire of lesbian and bisexual women to pass as heterosexual.

Neither the single-question/direct-comparison nor the paired-question/identical-wording format could be used to measure the beliefs that bisexuals are really lesbians and that bisexuals are in transition to lesbianism because the questions would have sounded awkward or nonsensical. For example, imagine a question that asked respondents to agree or disagree with the statement, "Bisexual women are more likely to really be lesbians than lesbians are to really be bisexual"—the statement is too confusing to produce meaningful responses. Or, imagine a pair of questions that asked respondents to estimate "How many bisexual women will eventually come out as lesbians?" and "How many lesbians will eventually come out as bisexual?" The first question of the pair makes sense because the idea that bisexual women are in transition to lesbianism is a familiar one and respondents would be able to respond to it without further thought. But the second question would probably leave many respondents scratching their heads because the idea of lesbians coming out as bisexual is unfamiliar; there is no cultural image for this question to evoke that would make it meaningful to lesbian respondents. Questions that ask about phenomena that are not meaningful to respondents are not fruitful questions; they create phenomena instead of measuring them.

Therefore, the beliefs that bisexual women are really lesbians and that bisexual women are in transition to lesbianism were measured using a third question format, paired-question/equivalent-wording, which allowed each question in the pair to be worded meaningfully. This format consisted of paired statements, each of which was worded to sound as realistic and natural as possible while retaining as much objective equivalence in the meanings of the paired statements as possible. For example, the pair of questions used to measure the belief that bisexuality is a transitional phase that women go through before coming out as lesbians was:

> "Women who say they are bisexual will eventually realize that they are lesbians." What proportion of women who say they are bisexual do you think will eventually realize that they are lesbian?

> "Some women who claim to be lesbians will eventually find out that they actually are bisexual, or straight." What proportion of women who say they are lesbians do you believe will eventually realize that they are actually bisexual or straight?

Each of these two statements was followed by a seven-point response scale ranging from "None" (1) to "All" (7). Although the statements are worded slightly differently, their meanings are similar. The first statement asserts that bisexuality is a transitional phase that women go through before they come out as lesbian, whereas the second statement asserts that lesbianism is a transitional phase. The arithmetic difference between a respondent's responses to these two statements gives a measure of the degree to which she is more or less likely to think that bisexuality is a transitional phase, as compared to lesbianism.

The variety of formats used to assess lesbians' beliefs about bisexual women has both advantages and disadvantages. The primary advantage is that each measure could be designed to optimally measure a particular belief. Since this study was the first to systematically explore many of lesbians' beliefs about bisexual women, a certain flexibility of measurement was necessary and appropriate; rigid measurement methodologies would be premature. The primary disadvantage is that results obtained from measures with different formats cannot be compared to each other. Each measure provides a rough indication of the prevalence or strength of a particular belief among lesbians, subject to the caveats outlined in chapter 3, but these measures cannot be compared to each other to determine which beliefs are most prevalent or most strongly held among lesbians.

In the discussion below, respondents' answers to closed-ended questions about their beliefs about bisexual women will be used to buttress information gathered from the spontaneous comments they made in answer to the question "What is your opinion of bisexuality?" Readers who are interested in a more detailed and scientific discussion of lesbian respondents' answers to the closed-ended questions are referred to Rust (1993b).

Unflattering Images

In their responses to the question "What is your opinion of bisexuality?" many lesbians were less than flattering in their comments about bisexual women. Most of these comments simultaneously invalidated bisexuality as a form of sexuality or as a political stance. Few lesbians described bisexual women in terms that were simply and purely unflattering without impugning the existence or politics of bisexuality (figure 4.2). In fact, only four such images were spontaneously mentioned by more than two lesbian respondents: sexual indiscriminacy, promiscuity or nonmonogamy, inability to commit, and carriers of sexually transmitted diseases.

Some of these beliefs tend to be more generalized than others. Of the 7 lesbians who described bisexuals as sexually indiscriminate or "switch hitters," only 2 implied that the charge applies to all bisexual women. The other 5 accused only a portion of the bisexual population of sexual indiscriminacy, although most charged the remainder of the bisexual population with having other unflattering characteristics. For example, Trudy wrote that bisexuals "are one of two things: . . . into . . . sex with anybody just for a thrill, [or] confused about sexuality." In contrast, most of the 10 lesbians who described bisexual women as promiscuous or nonmonogamous implied that this is a characteristic of all bisexual women. This is largely a matter of definition, however, since these are also the lesbians who define bisexuality in terms of simultaneous homosexual and heterosexual involvements or needs. Similarly, 8 lesbians described bisexual women as unable or unwilling to commit themselves to a relationship. Most of these women apply this image generally to all bisexual women, or believe that it is an inherent characteristic of bisexual women.

The 8 women who described bisexuals as unable to commit represent only 2.5% of the entire lesbian sample; is it possible that only one in forty lesbian respondents believes that bisexual women are less able or willing to commit themselves to a relationship? Or, are there other lesbians in the sample who would agree that bisexual women tend to be less committed, but who did not happen to mention it in answer to the question "What is your opinion of bisexuality?" What proportion of the sample does this 2.5% speak for? When asked directly to agree or disagree with the statement "Bisexuals are not as committed to other women as lesbians are; they are more likely to desert their female friends," 61% of lesbian respondents agreed (figure 4.3). When asked to agree or disagree with the statement "It can be dangerous for lesbians to trust bisexuals too much, because when the going really gets rough, they are not as likely to stick around and fight it out," 53% agreed. Apparently, concerns about bisexual women's loyalty to their female friends and the lesbian community are much more widespread than the spontaneous comments made in answer to the question "What is your opinion of bisexuality?" would lead one to believe. The majority of lesbian respondents share these concerns, although only a handful thought of mentioning it until they were asked about this issue specifically.

Finally, 7 lesbians spontaneously mentioned a concern that bisexual women would bring diseases into the lesbian population in answer to the question "What is your opinion of bisexuality?" Given the publicity surrounding AIDS and other sexually transmitted diseases, it is surprising that so few women would mention this concern. Are lesbian respondents unconcerned about sexually transmitted diseases? Or, are they concerned about disease but not given to blaming bisexual women for transmitting disease? In a separate question, respondents were asked specifically whether they felt that the existence of AIDS had affected lesbians in any way. Eighty-three percent said "yes," but most explained that AIDS affected lesbians by increasing homophobia or by infecting their gay men friends, not by infecting lesbians. Of those who expressed concern about the risk of HIV infection among lesbians, 14 specifically mentioned bisexual women as a risk. Some said that they were now more careful about relating to bisexual women than they had been, and others said that lesbians in general should be more careful about relating to bisexual women or that bisexual women could spread AIDS from gay men to lesbians. Three said that they themselves are less willing to relate sexually to men than they have been; that is, they are less willing to be behaviorally bisexual. In short, concern about HIV infection is low among lesbian respondents but among those who are concerned, a number single out bisexual women as AIDS risks.

Other unflattering images of bisexuals that were mentioned by one or two lesbian respondents in answer to the question "What is your opinion of bisexuality?" include mental illness, insecurity, self-abusiveness, willingness to settle for mediocrity (i.e., heterosexuality), lack of political consciousness, male identification, lack of self-knowledge or self-awareness, a tendency to be more "sexually" than "emotionally" oriented, faddishness, a potential or tendency to exploit or hurt others, and a lack of fulfillment. A total of 44 lesbian respondents, or 14.2% of lesbians, spontaneously mentioned one or more unflattering images of bisexual women.

Positive Images

Among the positive images associated with bisexuality in the minds of some lesbian respondents are naturalness, health, and idealism. Positive images of bisexuality were mentioned much less often by lesbian respondents than unflattering images were (figure 4.2). Only 4.4% of lesbian respondents—one-third of the number that described bisexuality in unflattering terms—spontaneously described bisexuality as natural, healthy, or ideal.

Mentioned by only 8 lesbian respondents, naturalness was nevertheless the most commonly mentioned positive image. Whereas some lesbians simply said that bisexuality is "as natural as any other sexual orientation," or "a natural state for some people," some went farther, arguing that bisexuality is "probably the most 'natural' state of sexuality."

As discussed earlier in this chapter, many respondents believe that bisexuality would be more common in an ideal society, the implication being that bisexuality is itself an ideal form of sexuality in which one is "more conscious about people than sex." Many of these women made it very clear, however, that they do not consider bisexuality to be an ideal in contemporary society.

Existentially Invalidating Images

Although the majority of lesbians believe that bisexuality exists, a substantial number believe that there is no such thing as bisexuality or that bisexuality is very rare. What do lesbians who don't believe in bisexuality think about women who engage in sexual activity with both women and men, who claim to be attracted to members of both sexes, or who call themselves bisexual? They cannot all be bisexual; all or most of them must be either lesbian or heterosexual. But then why are they behaving bisexually or claiming to be bisexual? Perhaps they are innocently unaware of their true sexuality and behave bisexually or call themselves bisexuals because they are confused. Perhaps they are merely experimenting with same-sex sexuality, or have not yet decided what their sexual orientations are. Perhaps they are in the process of coming out as lesbians and are using bisexual behavior or identity as a comfortable stepping stone during this transitional period. Or, perhaps they know full well that they are really lesbians (or possibly heterosexuals), but they call themselves bisexuals to escape the painful effects of homophobia, their own as well as other people's. All of these images of bisexual women—confused, undecided, transitional, and closeted lesbians—exist among the lesbians who participated in this study, and all of them effectively discredit bisexuality as an authentic form of sexuality. These different images have different implications, however, and some are typically accompanied by greater tolerance of bisexuals than others.

Confusion, for example, is understandable. Many lesbians experienced some confusion over their own sexuality at some point in their lives; after all, growing up lesbian in a heterosexual society is a confusing experience. It is not surprising that some women would mistakenly call themselves bisexual during this period of confusion. Sally noted that, "the bisexual people I know are rather confused ... This is the way I felt pretty much during the two years I thought I might be bi." For this reason, lesbians who perceive bisexual women as confused rarely condemn them for their confusion. Although such condemnation was expressed by a few respondents,

> I don't like it. The women I've known who are bi are not only very confused about their sexuality but their personal life as well. (Joyce)

it was more common for these lesbians to take a disinterested stance in which mild disapproval was mixed with a verbal shrug of the shoulders as if they were simply writing bisexual women off, as Rhoda did: "Some people are just plain confused."

The images of bisexual women as experimenting with lesbian sex or as indecisive generate slightly harsher reactions among lesbians. A couple of lesbian respondents criticized bisexual women for being sexual "tourists" or "adventurers," and many lesbians fault them for their inability to decide whether they are lesbian or heterosexual, impugning their strength of character. For example, Celia "avoid[s] bisexuals of both sexes. I don't respect or like them. I think they haven't the courage to make a choice, or will grab anything that comes along." Other lesbians, like Holly, nonchalantly dismiss bisexuals as people who have not yet decided whether they are lesbian or heterosexual: "Doesn't interest me. I feel a bisexual is a lesbian/gay who hasn't made up her/ his mind."

Many lesbians believe that bisexuality is a transitional phase that some women go through before coming out as lesbian. This transitional period is characterized by some as a period during which a woman is actually changing from being heterosexual to being a lesbian. Others characterize it as a period during which a woman is realizing that she is and has been a lesbian all along, during which she is becoming comfortable enough with her lesbianism to identify herself as a lesbian, or during which she behaves bisexually because she has not yet committed herself to a lesbian lifestyle. For example, Lee wrote, "For some I think it is a 'phase' before one becomes comfortable with one's lesbianism/ gayness."

Like confusion, transitional bisexuality is understandable and acceptable; many lesbians called themselves bisexual before identifying themselves as lesbians, and therefore they see bisexuality as a legitimate stepping stone toward lesbian identity:

When I used this label it was during a transition period of courage. Once I decided life was not going to just happen to me I acknowledged my true identity as a lesbian. (Sheila)

Instead of dismissing bisexual women, as lesbians who perceive them as confused do, or berating them, as lesbians who perceive them as undecided do, lesbians who perceive bisexual women as transitional lesbians generally adopt a friendly but reserved "wait and see" stance. If bisexual women are simply going through a predictable stage in the process of coming out as a lesbian, then one merely needs to wait a reasonable period of time for them to finish coming out.

Finally, many lesbians perceive bisexual women as lesbians whose internalized homophobia prevents them from adopting a lesbian identity, or as lesbians who want to avoid the stigma associated with lesbianism in this heterosexist culture. Some believe that bisexual-identified women have not even admitted their lesbianism to themselves, usually because of their own internalized homophobia,

Personally, I feel a bisexual is one who, for whatever reasons, does not allow themselves to identify one way or the other. That is, she's really a lesbian but will not allow herself to realize that fully. (Janene)

whereas others believe that bisexual-identified women know that they are really lesbians, and are using bisexual identity to deny their lesbianism to other people in order to avoid stigma,

> It is sometimes an easy label to hide behind when "gay" is too difficult. (Eleanore)

or to avoid emotional commitments, or to maintain heterosexual privilege:

> I think many people who call themselves bisexual are lesbian but afraid to make a commitment re: their feelings. (Dorothea)

> I think most people who claim to be bisexual are afraid to claim one lifestyle and don't want to give up their heterosexual privilege. (Hilary)

Some believe that all women who call themselves bisexual are really lesbians, whereas others believe that some, but not all, might be true bisexuals. Generally, the former condemn all bisexual-identified women and the latter approve of bisexual identification only if it reflects true bisexuality:

> I believe true bisexuality is just another hue on the spectrum of human sexual orientation. I think sometimes fearful lesbians will hide behind the bisexual label, and I despise this. (Sonya)

The condemnatory tone of lesbians who believe that bisexuals are really lesbians who are intentionally avoiding the stigma of lesbianism contrasts sharply with the neutral, nonjudgmental tone of lesbians who believe that bisexuality is a transitional identity. The former resent women who fraudulently use the bisexual label to protect themselves, and they do not sympathize with them. Once a woman has realized her own lesbianism, they expect her to come out as a lesbian and begin shouldering her share of the burden of living as a lesbian in a heterosexist society. But as a transitional phase, bisexual identification is understandable in light of the homophobia that women must overcome in order to come out as lesbians, and it is therefore acceptable. Danielle expressed the moral distinction between transitional bisexual identity and fraudulent bisexual identity clearly:

> People have a right to use available information (or to make a conscious decision) as to what to do with their lives. The time spent making an informed decision could be interpreted as bisexual. I do

*have problems with understanding a long term or convinced bisexual
as I wonder if it is a cop out or inability to make a decision. Often I do
not trust this group because I doubt their motives. (Danielle)*

The beliefs that bisexual-identified women are really lesbians who
are avoiding the stigma of lesbianism and that bisexual identity is a
transitional stage toward coming out as a lesbian are not mutually
exclusive beliefs. Many respondents, like Danielle, referred to both beliefs, explaining that some bisexual-identified women are aware of their
lesbianism, whereas others have yet to realize it.

Images of bisexual women as confused, indecisive, transitional, or
closeted lesbians effectively invalidate bisexual identity. Even among
lesbians who believe that there are some true bisexuals, these beliefs
have the effect of casting doubt on the identities of all women who claim
to be bisexual. As long as a lesbian believes that bisexual women are
likely to have these characteristics—or at least more likely than lesbians—she will tend to react suspiciously whenever another woman
claims to be bisexual. Bisexual identity cannot be accepted at face value,
because the woman who claims to be bisexual might not be a true
bisexual. Therefore, these images, even if they are not generalized to all
bisexual women, function to invalidate bisexual identity generally and,
therefore, to invalidate bisexuality.

Given the high percentage of lesbian respondents who are skeptical
about the existence of bisexuality, it is not surprising that existentially
invalidating images of bisexuals as confused, indecisive, transitional,
or closeted lesbians are popular among lesbians. Thirty-eight lesbians
(11.8%) spontaneously described bisexual women as confused or indecisive; 28 (8.7%) characterized bisexuality as transitional; and 26 (8.1%)
described bisexual women as lesbians who are closeted by homophobia
(figure 4.2). The results of closed ended questions suggest that these
lesbians represent a much larger number of lesbians who agree that
bisexual women are confused, indecisive, transitional, or closeted lesbians, but who did not happen to mention these beliefs spontaneously
(tables 4.1, 4.2). When asked to estimate the number of "women who
say they are bisexual [who] will eventually realize that they are lesbians," 67% of lesbian respondents replied that they thought at least half
of bisexual women will eventually come out as lesbians, and when asked
to agree or disagree with the statement, "Society makes it difficult to be
a lesbian, so some women claim to be bisexual when they are really

lesbians who are afraid to admit it," 83% agreed. Comparing these responses to lesbians' responses to closed questions about lesbian identity reveals that 79% believe that bisexual identity is more likely than lesbian identity to be transitional, and 50% believe that women who identify as bisexual are more likely than women who identify as lesbian to be denying their true sexuality (Rust 1993b). In other words, most lesbians believe not only that bisexual identity is likely to be transitional or fraudulent, but that it is more likely than lesbian identity to be so. These figures indicate that most lesbian respondents silently share the existentially invalidating images expressed by their more vocal sisters.

Political Images

Are bisexuals political cowards who want the joys of lesbian sex but refuse to shoulder their share of the burden of fighting against the oppression of same-sex love? Or, are they political victims who bear the brunt of oppression because they are not accepted by either heterosexual society or the lesbian community? Lesbians hold very different and conflicting views of the forms of privilege and oppression bisexuals experience, and very different views of the political status of bisexuals vis-à-vis the lesbian community and heterosexual society.

Images of Bisexual Privilege—"The Best of Both Worlds" and Political Distrust

Many lesbian respondents feel a great deal of anger toward women whom they believe call themselves bisexual in order to enjoy the pleasures of lesbian sexuality and the comfort of a nurturing community of women while maintaining heterosexual privilege and avoiding the costs associated with being lesbian in a heterosexist society. These costs include the personal cost of acknowledging one's own lesbianism or living a lesbian lifestyle,

> Most bisexuals are gay/lesbian but think it is too hard a life to choose. (Leah)

the social costs associated with committing oneself publicly to a lesbian identity,

> *. . . some claim to be bisexual so they can be somewhat accepted by both "sides." (Jodie)*

and the political costs associated with aligning oneself with a stigmatized minority:

> *. . . in contemporary culture, I think sexuality is so tied to . . . political issues that to be bisexual is to refuse to make a stand . . . to be bisexual seems [to be] a statement of political wishiwashiness. (Margaret)*

No matter what the reason, in the eyes of many lesbians, identifying as bisexual amounts to a "cop-out" or to "fence-sitting." A total of 32 (10%) lesbians spontaneously accused bisexual women of copping out, fence-sitting or trying to maintain heterosexual privilege. The most bitter feelings toward bisexual women were expressed by these lesbians. At best, they see bisexual women as weak-willed and, at worst, as traitors to the lesbian community because they are unwilling to own their lesbianism. Janice spoke for many when she wrote, "I have a lot of anger towards women who identify themselves as bisexuals—I see them as reaping both lesbian and heterosexual privileges."

Some lesbians concede that not all bisexual women are necessarily lesbians who are avoiding the stigma of lesbianism or hanging onto heterosexual privilege. These lesbians believe that some women who claim to be bisexual are in fact truly bisexual, and they reserve their disinterest, disapproval, or condemnation for those women who are dishonestly clinging to a bisexual identity for selfish personal or political reasons:

> *I don't like it when it is chosen because of heterosexual privilege, but if a person truly feels bisexual, I think it is a valid choice. I am willing to defend that choice for any person who is willing to defend my choice to be a lesbian. (Rachel)*

Regardless of whether women who call themselves bisexual are truly bisexual or whether they are really dishonest lesbians, claims of bisexuality amount to keeping a foot in the door to the heterosexual world. Because they maintain ties to heterosexuality, bisexuals appear to have the option of passing as heterosexual when it is convenient. When asked to estimate how easy or difficult it is for bisexuals to pass as heterosexual, 71% of lesbian respondents replied that it is somewhat to very easy for bisexuals to pass (table 4.3), and 83% gave higher estimates of the ease of passing for bisexuals than they did for lesbians

(Rust 1993b). When asked to estimate the proportion of bisexuals who would *want* to pass, 61% estimated that more than half would (table 4.4), and 65% gave higher estimates of the prevalence of desire to pass among bisexuals than they did for desire to pass among lesbians (Rust 1993b). Very few lesbians made exceptionless generalizations—only 4% stated that all bisexuals want to pass as heterosexual, and only 6% stated that no lesbians want to pass—but the majority of lesbians stated that bisexuals are both more able, and more willing, to pass as heterosexual. By implication, the majority of lesbians believe that bisexuals are more able and more willing than lesbians to avoid the stigma of lesbianism.

By the same token, because bisexuals have one foot in the door of the heterosexual world and are able to live in the heterosexual world, they appear to have the option of abandoning the lesbian lifestyle altogether when the consequences of being lesbian in a heterosexist society are too great. Therefore, lesbians fear that they cannot trust them to stick around at exactly the moment when trust is most important. Trust is necessary in platonic, romantic, and political relationships, and many lesbians have concerns about bisexual women's loyalties at these various levels. Some, like Deborah, fear that bisexual women would be less committed to them as friends or as lovers: "I've yet to see a woman be a practicing 'bisexual' who doesn't end up hurting her lesbian lover and retreating back into the ease of heterosexuality with a male lover." Others, like Miriam, do not trust bisexual women to remain committed to the lesbian community or the lesbian movement: "As a personal choice it is OK. As a political choice—it's shortsighted. I do not trust bi women to 'be there' for me because of their divided loyalties."

The apparent fact that bisexual women have the options of passing as heterosexual and of abandoning their lesbian friends, lovers, and community causes no small resentment among lesbians. Even lesbians who harbor no ill will toward bisexual women perceive that their bisexuality does avail them the opportunity to blend into heterosexual society. Although these lesbians do not blame bisexual women for having this opportunity, they do resent it. As Nancy apologetically put it, "I'm afraid [bisexuality] does indeed hurt lesbians, because bisexuals, consciously or unconsciously, 'run' to men, male approval, mainstream society for 'shelter.' " The fear that they would be abandoned leads some lesbians to avoid becoming involved in personal or political relationships with bisexual women, or to enter into these relationships carefully and reservedly, a reaction that will be explored more fully below.

But some lesbians' concerns about the politics of bisexuality extend beyond the possibility that bisexual women would abandon their lesbian friends, lovers, and communities for a heterosexual lifestyle. These women object to bisexuality for political reasons, arguing that bisexual women are political weak links or political energy sinks simply by virtue of their connections to men and male power. At best, they view bisexuality as an apolitical stance adopted for purely sexual reasons, as opposed to lesbianism, which is a political orientation and lifestyle. At worst, they view bisexuality as not merely apolitical but, in fact, antithetical to lesbians' and women's interests. For example, Hilary believes that women should support each other and work toward social and political solutions to sexual inequality rather than wasting their energy trying to forge personal solutions with individual men. She argued that women who invest energy in relationships with men reinforce women's oppression:

> . . . any long term investment in an intimate relationship with a male reinforces the oppression of women. I know that there are sensitive, loving, etc. males out there but for all their individual qualities, there is no denying they are still viewed as the privileged gender. I believe women need to support, nurture, and unite with one another first and then, when the reality of our world has changed, extend a hand in love and friendship to men. A collective consciousness raising is needed more than a few isolated cases of equality in relationships between women and men. (Hilary)

Similarly, Nadine feels that women who direct their energy toward men hinder their own development as women,

> I don't trust bisexual women because I feel too much of their energy goes to men and I think that it detracts from their own development as well as other women. (Nadine)

and Patricia feels that bisexual women drain energy from the lesbian community, giving it to the male enemy:

> Not good for the lesbian community because it gives energy (from women) to the "enemy" (men). (Patricia)

In short, bisexuality is bad politics.

Perhaps, in the ideal world of the future, in which sexual inequality has been eradicated, men will no longer be the enemy and relations between women and men will be egalitarian. In that world, heterosexual relations will not drain women's energy for the purposes of men, and heterosexual relations will not be detrimental to women's well being. Under the patriarchy, however, many lesbians believe that bisexuality amounts to sexual heresy and personal treason.

Images of Bisexual Oppression—"The Worst of Both Worlds" and Political Sympathy

In contrast to lesbians who resent bisexuals for reaping double benefits, other lesbians sympathize with bisexuals because of the double difficulties they face. Lesbians in the current study mentioned two types of difficulties: difficulties that are inherent in the nature of bisexuality itself, and difficulties that arise from a society that is not equipped to accommodate bisexuality.

Lesbians who are concerned about the former usually perceive bisexuals' difficulties as resulting from the dual nature of bisexuality, asserting that the combination of homosexuality and heterosexuality poses problems of management or integration:

> *I think that it would be a very hard way of life for me. I could not juggle the two. (Gina)*

> *It must be very difficult to be a bisexual because of the tremendous difference between loving women and loving men. (Georgia)*

Lesbians who are concerned about the latter pointed to heterosexual and lesbian societies, rather than to the inherent nature of bisexuality, as the sources of bisexuals' problems. These lesbians think that instead of getting the best of both worlds, bisexuals usually end up with rejection from both worlds because neither heterosexuals nor lesbians are willing to accept them. Fanny expressed concern that "bisexuality would be a very difficult way to live" because "bisexuals are never really accepted into either heterosexual worlds or the homosexual support groups." Some lesbian respondents singled out the lesbian community as the more egregious offender. For example, Lucy commented that "there is a lot of hostility toward it by lesbians that I don't understand."

Concerns about bisexuals' particular disadvantages are as common among lesbians as concern over their double advantages (figure 4.2). In all, 36 lesbian respondents, or 11.2%, expressed concerns about the difficulties that bisexual women face, whereas 38 (11.8%) made disparaging remarks about bisexuals getting the best of both worlds or being political cop-outs. Lesbians who sympathize with bisexuals' difficulties, however, are more likely to believe that these difficulties arise from the inherent nature of bisexuality itself than from bisexuals' social or political circumstances. Only 14 (4.4%) lesbians perceive bisexuals as political victims who get the worst of both worlds because they are rejected by both heterosexuals and by lesbians; the other 22 stated or implied that bisexuals are victims of their own bisexual condition. Thus, when only political images of bisexuality are considered, it appears that lesbians are much more likely to resent bisexuals for being political opportunists than to sympathize with them for being political victims.

Overall Perceptions of Bisexual and Lesbian Oppression

How do lesbians perceive the difficulties bisexuals face in comparison with the difficulties they face as lesbians? Respondents were asked to estimate the degrees of prejudice and discrimination faced, respectively, by lesbians and bisexual women, and the overwhelming majority of lesbians said that bisexual women experience less oppression than lesbians (table 4.5, figure 4.4). Seventy-one percent said that lesbians experience a great deal of prejudice, and 11% said that lesbians experience more prejudice than any other single group in society. In comparison, only 20% said that bisexuals experience a great deal of prejudice, and none said that bisexuals experience more prejudice than any other group. When individual lesbians' estimates of prejudice against bisexual women and lesbians are compared, the results show that 79% believe that lesbians experience more prejudice than bisexual women do. Similarly, 81% believe that lesbians experience more discrimination than bisexual women do. It seems that the 11.8% of lesbians who answered the question "What is your opinion of bisexuality?" with remarks about bisexuals' having the best of both worlds were expressing a very popular view; other lesbians may or may not believe that bisexuals actually have an advantage, but they certainly agree that bisexuals are less oppressed than lesbians.

What about the 4.4% of lesbians who expressed concerns about the difficulties bisexuals face because they are rejected by both heterosexuals and lesbians? Were they also speaking on behalf of a larger group? Apparently not—only 1% of lesbians feel that bisexuals experience more prejudice or more discrimination than lesbians, indicating that even those who are concerned about bisexuals' special oppression do not believe that bisexuals are therefore more oppressed than lesbians.

Underlying Conceptualizations: Two Different Kinds of Hybrids and Apoliticality

The "best of both worlds" and the "worst of both worlds" represent two radically different views of the political status of bisexuals vis-à-vis heterosexual society and the lesbian community. From the "best of both worlds" perspective, bisexuals are—whether intentionally or not—apolitical opportunists who enjoy privilege, avoid oppression, and abdicate their political responsibilities in favor of personal comfort. They are fence-sitters who refuse to cast their lot with either interest group, hedging all bets by "playing it both ways." From the "worst of both worlds" perspective, bisexuals are political victims who suffer from not only heterosexism, but also homosexism. They are caught in the middle, unable to belong to either world and rejected by both. Both perspectives rest on a conceptualization of sexuality as dichotomous and a conceptualization of bisexuality as a hybrid form of sexuality. In the "best of both worlds," bisexuals combine the advantages of homosexuality and heterosexuality and, in the "worst of both worlds," they combine the disadvantages. But closer analysis shows that the concepts of hybrid bisexuality underlying these different political beliefs are different.

The "best of both worlds" view is grounded in a concept of bisexuality as a hybrid *combination* of heterosexuality and lesbianism. Bisexuals can live a heterosexual lifestyle, feel comfortable in heterosexual society, and appear to be one hundred percent heterosexual. Or, they can live a lesbian lifestyle, feel comfortable in the lesbian community, and appear to be one hundred percent lesbian. Like a chameleon, at any given moment the hybrid bisexual appears to be either heterosexual or lesbian, depending on how she presents herself, whom she is dating, or whether she is among heterosexuals or lesbians. Since she is at all times both heterosexual and lesbian, she can move freely back and forth between these two lifestyles and societies. It is this ability to move freely back and forth between heterosexuality and lesbianism, and to appear to belong in all situations, that allows bisexuals to reap the benefits of both heterosexuality and lesbianism while avoiding the costs of both.

The "worst of both worlds" view of the political status of bisexuality is based on a concept of bisexuality as a hybrid *mixture* of heterosexuality and lesbianism. This type of hybrid bisexual is analogous to a biracial person whose features combine the characteristics of her two biological parents. Among people of her mother's race, she cannot hide the features she inherited from her father, and among people of her father's race, she cannot hide the features she inherited from her mother. Instead of appearing to belong completely to both communities, she appears out of place in both and might not be fully accepted by either. Likewise, the bisexual woman is *bi*sexual at all times; she is bisexual in heterosexual situations and she is bisexual in lesbian situations. She is, therefore, rejected by heterosexuals for her bisexuality or perhaps for her lesbian side, and she is rejected by lesbians for her bisexuality or perhaps for her heterosexual side.

Both forms of the hybrid conceptualization of bisexuality lead to a depoliticized view of bisexuality. As combinations or mixtures of heterosexuality and lesbianism, bisexuals have no political interests of their own as bisexuals. Their interests consist of a combination or mixture of the interests of heterosexuals and lesbians. Seen as combination hybrids, they have the ability to pick and choose their interests and so, of course, they choose the best of both worlds. Seen as mixture hybrids, they are excluded from the advantages of both and cannot escape the disadvantages of both. They are to be resented to the extent that they share all the advantages of both groups, or pitied to the extent that they share all the disadvantages of both groups. Either way, they have political interests only insofar as they share the interests of the two authentic interest groups, heterosexuals and lesbians; they have no unique political interests of their own.

Dissenting Voices

A few lesbians took exception to the charges that bisexual women are sexually indiscriminate, nonmonogamous, confused, indecisive, transitional, fence-sitting, untrustworthy lovers, or political traitors. In comparison to the number of lesbians who expressed these beliefs about bisexual women, the number who rejected them is minuscule. But the import of their comments lies not in their number. The fact that some lesbian respondents expressed negative images demonstrates that they exist at least in the minds of some lesbians, but the fact that other women felt the need to refute them demonstrates something even more significant from a sociological point of view. That is, that these images exist as ideas to be reckoned with in lesbian culture. Even if only a few lesbians actually ascribe to a given negative image of bisexual women, the fact that other lesbians found it necessary to refute that image is evidence that the image enjoys a lively existence in the symbolic world of the lesbian community.

Take, for example, the image of bisexual women as confused. In all, only one in ten lesbians spontaneously expressed the belief that bisexual women are confused. But the experiences of women like Rhonda, who recalled that she had begun to call herself a lesbian because her lesbian friends said she was confused and who found greater acceptance as a lesbian than she had as a bisexual, show that these women's attitudes are influential enough to set the tone of the atmosphere in which bisexuals find themselves. Likewise, regardless of how many lesbians actually believe that bisexuals are sexually indiscriminate and nonmonogamous, Lydia's impression is that "lesbians in general" do; she wrote, "bisexuality tends to be misunderstood by heterosexuals and homosexuals alike as the indecisive person who will 'screw around' with just about anybody."

Some lesbians implicitly accused those lesbians who do accept negative images of bisexuality of being uninformed or politically outdated by commenting that they, too, used to believe in these images before they were enlightened.

> I used to feel negative toward people who said they were bisexual because I felt it was a cop-out—just a homosexual who couldn't handle being gay. But now I truly believe that some people, many people, are bi and I feel for them because I think it would be hard to be "middle of the road" sexually. (Lily)

The charge that lesbians who perceive bisexuals as political fence-sitters or closeted lesbians are politically outdated is an ironic one, because lack of political acumen is exactly what these lesbians find objectionable about bisexual women.

Summary

Lesbians have a variety of images of bisexual women, both positive and negative, but negative images outnumber and are far more widespread than positive images. Lesbians' spontaneous comments about bisexuality reveal that more than one in ten lesbians perceive bisexuals as confused or undecided, and similar proportions perceive them as transitional lesbians and/or closeted lesbians. In addition, one in seven holds other unflattering beliefs about bisexual women, for example that they are sexually promiscuous or unable to commit themselves to a relationship, whereas less than one in twenty holds a positive image of bisexuality as natural or healthy. Finally, those lesbians who sympathize with bisexuals for getting the worst of both worlds are as numerous as lesbians who resent them for getting the best of both worlds, but most of the former pity bisexuals for being victims of their own bisexual condition, rather than victims of political circumstances.

Lesbians' responses to closed questions reveal that these negative attitudes toward bisexuality are even more widespread than spontaneous comments suggest. Whereas only 8.7% of lesbians spontaneously characterized bisexuality as transitional, in response to closed-ended questions 79% of lesbians described bisexual identity as more likely to be transitional than lesbian identity. Whereas only 8.1% of lesbians spontaneously characterized bisexuals as closeted lesbians, in response to closed-ended questions 50% indicated a belief that bisexual identity was more likely than lesbian identity to be fraudulent. Whereas only 2.5% spontaneously described bisexuals as unable to commit to a relationship, in response to closed-ended questions 61% stated that bisexuals are less committed to other women than lesbians and 53% stated that bisexuals are less trustworthy than lesbians. Eighty-three percent believe that it is easier for bisexuals to pass as heterosexual, 65% believe that bisexuals are more likely to want to pass, 79% believe that bisexuals experience less prejudice, and 81% believe they experience less discrimination. Apparently, the minority of lesbians who made these comments about bisexual women spontaneously were speaking for the majority of lesbians, most of whom simply did not express their opinions on these issues until specifically asked to do so.

Lesbians very rarely generalize these negative images to all bisexual women; most lesbians stopped short of saying, for example, that *all* bisexual women are confused or in transition to lesbian identity. Most lesbians also agreed that some lesbians share the traits that are so common among bisexuals; for example, some lesbians are also confused or in transition. In fact, the only beliefs that were generalized to all bisexual women by the lesbians who held them were those that followed from particular definitions of bisexuality. For example, lesbians who characterized bisexuals as nonmonogamous typically defined bisexuality behaviorally, a definition that virtually guarantees that bisexuals will be nonmonogamous. In general, therefore, lesbians' images of bisexuality have not prevented lesbians from perceiving either differences among bisexuals or similarities between lesbians and bisexuals.

But the fact that most lesbians do not generalize their images of bisexuality to all bisexuals does not imply that these images do not affect bisexuals generally. Even when exceptions are allowed, images of bisexuality function to implicate all bisexuals. This is particularly true of existentially invalidating images. Because there are no clear markers to distinguish the few "true" bisexuals from the greater number whose claims to bisexual identity are illegitimate, existentially invalidating images cast suspicion on any woman who claims to be bisexual and thereby invalidate bisexual identity generally. The lesbian who believes that bisexual identity is more likely to be fraudulent than lesbian identity, for example, is likely to be suspicious of *all* claims to bisexual identity, even though she believes that some of these claims to bisexual identity will eventually prove to be authentic. Thus, every bisexual is affected by her belief that some bisexuals are inauthentic.

Although negative images of bisexuality are far more numerous and common than positive images, lesbians are not unanimous in their opinions about bisexuality. To characterize lesbians as such would be to commit the sin of stereotypy ourselves. A few lesbians dissent from the general attitude toward bisexuality, arguing that bisexuals are also oppressed in their own right and that lesbians should try to understand and be sympathetic toward the special difficulties faced by bisexuals. Some have positive images of bisexuality as natural, healthy, and honest. Even among lesbians who are critical of bisexual women, many are quick to assert that there might be bisexual women who do not fit their stereotypes or that their impressions of bisexual women might be just that – stereotypes.

Despite the variety in lesbians' images of bisexuals, most have two things in common. First, most of lesbians' images of bisexuals, both positive and negative, are based on a conception of sexuality as dichotomous. If sexuality is dichotomous, then bisexuality either does not exist or is a hybrid form of sexuality. If it doesn't exist, then women who call themselves bisexual must be confused, in transition to lesbianism, or closeted lesbians. If bisexuality is a hybrid form of sexuality, then bisexuals are either psychologically healthy individuals who are able to enjoy their natural attractions to both women and men, or they are incomplete lesbians who share a watered-down version of lesbian politics and political interests but who also maintain friendly ties with an oppressive heterosexual society. Bisexuality might be a valid sexual identity or it might not, but either way, it is a derivative identity without a unique essence or politics of its own.

Second, most lesbians' images of bisexuals are laden with emotional implications. These emotions find their outlet in lesbians' feelings toward bisexual women.

HOW DO LESBIANS FEEL ABOUT
BISEXUAL WOMEN?

Lesbians' feelings toward bisexual women range from mistrust, hatred, and anger to respect and admiration. I discussed many of these feelings earlier in this chapter, because they are typically associated with certain images of bisexual women. For example, lesbians who believe that bisexual women are really lesbians who want to maintain heterosexual privilege or avoid the stigma of lesbianism generally resent bisexual women, and sometimes feel anger and hatred toward them. Lesbians who believe that bisexual women are likely to escape to heterosexuality when life as a lesbian becomes too difficult generally do not trust bisexual women. Very few lesbians have positive feelings, such as respect or admiration, for bisexual women, although a number do empathize with them or deplore other lesbians' harsh judgments of them.

Lesbian respondents frequently expressed their feelings about bisexual women by discussing the limitations of their own willingness or ability to relate to them. Many made general statements to the effect that they prefer not to interact with bisexual women, that they find it difficult to relate to bisexual women, or that they feel uncomfortable interacting with them. Deirdre, for example, feels that "in theory . . . bisexuality is okay" although "in practice I don't like dealing with bisexuals," and Juanita, who defines bisexuality as an equal attraction to both sexes, said "I find it hard to relate with them because I lean heavily towards women."

Some, like Deirdre, experience a conflict between their heads and their hearts. Their heads tell them to be tolerant of bisexuality but their hearts tell them to avoid bisexual women. Sharon resolves the problem by acknowledging her negative feelings about bisexuality to herself, but concealing them from bisexuals:

> My gut reaction is to think it's a cop-out for people who can't admit their homosexuality, but my intellectual reaction is much more positive. I have to think a lot to hold these negative feelings in check when dealing with bisexuals. (Sharon)

Chris, on the other hand, has not resolved her conflicting feelings; she welcomes bisexuals into her community, but cannot trust them:

> At times—I definitely stereotype and feel anger towards bisexuals . . . But I also admire them and welcome them into our community. I don't trust them as a group, though, because of their ties to men. (Chris)

Other lesbians' feelings about interacting with bisexual women are less ambiguous, and these women were often quite specific about the circumstances under which they are willing to interact with bisexual women or the levels of intimacy to which they are willing to admit bisexual women. One of the most intimate relationships two people can have is a romantic relationship, and more lesbians spontaneously commented on their feelings about dating bisexual women than about any other type of relationship. For example, Maxine and Angelina are willing to date bisexual women, but Maxine would do so only under certain conditions and Angelina finds her current relationship with a bisexual woman problematic:

> I would have no problem dating or loving a bisexual woman as long as she was monogamous and understood that leading a lesbian life is harder than a hetero. life. (Maxine)

> Since my current lover is bisexual it does not make for a very secure relationship. There is always the fear that she will go to the other side. It's very stressful in a love relationship. (Angelina)

Other lesbians are more reluctant to become romantically involved with bisexual women. Like Maxine and Angelina, their objections to involvement with bisexual women usually center around the belief that bisexual women are less likely to be loyal or monogamous lovers. Molly said that she doesn't "like to have relationships with [bisexual women], because I think they tend to leave."

Finally, some lesbians refuse to even entertain the thought of dating or becoming romantically involved with bisexual women. Although generally concerned about bisexual women's loyalty and monogamy, many of these lesbians are particularly concerned by the prospect that the bisexual woman's other sexual partner might be male rather than female. Why would a male lover be more objectionable than a female lover? There are several different reasons. First, many lesbians, like Bobbi, explained that they would be unable to "compete with a man to win the love of a woman." Arguing that bisexual women have both homosexual and heterosexual needs, they feared that as lesbians they could not fulfill all of a bisexual partner's needs nor could they wage a fair battle against a male lover.

Second, because the larger society condones heterosexuality and condemns lesbianism, lesbians fear that bisexual lovers will eventually retreat back to the comfortable world of heterosexuality when the stress of living in a lesbian relationship becomes too much. Bisexuals are, therefore, less likely to remain committed to their lesbian relationships because they can also enjoy socially approved heterosexual relationships. Although some lesbians find it incredible that a woman who once tasted lesbian sexuality could ever return to heterosexuality,

> I don't understand how a woman who has slept with a woman could ever want to sleep with a man again. (Lynda)

the fear that the desire for social approval would lure bisexuals back to heterosexuality remains:

> I'm afraid it does indeed hurt lesbians, because bisexuals, consciously or unconsciously, "run" to men, male approval, mainstream society for "shelter." (Nancy)

Other lesbians object not only to the tendency of bisexual women to become involved with men or to leave women lovers for men lovers, but to the heterosexual aspect of the bisexual woman herself. Some would not want to have intimate sexual contact with a woman who had also been in close sexual contact with a man because they find heterosexuality or male sexuality disgusting. For example, Alison "wouldn't want to have sex with an active bisexual female if she was presently having sex acts with men. No way." For a few lesbians, the desire to avoid heterosexually-involved bisexual women is related to a fear of the diseases that a bisexual woman might bring into the lesbian population, whereas for others it is simply a desire to exclude all things male from their own lives.

The heterosexual aspect of a bisexual woman becomes especially difficult to ignore when she actually does become heterosexually involved; as Carrie said, "I have a hard time getting really close with a bisexual woman, even as a friend, for fear she'll start dating a man and our different lifestyles and interests will come between us." Beth, who defines bisexuality behaviorally, feels that a bisexual woman's male lover is antithetical to her lesbianism, compromising the quality of her lesbian relationships. She wrote, "Loving women means more than physical relationships—it's more like a woman identification in lifestyle and beliefs—this would seem difficult with a man between the sheets."

The lesbian who becomes involved with a bisexual woman indirectly connects herself to heterosexuality and to men, a connection that is anathema to some lesbians. A comment by Thelma is perhaps the most revealing. She objects to the idea of becoming involved with a bisexual woman because of her own *identity* as a lesbian. In other words, becoming involved with a bisexual woman would endanger her lesbian identity. Even though the bisexual woman is a woman, and hence Thelma's involvement with this woman would be in itself a lesbian relationship, the fact that the bisexual woman is not a lesbian would compromise Thelma's lesbianism. For her, being a lesbian does not mean merely sleeping only with women; it means sleeping only with other lesbians and eliminating all connections, even indirect connections, to non-lesbians, including bisexual women and the men to whom they are connected:

> *I feel accepting of my friends who identify themselves as bisexual . . . Because of my strong identity as a lesbian I feel I would not want to be sexually involved with a bisexual woman. (Thelma)*

Do lesbians who reject bisexual women as lovers also reject them as friends? Some do, and some don't. Women like Thelma refuse only romantic involvement; Thelma is willing to accept friendship with bisexual women and reported that she did in fact have bisexual friends. Eileen is also open to the idea of friendship with bisexual women, but like Carrie, she does not feel that her friendships with bisexual women are as close as her friendships with lesbians:

> *I seem not able to connect with them in the same way as I do with my lesbian friends. But, I am open to friendship with bisexual women. (Eileen)*

In contrast, Celia and Keesha emphatically reject bisexual women at any and all levels of intimacy:

> *I avoid bisexuals of both sexes. I don't respect or like them . . . I won't relate socially or sexually to bisexuals. I won't relate socially or sexually to anyone who relates to bisexuals. (Celia)*

> *I prefer not to socialize with them. When they do I feel intruded upon . . . They have men in their lives and I want nothing to do with them. (Keesha)*

Apparently, there is considerable antipathy toward bisexual women within the lesbian community. Some lesbian respondents prefer to avoid bisexual women altogether, and those who are willing to accept bisexual women as friends often draw the line at romantic relationships.

This is not, however, the attitude of all lesbian respondents. Several commented disapprovingly on their sisters' rejection of bisexual women, chastising them for their intolerance:

> *There is a lot of hostility toward it by lesbians that I don't understand . . . I feel sorry for bisexual women because they have no support in the straight or lesbian community. I don't mean that I pity them, it would just be a hard place to be. (Lucy)*

Despite the sentiments of lesbians who deplored the lesbian community's intolerance of bisexuality, the antipathy expressed by those lesbians who prefer not to associate with bisexual women permeates the atmosphere in the lesbian community. Evidence of the pervasiveness of this antipathy exists not only in the observations of lesbians themselves, but also in the fact that some lesbians found it necessary to apologize for it. The number of such apologies leads one to wonder, however, whether this antipathy in fact reflects the feelings of the majority of lesbians, or whether the atmospheric tone is being set by a vocal minority of lesbians with extremely negative attitudes about bisexuality. After all, when

asked for their opinions on bisexuality, most lesbian respondents made
no spontaneous statements whatsoever about whether they would accept
bisexual women as friends or lovers or about whether they condone or
condemn the lack of acceptance bisexual women find in the lesbian
community. What does this silent majority think?

To find out what the majority thinks, all of the women who participated in the study were presented with a series of seven closed-ended
questions that asked specifically about their feelings toward bisexual
women in comparison to lesbians. All seven questions used the direct
comparison format described earlier in this chapter. One of these questions measured respondents' general comfort level with bisexual women,
three measured respondents' feelings about interacting with bisexual
women at various levels of social intimacy, and three measured the
degree to which respondents trusted bisexual women in various political
circumstances.

The results show that overall, lesbians do prefer to associate with
other lesbians rather than with bisexual women, and many feel very
strongly about the issue (figure 4.5). For example, 96% said that they
would prefer to date a lesbian, and 74% said that their preference to
avoid dating bisexual women is very strong. Only 13 lesbians said that
they don't care whether the women they date are bisexual or lesbian.
Many are willing to be friends with bisexual women, however; when
asked whether they are more likely to make friends with a woman they
had just met if she were lesbian or if she were bisexual, one out of four
lesbians said that it doesn't matter—seven times the number who don't
care whether their dates are lesbian or bisexual. But the other three out
of four (74%) do care, saying that they are more inclined to make
friends with a lesbian woman. Most lesbians also prefer lesbian-domi-
nated rather than bisexual-dominated discussion groups (89%) and feel
more comfortable when they are among lesbians than when they are
among bisexuals (81%).

Lesbians also prefer to share their political lives with other lesbians,
not with bisexuals (figure 4.6). Eighty-three percent would rather
have lesbian coworkers if they were involved in a gay rights campaign, 80% would rather have a lesbian lobbyist in Washington, DC,
and 73% would not trust a bisexual woman to give a speech about
alternative lifestyles to a general audience as much as they would trust
a lesbian.

Summary

In summary, the majority of lesbian respondents are reluctant to be socially or politically associated with bisexual women. Most even prefer not to become friends with bisexual women, and those who do not mind having bisexual friends usually draw the line at intimate romantic relationships. Those who are willing to date bisexual women would do so only under certain conditions; very, very few said that they do not care whether their romantic partners are bisexual. A fundamental issue underlying lesbians' unwillingness to associate closely with bisexual women is trust. To people who feel threatened, trust is a very important issue; in a heterosexual world, lesbians are threatened, and they do not trust bisexual women because bisexual women appear to be connected to that world.

5

WHO BELIEVES WHAT? THE IMPACT OF LESBIANS' PERSONAL POLITICS AND EXPERIENCES ON THEIR ATTITUDES TOWARD BISEXUALITY

One thing is clear: lesbians have a variety of attitudes, beliefs, and opinions about bisexuality. This variety is interesting in and of itself because it shows how diverse lesbians are and how many different ways there are to understand sexuality. Merely describing this diversity— which I did in chapter 4—provides insight into the controversy over bisexuality within the lesbian community because it shows the exact points of agreement and disagreement. If we can isolate these points, we can begin to understand each others' points of view.

But understanding each others' points of view also means that we must understand why we each hold the attitudes we do. For example, why do some lesbians believe that bisexuality doesn't exist while others believe that it is an ideal form of sexuality? Who among us is most likely to believe that women who identify as bisexual are really closeted lesbians, and who is most likely to chastise her lesbian sisters for invalidating bisexual identity in this way? What distinguishes the majority of lesbians, who prefer to maintain some social and political distance from bisexual women, from the handful of lesbians who don't care if their

dates, friends, and comrades are bisexual? Are there racial or generational differences in lesbians' attitudes toward bisexual women? Political
differences? Do lesbians' experiences of their own sexuality influence
their beliefs and feelings about bisexual women? Or, do lesbians' attitudes toward bisexual women crosscut demographic, political, and personal differences? If we discover who among us holds which attitudes,
we can gain some insight into why we hold the attitudes we do, and then
we can begin to understand the roots of the controversy over bisexuality
in the lesbian community.

RACE, EDUCATION, CLASS, AND OTHER DEMOGRAPHIC DIFFERENCES

Because the women who participated in this study are predominantly
White and well-educated, it is important to look closely at the opinions
of Women of Color and women with less education to see if their beliefs
and feelings differ from those of White and/or well-educated lesbians. If
they do, then the opinions expressed by the majority of lesbians in this
survey are really the opinions of the majority of White, well-educated
lesbians, not the opinions of the majority of lesbians. For similar reasons, it is also important to see if there are differences in the opinions
of lesbians of different social classes, incomes, employment statuses,
and ages.

Although there are some scattered differences in the opinions of the
African-American and White lesbians who participated in this study, the
attitudes of these two racial groups resemble each other much more than
they differ. For example, on the issue of whether bisexuality exists, two
out of ten Whites and three out of ten African-Americans indicated that
they believe it does not exist. One out of ten in each group explicitly
stated that it exists, and four out of ten implied that it exists without
saying so explicitly. According to these results, the entire range of opinions on this question is present within both racial groups, and no opinion appears to be more popular in one racial group than the other.
Quotes from African-American lesbians, other lesbians of Color, and
White lesbians show more similarity than difference. Compare, for ex-

ample, these three quotes from lesbians who do not believe that bisexuality exists as a legitimate form of sexuality:

> *I feel that bisexuals are very confused people, and will probably become lesbians. It's just that they are still on phase one. (Monifa)(African-American)*

> *I feel people who think they are bisexual are confused about it, or in transition. (Isabelle) (Euro-American)*

> *Usually it means a transition or a confusing part of life. It really doesn't exist. (Kamala) (Indian-American)*

There are also no apparent differences between the definitions of bisexuality used by lesbians of Color and White lesbians, nor in the ways different racial groups conceptualize sexuality.[1] Approximately equal percentages of lesbians in each racial group define bisexuality in terms of behavior, approximately equal percentages define bisexuality in terms of feelings of attraction, and the majority of every racial group conceptualizes sexuality dichotomously.

Comparisons between the images of bisexuality and feelings about bisexual women held by lesbians of different racial groups gave mixed results. For example, on average, African-American lesbians believe more strongly than White and Indian-American lesbians that bisexuals are really closeted lesbians, but there are no racial differences in the belief that bisexuality is a transitional stage that some women go through before they come out as lesbians. On the other hand, African-American lesbians and Indian-American lesbians believe more strongly than White lesbians that bisexuals lack commitment and that they are more likely than lesbians to want to pass as heterosexual, but there are no racial differences in lesbians' assessments of bisexuals' trustworthiness or of the relative ease with which bisexuals could pass compared to lesbians. Findings about racial differences in lesbians' willingness to associate socially and politically with bisexual women are equally mixed. None of the differences between African-American, Indian-American, and Euro-American lesbians are statistically significant, and it is very possible that they reflect random variations in individuals' beliefs rather than true racial differences. To impute great importance to these findings or to try to use them to argue that there are racial differences in lesbians' attitudes about bisexuality would be to overstate them, and perhaps to engage in racial stereotyping.

There are no educational and few social class differences in lesbians' attitudes toward bisexuality. Lesbians who dropped out of high school hold the same variety of beliefs about bisexuality and feelings about bisexual women as lesbians with college degrees or postgraduate educations. Working-class, middle-class, and upper-class lesbians also hold a variety of attitudes about bisexuality, with only one statistically significant difference between the classes. Specifically, working- and middle-class lesbians were more likely (21%) than upper-class lesbians (7%) to state explicitly that bisexuality exists as a valid sexual orientation, although upper-class lesbians were not more likely to say that bisexuality does not exist. This class difference cannot be accounted for by differences in education—for example, upper-class lesbians did not learn to think differently about sexuality in college—because lesbians with different levels of education do not have different attitudes toward bisexuality. Nor can the class difference be accounted for by differences in income or employment status, because lesbians with different incomes and employment statuses do not have different attitudes toward bisexuality. Whatever the explanation, the finding that there is a statistically significant class difference in lesbians' beliefs about bisexual existence must be placed in perspective; there are no class differences in any of lesbians' other beliefs about or feelings toward bisexuality. It is, therefore, likely that the one class difference found in the sample is a "false positive" that does not accurately reflect lesbians in general.

Lesbians of different ages and lesbians who came out in different decades experienced different social and political circumstances and might be expected to have different attitudes about sexuality and bisexuality. For example, the 1970s were the heyday of the feminist sexuality debates. The debates over the relationship between lesbianism and feminism, the merits of lesbian separatism, and the question of who is a lesbian—debates I will explore in chapter 6—raged more fiercely in the 1970s than ever before or after. During the 1970s, lesbian feminists were building Lesbian Nation and guarding its borders. Women who were involved in this struggle were deeply affected by it. Those who came out during this period learned to think about their sexuality in the context of these debates and formed sexual attitudes and sexual identities that reflected the issues of the day.

Women who came out before or after the 1970s experienced very different historical circumstances. Lesbians who came out before Stonewall did not have the luxury of debating the relative political merits of lesbianism and bisexuality or the relationship between lesbianism and feminism. Relationships with men were often a necessary cover, and support for one's relationships with women was too rare and precious to be compromised by quibbles over the meanings of these heterosexual relationships. For younger lesbians who came out in the 1980s, lesbian feminism was an established order against which to rebel. The time for separatism had passed, they said; the wave of the future is the destruction of gender and sexual categories, and the elimination of all boundaries between people. Lesbian feminist rules of political correctness were remnants of a political defense that was no longer necessary. Lesbian Nation was replaced by Queer Nation.

Do the attitudes of different generations of lesbians reflect these historical changes? Is the Lesbian Nation generation more critical of bisexuality than the pre-Stonewall and the Queer Nation generations? Among the lesbians in this study, women aged 30 to 34—who were college-aged in the early and mid 1970s—were indeed most skeptical about bisexual existence; over one-quarter of women in this age group either did not believe that bisexuality exists, or had serious doubts about its existence. Lesbians aged 25 to 29 or 35 to 39 were nearly as skeptical, and older and younger lesbians were less skeptical; less than one-fifth of lesbians under 24 or over 40 doubted or disbelieved the existence of bisexuality. But lesbians aged 25 to 39 were also most likely to explicitly validate the existence of bisexuality. Older and younger lesbians were less likely to raise the issue at all, reflecting the fact that bisexuality was not as important an issue for these women as it was for the generation that came out largely in the 1970s.[2] Although these findings suggest that lesbians of different ages have different beliefs about bisexuality, none of the differences are statistically significant; therefore, they cannot be taken as conclusive evidence of generational differences between lesbians in their attitudes toward bisexuality. At most, these findings suggest that generational differences might exist and should be explored further in future research.

Aside from the suggestion that there might be differences in the salience of the question of bisexual existence to lesbians of different generations, there are no meaningful age-related differences in lesbians' attitudes toward bisexuality. Perhaps there used to be differences that have been extinguished over time as lesbians of different ages and lesbians who came out at different stages of their lives mingle in the community and share their opinions with each other.

POLITICAL DIFFERENCES: DO POLITICAL LESBIANS SPEAK FOR US ALL?

In the late 1970s, Blumstein and Schwartz reported that antagonism toward bisexuality was particularly prevalent among lesbian feminists. Lesbian feminists in the current study also linked their own attitudes about bisexuality to their lesbian feminist political beliefs. For example, Chava wrote:

> I can understand bisexuality in an ideal society, but not under the patriarchy. I don't see how a woman could turn from a woman to a man if she had high standards and a desire for mutuality. I think bisexual women are more likely to give up on a relationship that needs work than lesbians are. (Chava)

If lesbian feminists' objections to bisexuality are based on political concerns, then it is tautological to conclude that lesbian feminists are more critical of bisexuality than other lesbians, because other lesbians would not have the same political objections to bisexuality that lesbian feminists do. Or is it? There are two flaws in this line of reasoning. First, the fact that other lesbians do not share lesbian feminists' political objections to bisexuality does not necessarily mean that they find bisexuality less objectionable. They might find bisexuality equally objectionable, but for other reasons.

Second, people often provide explanations for their opinions that do not reflect the original bases of those opinions. Because our culture values rationality we often underemphasize the emotional bases of our opinions and overemphasize the intellectual bases. We construct rationales that make our opinions appear to have grown logically out of our overall values and philosophies even if they did not. Sometimes we ourselves are unaware of the emotional motivations we have for our opinions, because we have learned to devalue—and hence discredit and ignore—our gut feelings. While it is quite possible that lesbian feminists' objections to bisexuality are in fact fundamentally based on political concerns, it would be naive to assume that this is true simply because lesbian feminists say that it is. This explanation for lesbian feminists' antipathy toward bisexuality is a hypothesis like any other, and must be tested before we accept it.

Politics and the Issue of Bisexual Existence

Before we can test whether lesbian feminists have different attitudes toward bisexuality than lesbians of other political orientations do, we have to find out whether they are more or less likely to believe that bisexuality exists at all. To identify respondents' political orientations, I asked them to list all political and social issues in which they are interested and to indicate whether they are actively involved in each issue. They listed a great variety of issues ranging from the environment, to homelessness, to U.S. intervention in Central America. Nearly half mentioned a concern about "gay rights" in general, and one-third wrote that they were concerned about "lesbian rights" in general or about particular lesbian issues, such as job discrimination, the rights to marry and maintain child custody, media images of lesbians, social attitudes, and lesbian health issues, including alcoholism. Seventy percent mentioned a concern about women's issues, including women's rights in general, ERA, reproduction rights and abortion, equal pay and occupational opportunity, discrimination, economic inequality, lack of political representation, violence (including rape and domestic abuse), pornography, sexual harassment, and health issues. In terms of active involvement in these issues, respondents range from those who are not politically involved at all, to those who donate money or confine their activism to personal talks with friends and coworkers, to those who give over ten hours a week to organizing and running meetings, protests, and other political action projects.

Neither the types of issues lesbians are concerned about nor the degree to which they are actively involved in these issues is related to whether they believe that bisexuality exists. Lesbians who indicated a concern about lesbian, feminist, or gay issues are no more skeptical than lesbians who did not. Among those who are concerned about lesbian issues, the degree of their active involvement in these issues is not related to their beliefs about bisexual existence; lesbian activists are no more likely than nonactivists and pocketbook or armchair activists to believe that bisexuality does not exist. Nor is the degree to which lesbians are actively involved in feminist issues significantly related to their beliefs about bisexual existence. Overall, there is no convincing evidence that politically active lesbian feminists—or politically active lesbians—have substantially different opinions on the question of bisexual existence than other lesbians do.

Politics and Sexual Conceptualizations, Beliefs, and Feelings about Bisexuality

Is the same true of lesbians' opinions on other matters? That is, do politically active lesbians' definitions of bisexuality, beliefs about bisexual women, and feelings about bisexual women also resemble the definitions, beliefs, and feelings of less active, less vocal lesbians? The findings of this study indicate that, for the most part, politically active lesbians' attitudes do reflect the attitudes of lesbians in general. Lesbian respondents of all political bents share the same variety of definitions of bisexuality and many of the same beliefs and feelings about bisexuality. For example, by all measures of political interest and activity, politically active and nonactive lesbians are equally likely to believe that bisexuality is transitional, that bisexuals are closeted lesbians, and that bisexuals are more able and willing to pass as heterosexual, and they are equally likely to prefer not to date bisexual women.

Although politically active lesbians generally do not have *different* feelings or beliefs than nonactive lesbians, they are more likely to express these feelings and beliefs, and they are more enthusiastic about doing so. In particular, they are more distrustful of bisexual women and less willing to associate with them as friends or in political situations than nonactive lesbians are. Lesbians who listed lesbian issues among the social and political issues they are concerned about tend to distrust bisexual women more than lesbians who did not mention lesbian issues; they agreed more strongly that bisexual women are likely to desert their woman friends, and that bisexuals can't be trusted to "stick around" when "the going gets rough" (figure 5.1). The difference is not so much a matter of the prevalence of doubt among those who mentioned lesbian issues and those who did not as it is a matter of the depth of their doubt. Sixty-seven percent of the former and 58% of the latter agreed that bisexual women lack commitment to their woman friends—a very small difference—but the former were more than twice as likely as the latter (25% versus 11%) to agree "very strongly."

In contrast, lesbians who mentioned "gay" issues are *less* likely to doubt bisexual women's commitment and trustworthiness. In fact, even among lesbians who listed lesbian issues, those who also listed gay issues expressed little more doubt about bisexual women than lesbians who did not list lesbian issues at all. Apparently, it is not concern for lesbian issues per se that is associated with the strength of lesbians' doubts about bisexual women; instead, it is the *exclusivity* of concern about lesbian issues that is associated with doubts about bisexual women. Similarly, lesbians who mentioned a concern about "women's" issues are no more likely to doubt bisexual women than lesbians who did not mention women's issues are. These findings indicate that strong doubts about bisexual women characterize lesbians whose political concerns are limited to lesbian issues, not those with broader political concerns that include both lesbian and gay issues or women's issues in general. This finding makes sense in light of the history of lesbian feminism. Early lesbian feminists took care to distinguish themselves from both women's liberationists and gay liberationists. They argued that lesbians have particular interests that arise out of their dual status as women and homosexuals, and that these interests differ from those of heterosexual feminists who are not lesbians as well as those of gay men who are as sexist as heterosexual men. Lesbians who carry on this lesbian feminist tradition are concerned about lesbian issues specifically; they are not concerned about gay rights or women's rights more generally. It is these women who expressed the strongest doubts about bisexual women's commitment and trustworthiness in this study.

Similar patterns exist in lesbians' feelings about bisexual women (figure 5.2). Lesbians who are exclusively concerned about lesbian issues care more strongly about the sexual identities of their friends and political coworkers than lesbians who did not mention lesbian issues or who mentioned both lesbian and gay issues. Differences were found in both the percentage of lesbians who preferred to associate with other lesbians, and in the strength of their preferences. For example, 92% of lesbians who mentioned a concern about exclusively lesbian issues would prefer their friends to be lesbian and not bisexual, whereas "only" 69% of those who did not mention lesbian or gay issues, and 73% of those who mentioned gay issues would prefer their friends to be lesbians. Lesbians who mentioned lesbian issues were also more than twice as likely as other lesbians to indicate that their preferences for lesbian friends were very strong. Similarly, 96% of lesbians who mentioned a concern about exclusively lesbian issues would prefer to be represented by a lesbian lobbyist compared to 82% of all other lesbians, and the former were over three times more likely than the latter to indicate that their preferences are very strong. In other words, most lesbians prefer other lesbians over bisexual women in both social and political situations, but lesbians who are exclusively concerned about lesbian issues have particularly widespread and strong preferences in these areas.

Politically active lesbians are more vocal than most lesbians and their opinions are therefore more likely to be heard by both lesbians and non-lesbians than the opinions of closeted or nonactive lesbians are. If politically active lesbians had very different attitudes from those of the majority of lesbians whose voices are rarely heard, the effect of their outspokenness would be to create an inaccurate impression of the attitudes of lesbians in general. This does not appear to be the case, however. Politically active lesbians have more extreme attitudes than other lesbians, but in substance their beliefs and feelings are similar to the beliefs and feelings of lesbians at large. As representatives of the lesbian community, they might be overstating the general attitude toward bisexuality, but they are expressing beliefs and feelings that are shared by a great majority of lesbians.

PERSONAL EXPERIENCES—THE ROLE OF EMPATHY

If lesbians of different races, ages, social classes, and political orientations share a similar variety of attitudes toward bisexual women, what does account for the differences among lesbians in their attitudes toward bisexual women? Of all the possibilities examined, lesbians' personal experiences of bisexuality in their own lives were found to be the most important factors distinguishing lesbians who accept bisexual women from those who want nothing to do with them. Many lesbians identified themselves as bisexual before coming out as lesbian, and many lesbians reported that they feel sexually attracted to men; these women's attitudes about bisexuality are different from those of lesbians who have no personal history of bisexuality.

When I began exploring the relationship between lesbians' personal experiences and their attitudes about bisexuality, I expected to find that lesbians whose own lives include a history of bisexuality would be the least tolerant of other women who call themselves bisexual. I had hypothesized that one reason lesbians discredit bisexuality in others is because, for women whose own histories include bisexual identities and feelings, discrediting bisexuality is necessary to maintain their own lesbian identities. For example, imagine a woman who calls herself a lesbian although she feels attracted to both women and men and has had romantic or sexual relations with both women and men—a description that fits more than half of the lesbians who participated in this study. To avoid hypocrisy, she has to define lesbianism in a way that includes herself. In other words, her definition of lesbianism has to include women who feel attracted to men and who have had heterosexual relationships. She might, for example, define a lesbian as a woman whose feelings of attraction for women are stronger than her feelings of attraction for men—a broad definition that is as legitimate as any other definition of lesbianism, and that is consistent with her own lesbian identity. If she believes bisexuality exists at all, she has to define it very narrowly to avoid defining herself as a bisexual. If she then applies her definitions of lesbianism and bisexuality to other women, she will conclude that many women who call themselves bisexual are actually, by her definition, lesbian. In order to maintain her identity as a lesbian without being hypocritical, she must reject others' bisexual identities. In contrast, a lesbian who has never had a heterosexual relationship and whose sexual feelings are exclusively for other women can afford to believe that bisexuality exists, and she can afford to define it broadly. She can afford to agree with women who have feelings of attraction for both women and men—no matter what the ratio—who call themselves bisexual, because accepting these women's definitions of themselves as bisexual does not threaten her own definition of herself as a lesbian. But such pure lesbians are rare; most of us cannot afford the luxury of allowing any woman who has the slightest history of bisexuality or heterosexuality in her past to define herself as bisexual, because most of us have the same experiences she does.

What I found among the lesbians who participated in this study does not support the argument that lesbians who have a history of bisexuality will be less tolerant of bisexually identified women than women with purely lesbian experiences, a hypothesis that I will call the "Identity Defense" hypothesis. In fact, I found quite the opposite to be true. Lesbians who reported that they feel some sexual attraction toward men are more, not less, likely to believe that bisexuality exists and more willing to associate with bisexual women. They also perceive greater similarity between bisexual women and lesbians than lesbians who are not attracted to men at all. Also, lesbians who have identified themselves as bisexual in the past tend to be more, not less, tolerant of bisexuality, *unless* they identified themselves as bisexual only *before* they came out as lesbians.

Why would women who call themselves lesbian in spite of their own heterosexual feelings be more, rather than less, tolerant of bisexuality than lesbians who are exclusively attracted to women? To understand the role of heterosexual attraction in lesbians' attitudes about bisexuality, we have to examine the actual differences between the attitudes of lesbians who had varying degrees of attraction to men. First, although lesbians who have some heterosexual feelings are as likely to be skeptical about the existence of bisexuality as lesbians who are exclusively attracted to women (40% versus 38%), they are twice as likely to be equivocal about their skepticism. Lesbians whose feelings are exclusively toward women are more certain in their belief that bisexuality does not exist.

The most likely explanation for this finding[3] is that lesbians who have heterosexual feelings themselves are more sympathetic to the idea that attractions to women and attractions to men can coexist within a single person, an explanation I will call the "Bisexual Empathy" hypothesis. They experience both attractions themselves, they readily acknowledge that they feel both attractions and, although they choose to call themselves lesbians, they can believe therefore that people who choose to call themselves bisexual do, in fact, experience real attractions to both women and men. Lesbians who are exclusively attracted to women, on the other hand, have no reason to believe that other people could be truly attracted to both women and men. Heterosexual society and lesbian subcultural ideology teach that attractions to women and men are distinct, if not mutually exclusive, feelings, and nothing in the personal experience of lesbians who are exclusively attracted to women contradicts this cultural wisdom. One woman made exactly this point:

> *I find it hard to understand being attracted to both men and women since I am so totally attracted to women, I have an easier time understanding heterosexuality in the sense that it is a total attraction. (Ginny)*

Because Ginny is totally attracted to women, she can understand heterosexuality as a total attraction to men. But bisexuality is less comprehen-
sible because her own experience as a lesbian who is exclusively attracted to women gives her no basis for identifying with bisexuals or
understanding their bisexuality. It is not surprising, therefore, that lesbians who are exclusively attracted to women disbelieve other women
who claim to be bisexual; nothing in their own experience gives them
reason to believe otherwise.

Second, lesbians who are attracted exclusively to women and lesbians who are attracted to both women and men have different beliefs
about the differences between lesbian and bisexual women. This is not
because they have different images of bisexual women—in fact, their
images of bisexual women are strikingly similar—rather, it is because
they have different images of lesbians. In general, lesbians who are
exclusively attracted to women have images of lesbians that differ
sharply from their images of bisexual women, whereas lesbians who
have heterosexual feelings have images of lesbians that resemble their
images of bisexual women more closely.

For example, most lesbians, regardless of whether and to what
degree they are attracted to men, agreed that "Society makes it difficult
to be a lesbian, so some women claim to be bisexual when they are
really lesbians who are afraid to admit it" (table 5.1). But lesbians who
have heterosexual feelings were much more likely than lesbians who are
exclusively attracted to women to agree that "some lesbians are really
attracted to men, but they are afraid to express these feelings because
other lesbians would not approve of them" (75% versus 56%). In other
words, lesbians who have heterosexual feelings tend to believe that
lesbians, like bisexual women, have heterosexual feelings and that, like
bisexual women, they hesitate to express their true sexuality for fear of
others' reactions. Lesbians who are exclusively attracted to women see a
greater difference between lesbians and bisexual women; they tend to
believe that lesbian identity, unlike bisexual identity, is an expression of
true sexuality (figure 5.3).

Probably, many of the lesbians who have heterosexual feelings
agreed with the statement that "some lesbians are really attracted to
men . . ." because their own personal experience told them it is true;
they themselves have heterosexual feelings they are afraid to express. If
not for this fear, these lesbian respondents might call themselves bisex-

ual. To the extent that this is the case, their interest lies not in defending a broad definition of lesbianism that would permit them to continue identifying as lesbians without hypocrisy—as I assumed in my original Identity Defense hypothesis—but in fostering acceptance of heterosexual feelings, or bisexuality, among lesbians so that they would no longer have to hide their heterosexual feelings.

Lesbians who have heterosexual feelings also perceive less difference between bisexuals' and lesbians' loyalties than lesbians who are exclusively attracted to women do (figure 5.4). When asked to agree or disagree with the statement "It can be dangerous for lesbians to trust bisexuals too much, because when the going really gets rough, they are not as likely to stick around and fight it out," lesbians with heterosexual feelings were more likely to disagree, and less likely to agree strongly, than lesbians who are exclusively attracted to women were. Furthermore, among lesbians with heterosexual feelings, the strength of these feelings is correlated with their perceptions of bisexuals' trustworthiness; the stronger their heterosexual feelings, the more willing they are to trust bisexual women.

Finally, lesbians who have heterosexual feelings are much more willing than lesbians who are exclusively attracted to women to associate with bisexual women socially and politically, and the stronger a lesbians' heterosexual feelings are, the more willing she is to associate with bisexual women (figure 5.5). For example, among lesbians who feel no attraction toward men whatsoever, 84% prefer that their friends be lesbian, not bisexual. Among lesbians who reported that one-tenth of their feelings are heterosexual, 75% prefer to associate with other lesbians. Among lesbians whose feelings are two-tenths heterosexual, the percentage decreases to 67%, and among lesbians whose feelings are three-tenths or more heterosexual, just over half (58%) care whether their friends are lesbian or bisexual.

If lesbians who have heterosexual feelings are more tolerant of bisexual women, then what about lesbians who have had actual heterosexual relationships? One would expect that, if heterosexual feelings predispose a lesbian to empathize with bisexual women, having had a heterosexual relationship would have an even greater effect on her feelings toward bisexual women. But the results of this study show that this is not the case at all. There are no differences whatsoever in the attitudes toward bisexuality of lesbians who have and have not had heterosexual relationships; they are equally likely to believe that bisexuality exists, equally likely to believe that bisexual women are really lesbians or in transition to lesbianism, equally likely to doubt bisexual women's political and personal loyalties, and equally unwilling to associate with bisexual women socially and politically. Moreover, among those who have had heterosexual relationships, the seriousness of those relationships does not matter; lesbians who have been heterosexually married or involved in serious, committed heterosexual relationships have the same thoughts and feelings about bisexuality as lesbians who have only dated men.

Given that the experience of heterosexual feelings apparently has such an influence on lesbians' thoughts and feelings about bisexuality, why would actual heterosexual relationships have no effect whatsoever? The explanation probably lies at least partially in the ubiquitousness of past heterosexual relationships among lesbians. As I reported in chapter 3, 91% of the lesbians who participated in this study have had heterosexual relationships. Because of their prevalence, lesbians have developed subcultural explanations for these relationships; for example, that they are a result of socialization, a response to social pressure, or a test of one's lesbianism. Whether or not these explanations are true—they are probably true in some cases and not in others—they effectively discredit past heterosexual relationships as reflections of one's true sexuality. Heterosexual relationships that are "explained away" in this fashion can no longer serve as the basis for empathy with bisexual women. For example, a lesbian who dated heterosexually as a teenager because of social pressure has little basis for empathy with someone who identifies herself as bisexual and dates men because she wants to.

Heterosexual feelings are much more difficult to explain away for several reasons. First of all, feelings, unlike behavior, emanate from one's internal self; whereas it is relatively easy to distance oneself from one's behavior, e.g., "I wasn't myself when I did that," it is much more difficult to distance oneself from one's feelings; claiming that one's feelings are not one's own seems to border on psychosis. Second, the heterosexual relationships of the lesbians in this study occurred in the past. Only 5 lesbian respondents were involved in heterosexual relationships at the time of the study, and the average lesbian had not been heterosexually involved for 7.2 years. But the heterosexual feelings reported by women in this study were feelings they had at the time of the study, not feelings they had had in the past. The passage of time creates a psychological distance; it is easier to distance one's self from past experiences than from current experiences. Third, even though heterosexual feelings are common among lesbians according to the results of this study, lesbians are afraid to reveal their heterosexual feelings to other lesbians for fear of their reactions. Therefore, subcultural explanations have not been developed for heterosexual feelings as they have been developed for heterosexual relationships. The individual lesbian is left to her own devices to decide the implications of her heterosexual feelings and, apparently, many lesbians find in their heterosexual feelings a basis for empathy with bisexual women that they do not find in their heterosexual relationships.

What about the role of bisexual identity in lesbians' lives? Many lesbians identified themselves as bisexual at some point in their lives. For some, this identity preceded their identity as lesbians and, in hindsight, appears to have been a stepping stone toward lesbian identity, i.e., a transitional identity. Others came out as lesbians and later temporarily adopted a bisexual identity. Some of these women switched back and forth between lesbian and bisexual identities numerous times. If having heterosexual feelings leads lesbians to empathize with bisexual women, then what effect does previously identifying oneself as bisexual have on lesbians' thoughts and feelings about bisexual women? Does it also lead to empathy or is it dismissed as a historical occurrence without current implications, as past heterosexual relationships are dismissed?

Having a history of bisexual identification is not as closely associated with lesbians' attitudes about bisexuality as heterosexual feelings are, but there are some connections. In general, lesbians who once identified themselves as bisexual see less difference between lesbians and bisexuals and are more tolerant of bisexuality than lesbians who never identified themselves as bisexual. Closer analysis reveals, however, that the role played by bisexual identity in a lesbian's past is very important. Specifically, lesbians who identified themselves as bisexual since coming out as lesbians see less difference between lesbians and bisexuals and are more tolerant of bisexuality than those for whom bisexual identity played a transitional role.

For example, lesbians who identified themselves as bisexual in the past are more willing to trust bisexual women's political loyalties than lesbians who never identified themselves as bisexual (figure 5.6). Thirty-seven percent of lesbians who previously identified as bisexual, compared to 28% of lesbians who did not, disagreed with the assertion that it is "dangerous for lesbians to trust bisexual women too much." But among those who previously identified as bisexual, those for whom bisexual identity was a transitional stage were just as likely as those who never identified as bisexual to agree that bisexual women should not be trusted. Only lesbians who interrupted their careers as lesbians with an interval of bisexual identification expressed an elevated degree of trust in bisexual women; nearly half of them (45%) disagreed with the idea that it is dangerous for lesbians to trust bisexual women too much, and an additional 14% remained neutral on the issue.

The same pattern is found with regard to lesbians' beliefs that some lesbians have heterosexual feelings that they are afraid to reveal. Lesbians who previously identified themselves as bisexual are more likely to believe that some lesbians have heterosexual feelings than lesbians who never considered themselves bisexual are (table 5.2). But among lesbians who previously identified themselves as bisexual, those who identified themselves as bisexual since coming out as lesbians see the least difference between lesbians and bisexuals; in fact, as a group they believe that lesbians are as likely to have concealed heterosexual feelings as bisexuals are to be closeted lesbians (figure 5.7).

There is also a general tendency for lesbians with a history of bisexual identification to be more willing to associate with bisexual women socially and politically, but this tendency is only statistically significant in the areas of friendship and dating, and in one of the three political contexts (figure 5.8). Lesbians who never identified themselves as bisexual or who did so only during a transitional period are more likely to care whether their friends are lesbian or bisexual than lesbians who identified themselves as bisexual since coming out as lesbians (79% and 85% versus 59%) and, among those who care, more likely to be adamant about their desire to avoid having bisexuals as friends. Those for whom bisexual identity was transitional are particularly adamant, even more so than lesbians who never identified as bisexual; nearly half of them expressed their preference for having lesbian, not bisexual, friends in the strongest terms possible. All three groups of lesbians have strong preferences when it comes to dating. Even lesbians who identified themselves as bisexual since coming out as lesbians are extremely unwilling to date bisexual women: 90% prefer to date lesbians, and 65% have very strong preferences in this area. But the desire to avoid dating bisexual women is even more prevalent and strong among lesbians who never identified as bisexual (95%, 82%) and lesbians for whom bisexual identity was transitional (98%, 76%). The only political situation in which lesbians' identity histories are significantly related to their willingness to work with bisexual women is the situation in which respondents were asked whether they would prefer a lesbian or bisexual woman to speak to a community group about alternative lifestyles. Again, lesbians who identified themselves as bisexual since coming out as lesbians are less likely to care whether the speaker is lesbian or bisexual, and less likely to care strongly, than lesbians who never identified as bisexual or lesbians for whom bisexual identity was transitional.

Identifying oneself as bisexual apparently has an effect on lesbians' attitudes toward bisexuality that is similar to the effect of having heterosexual feelings—like lesbians who have some heterosexual feelings, lesbians who previously identified themselves as bisexual perceive less difference between lesbians and bisexual women and are more tolerant of bisexuality than lesbians who did not. It seems that a history of bisexual identification leaves lesbians with an enduring empathy with bisexual women that enhances their sense of similarity to bisexual women and decreases their distrust of them. Lesbians who never identified themselves as bisexual, like lesbians who do not have any heterosexual feelings, lack this sense of similarity or connection to bisexual women and, therefore, perceive greater differences between bisexual women and themselves and have greater distrust of bisexual women. However, the usual moderating effect of a bisexual identity history is absent among lesbians who identified as bisexual only before they came out as lesbians. This is probably because, in hindsight, these women perceive their bisexual identities not as reflections of their true sexuality, but merely as a way of easing the transition to lesbian identity. Lesbian subcultural ideology encourages lesbians to dismiss bisexual identity as a transitional stage, as it encourages them to dismiss past heterosexual behavior as a response to social pressure. Dismissed, previous bisexual identity does not provide a basis for empathy or connection with bisexual women. In fact, it provides a basis for dismissing bisexual women themselves. Hence, the attitudes of lesbians for whom bisexual identity preceded lesbian identity resemble those of lesbians who never identified themselves as bisexual and, in some cases, are even more extreme.

Some readers might wonder whether the effects of heterosexual feelings and bisexual identity history might be one and the same effect. After all, lesbians who have heterosexual feelings are much more likely than lesbians who do not to have identified themselves as bisexual; 19% of lesbian respondents who are exclusively attracted to women, compared to 51% of those with heterosexual feelings, have at some time in their lives identified themselves as bisexual. Perhaps it is not a history of bisexual identification, but rather the heterosexual feelings that many lesbians who used to identify as bisexual still have, that produces their increased empathy and tolerance for bisexual women. Statistical analysis shows that this is not the case. But the effects of the two factors are not entirely independent of one another, either. The results suggest that each enhances the other. For example, among lesbians who are exclusively attracted to women, a history of bisexual identification has virtually no impact on their attitudes toward bisexual women, whereas among lesbians who have heterosexual feelings, the stronger these feelings are the greater the impact of bisexual identification is on their attitudes toward bisexual women. Conversely, among lesbians who never identified as bisexual, having heterosexual feelings is only slightly associated with increased tolerance for bisexual women, whereas among lesbians who identified as bisexual since coming out as lesbian, those with heterosexual feelings are substantially more tolerant of bisexual women than those who are exclusively attracted to women.

The explanation for the finding that each experience enhances the other might be that each experience is "necessary but not sufficient" to increase lesbians' tolerance for bisexual women. For example, a lesbians' heterosexual feelings might have no impact on her attitudes toward bisexual women unless, at some point in her life, she has interpreted these feelings as bisexual. Having had a bisexual identity indicates that she has interpreted these feelings as bisexual, and suggests that she still sees in them a basis for empathy with bisexual women even though she now calls herself lesbian. If she has heterosexual feelings but has never entertained the thought of herself as bisexual, then she probably does not make a connection between her own heterosexual feelings and the experience of being bisexual; she is a lesbian who happens to have some heterosexual feelings, not a bisexual. Conversely, having had a bisexual identity might have no impact on a lesbians' attitudes toward bisexual women unless she currently feels some attraction to men. If she does not, then she is either no longer bisexual or she never was, and again she sees little resemblance between herself and bisexual women.

SUMMARY

Lesbians of different races, educational levels, and social classes appear to share the same range of attitudes toward bisexual women. There is no evidence to suggest that there are any substantial demographic differences in the ways in which lesbians define bisexuality, or in their beliefs about and feelings toward bisexual women. Instead, the findings suggest that a great variety of attitudes are found among lesbians of all races, educational levels, and social classes.

Lesbians who are politically active tend to be more vocal about their attitudes toward bisexuality and, sometimes, more extreme in their opinions. For example, lesbians whose political concerns focus on lesbian issues in particular rather than on general gay or women's issues are less willing to trust or associate with bisexual women. On the whole, however, politically active lesbians have attitudes that resemble the attitudes of nonactive lesbians. The findings of previous researchers that lesbian feminists are more antagonistic toward bisexual women than other lesbians appear to be the result of lesbian feminists' greater outspokenness and strength of conviction, not an indication that lesbian feminists have substantively different attitudes about bisexuality than other lesbians do.

The most important factor in lesbians' attitudes toward bisexuality is whether or not their own experiences give them a basis for understanding the sexual experiences of bisexual women. Lesbians who have heterosexual feelings themselves or who identified themselves as bisexual in the past are more empathic and tolerant toward bisexual women than lesbians who are either exclusively attracted to women or never identified themselves as bisexual. The former are more likely to believe that bisexuality exists and are more willing to associate socially and politically with bisexual women. They also have images of lesbians that closely resemble their images of bisexual women, and are more willing to trust bisexual women. The latter are more skeptical about bisexuality, prefer more strongly to confine their social and political interactions to other lesbians, and believe that lesbians are very different from bisexual women.

The impact of previous bisexual identification on a lesbian's attitudes toward bisexuals is lost, however, if it occurred before she came out as a lesbian. Women who identified themselves as bisexual before they came out as lesbian can look back on their own histories and perceive their period of bisexual identification as a transitional phase. As a transitional phase, it has no lasting implications for their own sexuality and provides no basis for empathy with bisexual women. In fact, it tends to make these lesbians even less willing to interact socially with bisexual women, whom they probably expect are going through a transitional phase as they themselves have done.

Unlike heterosexual feelings and a history of bisexual identification, having had actual heterosexual relationships does not lead lesbians to empathize with bisexual women. This is probably because heterosexual experience is ubiquitous among lesbians. Subcultural explanations have developed that eliminate the implications of heterosexual experience for lesbians' own sexuality, thus neutralizing it as a basis for empathizing with bisexual women. In contrast, feelings of sexual attraction and a history of bisexual identification subsequent to coming out as a lesbian are difficult to explain away, leaving the lesbian who feels attracted to men or who has identified as bisexual with an enduring empathy for bisexual women.

The fact that lesbians' experiences of their own sexuality are closely related to their attitudes toward bisexual women suggests that the controversy over bisexuality among lesbians is intimately related to controversies over what it means to be a lesbian. Particularly noteworthy is the finding that lesbians who are attracted to men or who have identified themselves as bisexual in the past differ from other lesbians not in their definitions of bisexuality and their images of bisexuals, but in their definitions of lesbianism and their images of lesbians. In other words, lesbianism, not bisexuality, is the real issue.

6

THE PINK AND BLUE HERRING:¹ THE ISSUE IS LESBIANISM, NOT BISEXUALITY

Why is the topic of bisexuality so controversial among lesbians? Why does it arouse such passion in us, sparking heated debates in our newspapers and magazines? Why do most of us prefer to keep our distance from bisexual women, avoiding romance and even friendship with them? Although we often couch our arguments in political or intellectual terms, the emotional force behind them suggests that bisexuality touches a nerve in us. In fact, the question of bisexuality strikes to the core of our being because it is intimately related to the question of who we are as lesbians. As individuals and as a historically evolving community, we have struggled to form an identity. We have struggled to distinguish ourselves from heterosexuals in order to assert our existence in a society that assumes heterosexuality, and at the same time we have struggled to define ourselves positively in terms of what we have in common as lesbians. But these two processes—the process of distinguishing ourselves from heterosexuals and the process of defining ourselves as lesbians—lead to different conceptions of who we are. Disputes occur over how we should classify that which is lesbian by one definition, but not by another. Sometimes we refer to it as heterosexuality, sometimes we refer to it as lesbianism, and sometimes we refer to it as bisexuality. It exists at the edges of lesbianism, and it blurs those edges. It prevents us from defining clear boundaries as a community. To develop a sense of who we are as lesbians, we have had to overlook these boundary disputes. Bisexuality forces us to reexamine our own boundaries. It calls into question the clarity of our sense of ourselves as lesbians and reveals the disagreements we have with each other over the question of who we are as a community. It opens old wounds that are still painful. We have spent years defending our existence in a heterosexist society, and our identities as lesbians are hard won; any threat to these identities touches a sensitive nerve indeed, and bisexuality is a threat.

In this chapter, I will examine the development of our concept of ourselves as lesbians, including the disagreements we had—and still have—with each other along the way. I will then show how our current beliefs and feelings about bisexuality as described in chapters 4 and 5 stem from these disagreements, and have more to do with the schisms in our own conception of ourselves than they have to do with bisexuality.

Much of the debate over what constitutes lesbianism took place within the context of defining the political meaning of lesbianism, particularly in relation to feminism. A superficial overview of the history of the relationship between lesbianism and feminism locates the early 1970s as a pivotal point. The oft-told story goes like this:[2] In the early days of the second wave of the feminist movement, lesbians immediately recognized that feminist goals, for example, women's economic independence, mirrored their own needs as lesbians. Because of their particular interest in feminist goals, lesbians became some of the most active leaders in the feminist movement. But lesbianism was feminism's skeleton in the closet. Nonfeminists used the charge of lesbianism to intimidate feminists and would-be feminists. Heterosexuals in the women's liberation movement responded to these attacks defensively by declaring their heterosexuality, and lesbians remained hidden to avoid tainting the movement. Heterosexual feminists constructed lesbianism as a "lavender herring," i.e., a trivial issue that would distract feminists from the "real" issues. By constructing heterosexual women's issues as the proper focus of feminism, they constructed the heterosexual woman as the "real" woman and lesbians as a special interest group.

By the early 1970s, some lesbians were no longer content to remain hidden and no longer willing to let their concerns as lesbians be dismissed or put on the back burner. Encouraged by the development of gay liberation and tired of being second-class citizens in both the feminist (as lesbians) and the gay (as women) movements, they began to come out within the feminist movement. Eventually, after finding that their needs were not met within the feminist movement, they formed a splinter movement that became lesbian feminism. But in the meantime, through the debate over lesbianism in the feminist movement, a new concept of the political relationship between feminism and lesbianism evolved. No longer the skeleton in the closet, lesbianism became the ultimate expression of feminism, and lesbians became the vanguard of the movement.

This brief overview or "origin story" (King 1986) sketches the outlines of the historical evolution of the relationship between feminism and lesbianism, but it glosses over the twists and turns we took along the way. The transition was neither easy nor universal; on the contrary, it was hotly debated and never resolved. The story also ignores the fact that the debate over lesbianism within the feminist movement took place in the context of a larger society. This larger society, as a result of the increasing visibility of racial and ethnic liberation movements, such as the Black[3] civil rights movement, was familiar with "ethnic" modes of political discourse that differed from "feminist" modes of political discourse. Lesbians, as heirs to both political traditions, used both languages of political protest and thereby produced a variety of sometimes conflicting political arguments based on different concepts of lesbianism.

To understand how our contemporary concepts of lesbianism were shaped by the debate over lesbianism in the feminist movement and by the competition between ethnic and feminist modes of argument, we have to look closely at the exact nature of the arguments that were made on all sides of the debate, identify the points of contention, and analyze the faultlines in lesbian ideology that were created by these disagreements—faultlines that are exposed today when we talk about bisexuality. Because my goal is to identify the contradictions within lesbian ideology that arose from its multiple ideological roots, the discussion to follow is organized in terms of the differences between various ideological arguments and not by the historical integrity of each ideological argument. Readers who are interested in historical treatments of the development of particular strains of feminist or lesbian ideology, such as radical feminism, cultural feminism, lesbian separatism, and lesbian feminist reformism, are referred to many excellent works by other authors.[4]

THE PERSONAL AND THE POLITICAL: CONSTRUCTING LESBIANISM AS A FEMINIST ISSUE

To legitimize lesbianism as an issue in the eyes of feminists, lesbians had to construct an argument whereby lesbianism would become an important feminist issue. To do so required constructing a connection between an issue that had heretofore been considered personal, or private—lesbianism—and an issue that feminists had already politicized—women's oppression.

The politicization of the personal was an established feminist strategy. In fact, the entire second wave of the feminist movement was built on the redefinition of "women's issues"—such as abortion, child care, and physical abuse, issues that were formerly considered private matters—as political issues. In this feminist tradition, the "politicization of the personal" means first recognizing that problems that appear to be individual problems are in reality part of a larger social pattern that systematically disadvantages women as a group. As part of a larger social pattern, these problems must be the consequences of social, not individual, forces. Furthermore, the pattern was created and is perpetuated by power differentials between women and men in society; that is, the social pattern, and therefore the personal problems of women, are political in origin. The solution, therefore, must be a political—not an individual—one, in which the problems are attacked at their root, i.e., the power differential between women and men. Thus, feminism reconstructs individual problems as social problems, argues that the personal is a reflection of the political, and then prescribes a political solution to problems that were formerly considered private matters.

To legitimate lesbianism as a feminist issue, therefore, lesbianism had to be reconstructed as a political issue. Different lesbian feminists accomplished this reconstruction in different ways. In their famous essay, "The Woman-Identified Woman," the Radicalesbians[5] argued that "lesbian" is a term that is used to keep women in line; it is thrown at women who do not conform to the feminine gender role, and it is used to keep women from becoming too militantly feminist. Audre Lorde also described this tactic and urged Black women to recognize and resist it:

> let anyone, particularly a Black man, accuse a straight Black woman of being a Black Lesbian, and right away that sister becomes immobilized, as if that is the most horrible thing she could be, and must at all costs be proven false. That is homophobia. It is a waste of woman energy, and puts a terrible weapon into the hands of your enemies to be used against you to silence you. (Lorde 1988/1990:322–323)

In other words, homophobia is a tool that the oppressor can use to forestall feminist struggle. This argument constructs homophobia as a barrier to feminist progress, a point of weakness that the oppressor can use to perpetuate the oppression. Therefore, in order to advance the cause of feminism, it is necessary for feminists to defuse this weapon by confronting their own fear of lesbianism. Addressing the issue of lesbianism, and overcoming homophobia among feminists, then, becomes a necessary step in feminist progress or a means toward feminist goals.

The accusation of lesbianism also uses homophobia to control women in another way. Implicit in the accusation is the message that lesbians are not real women and that "the essence of being a 'woman' is to get fucked by men" (Radicalesbians 1970:51).[6] By accusing feminists of lesbianism, the patriarchy uses male-defined womanhood as the carrot to keep women submissive. By accepting this definition of womanhood and the homophobia implicit in it, feminists allow the patriarchy to subvert feminism. By rejecting homophobia and broadening the concept of womanhood to include lesbians, feminists could resist the patriarchy's attempts to retard feminist progress.

The Radicalesbians argued that overcoming homophobia is a means toward feminist goals in a more direct way as well. They argued that fear of lesbianism keeps women from forming intimate, supportive, and loving relationships with each other.[7] First, it scares women away from intimate relationships with each other because of the implicit lesbianism in those relationships. It prevents women from forming primary relationships with other women, and therefore from committing themselves primarily to women. Conversely, it ensures that women will remain primarily committed to men, and therefore under the control of men. Second, the lesbian label (hetero)sexualizes relations among women and causes women to perceive intimate relations between women according

to the heterosexual models they have been taught, e.g., to lay "a surro-
gate male role on the lesbian" and "make herself into an object" (Radicalesbians 1970:51). Thus, women are kept from forming real solidarity
among themselves because they are only able to understand intimate
relations in terms of heterosexual roles. But "[i]t is the primacy of
women relating to women, of women creating a new consciousness of
and with each other which is at the heart of women's liberation, and the
basis for the cultural revolution" (Radicalesbians 1970:55). Feminist
struggle requires that women commit themselves primarily to women,
not to men; to do so requires overcoming fear of lesbianism. Therefore,
addressing the issue of lesbianism and overcoming fear of lesbianism is
not only necessary to deprive the oppressor of one of his tools of
oppression, but also to create the most important tool of liberation—
solidarity among women.

Taking a slightly different approach, other feminists agreed that
homophobia divided women, but they argued that it divided women not
because it prevented women from forming intimate relations with each
other, but because it divided heterosexual women from lesbian women.
For example, Val Carpenter (1988) observed that anti-lesbianism kept
heterosexual and lesbian women separated from each other by distrust
and prejudice and encouraged them to undercut each other, thus
allowing men to consolidate their power as men over both heterosexual
women and lesbians. Audre Lorde characterized this as a "divide-and-
conquer routine" (1988/1990:324), which wastes women's energy and
prevents heterosexual women from benefiting from the insights of strong
Black Lesbian feminists.

The above arguments assert that homophobia is a barrier to feminist
progress and that, therefore, feminists must recognize lesbianism as a
political issue and work to eliminate their own homophobia in order to
achieve liberation for women. Addressing the issue of lesbianism is
presented as a means toward a feminist end; once the barrier of homophobia is removed, feminists will be able to get on with the real business
at hand, i.e., dismantling sexism.

A more radical approach to the problem of establishing lesbianism
as a legitimate political issue of concern to feminists was to argue that
lesbianism *itself* is political, and that lesbianism per se is a feminist
political issue. Again, different theorists used different arguments to
construct lesbianism as a political issue. The Furies, a lesbian-feminist

collective in Washington, D.C., and the Leeds Revolutionary Feminist Group began by politicizing heterosexuality, then constructing a relationship between heterosexuality and the politics of male supremacy, and finally arguing that lesbianism, as an alternative to heterosexuality, is a political response to male supremacy. For example, in the Introduction to their collection of essays written by members of The Furies or published in *The Furies* newspaper, Nancy Myron and Charlotte Bunch argued that heterosexuality is a political institution and an ideology that supports male supremacy (1975).[8] In an essay in the collection, Bunch further explained that heterosexuality is political because relationships between women and men involve power and dominance, i.e., they are political. Heterosexual relationships are the most individual form of male domination, in which a man dominates a woman. In an essay in the same collection, Rita Mae Brown helped construct the relationship between male domination in society and male domination within individual heterosexual relationships by arguing that the man in a heterosexual relationship "has the entire system of male privilege to back him up" (1972/1975:70–71). Or, as Jill Johnston put it in *Lesbian Nation*, "Sexual dependence on the man is inextricably entangled in the interdependence of man and woman at all levels of the social structures by which the woman is oppressed" (1973:165). In other words, male domination in heterosexual relationships is the expression of and is supported by male social domination.

Because heterosexuality is a tool of male domination, it is enforced by patriarchal society via socialization and social norms. Gerre Goodman et al. argued that gender role socialization fractures human integrity by transforming women and men into complimentary emotional cripples, and thereby compelling women and men to bond together to reestablish their integrity (1983). This socialization, or "heterosexual conditioning" as the staff of *Purple September* called it, is especially crippling to girls because it teaches them to deny their human identities and see themselves and their sexuality through male eyes so that they will provide a good match for males who have also been taught to see through male eyes (1975:81). Coletta Reid cited the myth of the vaginal orgasm as evidence that heterosexual meanings are culturally constructed to benefit men (1975), and Brown argued that a woman's entire identity in male supremacist heterosexual society is defined by her sexual function (1976a). Heterosexual socialization is backed up by norms that proscribe non-heterosexual forms of sexuality (*Purple September* 1975), and by male behaviors, cultural myths, and economic realities that conspire to create the "lie of compulsory female heterosexuality" (Rich 1980/1983:199). Thus, heterosexuality is not a personal choice, but a politically prescribed outcome. This normative prescription, or heterosexism, is the mechanism by which heterosexuality is transformed into a coercive institution, i.e., the mechanism by which women are forced to make themselves available to serve men within individual heterosexual relationships (Goodman et al. 1983). Heterosexuality is therefore a political institution that not only perpetuates sexist gender roles, but guarantees that men's control over women will extend into the most personal aspects of women's lives and psyches.

Because heterosexuality is a political institution that supports male supremacy, lesbianism, as an alternative to and implicit critique of heterosexuality, is itself political. By rejecting heterosexual relationships and choosing to love women in a culture that despises women, the lesbian is in revolt against male supremacy. At the cultural level, the lesbian "threatens male supremacy at its core" (Bunch 1972/1975:29) by rejecting the cultural valuation of the male (Brown 1976a). At the structural level, by forming same-sex pairs the lesbian subverts the division of humanity into two emotionally crippled but complimentary female and male groups; i.e. she challenges gender roles (Goodman et al. 1983). She is "the person who is outside of the collaborating categories of male and female" (Wittig 1981/1991 cited by King 1986:82) and who refuses to collaborate in her own oppression (Rich 1980/1983). She "is a terrible threat to male supremacy" because she "is totally independent of men" (Shelley 1969/1970:345).

At the personal level, the lesbian "undermines the personal power that men exercise over women" (Bunch 1972/1975:33) and withdraws support for individual men (Brown 1972/1975) by refusing to participate in heterosexual relationships. Reid asserted that this deprives men of their personal servants (1975), and Brown suggested that men will change if they are deprived of the support of women. Carrying this thought to an extreme, Brown pointed out that "if all women were Lesbians male supremacy would have the impossible task of maintaining itself in a vacuum" (1976f:122). Marilyn Frye defined power in terms of differential access; power is the right of access by the powerful to the powerless. Therefore, lesbianism, insofar as it represents a denial of men's right to sexual access to women on the part of individual women, reclaims women's power and challenges men's power over women (1977/1983a). Finally, at the psychological level, the lesbian challenges male-defined sexuality by demonstrating that sexuality need not involve a penis, and she challenges male-defined images of women by rejecting "male definitions of how she should feel, act, look, and live" (Bunch 1972/1975:29), including the definition of a woman as a person who is fucked by men. In multiple ways, therefore, the lesbian offers "the beginning of the end of collective and individual male supremacy" (Bunch 1972/1975:33).

This argument presents lesbianism as inherently subversive because lesbians' very existence challenges male supremacy. Lesbians, by virtue of being lesbians, are living feminism. Through their personal lives, lesbians present a political challenge to the enemy of feminism, male supremacy. Therefore, the lesbian lifestyle is a political act. As Reid stated so eloquently, "In the context of the institutional nature of enforced heterosexuality, lesbianism is an act of individual rebellion" (1975:103).[9] Feminists have an interest in fighting heterosexism not only because it is a barrier to feminist progress, but because lesbianism itself is feminist.

The argument that lesbianism is political because it implicitly challenges male supremacy constructs lesbianism as not merely a feminist issue, but a key feminist issue. If heterosexuality is the fundamental basis of male supremacy, then lesbianism is the cornerstone of women's liberation. In other words, lesbianism is necessary to feminism. This opinion was expressed by many lesbian feminist writers of the early 1970s. For example, Bunch commented that "Lesbianism is the key to liberation" (1972/1975:36), Johnston quipped in *Ms.* magazine, "Feminism at heart is a massive complaint. Lesbianism is the solution,"[10] and Ti-Grace Atkinson wrote, "Lesbianism is to feminism what the Communist Party was to the trade union movement. Tactically, any feminist should fight to the death for lesbianism because of its strategic importance" (Atkinson 1970/1974:134). Whereas a few short years earlier lesbianism had represented a threat to feminism, it now represented the hope for women's liberation.[11] As Katie King (1986) observed, lesbianism had become "feminism's magical sign."

Some lesbian feminists argued that lesbianism is a feminist lifestyle in practical, as well as theoretical, ways. Myron and Bunch (1975) argued that lesbianism is feminist not merely because lesbians' existence poses an implicit challenge to the interrelated institutions of heterosexuality and male supremacy, but also because lesbians' personal lives are more likely to embody feminist ideals. For example, whereas heterosexual women are able to depend on the men to whom they are attached, lesbians must provide for themselves economically and psychologically. Lesbians represent "the ultimate in an independent life style" (Abbott and Love 1971:602) because the lesbian "is freed or has freed herself from the external and internal dominance of the male" and "has sought wholeness within herself, not requiring, in the old romantic sense, to be 'completed' by an opposite." [12] Freedom from dependence on men is a feminist goal; lesbians, by virtue of being lesbians, are already living lives in which they have attained this feminist goal. Moreover, this independence leads to "strength and spirit in individual women" (Myron and Bunch 1975:13), qualities that are desirable from a feminist perspective.

In addition to independence, freedom from men and relationships with women provide the lesbian with the opportunity for greater self-knowledge, the opportunity to shed male definitions of womanhood, and the opportunity to learn to love and value herself through learning to love and value another woman. This is how Jessica Wood experienced her lesbian desire; inside her, struggling to emerge, was not a "woman attracted to women" but a "completely woman-defined-woman" (1981:53). The Radicalesbians wrote that "Only women can give each other a new sense of self" because this new sense of self has "to develop with reference to ourselves, and not in relation to men" (1970:54). Recognizing the connection that the Radicalesbian argument constructed between the individual and the collective woman, Brown explained how relationships with women can lead an individual woman to greater self-knowledge: "A woman can best find out who she is with other women, not with just one other woman but with other women, who are also struggling to free themselves from an alien and destructive culture" (1976d:76). Similarly, Goodman et al. explained how loving other women can lead individual women toward greater love for themselves as women:

> To completely love ourselves, it may not be necessary to love other women. However the conditioning that we are weak, incomplete—needing a man for strength, fulfillment, and protection—tells us that

we cannot love women, even ourselves, that we must serve men; it also tells us to include ourselves under a category meaning inferior and not worthy of commitment. Loving another woman, because it contradicts this conditioning, inevitably leads to greater self-love. (1983:32–33)

Self-knowledge is a feminist ideal because to build a strong feminist movement, women must first discover who they are as women, apart from the male-defined images of themselves they have been taught in a male supremacist culture. They must also learn to value themselves as women, shedding the devaluation and negative valuations imposed on women by a male supremacist culture. Lesbians, by virtue of their relationships with women, have greater opportunities for developing feminist self-knowledge and self-love than heterosexual women do.

Another feminist ideal is the egalitarian relationship. Heterosexual relationships, by virtue of the differential power of women and men and the gender roles imposed by society, are necessarily unequal. Heterosexual women must confront the sexism of their male partners and the sexist expectations other people place on heterosexual relationships on a daily basis. In contrast, a lesbian relationship is a relationship between two social equals that has the potential to be egalitarian, and therefore feminist. As Sasha Gregory Lewis (1979) argued, lesbians were never included in the heterosexual gender role system and therefore are free from its rules and roles. A woman in a relationship with another woman avoids having to deal with sexism in the most personal area of her life. Therefore, lesbians are free to live feminist lives without the burden of a constant struggle. Lois Hart described her personal experience of this freedom: [13]

in living with another woman, and in developing a relationship with another woman . . . I don't have to deal with a lot of my own feelings of oppression as when I'm with a man. I don't have to deal with that part of me that's been trained to respond to men in certain ways and to have certain emotional reactions towards men. It's very clear to me, when I'm with another woman, that I am responsible for myself . . . I see that as a political thing. [14]

The argument that lesbians' lifestyles are more likely to embody feminist ideals utilizes a strategy for the politicization of lesbianism that is different from the strategy underlying the argument that lesbianism is inherently subversive. Instead of politicizing heterosexuality and then linking heterosexuality to the political institution of male supremacy in order to conclude that lesbianism, as an alternative to heterosexuality, is politically feminist, the argument that lesbian lifestyles embody feminist ideals draws the connection between lesbianism and feminism first at the personal level, and then shifts this connection to the political level. The quote from Hart illustrates this strategy. Hart asserted that when she is in a lesbian relationship, she experiences a freedom from sexism; this personal relationship is therefore feminist. Because the personal is a reflection of the political, the relationship itself, embodying the connection between lesbianism and feminism, is political. As Hollibaugh and Moraga wrote in the early 1980s, lesbianism "came to be seen as the practice of feminism" (1981/1983:395).

In a letter to *The Ladder* in 1969, Martha Shelley added a subtle but critical twist to the argument that the lesbian lifestyle is feminist. She encouraged lesbians to be proud of themselves because "We are a body of women independent of [men's] domination, willing to compete with them on an equal basis—not willing to reduce ourselves to the lowest common denominator so that every living male can feel himself superior to us." [15] Writing during a historical period during which most lesbians accepted the "experts' " opinion that homosexuality was a form of perversion, Shelley's intent was undoubtedly to counteract lesbians' negative self-images by pointing out the positive aspects of lesbianism. However, by urging lesbians to be proud of their lack of subordination to men, Shelley implicitly suggested that lesbians could somehow take credit for the fact that their lives conformed to feminist ideals. In other words, she suggested that lesbians not only lived feminist lives but that they *were* feminists, and that they had become feminist not by default but through their own volition. This might have been one of the first written implications that lesbianism is a matter of choice, an idea that became the subject of explicit controversy among lesbians and feminists a few years later. It was also the beginning of the idea that the lesbian lifestyle is not only *consistent* with feminism's vision for all women, but that the lesbian lifestyle is in fact an *expression* of feminism. [16]

Once lesbianism per se had been reconstructed as political and feminist, lesbian feminists could begin to argue that lesbians, as individuals and as a collective, have something to offer heterosexual feminists. Many claimed that lesbians have a special vantage point or analysis of heterosexuality as an institution, which they possess by virtue of their perspective as outsiders to the institution. In good feminist fashion,

Coletta Reid drew on her own personal experience to explain that lesbianism reveals the workings of heterosexuality: "I had heard the term 'heterosexual privilege' before, but I never really understood how it worked. Now I knew. . . . As I tried to live as an open lesbian I began to see the privileges I had taken for granted when married" (1975:95– 96). In other words, as a lesbian, Reid could see the forces that coerce women to participate in the heterosexual institution.

Marilyn Frye made the same point in a more philosophical fashion. Frye metaphorically described the male supremacist world as a Reality play. In this play, men are the actors toward whom the audience's attention is properly drawn, and whose actions define Reality. Women are stagehands who are necessary to the performance but whose movements must be ignored to maintain the illusion of Reality. In this phallocratic Reality lesbians do not exist, but we can begin to understand lesbians by imagining them as seers who look beyond male-defined Reality and perceive the women instead. The individual lesbian might not pose a threat to Reality, but as a seeing woman she signals the possibility of seeing, and therefore authoring reality, to other women. As a seer of women, she also signals the possibility of women being seen. The danger to male supremacist society lies in the potential contagion of this perception "to the point where the agreement in perception which keeps Reality afloat begins to disintegrate" (1983c:171). The lesbian is, therefore, a threat to male supremacist Reality. [17]

The message to heterosexual women in these arguments is that they are blinded by their own involvement in heterosexuality, and that they must rely on the superior insight of lesbians to achieve a greater understanding of their own oppression as women. Heterosexual women cannot liberate themselves; their hope for liberation lies in trusting the vision of lesbians.

In addition to a special vision, lesbians have greater opportunities and resources to offer in the struggle for women's liberation than heterosexual women do. Because lesbians are free of personal obligations to men, they are free to devote their time and energy to the advancement of women's liberation (e.g., Packwood 1981). Because they are not servants to men and do not derive benefits from the heterosexist patriarchal system, they are in a position of independent political strength from which they can attack the patriarchy (e.g., Abbott and Love 1972). Because they have no vested interest in male-dominated culture, they are free to develop a different culture; lesbian musicians, healers, etc., have been the source of much women's culture (Goodman et al. 1983). Lesbians are also best situated to develop revolutionary feminist consciousness. The creation of feminist consciousness depends on women sharing their experiences as women and discovering themselves as women apart from male definitions. Because their closest relations are with women, lesbians are in the best position to escape male-defined reality and create the women-only spaces necessary to develop a revolutionary feminist consciousness (Radicalesbians 1970).

Because lesbians are best situated to discover that which is truly womanly apart from male definitions, lesbians are the most womanly of women. In other words, lesbians are not only the best feminists; they are the best *women*. Who could be more womanly than a woman's woman, whose life is centered around women? Among the groups that ascribed to this belief was The Caucus, a group of reformist lesbian feminist members of DOB-New York, whose members felt that "homosexual women, as women with the ability to be totally intimate with other women, had quintessentially female sensibilities" (Marotta 1981:265). Johnston put it a bit more crudely, "You are who you sleep with. Thus the lesbian rightfully says she is the woman par excellence" (1973:175). The proof that lesbians are the most womanly of women, argued Johnston (1973) and Brown, is the fact that lesbians are the most oppressed of women. Lesbians experience the "ultimate sexist oppression" (Brown 1976f:128). In other words, lesbian oppression is not distinct from women's oppression. On the contrary, it is an extreme form of the same oppression, or, as Gay Liberation Front Women put it, "the core oppression of women is the lesbian's oppression" (1971/1972:202). Because heterosexual women are male-identified and male-defined—i.e., less womanly—they receive benefits for participating in male supremacy that mitigate their oppression as women. Lesbians, on the other hand, suffer the most brutal manifestations of male supremacism because they reject male definitions of womanhood—i.e., because they are the most womanly of women. Heterosexual women have much to learn from lesbians; not only about feminism and women's oppression, but about being women. The concepts of the lesbian as the quintessential woman and of lesbian liberation as the ultimate feminist liberation represented a radical shift from the concept of lesbianism as a "lavender herring" that would distract feminists from the needs of "real," i.e., heterosexual, women.

The arguments that lesbians have greater vision, resources, opportunities, and superior womanhood constructed lesbians as the most suit-
able and likely leaders of the feminist movement. This fundamental
lesbian feminist principle was clearly articulated as early as 1970 by the
Radicalesbians, whose essay "The Woman-identified Woman" characterized lesbians as the vanguard of the feminist movement.[18] Ti-Grace
Atkinson arrived at the same conclusion by conceptualizing lesbians as
the "buffer" zone between women and men in patriarchal society. As
long as lesbians remain unpoliticized, patriarchal society can use them
as an object lesson to keep heterosexual women in line. But by the
same token, lesbians are the potential source of the leaders of women;
politicized lesbianism threatens to turn the "buffer" zone that protects
heterosexual patriarchs into the "shock troops" that lead the attack
on heterosexual patriarchy (Atkinson 1972/1973:13). Brown, who saw
sexism as underlying all other forms of oppression, saw lesbians not
only as the vanguard of the feminist movement, but as the vanguard of
a larger revolutionary Movement that would end oppression based on
race and class, as well as oppression based on gender and sexuality
(Marotta 1981).

The conclusion that lesbians are the vanguard of the feminist movement represented the completion of the transformation of the relationship between lesbianism and feminism. Lesbianism had been politicized
and then catapulted to the front of the feminist agenda. No longer the
skeleton in the feminist closet, lesbianism had been reconstructed as a
key feminist issue. Lesbianism represented the heart of feminism and the
hope for women's liberation. Lesbians were no longer the untouchables
of the feminist movement and the heterosexual woman was no longer
defined as the "real" woman who was the true constituent of the feminist movement; lesbians had been reconstructed as the political elite, the
most feminist of feminists, and the most womanly of women.[19]

If lesbians are the feminist elite, what of heterosexual women? Arguments that were originally intended to establish lesbianism as a feminist
issue and to counter accusations that lesbians are detrimental to feminism had led lesbian feminists to the conclusion that lesbians play a
critically important role in the feminist movement. What then, could be
said of the quality of heterosexual women's feminism? At the very
least, many lesbian feminists believed that heterosexual feminists face
contradictions or conflicts between their personal and political commitments, and that these conflicts prevent them from achieving the full

understanding of sexism that lesbians can achieve. Val Carpenter, for example, felt that heterosexual feminists have something to contribute to the analysis of sexism even though "Their position is complex, sometimes contradictory and occasionally uncomfortable" and their investment in men blinds them to the dynamics of male domination (1988:171). Heterosexual women experience conflicting interests on both personal and political levels. On the personal level, they have to struggle with sexism on a daily basis in their relationships with men, yet they receive benefits from their individual relationships with men. On the political level, as heterosexuals they participate in the very institution that perpetuates the sexism they are committed to fighting as feminists.

Because of the inherent conflicts between heterosexuality and feminism, many lesbian feminists—for example, Johnston (1973), and Bunch (1972/1975) and Reid (1975) of The Furies collective—argued that heterosexual women are less likely to be revolutionary feminists than lesbians are. Because of their ties to men, heterosexual women receive privileges that give them a stake in the heterosexual system. Heterosexual women therefore seek to minimize their oppression within that system by seeking greater privileges from it, rather than seeking to overturn the system itself. Lesbians, who receive no benefits from the heterosexual system, are less likely to be co-opted into adopting reformist feminist politics.

But Johnston and many members of The Furies collective went even farther in their arguments, asserting that heterosexual women are not merely less radical as feminists, but that they are in fact unhelpful or even detrimental to the feminist movement. Brown argued that heterosexual women pour their energy into changing their individual men and have little energy left over to fight larger battles. Bunch argued that heterosexual women will inevitably betray their lesbian sisters, because "the very essence, definition, and nature of heterosexuality is men first," and therefore "only women who cut their ties to male privilege can be trusted to remain serious in the struggle against male dominance" (1972/1975:36). Brown explained this point more clearly: "How can a woman tied to men through heterosexuality keep from betraying her sisters. When push comes to shove, she will choose her man over other women; heterosexuality demands that she make that choice" (1972/1975:72). As Johnston put it, "If you're not part of the solution you're part of the problem" (1973:181).

Barbara Solomon argued that the reformist politics of heterosexual feminists are not only nonrevolutionary, but counterrevolutionary; she felt that the privileges heterosexual women receive and fight for within heterosexual patriarchy are gained at the expense of other women. Heterosexual women live the perpetuation of patriarchy; they are, therefore, responsible for the perpetuation of patriarchy and the oppression of other women (1972/1975).[20] Heterosexual women make the job of fighting for women's liberation more difficult because, by giving in to oppression, the heterosexual woman "exposes her sisters who are fighting that oppression," thus increasing the burden on them (Brown 1972/1975:70). Furthermore, Solomon felt that heterosexual women directly obstruct feminist progress by draining women's energy to fill needs created by their relationships with men, energy that would otherwise be available for feminist purposes. Heterosexuality, therefore, is a form of stealing; heterosexual women not only give their energy toward the perpetuation of heterosexual patriarchy, but they drain energy from the revolutionary struggles of lesbians. Solomon, voicing an opinion she shared with other members of The Furies collective, concluded that heterosexuality and feminism are antithetical; "any woman relating to a man cannot be a feminist" (1972/1975:46).

If a lesbian lifestyle is consistent with feminist politics and a heterosexual lifestyle is inconsistent with feminist politics, then it follows that to be a good feminist a woman must be a lesbian. Atkinson said so, very clearly. She pointed out that when one is engaged in a struggle in which one truly believes, one commits one's whole self to the struggle. One's personal life and one's political life both become part of the struggle, and they are consistent with each other because one will want to live a personal life that furthers one's political goals. Therefore, the committed feminist will live a lesbian life. Asking her reader, "Can you imagine a Frenchman serving in the French army from 9 to 5, then trotting 'home' to Germany for supper and overnight?" (1970/1974:132), she accused heterosexual women of collaborating with the enemy in the battle of the sexes. In war, she argued, there is no "private life" within which you may participate in social relations that undermine your political struggle; if you want such a private life, then you are not committed to the struggle. Anything less than full commitment is treason.

Brown agreed that a good feminist must be a lesbian. Choosing to concentrate on love instead of war, she asked: "If you cannot find it in yourself to love another woman, and that includes physical love, then how can you truly say you care about women's liberation? If you don't feel other women are worthy of your total commitment—love, energy, sex, all of it—then aren't you saying that women aren't worth fighting for? If you reserve those 'special' commitments for men then you are telling other women they aren't worth those commitments, they aren't important" (1972/1975:70). Brown argued that the giving of love is an expression of regard; the value you attach to others is indicated by whom you choose to love, and you will love those whom you value. Women who behave heterosexually demonstrate that they value men more highly than women, a sentiment that is contrary to the feminist principle that women are at least as important as men. But according to Brown, not loving men is insufficient to qualify one as a feminist. Women who do not love women—presumably regardless of whether they love men—demonstrate that they do not value women and that they do not value them*selves:* "If we can't find another woman worthy of our deepest emotions then can we find ourselves worthy of our own emotion [. . . ?]" (1976e:92). Therefore feminists, who by definition value women in general and themselves in particular at least as much as they value men, will love women; i.e., they *will be* lesbians. Solomon agreed with Brown, "Women who give love and energy to men rather than women obviously think men are better than women" (1972/1975:46). Bunch argued the same point from a slightly different angle by pointing out that women deserve to have the love of women that men traditionally receive; by not loving each other women deny themselves that deserved pleasure (1972/1975). Johnston went one step further to argue that love between women is more than an expression and recognition of women's value; it is also an expression of commitment to the women so valued. She referred to "sex with another woman as the basic affirmation of a powerful sisterhood" and to lesbian feminism, which she called "Gay/Feminism," as "the proper sexual-political stance for the revolutionary woman" (1973:149, 165).

These arguments constructed one's lifestyle as an expression and reflection of one's politics; consequently, one's politics could be inferred from one's lifestyle. Janet Dixon, writing about her experiences as a lesbian separatist in the early 1970s, spelled out the new prescriptive[21] relationship between the personal and the political: "We demanded proof of intent, and that could only be achieved through living a separatist lifestyle" (1988:77). Atkinson, Johnston, and the three Furies members quoted above all specifically included sexual love in their arguments, clearly arguing that sexual love of women is an integral expression of feminism and that lesbianism is therefore proof of a true commitment to feminism. Herein arises a moral imperative to would-be feminists, "Thou shalt be a lesbian." In other words, all feminists must be lesbians; any woman who is not a lesbian cannot be a feminist.

If one must be a lesbian to be a feminist, is the converse also true? In other words, are all lesbians necessarily feminists? In the 1970s, Dixon would have answered "yes" without reservation or qualification. She wrote, "To us, lesbianism and feminism were synonymous, either one without the other was untenable. A non-feminist lesbian was just a failed heterosexual. A non-lesbian feminist was just a male apologist" (1988:77).[22]

Other lesbian feminists were more hesitant to conflate the two terms. Solomon stated explicitly that all lesbians are not feminists, "Implicit in the Lesbian lifestyle is a Feminist political principle. That does not mean that all Lesbians are Feminists" (1972/1975:42). Similarly, Adrienne Rich wrote that there is a "*nascent* feminist political content in the act of choosing a woman lover or life partner in the face of institutionalized heterosexuality" but that for lesbian existence to reach its full political potential it must deepen into "conscious woman-identification—lesbian/feminism," thereby distinguishing between lesbianism and lesbian feminism (Rich 1980/1983:201). Bunch agreed that Lesbianism is the necessary starting point for feminism, but that it is not sufficient: "Of course, not all Lesbians are consciously woman-identified, not are all committed to finding common solutions to the oppression they suffer as women and Lesbians. Being a Lesbian is part of challenging male supremacy, but not the end" (1972/1975:31), and Brown quipped, "Becoming a Lesbian does not make you instantly pure, perpetually happy and devotedly revolutionary" (1972/1975:75).

Brown explained that some lesbians lack feminist consciousness because they protect themselves from the pain of heterosexism by viewing themselves as imitation men. These women, who are generally found working with gay men in Gay Liberation rather than with feminists in the feminist and lesbian feminist movements, are male-identified instead of woman-identified. They have accepted the patriarchy's valuation of the male and chosen to identify with the powerful male rather than challenge society's valuation of him. Lesbians who buy into romantic notions of monogamous love or who participate in either butch or femme roles are also examples of lesbians who are not feminists, according to Johnston (1973). Even lesbians who have feminist consciousness are at risk of losing it without vigilance. Goodman et al. argued that lesbians could not rest on their feminist laurels: "It is crucial for a feminist who becomes a lesbian to keep her political analysis in mind and not to imagine her oppression as a woman has ended just because she now has a woman lover" (1983:81). Lesbian sexuality is not a magical antidote to oppression, nor to the oppressive ways of relating that women have been taught through heterosexual conditioning (Hollibaugh and Moraga 1981/1983).

These arguments distinguish the lesbian who is not a feminist from the lesbian who is a feminist by constructing the latter as a distinct type of lesbian. The Furies—represented here by Brown, Bunch, and Solomon—called her a "woman-identified woman." Johnston called her "the woman in relation to herself."[23] Whatever she is called, she is the woman who is not only a lesbian, but who has succeeded in her lesbianism to overcome male-identification and heterosexual styles of relating.

But then Brown and Bunch added a twist to their argument. Having created the Woman-Identified Woman by distinguishing her from the Lesbian, both authors proceeded to collapse the distinction between these two constructs by redefining the Lesbian in terms of Woman-Identification. Both argued that the definition of the Lesbian as a woman who has sex with other women is a male definition of Lesbianism that reflects the patriarchal practice of defining women in sexualized terms. For example, Brown wrote, "Men, because they can only think of women in sexual terms, define Lesbian as sex between women. However, Lesbians know that it is far more than that, it is a different way of life. It is a life determined by a woman for her own benefit and the benefit of other women. It is a life that draws its strength, support and direction from women. About two years ago this concept was given the name woman-identified woman" (1972/1975:69). Bunch also argued that the deemphasis of sexuality is an integral part of the process of politicizing lesbianism. Because sexuality is considered a private matter, moving lesbianism into the political realm required the deemphasis of its sexual aspect.

Thus, Brown and Bunch distinguished the original concept of the

Lesbian as a sexual type from the concept of the woman-identified woman, and then dismissed it as a male fiction and entirely replaced it with the concept of the woman-identified woman. The Lesbian as a woman who has sex with other women no longer exists, and those who would argue that she does are antifeminists guilty of buying into male sexual definitions of women. The woman who has sex with other women but who is not woman-identified might be a gay woman, but she is no longer a Lesbian. This conceptual reshuffling leads to the conclusion that feminism is indeed a necessary condition for lesbianism. In other words, notwithstanding their initial resistance to the conflation of lesbianism and feminism, both Brown and Bunch ultimately constructed all lesbians as feminists by definition, thereby arriving at the same conclusion that Dixon and her separatist friends had reached via a less circular argument.

The construction of a relationship between lesbianism and feminism was now complete. Not only had lesbianism been established as a feminist issue, but lesbianism and feminism had become inextricably intertwined political issues. Lesbianism, once considered a menace to the feminist movement, was now considered an expression of feminist commitment and a requisite for feminists. Conversely, all Lesbians were now feminists by definition. For all practical purposes and in the minds of many lesbian feminists, lesbianism and feminism were not only mutually necessary, but synonymous.

The lesbian feminist reconstruction of the relationship between lesbianism and feminism did not meet with universal acceptance. On the contrary, it sparked intense debate. Heterosexual feminists objected to the construction of any relationship between lesbianism and feminism, particularly a relationship in which lesbianism became a prerequisite for feminism. Some lesbians, including less radical lesbian feminists, questioned the reconceptualizations of lesbianism that had been necessary to establish lesbianism as a feminist issue and construct a relationship between lesbianism and feminism. A particularly controversial issue was the role of lesbian sexuality in the definition of lesbianism. A second controversial issue was the nature of gender and the interests of lesbians and feminists vis-à-vis gender. But perhaps the most problematic controversy arose because the route taken by lesbian feminist discourse in the 1970s conflicted with a more established political tradition, the ethnic political tradition that had become increasingly prominent in mainstream politics since the popularization of the Black civil rights movement of the 1950s. The concepts of lesbianism created within lesbian feminist discourse could not be used to make claims for lesbian rights outside the feminist context because they were inconsistent with the modes of argument available in mainstream politics, modes that had developed to express the demands of racial and ethnic minorities.

The remainder of this chapter provides an overview of the debate that followed the lesbian feminist construction of a relationship between lesbianism and feminism, followed by a detailed look at the specific controversies over sexuality, gender, and ethnicity that arose in this debate, and concluding with a discussion of the ways in which these controversies resurfaced in the 1980s and 1990s in the debate about bisexuality.

DEBATE OVER THE RELATIONSHIP BETWEEN LESBIANISM AND FEMINISM

Not surprisingly, the assertion that lesbians are better feminists than heterosexual women—not to mention the assertions that all feminists should become lesbians or that lesbianism and feminism are synonymous—met with considerable protest on the part of heterosexual feminists and some lesbian feminists. The dialogue that followed the articulation of the lesbian feminist position of the Leeds Revolutionary Feminist Group is documented in a book called *Love Your Enemy?* This book begins with the Leeds paper "Political lesbianism: The case against heterosexuality." The paper is organized in a Q & A format in which group members respond to some of the questions they had been asked by other feminists. Following this essay are dozens of letters responding to it and to each other,[24] and finally, an afterword from the Leeds Revolutionary Feminist Group. The criticisms are similar to those made against the lesbian feminist ideologies of the Radicalesbians, The Furies, and other groups. *Love Your Enemy?* is one of the most detailed written accounts of the debates that surrounded the construction of a relationship between lesbianism and feminism.

One criticism raised against the Leeds "Political lesbianism" paper was that it was reductionist; it reduced the problem of male supremacy to the act of heterosexual intercourse, and it reduced feminist strategy to the withdrawal of sexual services from men. As Alexandra Stone, a member of Onlywomen Press, which published *Love Your Enemy?*, put it, "not fucking is not the end of heterosexuality as institution and compulsory lifestyle, [nor] our oppression as women" (1981:61). Sophie Laws charged the Leeds feminists with taking the easy way out by reducing oppression and liberation to sexuality, asserting that it was easier for them "to make heterosexual feminists feel guilty than it is either to confront the structures of the patriarchy which go beyond immediate personal relationships or to examine in depth the reasons why heterosexual relationships have the hold over women that they do" (1981:12).[25] In other words, the Leeds feminists—not heterosexual feminists—were the ones who were avoiding the real issue.

The paper was also criticized for dictating women's politics and behaviors. Frankie Rickford reminded readers that feminism is built on the principle that "every woman's experience is real, and valid" (1981:11) and pointed out the irony of a group of feminists telling other women what's good for them. Similarly, Ann Pettitt felt that a central feminist demand is the "right to a self defined sexuality" (1981:14) and argued that by prescribing lesbianism, the Leeds feminists were trying to deny women this right. Penny Cloutte wrote that she did not appreciate the growing perception of feminism as "some sort of established church" with rules that had to be followed (1981:15). She was struggling to get away from such rules in her life, and argued that feminism should serve women, not vice versa. Diane Grimsditch also objected to the idea of a feminist orthodoxy and resented being made to feel "that I'm not a proper feminist and don't deserve liberating because I'm not behaving properly" (1981:19), i.e., because she is not a lesbian.

Other critics did not object per se to the idea of a feminist standard of sexual behavior, but focused their attention on the particular rules of behavior with which they disagreed. For example, Justine Jones agreed that feminists should cease having sex with men, but she found the idea that feminists should practice lesbianism incredible. In a paper she gave at the Leeds Conference on Sexual Violence Against Women, she said, "Yes, I think we have to get out of men's beds as part of achieving this [self-defined sexuality and the end to male supremacy]—but no, I'm not advocating going to bed with a woman 'for political reasons', or 'to further the revolution'—would any woman do so anyway? Saying lesbianism can be and is a political as well as a personal choice doesn't imply that, does it?" (1981:22). Janet Wright agreed that having sex with women should not be a requirement for feminists, because nonsexual relationships among women were just as important and valid as sexual relationships among women (1981). Similarly, Grimsditch objected to the implication that lesbian sex was proof of woman loving; she explained that she did not sleep with women, not because she did not value women, but because she valued women too much to "trust herself" with them.

Pauline Maniscalco disagreed with the idea that heterosexual behavior is contrary to feminism (1981). She argued that men had played a share in the development of her feminism, albeit in a negative way, and that she took pleasure in educating men. She saw her feminism as a process, not a state of being; her relationships with men were part of that process. In other words, her relationships with men were part of her feminism, not antithetical to it. Gregory agreed that heterosexuality did not preclude feminism, saying "I don't want any woman to feel she is unable to be a serious feminist. I don't want any woman to feel she cannot make meaningful changes in her life unless and until she stops having sexual (physical-emotional) relations with all men" (1981:40–41). Gilly Heron echoed this sentiment, writing "a lot of heterosexual feminists have spent—and are spending—a lot of energy trying to work out their situation. . . . Is this not taking one's feminism 'seriously', given that one is open to change?" (1981:17).

Although Maniscalco, Gregory, and Heron argued that heterosexual behavior does not preclude feminism and intended to assert that heterosexual women could be as feminist as lesbians could be, the arguments they used to support their claims implicitly accepted the feminist superiority of lesbianism. For example, Heron gave herself away when she wrote "given that one is open to change." In other words, heterosexual women can be feminists but they must live with the contradictions between their heterosexuality and their feminism, and continue to work on these contradictions in order to retain the right to call themselves feminist. If feminism is a process, then the implicit end of that process is still lesbianism, whether every individual woman attains that end or not. This argument establishes a "feminist continuum" on which all women, regardless of whether they are heterosexual or lesbian, can be feminists; it's just that some women—namely, lesbians—are "more feminist" than others.

Finally, the Leeds feminists and other lesbian feminists who put forth similar arguments were criticized for "man hating," for equating man hating with woman loving, and for defining lesbianism in terms of the former instead of the latter. Grimsditch wrote, "I still believe that loving women isn't the same as hating men" and explained that she loved women "because they are women, not because they are not men." As a feminist who loved women but did not sleep with them, Grimsditch did not want to "be a lesbian by default." Frances M. Beal pointed out that lesbian feminists' anti-male sentiments reflected a lack of sensitivity to Black women's issues: "Black people are engaged in a life-and-death struggle and the main emphasis of black women must be to combat the capitalist, racist exploitation of black people" (1970:394). The problem, Beal argued, lies in the System, not in individual men seeking pleasure from women's bodies.

In response to these protests, lesbian feminists clarified and refined their arguments. The Leeds feminists objected to the characterization of their argument as "reductionist," explaining that the "withdrawal of sexual services from men" was not the "sum total" of their political strategy; it was necessary, but not sufficient (1981:67). Moreover, they claimed that they had not meant to prescribe lesbian sexuality for all feminists; they did believe that all feminists should be lesbians, but explained that they meant *political lesbians:* "We do think that all feminists can and should be political lesbians. Our definition of a political lesbian is a woman-identified woman who does not fuck men. It does not mean compulsory sexual activity with women" (1979/1981:5). "Political lesbians" were therefore defined not by sexual relations with women—which many did not have and did not want—but by their feminist political convictions and their lack of relations with men.[26] With the advent of the "political lesbian," lesbianism came to be defined not in terms of sexual activity but in terms of nonsexual forms of commitment to women. Presence or absence of sexual activity with women merely distinguished two types of lesbians, the political lesbian and the "real lesbian," from each other. Thus, the Leeds feminists joined Brown, Bunch, and others in desexualizing the lesbian per se.

The Leeds feminists responded to the criticism that they were missing the real issue because it was easier to attack heterosexual women than to attack the patriarchy by explaining that they had meant to criticize heterosexuality as an institution, not heterosexual women. They wrote, "Some lesbians and some heterosexual feminists saw the paper as

an attack on heterosexual women: in fact, we were criticizing heterosexuality as the accepted form of sexuality under male supremacy, and
saying that it is used to oppress us" (1981:66). To conciliate heterosexual women, they reconsidered the word "collaborators," which they had
used to describe heterosexual women in the "Political lesbianism" paper:
"We now think that 'collaborators' is the wrong word to describe
women who sleep with men, since this implies a conscious act of be-
trayal. Even if applied solely to heterosexual feminists, rather than to
heterosexual women in general, it is inaccurate: most feminists do not
see men as the enemy, or heterosexuality as crucial to male supremacy"
(1981:66). Thus, the Leeds feminists exchanged criticism of heterosexual
women for paternalistic patience with women who were not to blame
for heterosexual behavior that arose out of false consciousness. Anna
Wilson, a member of the Onlywomen Press, was not willing to compromise even that much, "if you want to go on being heterosexual, that's
ok. but i want you to think about the fact that you're doing it because
you want to. you are responsible for being heterosexual" (1981:61).

The Furies and the staff of *Purple September,* whose arguments were
very similar to The Leeds Revolutionary Feminist Group's arguments,
made similar clarifications. In the introduction to a collection of Furies
writings, Myron and Bunch wrote defensively:

> Some feminists say that lesbians are "divisive to the women's move-
> ment" by demanding that every woman be a lesbian. We are less
> concerned with whether each woman personally becomes a lesbian
> than with the destruction of heterosexuality as a crucial part of male
> supremacy. Lesbians have been the quickest to see the challenge to
> heterosexuality as necessary to feminists' survival. However straight
> feminists are not precluded from examining and fighting against hetero-
> sexuality as an ideology and institution that oppresses us all. (1975:12)

The staff of *Purple September* agreed,

> from a feminist viewpoint it is indeed irrelevant whether feminists are
> straight or gay, but that is not the end of the story. Feminism does
> require that feminists critically assess the normative status of heterosex-
> uality whether or not they abide by that norm in their personal lives.
> (*Purple September* 1975:82).

In other words, there is no necessary connection between one's personal
sexuality and one's feminism; heterosexual women can also be feminists,
that is, they can also challenge heterosexuality. "The real difference is

between woman-identified women—those who are serious about feminist struggle and loving women—and women who are still allied mainly with men; and there are heterosexual, bisexual, and homosexual women on both sides" (Goodman et al. 1983:90). Of course, lesbians are still more likely to be feminists, because heterosexual women are less likely to challenge heterosexuality and lack the vantage point lesbians possess (e.g., Carpenter 1988; Goodman et al. 1983).

Lesbian feminists also defended themselves against the characterization of their position as "anti-male," and the charge that they equated man hating with woman loving. The Leeds feminists, for example, accepted the charge that their initial statements in the "Political lesbianism" paper had overemphasized man hating at the expense of woman loving. They explained that they had originally "defined a Political Lesbian as a woman-identified-woman who did not fuck men" but that they had "re-examined the phrase" and realized that it really meant "women who, by withdrawing their energy and support from men, have put women first. In doing so, they have found that it is incompatible with sleeping with men" (1979/1981:5). Thus, by shifting their emphasis, the Leeds feminists dodged charges of man hating while maintaining the connection between woman loving and sexual separatism. Goodman et al. took a different approach toward the same goal. They explained that separatism is necessary as an intermediate step for oppressed groups to gain strength, but that the "ultimate goal of this separation, however, is solidarity: all people living and loving together in mutual respect" (1983:76). Goodman et al. also argued that separation from individual men was not a reflection of man hating. On the contrary, separatism was a necessary technique that would lead women to perceive the systemic nature of their oppression and "recognize how they have been hurt without blaming it on each individual member of the oppressor class" (1983:76). In other words, separatism from men was not evidence of man hating; in fact, it was quite the opposite, i.e., a technique for overcoming the tendency to blame individual men for women's oppression.

These revisions and refinements of the lesbian feminist viewpoint brought the relationship between lesbianism and feminism full circle. Before the advent of lesbian feminism, lesbianism was dismissed as irrelevant to feminism at best and harmful at worst. To establish lesbianism as a feminist issue, lesbian feminists first politicized lesbianism as a feminist lifestyle and as a political challenge to the institution of heterosexuality. Having established the politics of lesbianism, lesbian feminists then divorced the political from the personal so that the institution of heterosexuality could be attacked without attacking the women within it, and the institution of male supremacy could be attacked without attacking the individual men who benefited from it. Because of the divorce between feminism and heterosexuality and the depersonalization of the attack on male supremacy, women within the heterosexual institution who had ties to individual men could now join in the attack, because the politics became available to every woman regardless of her personal sexual lifestyle. Personal sexuality was once again irrelevant, but the brief marriage between lesbianism and feminism had given birth to a new feminist politics. Heterosexual women were invited back into the feminist fold, but in their absence feminism had been redefined as a movement to challenge the norm of heterosexuality and they were allowed back in only insofar as they agreed to examine their own complicity in this norm.

Furthermore, the invitation to heterosexual women was tinged with the expectation that once they challenged the institution of heterosexuality, they would become lesbians. Brown, for example, wrote, "The inevitability of lesbianism is obvious to anyone who follows the logic of feminism," (1976g:184), and Faderman quoted a woman who observed, "once you're a feminist it's almost impossible to have any kind of whole relationship with a man. . . . That's the only way I can see myself going really, from a strong person, to a feminist to a lesbian. It's just a very logical progression" (1981:391).[27] Frye observed that "women with newly raised consciousnesses tend to leave marriages and families. . . . Many awakening women become celibate or lesbian" (1977/1983a:102). Goodman et al. chastised lesbian feminists for failing to support women who are involved in heterosexual relationships, admonishing them that they do not have the right to assume that all opposite-sex relationships are oppressive and encouraging women to support each other despite their sexual differences. But two pages later, the same authors encouraged lesbians to help heterosexual women overcome the barriers that keep them from loving women. Their tone was decidedly patronizing, "It is also important for lesbian feminists to remember that non-lesbian women are rigidly heterosexual only because of heterosexist training, and to find ways of showing them that this is the case. . . .

Lesbians oughtn't to try to force other women into it; just keep pointing out the blocks which keep them from realizing it" (1983:87).

Ironically, lesbian feminists' apparent concession to heterosexual feminism created a new opportunity for lesbian feminists to criticize heterosexual women. Once lesbian feminists conceded that heterosexual women could be feminist, they could criticize heterosexual feminists for any shortcoming in the quality of their feminism, including their continued heterosexuality itself. Although the invitation to heterosexual feminists was extended at the request of heterosexual feminists who hoped to free themselves from the lesbian feminist moral imperative to become lesbian, the effect was to place heterosexual feminists even more firmly under the jurisdiction of lesbian feminist ideology. [28]

While lesbian feminists and heterosexual feminists were debating the relevance of lesbian sex and heterosex to feminism, many non-lesbian women accepted the invitation to become lesbian feminists in the political sense. In keeping with the arguments of the Leeds feminists, these women were defined by their political convictions and their lack of relations with men, not by sexual relations with women. But once women began declaring themselves as political lesbians, some real lesbians began to resent what they perceived as a transgression. [29] Political lesbians, even those who did go so far as to have sexual relations with women, knew little of the day-to-day hardships of real lesbians, and real lesbians felt used by women who wanted to "try" lesbianism as if it were a new flavor or a way to earn their feminist credentials. Joy Pitman was angered because she felt that political lesbianism denied the hardships experienced by real lesbians like herself who had come out without the support of a Women's Movement (1981), [30] and Brown had some harsh words for the woman "who was going to liberate herself on my body" (1976e:90). Similarly, Alice et al. resented "nouveau" lesbians who "used lesbians in order to assuage their guilt and experiment with a 'lesbian experience' " and who would return to men and male privilege when lesbianism was no longer politically fashionable (1973/1991a:36). An anonymous member of the Birmingham Revolutionary Feminist Group, who initially chose to become a lesbian for feminist reasons, recalled that "lesbians moving within more conventional gay circles" were suspicious that women like herself were not "real" lesbians (1981:33). In hindsight, she agreed with them, acknowledging that lesbianism cannot be based on political convictions alone because it must involve female eroticism. As she developed this eroticism herself, she found herself sharing real lesbians' suspicions of political lesbians.

Political lesbianism was also criticized, ironically, for being male-identified. From her new standpoint as a "real" lesbian, the anonymous Birmingham feminist just cited rejected political lesbianism because it is defined in terms of (a lack of) women's relations with men, as opposed to lesbianism, which is defined in terms of relations with women. The concept of political lesbianism, she wrote, "ignores the importance of women's sexual relations with other women whilst making the question of whether women have sexual relations with men central to the whole definition of political lesbianism" (1981:34). Gregory took this point further, arguing that defining oneself as a lesbian out of hatred for men instead of love for women not only is an inappropriate expression of feminism, but is not feminist at all. Whereas lesbianism defined in terms of a positive attraction to women is "part of the process of getting rid of the man in our head," lesbianism defined in terms of rejection and hatred of men "makes [the man in our head] ever more powerful" (1981:43).

These reactions must have been confusing to well-meaning political lesbians who thought they were demonstrating their commitment to feminism and support for lesbians by identifying themselves as political lesbians. First they had been told that they should accept lesbianism as the expression of feminism; then they were told that they were oppressing lesbians by attempting to express their feminism through lesbianism. The conflicting viewpoints arising from the lesbian feminist elaboration of the relationship between lesbianism and feminism must have been confusing to other feminists as well. Feminists in general had been chastised for considering lesbianism "just a personal issue," only to be told later that whether one had sex with another woman was actually irrelevant not only to feminism but to lesbianism itself. Heterosexual feminists were told that they could not be feminists because they were heterosexual and therefore collaborators with the oppressive heteropatriarchal structure, but then they were invited back into the feminist fold and criticized for failing to challenge heterosexuality as an institution. The result of the lesbian feminist debate over the relationship between lesbianism and feminism was a confusing set of messages that reflect the controversies surrounding this relationship and, at a deeper level, the internal contradictions in lesbian feminist ideology.

Controversy over the Relationship of Lesbian Sex to Lesbianism

From the foregoing, it is clear that one controversy generated by the lesbian feminist construction and reconstruction of the relationship between lesbianism and feminism is the issue of the relationship of lesbian sexual behavior to lesbianism. This issue merits further attention here because of its centrality in the construction of bisexuality as an issue. To recap, in order to politicize lesbianism, lesbian feminists had expanded the definition of lesbianism well beyond the traditionally private realm of the sexual. Then, to appease heterosexual feminists and effect a reconciliation between lesbian and heterosexual feminists, some lesbian feminists created the "political lesbian" and trivialized the sexual aspect of lesbianism in order to attack male supremacist heterosexuality without attacking heterosexual women.

But the desexualization[31] of lesbianism was not merely a consequence of the politicization of lesbianism and the elaboration of the relationship between feminism and lesbianism; it was also a controversial process of reconstruction in its own right. For example, some lesbian feminists saw the desexualization of lesbianism as a direct challenge to patriarchy, because it represented a rejection of sexualized definitions of womanhood. At the (First) Congress to Unite Women in 1969, lesbian audience members accused panelists of ignoring the lesbian issue. Panel members responded by accusing lesbian audience members of reducing women to their sexuality, arguing that the sexualization of women is one aspect of women's oppression and that lesbians were buying into that oppression by giving importance to women's sexuality. Roxanne Dunbar tried to steer the discussion away from lesbianism by commenting from the panel, "Sexuality is not the key issue. What I want to do is get women out of bed." In "Say it isn't so," Brown countered with the accusation that Dunbar was doing exactly what she accused lesbian audience members of doing, that is, reducing women to their sexuality by perceiving women-identified women as lesbians, defined solely in terms of sexuality (1976b:50). Brown argued that it was heterosexual women who wanted to suppress the issue of lesbianism, not lesbians, who were buying into male definitions of women in terms of their "sexual activity and function." In other words, the redefinition of lesbianism in nonsexual terms not only de-privatized and politicized lesbianism, but challenged male-dominated views of women.

The desexualization of lesbianism was also fostered because it facilitated historians' attempts to construct a lesbian history. As lesbians began to develop a culture and communities of their own, they also began to desire a history of their own. Modeling themselves after the Black civil rights movement and other racial/ethnic movements—a process that will be explored in detail later in this chapter—they searched for the shared history that would give them a sense of shared origins and shared fate. Early collections of lesbian and gay writings mythologized Sappho, reconstructed ancient Greece as the golden era of male homosexuality, and pointed with pride to historical figures whose personal papers revealed passions for same-sex lovers. But a lesbian history was difficult to construct because the concept of the lesbian as a type of person is a recent invention and because the repression of women's sexuality had ensured little record of women's sexual activities in the past. Lesbian history could not, therefore, be constructed on the basis of sexual behavior.[32] The desexualization of lesbianism conveniently opened the door for the construction of a lesbian history.

In turn, the construction of a lesbian history in the absence of historical information about sexuality helped construct contemporary lesbianism in desexualized terms. For example, Blanche Wiesen Cook suggested that all independent women who choose to nurture and support other women are lesbians.[33] Using this definition, any strong woman-identified historical figure could be claimed as an ancestor of the modern lesbian, despite a lack of information about her sexual behavior.[34] For example, Brown saw herself as belonging to a long history of women who had become "women-identified" after they "questioned the system and found it destructive to themselves" (1976e:79). Carpenter referred to the leading figures in the Girls' Work Movement as "spinsters," and commented that the suppression of women's sexuality meant that "there was no public discussion of lesbianism and rarely any acknowledgment that these 'splendid,' 'dedicated' and strong examples of 'magnificent womanhood' were in fact lesbians" (1988:171–172). Carpenter, who presented no evidence of these women's sexual habits, was either using a definition of lesbianism similar to Cook's, or she was assuming that these strong, unmarried women did in fact engage in lesbian sex of which, of course, there is no record.[35]

Faderman was also not hampered in her construction of nineteenth-century romantic friends as the ancestors of modern lesbians by the lack of evidence about their sexual behaviors. In fact, she gratuitously granted that romantic friends probably were not sexually involved, "While romantic friends had considerable latitude in their show of physical affection toward each other, it is probable that, in an era when women were not supposed to be sexual, the sexual possibilities of their relationship were seldom entertained" (1981:414). She then analogized romantic friends with modern lesbians by asserting the asexuality of modern lesbians, "Contemporary women can have no such innocence. But the sexual aspects of their lesbian-feminist relationships generally have less significance than the emotional sustenance and the freedom they have to define themselves" (1981:414).[36] She strengthened the analogy by arguing that nineteenth-century romantic friendships became threatening to men for the same reason modern lesbian relationships are threatening; that is, not because of their sexual aspect but because of their political implications for the overthrow of patriarchy. In other words, the emphasis on the modern lesbian's politics at the expense of her sexuality provides her with access to a history and ancestry.

The rise of cultural feminism also facilitated the desexualization of lesbianism in the 1970s. Building on radical feminists' calls for women-only space, cultural feminists claimed that in this separatist space women would build an alternative world that would be very different from the world built by men. As cultural feminists elaborated their arguments about the world women would build, they lost sight of the radical feminist tenet that the differences between women and men are culturally created. Radical feminists had originally envisioned women-only space as an opportunity for women to examine the effects of socially imposed gender on their lives. Cultural feminists began to see women-only space as an opportunity for the natural essence of woman to emerge, and they believed that this essence was fundamentally different from the essence of man.[37] They argued "that women are essentially more pure, more temperate, and more moral than men, and that women's mission is to battle male lustfulness and corruption" (Adam 1987:146).[38] In the absence of men and the competitive, death-loving culture men had created, women would naturally create a nurturant, life-centered society.

The desexualized political lesbian was welcomed enthusiastically by cultural feminists. As a political woman committed to the class struggle of women, she was a champion of cultural feminism. Because her closest relationships were with women, she was as removed from the male death-culture as any woman could be. Surrounded by women, she lived in a world that approximated the woman-designed world envisioned by cultural feminists in which woman's essence would emerge. As "primitive" peoples are often stereotyped by "sophisticated" Euro-Americans as "closer to nature," the political lesbian was considered by cultural feminists to be closer to the true woman. Given the political lesbian's proximity to essential womanhood, her desexualization was comforting to cultural feminists for two reasons. First, it purified her of embarrassing sexual habits that would tarnish her womanly image—not necessarily because lesbian sexual habits would have been any more embarrassing than heterosexual habits, but because sexuality itself was vulgar and unwomanly. Second, it universalized her. By definition, womanly essence must exist in every woman. As long as the lesbian was defined by her sexuality, she could not represent the essence of all women because she could not represent the essence of heterosexual women. But stripped of her sexuality, the lesbian could become the essential woman. Because of her political nature, her sexual purity, and her universality, the political lesbian became cultural feminism's prototypical woman.

By essentializing womanhood, cultural feminists had taken a sharp right turn from the road that they had initially shared with radical feminists. Radical feminists accused cultural feminists of reactionism because the asexual womanly essence they glorified and strove to "recapture" bore a striking resemblance to nineteenth-century Victorian images of women that radical feminists had been struggling to destroy. As Echols put it, "Cultural feminist sexual politics really offer us nothing more than women's traditional sexual values disguised as radical feminist sexual values" (1984:64). Echols also played apologist for cultural feminists by explaining that any oppressed group finds it "tempting to seek solace in the reclaiming of that identity which the larger culture has systematically denigrated" (1984:50),[39] an option that is especially appealing when radical cultural change seems unlikely.

In addition to desexualizing lesbianism and essentializing womanhood, cultural feminism also revitalized the antipornography movement, critiqued the "sexual revolution" as a social movement that liberated men at the expense of women, and promoted other sex-negative views within the feminist movement. This provided another point for criticism, as other feminists charged cultural feminists with demonizing sexuality in order to suppress it rather than exploring it at the risk of discovering their own politically incorrect sexual desires (e.g., Echols 1984). Critics also questioned the motivation behind the refocusing of feminist attention on issues like pornography instead of issues concerning women's economic and political oppression and charged that the feminist movement had been co-opted into adopting a conservative political agenda (Adam 1987). Lesbians who had recently reclaimed their sexuality and developed a sense of pride protested the renewed deemphasis of their sexual experiences and feelings. In short, critics argued that in an effort to avoid complicity with male definitions of women solely in terms of their sex, cultural feminists had gone too far and ended up buying into the traditional denial of female sexuality in general and the trivialization of lesbian sexuality in particular.

The lesbian sex-positive movement of the 1980s arose from these protests.[40] Lesbian pornography magazines like *On Our Backs*, whose name carries an implicit protest against the asexual politics of *Off Our Backs*, arose to celebrate the joys of lesbian sexuality. Sexperts like Susie Bright taught women how to enjoy sex—including how to ejaculate. Gayle Rubin and the Samois collective proclaimed the pleasures—and political correctness—of sadomasochism. The "sex positivists" or "sex radicals" encouraged women to celebrate and explore their sexuality uninhibited by concerns about the political correctness of any form of sexual expression, including concerns about the appropriateness of the genders of their partners. Echoing the sentiments of earlier heterosexual feminists who defended themselves against the deification of lesbianism by claiming that they *liked* sex with men, Hollibaugh and Moraga argued that "There *is* heterosexuality outside of heterosexism" (1981/ 1983:395). In other words, women's sexual desires are real and arguments about the political implications of various forms of sexuality or the ways in which sexuality is socially controlled and perverted to serve the ends of the patriarchy do not help us understand these desires. The sex positivists reclaimed sexuality as a good in its own right, not merely a means to be used for political purposes by both sides in the war between patriarchy and feminism.

On the surface, the Sex Wars of the 1980s were debates over issues such as the correct feminist stance on pornography and whether sado-masochism challenged or re-inscribed patriarchal sex roles. But under-neath these debates, the real issue in the 1980s Sex Wars was the question of feminist attitudes toward sexuality itself. Should sexuality be rejected as the traditional source of women's oppression, or should it be embraced, enjoyed, and reclaimed by women who had rediscovered the sexual desires that patriarchy had attempted to suppress and vilify? Is sexuality a source of pleasure, or a source of danger?[41]

Despite the heated controversy over the role that sexuality *should* play in feminist theory and lesbian lives, many lesbians maintained all along that sexuality *is* an integral part of lesbianism by definition. Lesbianism means sexual lesbianism, and any attempts at redefining lesbianism are bound to fail for practical reasons. For example, a mem-ber of the Birmingham Revolutionary Feminist Group wrote, "lesbi-anism, whether we like it or not, has always been used by both the Women's Movement and our enemies to describe a relationship between women which includes a sexual commitment. The term is therefore not synonymous with women-identified women" (1981:34). In fact, she pointed out, it is the "centrality of sexuality to our feminist struggle" that initially motivated lesbian feminists to assert the centrality of lesbi-anism to feminist struggle (1981:34). Similarly, Pitman objected to the concept of a political lesbian for the simple reason that it was contrary to the traditional definition of a lesbian as a woman who is sexually attracted to other women: "To use the term 'lesbian' in this way (as in Political Lesbian) is to rob it of any meaning as a description of sexual orientation/preference/practice" (1981:44).

The argument that nonsexual definitions of lesbianism would not replace sexual definitions of lesbianism because the latter were already well established proved to be true. In 1983, Goodman et al. stated that lesbian relationships remained the cornerstone of lesbian identity for many lesbians. Notwithstanding the political nature of lesbianism, they asserted that the heart of lesbianism still consisted of lesbian relation-ships among women:

> The cornerstone of a lesbian identity for many lesbians is a relationship with a lover. . . . To say this does not deny the significance of the political analysis lesbians have developed, or the political nature of society's reactions to lesbianism, or the validity of women who come

to a lesbian identity out of political conscience—but it identifies the foundation of the entire lesbian culture: our right to love. (1983:69)

In other words, regardless of the outcome of the lesbian Sex Wars and the feminist debates and regardless of the political meanings erected around sexuality, most individual lesbians still perceive their sexuality as the basis for their personal lesbian identities. Lesbians still believe that lesbianism is about lesbian sexuality.

Controversy over the Nature of Gender

The critical difference between the early radical feminists and the cultural feminists of the 1970s was their understanding of gender.[42] Whereas the radical feminists saw gender as a social construct imposed via socialization and social structure, cultural feminists saw gender as essential. Whereas radical feminists struggled to free themselves from socially imposed gender, cultural feminists strove to discover and embrace their womanly essence. Each type of feminist envisioned a utopia of the future, but their visions of the role of gender in this utopia were very different. Because lesbianism—whether defined in terms of sexual relations with women, political commitments to women, or the absence of relations to men—is defined in terms of gender, these two visions therefore have very different implications for the future of lesbianism and the organization of sexuality in general.

If gender is socially imposed, then the liberated human being is androgynous and women are oppressed by a feminine role that is something less than human. The Radicalesbians were among the groups that ascribed to this perspective. They argued that "sex roles dehumanize women" (1970:50) by defining women in relation to men, and that a lesbian is a woman who "acts in accordance with her inner compulsion to be a more complete and freer human being" (1970:49). One cannot be both a "woman" and a whole person because to be feminine is to be only part of a person. But neither are men whole; men are also emotionally crippled by a gender that alienates them from "their own bodies and emotions in order to perform their economic/political/military functions effectively" (1970:50). The goal of feminism, therefore, is the elimination of gender, i.e., the removal of restrictions on humanness. When, at the end of "Woman-identified Woman," the Radicalesbians referred to "the cultural revolution," they did not mean a cultural revolution in which women's life-loving essence would triumph over men's death-loving essence; they meant a revolution in which gender would be elimi-nated and all people would "achieve maximum autonomy in human expression" (1970:55).

If gender is oppressive to both women and men, and the goal of femi-nism is the elimination of gender, then feminism will liberate men as well as women. In other words, feminism is really "human liberation." As Lois Hart said on "Womankind," "basically, what we're talking about is completely rejecting imposed definitions upon our humanity. I mean, we believe we're endless and infinite, in some kind of sense, and that we have the right to be ourselves, whatever that might be. It's human liberation, and it's for men and women" (Marotta 1981:232–233).

If the goal of feminism is the elimination of gender, then in the utopia that feminism will eventually create neither heterosexuality nor lesbianism, both of which are defined in terms of gender, will exist. Some lesbian feminists, including Shelley and Brown,[43] recognized this implication. Goodman et al., in fact, posited the elimination of hetero-sexuality and lesbianism per se as the ultimate goal of lesbian liberation, "Being gay and feminist, while it does mean supporting our right to be sexual with others of the same gender, also means commitment, struggle, and having a vision of what the world would be like if we were all free to act on our own feelings of love for one another" (1983:84). But most lesbian feminists who recognized that the elimination of gender would eliminate heterosexuality and lesbianism as forms of sexuality quickly asserted that utopia has not yet been reached and that in the current imperfect world, gender still matters. For example, Liz Wilkie wrote, "The idealist says that in a perfect world you should relate freely to all individuals, while the realist says that NOW we can't do that and relating to men is upholding the sexist status quo" (1981:30). Loretta Ulmsch-neider used the concept of bisexuality to make the same point: "One goal of our revolution is to have a society where no particular expression of sexuality is enforced. BUT, the revolution has not happened yet. This is not utopia. Women who practice bisexuality today are simply leading highly privileged lives that do not challenge male power and that, in fact, undermine the feminist struggle" (1973/1975:88). In other words, the elimination of gender might be the ultimate goal, but we do not yet live in a genderless world and if we pretend to live in that world before it exists, we will in fact prevent its actual achievement. Thus, lesbian feminists are justified in refusing to relate to men even as they argue that the ultimate goal is the elimination of gender.

Other feminists, notably cultural feminists, ridiculed the idea of "human liberation" as unsophisticated and naive. Liza Cowan, for example, explained that when she first became a feminist, she idealistically believed that there was no basic difference between women and men—until she realized that the notion of humanism merely serves to keep men in control (1978/1991). Alice et al. agreed, "We no longer believe that we are all just 'people'—just 'human beings.' Either you are a man or a woman; either you have male privilege or you don't; either you get benefits from that privilege as a straight woman, or you don't" (1973/1991a:33). Alice et al. sympathized with other feminists' perception of separatism as reverse sexism and avoided arguing that men were essentially different from women, but they did feel that sexism had put women and men in such different positions that humanism was untenable:

> Unfortunately for all our hopes and good vibes, patriarchy has created (or is reflective of) some very real divisions that can't be smoothed over with the term *human being*. Men get privileges *off* sexism and women are oppressed by sexism. Men are in power in patriarchy. Women are kept powerless by those men. We are not prepared to take a position on whether men are a separate biological species or not. At this time that question is somewhat irrelevant. Their male culture has created for them a daily life experience that is so different from that of women, and so diametrically opposed to that of women, that they behave as if they're from another planet. (1973/1991:391)

Julia Penelope was less sympathetic toward humanist feminism. Accusing lesbian as well as heterosexual feminists of abandoning the dream of feminist revolution and watering down their demands to make them "less threatening to men and their women," she wrote that "What is now being called 'feminism' is indistinguishable from the 'human growth potential' movement, and women who call themselves 'feminists' speak psychobabble fluently, a dialect that enables them to avoid talking about real pains and real issues" (1984/1991:515). She derisively compared the new "feminism" to "garden-variety liberalism," reminded feminists that men benefit from the oppression of women, and argued against naming "society" as an entity that oppresses both women and men, thereby removing the blame from men themselves.

Radical feminists, cultural feminists, and other feminists do not disagree so much about the fact that gender plays a role in women's oppression in the current society, as they disagree about the role gender should play in the future and about the goals of feminism with regard to gender. Should feminists strive to eliminate gender, meanwhile recognizing the very real implications that gender has in the current society, or should feminists strive to glorify feminine gender and create a matriarchal world in which women's life-loving essence will prevail? In the former scenario, sexualities and politics based on gender—including lesbianism and feminism—would be eliminated along with gender. The success of lesbian feminism, therefore, would result in its own deconstruction. In the latter scenario, the utopia of the future would be a world in which lesbian feminism not only survives, but dominates. The controversy over the role of gender in feminism is alive and well among lesbians in the 1990s, and like the controversy over the relationship between lesbianism and lesbian sexuality, it underlies the contemporary controversy over the role of bisexuality, as I will soon show.

Competing Political Traditions: The Feminist Tradition and the Ethnic Tradition

The lesbian feminist reconstruction of lesbianism as a political issue took place in a feminist context for the benefit of a feminist audience. Lesbian feminists used the language of feminism to develop political arguments that were effective within feminist discourse. But outside the feminist context, the dominant language of political protest in the 1970s was the language of ethnic politics popularized by the activities of racial and ethnic minorities, in particular African-Americans. As members of the larger society and, in many cases, veterans of earlier civil rights movements and/or members of racial and ethnic minorities themselves, lesbians are heirs to the ethnic political tradition as well as the feminist political tradition. The ethnic political tradition uses concepts and modes of argument that differ from those used in the feminist political tradition. As I will explain below, the fundamental difference is that feminist arguments rely on the assumption of choice, whereas ethnic arguments rely on the assumption of essence. Because of this fundamental difference, the concepts and arguments developed by lesbians in the feminist tradition conflict with the concepts and arguments that emerged from the ethnic political tradition. The conflict between feminist and ethnic modes of discourse produced another layer of controversy in the lesbian feminist debates over the nature and political implications of lesbianism. But before I can discuss the implications of this controversy for the issue of bisexuality, I must first examine the importance of choice in the feminist political tradition, the manner in which lesbian feminists constructed lesbianism as a choice, the importance of essence in the ethnic political tradition, and the construction of lesbians as an ethnic group.

The Importance of Lesbianism as a Choice in the Feminist Political Tradition

Many of the arguments radical lesbian feminists made in their efforts to establish a connection between lesbianism and feminism relied implicitly on the assumption that lesbianism is a possible choice for all women. From attempts to define lesbianism as a feminist issue by showing that homophobia impedes feminist progress to declarations that lesbians are the vanguard of feminism and that feminists should strive to be lesbians, the issue of choice is of critical importance to lesbian feminist ideology.

For example, the most basic argument linking lesbianism to feminism is the argument that lesbianism challenges male supremacy, and the concept of lesbianism as a choice underlies many lesbian feminists' arguments about why lesbianism is a threat. Reid, for example, argued that lesbianism deprives men of their personal servants, and Brown suggested that lesbianism is a feminist political tool because men would be forced to change if they were deprived of the services and support of women. But lesbianism could be such a tool only if women were able to choose lesbianism freely in response to men's patriarchal behavior, and men would only change their behavior if they believed that women were capable of responding to their behavior by withholding services (lesbianism) or granting services (heterosexuality). If, on the other hand, lesbian and straight women were essentially different from each other, there would be no threat and no motivation for men to change their behavior. The argument that lesbianism is a choice is, therefore, a critical component of the argument that lesbianism challenges the patriarchy.

Whereas heterosexual men are threatened by the possibility of losing their personal servants, heterosexual women are threatened because les-

bians represent the possibility that they themselves could become liberated. This threat, too, rests on the assumption that lesbianism can be
chosen: "My co-workers at the newspaper were threatened by my becoming a lesbian. If I could do it, they could do it. They could stop co-
operating in their oppression. They could choose to be lesbians, lesbians
weren't born, they were made" (Reid 1975:97). This is threatening to
heterosexual women because they are afraid to make this choice: "They
are angry at us because we have a way out that they are afraid to take"
(Shelley 1969/1970:347).

    Besides threatening individual men with the loss of their personal
servants and individual women with loss of their subject status, lesbianism threatens patriarchy as an institution with the loss of its entire
subject class. Brown wrote, "if all women were Lesbians male supremacy would have the impossible task of maintaining itself in a vacuum."
Similarly, Frye pointed out that the ability of a few lesbians to see
through male Reality is, in itself, not threatening to patriarchy; the
threat lies in the possibility that this vision will spread to other women.
If enough women begin to see through Reality, the illusion of Reality
will be destroyed. Such threats are only good insofar as all women have
the potential to become lesbians. If they do not, then patriarchy need
not fear the loss of its subject class and lesbianism presents no challenge
to patriarchy at all. So the threat of lesbianism to patriarchy as an
institution hinges on the assumption that it would be possible for all
women to become lesbians. This is why, Brown argues, men "heap the
worst abuse upon the Lesbian in order to keep women from becoming
Lesbians" (1976f:122); men's hostility toward lesbians becomes proof
of the argument that lesbianism is threatening to men because it can
be chosen.

    The argument that lesbianism "threatens male supremacy at its
core" (Bunch 1972/1975:29) by rejecting the cultural valuation of the
male also hinges on the assumption that lesbianism is a choice. If lesbianism could not be chosen, then it could not be understood as a rejection
of patriarchal values, including the valuation of the male and the normalcy of heterosexuality. As Frye pointed out, "The choosing challenges
the value placed on heterosexual normalcy" (1983b:150).

    Atkinson argued that the patriarchy protects itself from the threat of
lesbianism by portraying lesbians as women who *can* not, rather than
women who *will* not, fulfill their "proper political function in society"

(1972/1973:12). In other words, patriarchy co-opts lesbians by constructing them as failed heterosexual women, thus preserving its subject class by essentializing the difference between lesbian and heterosexual women, reaffirming the superior value of heterosexuality, and denying female sexual agency. The implication of Atkinson's analysis is that lesbians who believe that they are essentially different from heterosexual women or that they did not choose their lesbianism are allowing themselves to be co-opted by the patriarchy. The threat lesbianism poses to patriarchy is therefore dependent not only on lesbianism *being* a choice, but on lesbians *believing* that lesbianism is a choice.

Finally, lesbian feminist arguments concluded in a moral imperative that feminists *should* be lesbians. The lesbian imperative, as do all the arguments that led to it, relies on the assumption that lesbianism is an option for all women. If women could not choose to be lesbians, then it would make no sense to demand that they become lesbians or to admonish them for not becoming lesbians.

The Construction of Lesbianism as a Choice in Lesbian Feminist Discourse

> *Any woman can be a lesbian.*
> — Alix Dobkin, *Lavender Jane Loves Women*

As Katie King observed, lesbian feminists developed a "highly elaborated rhetoric of choice around the idea and practice of lesbianism" (1986:82). Because of the critical importance of choice in the construction of lesbianism as feminist, many lesbian feminists wrote about the issue of choice, each constructing lesbianism as a choice in her own way. Most did so by arguing that all women could be or are lesbians; if all women were potential lesbians, then there would be no essential difference between lesbians and non-lesbians. Therefore, the difference would necessarily be the result of mutable individual factors which, as such, are alterable by choice. Some lesbian feminists accomplished the task of arguing that all women are potential lesbians by reconceptualizing *womanhood,* some accomplished it by reconceptualizing *lesbianism,* and still others accomplished it by reconceptualizing *choice.*

One of the most common arguments began with the assertion that every woman is inherently bisexual. Therefore, every woman has a "lesbian aspect" which, most proponents of this view argued, had been suppressed by heterosexual training in a male supremacist culture. Becoming a lesbian is a process of rediscovering one's own suppressed lesbianism, a process that every woman can choose to undergo. For example, Loretta Ulmschneider wrote, "As lesbian/feminists we affirm the bisexuality of human nature. . . . Lesbians represent that part of every woman that male supremacy has destroyed or suppressed" (1973/ 1975:88).[44] Jill Johnston, referring to heterosexual women she observed while living in New York, wrote: "The lesbianism of all these women was inaccessible to them in direct proportion to the social definition of themselves exclusively in relation to the sexual needs of the man" (1973:151). In other words, male definitions of womanhood promote heterosexuality among women by cutting them off from their own lesbianism. Presumably, therefore, freeing oneself from male definitions should put a woman back in touch with her lesbianism. Faderman alluded to the same argument in *Surpassing the Love of Men,* when she predicted that the independent woman of the future would reject male definitions of womanhood and the myth that heterosexual marriage is necessary for fulfillment. Love between these liberated women would be more common because they would "have no need to repress natural feelings of affection toward other women" (1981:414). Similarly, Brown promised women that through lesbianism, they would discover their "woman-identified" selves, implying that all women had such selves (1972/1975).

The staff of *Purple September* took a different approach that involved a similar reconstruction of womanhood. Instead of arguing that lesbianism is a possibility for all women, they argued that heterosexuality is not inevitable for any woman. Pointing out that we live in a society that socializes women to be heterosexual, they asserted first of all that arguments that heterosexuality is either a personal choice or a matter of immutable personal preference are unconvincing. Secondly, axiomatically asserting that "if [heterosexuality] is a given in the life of one person, it has to be a given in the lives of all of us" (1975:82), they argued that heterosexual socialization would be unnecessary if heterosexuality were inevitable. Therefore, heterosexuality is inevitable for no one and, by implication, any woman can choose to be a lesbian.

Some writers argued that lesbianism is a choice by citing their own personal experience. For example, Barbara Solomon generalized her own experience to all lesbians when she asserted that "Lesbians are not born. We have made a conscious choice to be Lesbians" (1972/ 1975:40). Faderman asserted that many "old gay" women had initially become lesbians for feminist reasons, but that these reasons had been obscured within a gay subculture that accepted the "experts' " opinion that lesbians are born, not made: "Once the connection between lesbianism and feminism was widely acknowledged, older lesbians, whose feminism had up until now been buried under the rubbish of society's views, were able to reexamine in daylight what it was in the first place that made them decide to commit themselves to making women prime in their lives" (1981:383). As evidence, she cited a writer in *The Ladder* who stated that she is " 'a lesbian by choice,' because that choice (which she said had little to do with a desire for a particular sexual act) permitted her freedom from socially imposed female roles" (1981:381).

The argument that lesbianism is an alternative lifestyle that offers freedom from male domination constructs lesbianism as a route toward personal liberation that might be chosen by any woman. In contrast to arguments that resolve the problem of choice by asserting that all women are potential lesbians, this argument establishes lesbianism as a choice by reconstructing lesbianism itself. Lesbianism is the result not of essential feelings of attraction to women, but of a feminist desire to avoid male supremacism; in other words, lesbianism is a personal reaction to patriarchy. This is true even if the individual lesbian does not realize that the true motivation for her lesbianism is a desire for liberation.[45] Many lesbian feminists held lesbianism out to women as a solution to the oppression they experienced in their intimate lives. For example, Shelley wrote that "[l]esbianism is one road to freedom—freedom from oppression by men" (1969/1970:343). Rita Mae Brown asked rhetorically why heterosexual women would want to take on the burden of double oppression that lesbianism brought, and answered her own question by claiming that "[l]esbianism also offers you the freedom to be yourself. It offers you potential equal relationships with your sisters. It offers escape from the silly, stupid, harmful games that men and women play" (1972/1975:72). In case any woman did not feel the need for personal liberation, Brown promised women that lesbianism would bring a feminist consciousness and an awareness of the need for personal liberation: "You will discover the thousand subtle ways that heterosexuality destroyed your true power; you will discover how male supremacy

destroys all women and eventually the creators of it, men" (1972/
1975:73). The reconstruction of lesbianism as a feminist alternative to
oppressive heterosexual relationships gave new meaning to the idea that
lesbianism is necessary for feminist liberation. Not only does lesbianism
hold the hope for collective women's liberation, it is also the route to
individual liberation.

The reconstruction of lesbianism as an alternative to personal male
domination was one of a number of reconstructions of lesbianism that
effectively transformed lesbianism into a choice available to all women.
Other lesbian feminists, seeking a way to impress heterosexual feminists
with the relevance of lesbianism to their lives, reconstructed lesbianism
as the representation of all positive relationships among women. The
most famous version of this reconceptualization is Rich's (1980/1983)
"lesbian continuum," which includes all of women's relationships to
each other, ranging from casual to intimate. The implication of this
continuum is that the difference between sexual lesbianism and other
relations among women is not a qualitative difference, but merely a
difference in intensity. All women's relations with each other have a
single underlying dimension, and the name Rich gave the continuum
indicates that the underlying dimension is lesbianism itself. Sex with
women is merely the most intimate and intense expression of the lesbianism that is a component of all women's relations with each other.

The idea of defining lesbianism in terms of all positive relationships
between women did not originate with Rich's concept of a lesbian
continuum. In 1976, Brown equated lesbianism with ties among women,
and established a complete correspondence between lesbianism and ties
among women: "Lesbianism is the issue that deals with women reacting
positively to other women. All other issues deal with men and the society
they have built to contain us" (1976e:91). If *all* other issues deal with
men, then all issues not involving men must be lesbian issues; therefore,
all forms of positive interaction among women must be lesbian interactions. Although Brown's purpose was to establish lesbianism as a central
feminist issue and to argue that heterosexism is a barrier to feminist
progress because it prevents women from developing primary loyalties
to each other, her argument effectively defined all relations among
women as lesbian relations.

The equation of lesbianism with positive ties among women establishes lesbianism as a possibility for all women in two ways. First, it

defines any woman who has a friendship with another woman as a lesbian. Since few women have no female friends, nearly all women are thereby defined as lesbians. Lesbianism is not only a possibility for all women, it is a possibility that has already been realized; all women are lesbians. Second, since all of women's relationships with each other are qualitatively similar to sexual lesbianism, any woman who has a friendship with another woman need only intensify that relationship to become a lesbian in the traditional sexual sense. There is no essential difference between sexual lesbians and other women; all women have the capacity for lesbianism as evidenced by their friendships with other women. As Brown stated clearly in *Plain Brown Rapper,* "Every woman can confront the issue of Lesbianism because she has the potential to be a Lesbian" (1976c:69).

The construction of lesbianism as a choice—either by redefining womanhood or by redefining lesbianism—was threatened by the existence of "born lesbians" whose own experiences belied the claim that lesbianism was a matter of choice. Born lesbians experienced their lesbianism as an essential aspect of themselves that distinguished them from heterosexual women. For them, coming out had been a personal process of discovery, not a political process of feminist transformation, and the lesbian feminist idea that lesbianism was a choice seemed foreign. "Born lesbians" resented "political lesbians" who not only claimed lesbian identities without living lesbian lives, but then had the audacity to tell born lesbians that their lesbianism had also been a political choice rather than an essential discovery.

Lesbian feminists who had a stake in the construction of lesbianism as a choice needed to inoculate lesbian feminism from the challenge posed by born lesbians. Atkinson and Frye did so by redefining choice. For Atkinson, the importance of choice lies in its capacity to produce an effective movement. Drawing on her war metaphor, she wrote, "It is the association by choice of individual members of any Oppressed group, the massing of power, which is essential to resistance. It is the commitment of individuals to common goals, and to death if necessary, that determines the strength of an army" (1972/1973:11–12). In this passage, Atkinson did not refer to *lesbianism* as a choice, but rather to *association* as a choice. In other words, she bypassed the question of whether one chooses to be a lesbian and focused instead on the question of whether lesbians choose to unite in struggle, a choice that could be

made by born lesbians as well as political lesbians. But having incorporated born lesbians into her argument, Atkinson proceeded in the next
paragraph to define lesbianism as commitment to women: "It is this
commitment, by choice, full-time of one woman to others of her class
that is called lesbianism" (1972/1973:12). By using this reconstructed
concept of lesbianism, Atkinson returned to the argument that lesbianism itself must be chosen if the struggle for women's liberation is to
be successful.

Frye, who believed that choice is important because it allows lesbians to appreciate the visionary advantages of their marginal position,
provided a less circular argument. She explicitly stated that the choice to
be made is not the choice to become a lesbian, but a choice about how
to experience one's lesbianism: "Whether as individuals we feel ourselves to have been born lesbians or to be lesbians by decision, we claim
as morally and politically conscious agents a positive choice to go with
it; to claim our lesbianism, to take full advantage of its advantages"
(1983b:149). Lesbians can choose whether to "deny, resist, tolerate, or
embrace" their lesbianism, thereby choosing whether to avail themselves
of the benefits of lesbianism. By redefining choice, Frye made room in
her argument for women who experience their lesbianism as essential
and thereby neutralized the threat these women pose to the very cornerstone of lesbian feminism. One could say that Frye co-opted born lesbians into the lesbian feminist argument.

Other authors solved the problem of born lesbians more directly, by
simply dismissing their conscious experiences as evidence. Shelley, for
example, said "I think you can see the lesbian in a political sense as
unconsciousness propelled by whatever hidden motivations—say as a
rebel against the accepted mores of society. This is a political decision,
even if it happens on an unconscious level."[46] In other words, becoming
a lesbian is a political decision even if the woman becoming lesbian does
not experience it as such. Such a statement is unfalsifiable, and effectively inoculates lesbian feminism from any and all challenges on the
basis of personal experience—an ironic outcome for a movement that
began by politicizing the personal.

Each of the above arguments succeeded in constructing lesbianism
as a choice. The fact that each argument did so on the basis of very
different premises and arguments was immaterial because each succeeded in providing lesbian feminism with what it needed at the time.

But a problem arose nevertheless, because the concept of lesbianism as a choice, as critical as it was for feminist claims, provided a very poor basis for claims making within the political realm of the larger society. In this larger realm, the dominant language of political protest had been articulated by racial/ethnic protest groups and relied on the assumption of essence, not choice.

The Importance of Essence in the Ethnic Political Tradition and the Construction of Lesbians as an Ethnic Group

The ethnic political tradition involves a political language developed to articulate the concerns of racial and ethnic minorities, most notably African-Americans in the Black civil rights movement of the 1950s and 1960s. This language was borrowed by lesbians, who constructed themselves as an ethnic group in order to use it. The process of constructing lesbians as an ethnic group produced concepts of lesbianism and political arguments that were very different from those produced in the effort to establish lesbianism as a feminist issue.

Groups defined by race or ethnicity possess qualities that groups based on association or choice do not, and these qualities are integral to the ethnic model of political movement. First, racial and ethnic groups possess a common history and culture. By virtue of the fact that racial/ethnic identity is to a large extent inherited, children are usually born into and raised by members of their own racial/ethnic group. They learn their ethnic culture as children, and that culture survives from generation to generation. The connection between the parents' culture and the children's culture is direct, creating a feeling of a continuous history and a cultural tradition to which one belongs from birth. Individuals who are raised by people of other race/ethnicity often feel as if they need to "get in touch with their own heritage" by learning about the culture they were "deprived" of as children. Despite the fact that they did not learn this culture as children, they feel a connection to it and experience their unfamiliarity with it as an alienation from their own past. It is, in effect, their birth right.

Second, members of racial and ethnic groups have ancestors in the strictest sense of the term. One can look back on these ancestors with pride by claiming their accomplishments and contributions to society as the achievements of the ethnic group as a whole. One can look up to these ancestors—or to their contemporary equivalents—as role models for oneself. Racial and ethnic groups whose ancestors and contemporary figures are underrepresented in school curricula expend a great deal of energy encouraging schools to provide a multicultural education, so that their children will be exposed to individuals about whom they can feel a sense of ethnic pride and after whom they can model themselves.

Third, racial and ethnic groups have, at least apparently, clearly defined boundaries. Despite the socially constructed nature of racial and ethnic categories and the importance of identity, racial and ethnic physical characteristics are largely genetically determined. People in cultures with rigidly defined racial categories, such as the continental U.S., generally overlook the role of their own cultural categories in the interpretation of these racial and ethnic characteristics and believe that race and ethnicity are determined solely by the physical characteristics themselves. Therefore, race and ethnicity are widely perceived as essential, immutable, unambiguous, and out of one's own control. One is either a member of a particular racial or ethnic group or one is not, the fact of race and ethnicity is determined at the moment of conception, and one can neither choose one's race nor change races. Therefore, the boundaries of ethnic groups are clearly defined and fixed.

The ethnic model of political movement developed as a political strategy designed to serve the interests of racial and ethnic groups, i.e., groups with a shared history and culture, ancestors, and ostensibly clear and fixed boundaries defined by essential and immutable characteristics. It is a liberationist model that identifies an oppressor and an oppressed, whose group boundaries correspond closely to the boundaries between racial/ethnic groups. Although members of ethnic groups other than one's own can be perceived as allies or as "wise," they are rarely extended the same benefit of the doubt or expected to show ethnic allegiance until they have proven themselves trustworthy. Conversely, members of one's own ethnic group are expected to show allegiance and are subjected to criticism and charges of sedition if they do not. These distinctions between the oppressor and the oppressed would not be possible if the boundaries between ethnic groups were not apparently clearly defined and fixed.

Moreover, the oppressor has power and uses it to oppress the oppressed; therefore, the task of the oppressed is to empower itself. It can do this by asking the oppressor for a piece of the pie (the civil rights approach), by making the pie larger or baking a pie of its own (the nationalist approach), by transforming the pie or offering an alternative (the radical approach), or by destroying the pie altogether and replacing it (the revolutionary approach). Each of these approaches relies on certain characteristics of ethnic groups. Civil rights claims, for example, are usually based on the argument that it is unfair to discriminate on the basis of immutable characteristics over which one has no control. Nationalism and other, less radical forms of cultural empowerment depend on the preexistence of a culture, history, and ancestral accomplishments to which members of the ethnic group can claim special rights and in which they can take pride. Radicalism and revolutionism are less specifically tailored to the special characteristics of ethnic groups; groups based on choice or political convictions can also advocate the transformation or overthrow of the current system. For example, radical and revolutionary approaches were used by the New Left and countercultural movements as well as by racial and ethnic movements. But ethnic groups have a special advantage in that their preexisting cultural heritage can provide the blueprint for the visionary goals of radical and revolutionary action, and the fact that the clarity and immutability of their boundaries assure a level of group cohesion that is not dependent on the existence of an enemy.

As Black activists carefully hammered out civil rights, nationalistic, radical, and revolutionary arguments and worked to publicize these arguments, the ideology and language of ethnic politics became increasingly familiar to African-Americans and non-African-Americans alike. The more familiar the language and the arguments of ethnic politics became, the more valuable they became as political currency and the more available they became for use by other groups. Any group that could adapt the language of ethnic politics to its own ends could tap into a well-developed social change ideology. As the Black movement gained national attention, carefully constructed arguments were reduced to slogans—phrases that function as political shorthand. Slogans quickly develop an emotional charge that precedes the carefully reasoned arguments behind them, and they can be borrowed easily; even if the detailed arguments behind the slogans would not hold up under close examination when applied to another group, that group can use the slogans to elicit the associated emotional responses without much fear of scrutiny

by theoretical purists. Many non-African-American ethnic groups, including white immigrants as well as other Peoples of Color, followed the
lead taken by African-Americans and adapted the language of ethnic
politics to their own needs.

When the second wave of the feminist movement began, ethnic
political language was the primary language of protest available in the
sociopolitical arena. But women were limited in their ability to avail
themselves of ethnic political language because women as a group do
not possess all of the qualities of an ethnic group. Women are not
entirely unlike an ethnic group; femaleness is by and large a genetic
characteristic and, as such, it is as essential and immutable as race and
ethnicity. Women could, therefore, avail themselves of civil rights, radical, and revolutionary approaches to empowering themselves. For example, the National Organization for Women, formed in the fall of 1966,
adopted a liberal civil rights approach, whereas feminists who received
their political training in the New Left movement preferred a more
radical approach involving the cultural transformation of society, and
WITCH was sympathetic to revolutionary goals and tactics (Adam
1987; Marotta 1981).[47] However, women, unlike members of ethnic
groups, do not share a historically integral culture. To the extent that
women have a historically transmitted culture, it has permeable boundaries because it is intimately intertwined with men's culture, and, from a
feminist point of view, it is not *women's* culture because it developed as
a complement to men's culture. It was, for example, difficult to find
feminist pride in the historical and mythical figures traditionally offered
as representatives of women such as Betsy Ross and Mrs. Ward Cleaver.

To discover or create a women's culture, feminists used the strategy
of the consciousness raising group.[48] Recognizing that their perceptions
of their own experiences had been shaped by the patriarchal culture in
which they had been raised, feminists reasoned that the only way they
would be able to get in touch with who they were as women would be
to communicate with each other at the most basic emotional level. In the
absence of men, if they could help each other rediscover their own
emotions—those experiences that exist prior to cultural interpretation—
they might be able to discover who they were as women and build a
women's culture atop this discovery.

Women in consciousness raising groups and other separatist spaces
did succeed in producing a feminist women's culture. This new culture

includes feminist humor, women's music, a new genre of literature, and feminist social structures, such as feminist political organizations, battered women's shelters and other social services, bookstores, music festivals, and coffeehouses. As noted earlier in this chapter, the search for culture also involved a search for a herstory, particularly a herstory of notable women who could become the equivalent of ethnic ancestors. Women soon discovered historical figures of whom they could be proud. Sojourner Truth and Elizabeth Blackwell, for example, became role models for women. Their contributions to society became contributions on behalf of women as a class, and women as a class began to take pride in the contributions that their newfound ancestors had made. A sense of historical continuity—of heritage—emerged as women's culture and history took shape.

As women's feminist culture developed, women became more like a traditional ethnic group, and the language of ethnic politics became increasingly available to them. Not surprisingly, this coincided with the rise of cultural feminism and the incorporation of the concept of an essential womanhood that had been contaminated by men's domination. The matriarchy of the future was to be based on the blueprint of past (mythical) matriarchies that had been destroyed by patriarchal Christians. The effort to create a feminist culture became an effort to reclaim a women's ethnic culture from the past.

But to develop the culture necessary to become an ethnic group women had had to develop their own political dialect. Because women had created their culture by looking at their personal lives, the feminist political language that developed was based on the premise that the personal is political. In this feminist dialect, the political is legitimized by reference to the personal, rather than by reference to the essential or the immutable. This added a new political language to the existing ethnic political language. Lesbians, when they began protesting, were therefore faced with two political languages. I have already shown how the use of feminist political language led to a variety of arguments and constructions of lesbianism based on the premise that lesbianism is chosen; ethnic political language demanded a very different approach.

Like feminists, lesbians had to reconstitute themselves as an ethnic group in order to utilize ethnic political language to articulate their demands for social change. This task was even more problematic for lesbians than it was for feminists. Like women in general, lesbians in particular lacked a preexisting cultural heritage and ancestry. But unlike women, lesbians also lacked unambiguous group boundaries defined by apparently immutable and essential characteristics. Femaleness appears immutable and essential because it is genetically determined, but the causes of lesbianism are open to debate. Therefore, lesbianism might not be immutable and it might be subject to choice; if it is, then the boundaries of the lesbian group are ambiguous because women can enter and leave the group at will. This ambiguity is exacerbated by the relative invisibility of sexual orientation; whereas most women make their femaleness socially visible through widely recognized symbols of gender, lesbianism is usually invisible both because of the lack of widely recognized symbols and the desire of lesbians to conceal their sexual orientation from heterosexuals. The symbols that can be used to make lesbianism visible are generally known only to lesbians and "wise" heterosexuals; other heterosexuals who wish they could tell who is lesbian must content themselves with an illusion of knowledge based on stereotypy.

Therefore, to become an ethnic group, lesbians not only had to develop a culture, history, and ancestry, but they also had to construct lesbianism as an essential characteristic that is unambiguous, immutable, and involuntary. Lesbians received considerable help with the latter task from "experts" who proclaimed that sexual orientation is biologically determined. As discussed by Faderman, before the advent of lesbian feminism, gay women typically looked to the experts as sources of legitimate information about lesbianism. Faderman argued that preliberation gay women were so cowed by social stigma and internalized heterosexism that they accepted the experts' essentialist views even when these views conflicted with their own experience of having chosen lesbianism for feminist reasons. In this view, modern feminism was the savior that liberated gay women from the yoke of heterosexist expertise (1981). But, when we take into consideration the fact that the dominant model of political protest available to lesbians prior to gay liberation was the ethnic model, then we can see that gay women's acceptance of essentialist views of sexual orientation was, in fact, not merely a view imposed on them by heterosexist experts but a view that was consistent with their own interests. [49]

To create a lesbian culture, history, and ancestry, lesbians used the same methods used by feminists. In fact, to a large extent the development of lesbian heritage and the development of women's heritage were one and the same effort. Cultural radical feminists, for example, the members of Redstockings and The Feminists, were interested in the cultural transformation of society to eliminate sexism; they were, therefore, willing to critique the culture of heterosexism and welcomed lesbians as cultural workers (Marotta 1981). Much of what is now referred to as "women's culture" is really lesbian culture; most so-called "women's music" is composed by and for lesbians; "women's coffeehouses" expect to attract a lesbian clientele; and most "women's festivals" are attended primarily by lesbians. These institutions are no less than partial manifestations of the "Amazon Nation," a visionary society that represents the culmination of both feminist and lesbian nationalism. The role of lesbians and lesbianism in "women's culture" prompted Adam to refer to lesbianism in the 1970s as a form of "feminist 'nationalism' " (Adam 1987:91).

In addition to feminist "women's culture," lesbians also created a history and ancestry that is uniquely lesbian. As Goodman et al. wrote, "Since mainstream society provides no context for lesbianism, we have created our own culture, and its birth has spanned many centuries. From Sappho and her colony on the isle of Lesbos in ancient Greece, through the witches in medieval Europe . . . to the communal lesbian households of today, we have come together to share support, comfort, delight, despair, rituals, music, and magic" (1983:71). The romantic friends described by Faderman and the spinsters described by Carpenter are the ancestors of the modern lesbian, not the modern feminist; they are the ancestors of feminists only insofar as lesbianism is available to heterosexual feminists as a magical sign (King 1986).

Contemporary lesbian culture also reflects specifically lesbian needs and creativity, not general feminist concerns. For example, the high rate of alcoholism among lesbians has contributed to the development of a unique sensitivity to the needs of women in recovery, and the small size of the community produces ingrown "family trees" and rules for relating to ex-lovers that differ dramatically from the norms governing heterosexual ex-relationships. Concerns about cultural sensitivity have generated a complex form of political correctness that predated the distorted image of political correctness produced in the late 1980s by the religious and political right for its own ends. The mark of a mature culture might be the ability to make fun of itself; contemporary lesbian culture is

complex enough to support not only a serial comic strip, Alison Bech-
del's "Dykes to Watch Out For," but a growing number of lesbian
comedians. Although in the 1980s and 1990s lesbians became more
interested in traditional mainstream goals, such as economic success and
motherhood, and less interested in the building of Lesbian Nation, the
nationalist fervor of the 1970s produced a powerful cultural reality that
became even stronger as lesbians gained economic power.

The construction of lesbians as an ethnic group made ethnic strategies of political argument available to lesbians. If lesbianism is immutable and essential, then it is as unfair to discriminate against lesbians as it
is to discriminate against African-Americans or any other racial or ethnic
group. If lesbians have a culture, a history, and an ancestry, then they
can take pride in their heritage and the accomplishments of their ancestors. Using the cultural values and objects produced by this heritage,
lesbians have built institutions, an economy, and indeed an entire subsociety complete enough to permit at least temporary escape from the
oppressive heterosexism of mainstream society. Using this countercultural subsociety as a blueprint, radical and revolutionary lesbians can
hope to transform or supersede society at large. All of the strategies of
the ethnic political tradition—including civil rights, nationalist, radical,
and revolutionary strategies—become available to lesbians as an ethnic
minority.

Lesbians who participated in the construction of lesbians as an
ethnic group were often quite aware of what they were doing and of the
benefits to be had by using ethnic political strategies.[50] Many lesbian
feminist activists drew explicit parallels between women, lesbians, and
ethnic groups. Some drew these parallels based on simple similarity. For
example, Martha Shelley argued that heterosexism is based on sexism
and referred to sexism as "a form of racism where, because you are born
with a particular color, shape, sex, nationality, or into a family with a
particular religious orientation, you are automatically forced into a certain pattern."[51] In 1970, Brown also analogized gender and race in her
response to Roxanne Dunbar's dismissal of the lesbian issue as a trivial
personal issue of "sexuality," commenting in *Plain Brown Rapper* that
"[women] are continually seen in sexual terms, we are defined by our
genitals as brutally as a non-white is defined by pigment" (1976b:50).
Florynce Kennedy, a feminist lawyer and civil rights activist, told DOB-
New York that "being lesbian was like being black."[52]

Because of the similarities between female, lesbian, and ethnic oppression, many lesbian activists argued that people who experience one form of oppression should have an enhanced understanding of other forms of oppression. For example, Brown reasoned that lesbians are uniquely antiracist and anti-classist because "[o]nce you feel your strength you cannot bear the thought of anyone else being beaten down. All other oppressions constructed by men become horrible to you, if they aren't already" (1972/1975:75). White women cannot become Black and upper-class women do not become working class, so they cannot understand race and class oppression first hand. But every woman can be a lesbian. Therefore, Brown reasoned that the experience of lesbianism could be the stepping stone toward an understanding of race and class oppressions for all women. (1976c).

The connections lesbian activists drew between heterosexism, sexism, and racism were not limited to simple analogies based on similarity. Many writers constructed causal relationships between the various oppressions. For example, Brown and Bunch argued that sexism was the primary form of oppression and that racism, classism, and all other forms of oppression developed subsequent to and atop the foundation provided by sexism.[53] Under the subheading "Sexism is the Root of All Oppression," Bunch wrote, "The first division of labor was based on sex . . . . Having secured the domination of women, men continued this pattern of suppressing people, now on the basis of tribe, race, and class" (1972/1975:32).[54] She further explained that although white and upper-class lesbians might appear to enjoy race and class privilege, they lose these privileges if they are discovered to be lesbians. Therefore, lesbians really have no race and class privileges, lesbians who attempt to hang onto their illusory race and class privileges or fail to fight racism and classism are merely dividing themselves from their sisters, and all lesbians have an interest in fighting every form of oppression. Brown added that race and class divisions are in the interest of male supremacy because they fragment the oppressed and prevent effective protest. Moreover, because sexism is the most basic oppression, the struggle against sexism—particularly the struggle against heterosexism, the "ultimate sexist oppression" (1976f:128)—is an attack on the roots of racism and classism. Of lesbian communities, Brown wrote "We know they are a tiny space of freedom we have created in the male world. We know they are the beginning of the end for male supremacy and its hideous younger brothers, racial oppression and class oppression" (1976f:128).[55]

The argument that sexism is the most basic form of oppression contrasts sharply with socialist analyses that posit classism as the most basic form of oppression. Brown explicitly rejected the socialist analysis:

> The world has witnessed a number of class revolutions led by Marxist intellectuals. . . . In all those countries women still do not share political power commensurate with their number. . . . In Cuba for all its miracles, sexism is so fierce that homosexuals are 'rehabilitated.' To tell a woman, especially a working class Lesbian, to repeat the class struggle as defined by men . . . is to tell her to forget her own oppression . . . to . . . give herself over to politics as constructed by men. . . . Having seen what happens to women repeatedly in class revolutions it is clear that we must try another way. (1976f:126–127)

Barbara Smith and Audre Lorde disagreed with both positions. Both authors felt that attempts to identify a "primary" oppression were misguided and counterproductive because all forms of oppression share the same root. As Lorde wrote so eloquently, "there can be no hierarchies of oppression. I have learned that sexism (a belief in the inherent superiority of one sex over all others and thereby its right to dominance) and heterosexism (a belief in the inherent superiority of one pattern of loving over all others and thereby its right to dominance) both arise from the same source as racism—a belief in the inherent superiority of one race over all others and thereby its right to dominance" (Lorde 1983:9). Moreover, different oppressions are interconnected, if only because the groups affected by various oppressions overlap. As Black feminist lesbians, both women pointed out that they are oppressed by racism, sexism, and heterosexism, and that these various forms of oppression are inseparable in their lives. "As a Black woman, a lesbian, a feminist and an activist, I have little difficulty seeing how the systems of oppression interconnect, if for no other reason than that their meshing so frequently affect my life" (Smith 1983:7). Individuals who belong to only one oppressed group often think of oppressions as additive, as if the oppression experienced by Black lesbians equals the oppression experienced by a white lesbian plus the oppression experienced by a Black heterosexual woman. Such conceptualizations of oppression implicity define majority status as neutral status, as if one could remove the color and find a white person underneath, or remove the lesbianism and find a heterosexual underneath. The fallacy of this logic is evident to people who are members of multiple oppressed groups, for example lesbians of Color, who "have often been the most astute about the necessity for developing understandings of the connections between oppressions" and who recognize the significance of "those messy inconsistencies that occur whenever race, sex, class and sexual identity actually mix" (Smith 1983:7).

Because oppressions overlap, Smith reasoned that each oppressed group has an interest in combating other forms of oppression because some of its members experience those other forms of oppression. Contrary to the common perception among People of Color that "[h]omosexuality is a white problem or even a 'white disease'," Smith argued that homophobia is as much an issue for People of Color as racism is because "[h]omophobic people of color are oppressive not just to white people, but to members of their own groups—at least ten per cent of their own groups" (Smith 1983:8). Homophobic People of Color are, therefore, guilty of oppressing other People of Color; that is, of racism. Lorde agreed that homophobia and racism are indiscrete: "Any attack against Black people is a lesbian and gay issue, because I and thousands of other Black women are part of the lesbian community. Any attack against lesbians and gays is a Black issue, because thousands of lesbians and gay men are Black" (Lorde 1983:9). In other words, homophobia is racist and racism is homophobic.

Arguments about the similarities and connections between racism, classism, sexism, and heterosexism, especially within the context of claims that all oppressions are equivalent and none are "primary," implicitly construct lesbians as an ethnic group by equating them with groups defined by race or ethnicity. These arguments forego the question of whether lesbians are an ethnic group, assume an affirmative answer, and proceed to apply the language of ethnic politics to lesbians. As an ethnic group, lesbians became another in a series of groups that were able to avail themselves of the language of ethnic political protest.

Feminist Choice or Ethnic Essence: Internal
Contradictions Are the Legacy of a Dual Heritage

The concepts of lesbianism and strategies for liberation that arose from the feminist and the ethnic political traditions undermined and conflicted with each other, complicating lesbians' efforts to constitute themselves as a legitimate interest group. Within the feminist political tradition, political issues are legitimized by reference to the personal. The application of this strategy to lesbianism produced a lesbian feminist ideology that is heavily dependent on the construction of lesbianism as a choice. But within the ethnic political tradition, identity is treated as essential and the legitimacy of political claims depends on the assumption that minority identity is immutable, clearly defined, and historically integral. Claims to rights based on chosen identities fail in the ethnic political tradition. Therefore, lesbian feminists' efforts to legitimate lesbian claims in the eyes of feminists by constructing lesbianism as a choice simultaneously weakened lesbians' ability to make claims using the more familiar language of ethnic politics. The failure of choice in the ethnic political tradition is demonstrated by feminists' reactions prior to the elaboration of the politics of lesbianism as a choice. For example, in 1969, Roxanne Dunbar dismissed the issue of lesbianism by saying "I think homosexuality is a chosen oppression whereas being a woman is the root of oppression. I don't think it's that important" (Brown 1976b:50). Conversely, the construction of lesbianism as an ethnicity undermined lesbian feminists' efforts to legitimate lesbianism as a feminist political issue. For example, King reported that, to the extent that lesbianism was not seen as a matter of choice, feminists in the 1960s and 1970s considered it a civil rights issue, but not a feminist concern (1986).

If the contexts of ethnic and feminist discourse were distinct, the contradictory political strategies necessary in these contexts would not be problematic. But they are not distinct; Dunbar made the statement quoted above at the Congress to Unite Women. Feminist and ethnic discourses overlap and interconnect for the same reasons that sexism and racism overlap and interconnect. Were the two discourses not diametrically opposed, their mingling would have produced a workable synthetic ideology. But the two strategies are based on fundamentally different assumptions and their mingling has produced instead a collection of concepts and arguments full of internal contradictions that reflect the dual heritage of lesbian political philosophy.

These contradictions—like the controversies over the role of sexuality in the definition of lesbianism and the goals of the lesbian feminist movement with regard to gender—produced faultlines that rumbled under the surface of lesbian politics during the 1980s and 1990s. The issue of bisexuality exposes these faultlines, and the heated debates that occur among lesbians over bisexuality have less to do with bisexuality than with the controversies and contradictions in lesbian political ideology.

BISEXUALITY: THE ISSUE THAT EXPOSES CONTROVERSIES AND CONTRADICTIONS IN LESBIAN IDEOLOGY

In the 1980s, ideological debates among lesbians abated as many of us turned our attention to personal career and family goals. But the controversies that fueled these debates in the 1970s were never settled, and the contradictions in lesbian ideology that reflect them were never resolved. These controversies and contradictions lie submerged and largely unexamined by women who have worked out their own individual ideological solutions so that they could go on with their personal lives.

The issue of bisexuality uncovers these controversies and contradictions. The recent resurgence of bisexual activism, including demands by bisexuals within the lesbian community that bear a striking resemblance to the demands lesbians brought to feminists in the 1970s, has forced lesbians to deal with the issue of bisexuality. As lesbians debate the place of bisexual women in the lesbian community, the role of bisexuality in their own lives, and the political implications of bisexuality, they are forced to confront old controversies and contradictions in their conceptions of themselves as lesbians and their political goals as an interest group. The passion that marks the lesbian debate about bisexuality is none other than the passion with which lesbians struggled to define themselves and their issues in the 1970s.

Contemporary lesbians inherited a multiplicity of crisscrossing and contradictory definitions of lesbianism from the 1970s debates. Each of the arguments used by lesbian feminists to construct lesbianism as a political issue was based on a particular definition of lesbianism, and spelled out the political implications of lesbianism as so defined. But by defining lesbianism and its political implications, each argument defined what is not lesbianism and gave non-lesbianism political implications as well. That which is bisexual is not lesbian; otherwise bisexuality per se would not exist except as lesbianism. Therefore, if we disagree about what is lesbian, we disagree about what is bisexual, and if we disagree about the political implications of lesbianism, we disagree about the political implications of bisexuality.

To see how the controversy over bisexuality arises from the controversy over lesbianism, we have to analyze the arguments that were used to politicize lesbianism to discover the many different and conflicting consequences they had for the conceptualization and political meaning of bisexuality.[56] As we will see, the various definitions and images of bisexuality found among contemporary lesbians as described in chapters 4 and 5—including the belief that bisexuality does not exist as well as the belief that it does; the definition of bisexuality variously in terms of behaviors, attraction, identities, choices, and preferences; and images of bisexuals as healthy, confused, undecided, transitional, closeted lesbians, political cop-outs and political opportunists—are none other than the multiple and conflicting concepts and meanings that were implicitly ascribed to bisexuality during the struggle to construct lesbianism as a political issue.

A basic starting definition of lesbianism is, "a woman who loves other women emotionally and spiritually, and desires to express that love and commitment sexually" (Alice et al. 1973/1991a:31). This definition of "lesbian" was adequate to support the argument that feminists should overcome their own homophobia because homophobia was a barrier to feminist progress. But it quickly became inadequate when lesbians began arguing that lesbianism itself is political. Take, for example, the argument that heterosexuality is a male supremacist institution, and that lesbianism is a form of political protest because it represents a refusal to participate in heterosexual relationships. According to this line of reasoning, lesbianism is not defined in terms of emotional or sexual attractions and bonds between women but instead as a lifestyle involving an absence of relationships with men. Whether a woman chooses to become involved in relationships with women is secondary; lesbianism as a form of political protest is primarily defined in terms of the absence of heterosexual relationships.

If lesbianism is defined as a lifestyle characterized by refusal to become involved in heterosexual relationships, then bisexuality must involve willingness to become involved in heterosexual relationships—

otherwise it would be lesbianism. By this definition, a woman's feelings of actual sexual attraction are fairly irrelevant except insofar as they might make her more or less likely to refuse heterosexual relations. A woman who is attracted to men might still abstain from heterosexual relationships and if she did, she would be living a lesbian lifestyle as much as any other lesbian—that would make her a lesbian, not a bisexual. Bisexuality as a dual attraction to women and men is undefined; bisexuality is distinct from lesbianism only as it is defined as involving a willingness to become involved in heterosexual relations.

If lesbianism is a form of political protest because it represents a refusal to participate in the most intimate manifestation of male supremacy, then bisexuality is a form of cooperation with male supremacy because it represents a willingness to participate in the male supremacist institution of heterosexuality. Unlike the lesbian, the bisexual woman so defined has not rejected male supremacy's valuation of the male. Unlike the lesbian, the bisexual woman colludes in the separation of the human race into two emotionally crippled and complementary genders. Unlike the lesbian, who forces men to change by withdrawing her support from them, the bisexual woman makes her support available to individual men. By her willingness to participate in a male-dominated relationship, the bisexual woman supports the entire system of male domination instead of contributing to its breakdown. Finally, the bisexual woman fails to challenge the male definition of a woman as a person who is fucked by men. By being a person who can be fucked by men, she permits herself to be defined as a woman in male terms.

What about the woman who calls herself bisexual, but forswears heterosexual relations? Refusal to participate in heterosexual relationships has no value as a form of protest unless it is communicated to others, particularly men.[57] Therefore, the woman who calls herself bisexual is, for political purposes, bisexual. Men will perceive her as heterosexually available, and she will have no impact on male supremacist culture. By calling herself bisexual she presents herself as someone who is willing to participate in the institution of heterosexuality; her private refusal has no political consequence. Lesbianism is an act of rebellion; bisexuality—defined as a willingness to participate in heterosexual relations or as bisexual identity—is a form of complicity that is politically indistinguishable from heterosexuality.[58] Thus, the argument that lesbianism is form of protest against male supremacy because it is an alternative to heterosexuality defines bisexuality as a willingness to engage in heterosexual relationships and gives to bisexuality the same political meaning it gives to heterosexuality.

Other arguments used to politicize lesbianism had different consequences for the definition and political meaning of bisexuality. For example, lesbianism was also constructed as feminist via the argument that the lesbian lifestyle embodied feminist ideals, such as economic and psychological independence from men, self-knowledge and self-esteem as a woman, and egalitarian relationships. Psychological and economic independence from men can be achieved by any woman who is not involved with a man, regardless of which sex or sexes attract her, regardless of whether she calls herself lesbian, bisexual, or heterosexual, and even regardless of whether she is willing to become involved with a man. In terms of opportunity for independence, any single or celibate woman is the equal of the lesbian and this is no less true for bisexual women than for women of any other sexual orientation.[59] As long as the bisexual woman does not actually become involved with a man, she is the political equivalent of the lesbian, even if she is willing to become involved with men and even if she announces this willingness by calling herself bisexual.

Knowledge and respect for oneself as a woman, on the other hand, are achieved only through relationships with other women and egalitarian relationships can only be had with other women. Lesbians have greater self-knowledge and self-esteem because they develop these qualities through their egalitarian relations with women. Any bisexual woman who became involved with another woman could also experience egalitarian relations and develop self-knowledge and self-esteem. In this respect, as long as a bisexual woman is involved with another woman, she is the political equivalent of the lesbian, even if she calls herself bisexual and feels attracted to men. Thus, bisexuality as defined in terms of identity or sexual attraction has the same feminist political potential as lesbianism does.

But what if the bisexual woman becomes involved with a man? That would be problematic because a heterosexual relationship would not only fail to provide her with the benefits of a lesbian relationship, but it would also compromise any benefits she might have received from her relations with women. For example, any knowledge of herself that she gained through relations with women was gained because relations with women provided her with a context free from male definitions of women. By putting herself in a heterosexual context, she would expose herself once again to a male-dominated meaning system that would make it difficult to stay in touch with her newly discovered woman-defined self. If, therefore, the bisexual woman is defined as a woman who relates sexually to men as well as women, then the bisexual woman is less of a feminist than the lesbian is.

Once lesbianism had been constructed as political, lesbian feminists could argue that lesbians are feminists, and that lesbians have something to offer heterosexual women. Among the qualities lesbians have to offer are a special understanding of heterosexuality from their vantage point as outsiders to the institution, a greater opportunity to escape male-defined reality and develop feminist consciousness, more resources to devote to women because they do not spend their time and energy on men, and political independence because they have no vested interest in male-dominated culture. By this argument, a woman who is attracted to both women and men but who chooses to become involved only with women and to devote her time and energy to other women would be as politically acceptable as a lesbian who did the same. If she adopted a lesbian identity to symbolize her commitment to women, so much the better. She can participate fully in woman-only spaces and contribute equally to the development of feminist consciousness. Bisexuality as defined in terms of dual sexual attraction is not problematic.

On the other hand, bisexuality that involves any form of relating to men or any compromise of one's political commitment to women is the political equivalent of heterosexuality. A bisexual who relates to men enjoys heterosexual privilege and supports male supremacy by partici-pating in a male-dominated institution. Her feminist vision is clouded by her stake in the patriarchal system, and, like any other heterosexual, she must follow the lead of lesbians and be grateful for their insight and efforts to liberate her. Ultimately, she will betray her lesbian sisters because heterosexuality demands that she do so; therefore, lesbians cannot count on her any more than they can count on their heterosexual followers. But the real problem is the bisexual who relates to both women and men. She not only withholds her own time and energy from other women; she also drains other women's time and energy to fill the needs created by her relationships with men and to support her interest in the patriarchy. In doing so, she hampers other women's efforts toward feminist liberation. If the heterosexual woman is unhelpful, the bisexual woman—defined as a woman who relates to both women and men—is a hindrance and an adversary.[60]

If lesbians are better feminists than heterosexual women, lesbian feminists argued, it follows that feminists should become lesbians. The advent of the moral imperative to be lesbian signaled the birth of a new concept of lesbianism; lesbianism as a political statement. No longer an expression of sexual attraction to women, according to this argument, lesbianism—consisting of a lack of relationships with men, sexual relationships with women, and a political commitment to womankind—is an expression of commitment to feminism. A woman's sexual life no longer has anything to do with her sexual desires, and everything to do with her political commitments. Any woman who does not relate sexually to other women obviously does not consider women worthy of their most intimate love. Any woman who continues to call herself bisexual signals not her sexuality, but her lack of political commitment to women; what possible reason could a woman have for calling herself bisexual if not to retain her connection to men and heterosexual privilege? Either one expresses one's feminism by declaring oneself a lesbian and living a lesbian life, or one is not a feminist. There are no other options.

The criticism of lesbian feminism that arose in the wake of the advent of the lesbian moral imperative raised yet another set of political implications for bisexuality. The argument that a basic tenet of feminism is every woman's right to a self-defined sexuality effectively tossed all proscriptions against any form of sexual behavior or identity out the window. This argument led to the conclusion that a bisexual lifestyle or identity based on a recognition of one's bisexuality would be as consistent with feminism as a lesbian lifestyle or identity that was similarly based. What was not feminist was any woman's attempt to deny other women the right to bisexual behavior or identity.

But the argument that every woman has a right to define her own sexuality does not preclude the argument that one's sexuality has political meaning, political causes, or political implications. It merely reaffirms each woman's right to analyze the politics of her own sexuality as she sees them. Many who made this argument implicitly accepted the premise that lesbianism is more consistent with feminism than heterosexuality is, and expected that as women did examine the political implications of their sexuality, they would choose to move toward lesbianism. The feminist imperative therefore became not a behavioral prescription, but a demand that each feminist perform her own feminist analysis of her sexuality, whatever her sexuality might be and whatever changes in her sexual behavior or identity her analysis might precipitate. The arguments that these feminists applied to heterosexuals—that they should continuously examine the relationship between their politics and their sexuality—apply equally to bisexual women. Thus, bisexual identity and bisexual behavior are as politically respectable as any other sexual identity or behavior; as long as the bisexual is continually analyzing the political implications of her own bisexuality.

Other criticisms of the lesbian moral imperative were the higher value it placed on sexual than on nonsexual relations between women, the assertion that heterosexual behavior is antithetical to feminism, and the tendency to define lesbianism in terms of an absence of relations with men instead of positively in terms of relations with women. These arguments also lead to the conclusion that bisexuality per se is no more or less feminist than either lesbianism or heterosexuality. The former arguments posit that neither relations with women nor relations with men reflect a woman's political convictions; therefore, bisexual behavior has no necessary political implications and is no less feminist. The latter argument implies that lesbianism should be defined in terms of relations with women, regardless of the presence or absence of relations with men. By this positive definition of lesbianism, a woman who engages in relations with both women and men would be a lesbian. This definition of lesbianism effectively defines bisexuality out of existence by collapsing it into lesbianism and thereby giving it the same political implications as lesbianism.

In the face of objections to the lesbian moral imperative, lesbian feminists revised their definition of lesbianism once more. Because lesbianism was already divorced from sexual attraction to women, it was a relatively simple matter to divorce lesbianism from lesbian sex. Lesbian feminists appeased heterosexual women by agreeing that their heterosexual behavior and their lack of lesbian sexual behavior did not compromise their feminism. In fact, their lack of lesbian sexual behavior did not compromise their lesbianism; they could be political lesbians if only they would abstain from sex with men and declare a political commitment to women. The advent of the political lesbian reopened the feminist door to bisexual women, as it did to heterosexual women. Bisexual women, like heterosexual women, could be reinstated as feminists if only they would abstain from heterosexual relations. In this case, bisexual women had an advantage over heterosexual women because they did not have to become celibate to do so. But bisexuality per se still had no political meaning and, since "sexuality" was now defined in terms of politics and not sex, it therefore did not exist as a state of being distinct from lesbianism and heterosexuality. Either a woman abstained from heterosexual relations and earned her feminist credentials as a political lesbian, or she engaged in heterosexual relations and thereby demonstrated her lack of feminism; bisexuality, by any definition, was inconsequential.

Of course, once a woman extricated herself from heterosexuality and began to challenge the institution with a vision that was not clouded by an interest in it, she would begin to see the superiority of lesbianism. As she learned to value other women the way she previously valued men, she would become attracted to them and she would want to give them the love that she used to give men. As a woman who is able to understand the institution of heterosexuality from the vantage point of an outsider, and as a woman who has learned the value of women, the bisexual woman who undergoes feminist awakening should soon slip easily into a comfortable lesbianism. If she fails to do so, that is, if she continues to call herself bisexual or remains attracted to men as well as women—even if she abstains from heterosexual relations—she indicates that she values men at least as much as she values women. In doing so, she challenges the feminist valuation of women in the same way that lesbians themselves challenge the male supremacist valuation of men. She belies the lesbian feminist argument that in a sexist society lesbian relations are inherently superior to heterosexual relations, because she has had the opportunity to experience both and she does not agree. Her existence demonstrates that a woman might, with full knowledge of the joys of relating to women, continue to desire sexual relations with men. The implication that lesbian relations are not obviously superior to heterosexual relations cuts to the foundation of lesbian feminism, and is very threatening to it. The bisexual—defined as a woman who persists in being attracted to men after she should have realized the superiority of lesbianism—is therefore a greater political problem for lesbian feminism than the heterosexual woman whose continued heterosexual "desire" merely reflects her ignorance of the joys of relating to women.

The sex positivist movement that arose in reaction to the desexualization of the lesbian was better able to accommodate bisexuality. With its emphasis on pleasure and sexual exploration, it brought sexual desire back into sexuality and rejected any limits on sexual expression including limits on the genders of one's partners. To sex positivists, bisexuality as a sexual practice was as legitimate an area of sexual exploration as any other. Like any other form of sexuality, it should be celebrated and enjoyed.

The debate over the role of gender in feminism and lesbian/gay liberation is of even greater consequence in the controversy about bisexuality than the debate over the relationship between lesbianism and lesbian sex is. However controversial, lesbianism is definable without reference to sex, but it is not definable without reference to gender. In fact, the very feminists who are most eager to desexualize lesbianism—the cultural feminists—are the same feminists who emphasize the importance of gender. Therefore, the elimination of gender—a goal advocated by early gay liberationists and some feminists who hoped to create a world in which all people would be free to love whomever they chose without cultural, psychological, economic, or legal constraints—would effectively eliminate the lesbian as a social type because it would eliminate the basis for her definition. Such a possibility is very unsettling to lesbians who have struggled to create a lesbian identity in a hostile world, and who have considerable personal, social, and political investments in preserving that identity. It is particularly unsettling to cultural lesbian feminists whose world views are heavily based on a foundation of essential gender.

The issue of bisexuality is very closely related to the issue of the elimination of gender, a relationship that can be seen in the implications of the elimination of gender for bisexuality, which are two-fold. First, it implies that all people would be bisexual because no one would be constrained to choose a lover of a particular gender, and if a person did choose a lover of a particular gender that person would not be labeled lesbian/gay or heterosexual. For this reason, feminists and gay liberationists who strive to eliminate gender often conceptualize the ideal world of the future as a bisexual world. But by the same token, bisexuality would be as undefinable as lesbianism or heterosexuality in that world. Everyone would be bisexual, but no one would be bisexual, because if the concept of gender were truly eliminated the concept of bisexuality would be either meaningless in its failure to distinguish between people, or wholly unthinkable.[61] Conversely, the preservation of gender has two implications for bisexuality. First, it mediates against the realization of bisexuality because it tends to reify two types of sexuality corresponding to the two genders. As long as gender remains the basis for sexual distinction, homosexuality and heterosexuality remain conceptually distinct, and this distinction exerts a constructive influence on reality. At the same time, however, it retains the basis on which bisexuality can conceivably be defined in a meaningful way.

Because the issue of bisexuality is so closely related to the issue of gender, bisexuality takes on the same diametrically opposed implications. Whereas feminists and gay liberationists who see the elimination of gender as a political goal tend to welcome the prospect of bisexuality and envision an ideal world in which everyone would be bisexual, lesbian feminists foresee their own annihilation in such a world and struggle to preserve gender and defend themselves against the existential threat of bisexuality. Paradoxically, lesbians who protect the concept of gender in order to protect lesbian identity simultaneously preserve the basis for the meaningful conceptualization of bisexual identity.

The lesbian feminist reconstruction of lesbianism as a choice created additional political implications for bisexuality. In particular, the argument that all women are inherently bisexual and therefore have a "lesbian aspect," which is suppressed by patriarchy and liberated by feminism, has obvious implications for the discussion of bisexuality. The argument implies that bisexuality not only exists, but that it is universal and essential. Lesbianism, like heterosexuality, is at best only a partial expression of women's full sexuality. The argument was intended to support the lesbian moral imperative by constructing all women as potential lesbians, and succeeded in doing so because arguments that heterosexuality was antifeminist were already in place. Without these arguments, the assertion that all women are inherently bisexual would lead to the conclusion that bisexuality is a more complete form of sexual expression than lesbianism and that the goal of women's liberation— which is, after all, the struggle to provide women with the freedom to be all they can be—should be to promote the expression of bisexuality, not lesbianism. If the basis of the arguments that heterosexuality is antithetical to feminism were to disappear—if, for example, patriarchy were eventually overthrown—then the concept of universal bisexuality would come back to haunt lesbian feminists with its implication that bisexuality is the ultimate feminist form of sexuality. This argument, used as a means toward an end by lesbian feminists, provides a toehold bisexuals can use to insert claims about the legitimacy of bisexuality into lesbian feminist discourse and challenge the conclusion that lesbianism is the desired feminist outcome. It is, in effect, a time bomb planted by lesbian feminists themselves.

Attempts to construct lesbianism as a choice for all women by defining lesbianism in terms of all positive relationships between women also have different implications for bisexuality. Instead of defining bisexuality as universal, these arguments define bisexuality out of existence. In fact, they define heterosexuality out of existence in terms of political relevance. For example, Rich's lesbian continuum defines lesbianism as the common dimension underlying all of women's positive relationships with each other. If women have relations to men, they are irrelevant except insofar as they might weaken their ties to women; all women are more or less lesbians on the basis of the quality of their ties to women. Neither heterosexuality nor bisexuality is represented on this scale; it is a unidimensional scale ranging from less to more lesbian, not a bidimensional Kinsey-type scale ranging from heterosexuality through bisexuality to homosexuality. So-called "bisexuals," like so-called "heterosexuals," are really lesbians.[62]

If lesbianism is a choice for all women, then it is particularly important for bisexual women to choose lesbianism because in their case the fact of choice is indisputable. The patriarchy can attempt to co-opt lesbians into the heterosexist system by portraying "lesbians as women who *can* not, rather than women who *will* not,"[63] be heterosexual. But the woman who is bisexual and nevertheless chooses lesbianism cannot be constructed as a failed heterosexual; the fact of her rejection of heterosexuality is undeniable. Therefore, a bisexual woman who chooses to continue relating to men is a traitor because, having the opportunity to challenge heterosexism, she chooses instead to affirm it. In fact, she is the only true heterosexual, because only she can be said to have consciously chosen heterosexuality.

Like efforts within feminist discourse to construct lesbianism as a feminist issue and a choice, efforts within the ethnic tradition of political discourse to construct lesbianism as an ethnicity produced unintended implications for bisexuality. The greater impact of the ethnic argument vis-à-vis bisexuality, however, was not to create implications for bisexuality, but to make lesbian ethnicity vulnerable to claims of bisexuality. The construction of lesbians as an ethnic group involved the construction of lesbianism as an essential, immutable, unambiguous, and involuntary characteristic upon which to build a lesbian community with clearly defined and fixed boundaries, and the creation of a lesbian culture and history. The construction of lesbianism as an essential characteristic made lesbian feminism vulnerable by creating the unfalsifiable possibility that there might also be a bisexual essence. Lesbian essence itself cannot be observed, so essence must be discovered through observable characteristics such as identity and behavior. If there is a bisexual essence, then many women who had been declared to be lesbians on the basis of their identity or behavior might *really* be bisexuals. Consistent with their belief in the essentiality of lesbianism, lesbians would be morally compelled to recognize the bisexuality of these women to be as legitimate as their own lesbianism; in other words, it would compel them to acknowledge the "loss" of a number of lesbians whose lesbian essence could no more be proved than their bisexual essence could be disproved.

Moreover, if lesbian essence is subject to such uncertainty, then lesbian essence is not as immutable and unambiguous as is necessary to clearly define the boundaries of the lesbian ethnic group. A woman who is attracted to women and has sex only with women might, for example, be a lesbian—or she might not, because she might also be attracted to men. Bisexuals demonstrate that homosexuality and heterosexuality are not mutually exclusive and immutable characteristics, and the boundaries of the lesbian community are therefore not clearly defined and fixed. Bisexuality represents the "grey area" of sexuality that challenges the clarity of the distinction between homosexuality and heterosexuality. Suddenly, no one's lesbianism is guaranteed, allies cannot be distinguished from enemies, and the distinction between lesbianism and heterosexuality that is so necessary to the definition of lesbians as an oppressed ethnic group becomes vague and shifting. If lesbians cannot be clearly distinguished from heterosexuals, then lesbians are not an ethnic group and cannot use ethnic strategies of liberation.[64]

The manner in which lesbian culture and history was constructed also created a site of vulnerability to bisexuality. By desexualizing the lesbian in order to claim independent women as lesbian ancestors in the absence of information about their sexual behaviors, cultural feminists and historians effectively defined the bisexual out of existence not only in contemporary society but in history. Even women whose heterosexual behaviors are a matter of public record could be claimed as the ancestors of the modern lesbian because their heterosexual behavior was easily explained away as the result of the social constraints of the time period, or simply ignored as irrelevant to the definition of lesbianism. This practice effectively eliminated bisexuality from history as it constructed a lesbian history by claiming as lesbian ancestors women who would otherwise be described as bisexual. The process was not unlike the process in which heterosexist historians had "set history a little *too* straight" at the expense of lesbian and gay history. As bisexuals have become politically active in the late 1980s and early 1990s, some have chosen to participate in ethnic political discourse and construct themselves as an ethnic group. To do so, they are constructing a bisexual history; a project that necessarily depletes lesbian history and thereby threatens lesbian ethnicity. This and other efforts on the part of bisexuals, and the challenge they pose to lesbians, will be discussed in chapter 8.

Summary

The many different arguments that have been used to construct lesbians as a political interest group have simultaneously constructed bisexuality in a variety of ways, and ascribed to bisexuality a variety of different political meanings. Even if we were to agree on a particular definition of bisexuality, these different arguments would ascribe to that bisexuality different and conflicting implications.

If, for example, we choose to define bisexuality in terms of attraction to both women and men, most of the arguments used to politicize lesbianism lead to the conclusion that bisexuality is irrelevant, whereas others conclude that it is politically equivalent to lesbianism or, conversely, to heterosexuality. Specifically, the arguments that lesbianism is an implicit political protest against patriarchy, that relationships with women provide women with greater self-knowledge and self-esteem than relationships with men, that lesbians have superior insight and resources to offer the feminist struggle, and that all feminists should become lesbians in either the sexual or the political sense, are unconcerned about the possibility that women might be attracted to both women and men. In most of these arguments, what matters is how women behave; their sexual attractions per se have no political implications, and bisexual attraction is therefore unproblematic.

But a few arguments do ascribe political implications to bisexual attraction. Those who argue that feminists should fight for the right of every woman to a self-defined sexuality consider bisexual attraction no more or less feminist than either lesbianism or heterosexuality; in fact, they label as nonfeminist those who consider bisexual attractions less feminist than lesbian ones. Sex positivists also consider bisexual attraction politically equivalent to lesbian attraction, but in their case it is because they reject feminism as a standard for the relative moral assessment of various forms of sexuality altogether. In contrast, those who expound on the glories of lesbianism and believe that women who declare themselves political lesbians or who taste lesbian pleasures will immediately see the superiority of lesbianism, find continued bisexual attractions more troubling than heterosexual attraction. Bisexual attraction is more troubling because it demonstrates that women who know the pleasures of lesbianism can still feel heterosexual desire, thus calling into question the obvious superiority of lesbianism. Finally, bisexual attraction is threatening to the notion of lesbian ethnicity because it destroys the clarity of the defining characteristic of that ethnicity.

If we choose to define bisexuality in terms of identity, such that any woman who calls herself a bisexual is defined to be a bisexual, lesbians' arguments lead to a new set of political implications for bisexuality. In contrast to bisexual attraction, bisexual identity is rendered irrelevant by very few of lesbians' arguments. Among these are the arguments that lesbians obtain feminist self-knowledge and self-esteem from their relationships with other women, and that lesbianism should be defined positively in terms of women's relationships with other women instead of negatively in terms of the absence of relationships with men. Bisexual identity would not prevent a woman from obtaining feminist benefits from her relations with women, and it would be irrelevant if lesbianism is defined in terms of relations with women; if she related to women, she would be a lesbian—her bisexual identity notwithstanding and completely irrelevant.

Most of lesbians' arguments ascribe very definite political implications to bisexual identity. If lesbianism is an implicit protest against patriarchy, then bisexual identity is politically indistinct from heterosexual identity because a woman who calls herself bisexual conveys that she is willing to engage in heterosexual relations. The protest of lesbianism lies in the refusal to participate in heterosexuality and therefore patriarchy, and this protest is only political if it is made public; the woman with a bisexual identity makes no such protest and is therefore politically identical to the heterosexual-identified woman. Similar implications follow from the argument that all feminists should at least be political lesbians if not sexual lesbians; political lesbianism is an identity as well as a promise to reject heterosexual relations, and women who call themselves bisexual are avoiding their moral obligation to feminism by not becoming political lesbians.

On the other hand, the argument that lesbians embody the feminist ideal of independence from men leads to the conclusion that the bisexual-identified woman can be the political equivalent of the lesbian-identified woman as long as she refrains from heterosexual relationships. If she did become heterosexually involved, her lifestyle would become less feminist, but this would be because of her heterosexual relationship not because of her bisexual identity. Her bisexual identity per se is not problematic. Similarly, those who argue that lesbians have greater insight and resources to offer the feminist movement would not consider bisexual identity per se a necessary impediment to one's value to the feminist movement. Of course, it would be preferable if one adopted a lesbian identity to symbolize her commitment to women, but that would be icing on the cake. Those who argue that feminists should fight for every woman's right to a self-defined sexuality would observe that bisexual-identified women are merely taking advantage of their feminist right, and the sex positivists would encourage bisexual-identified women to enjoy their self-defined sexualities.

The implications of bisexuality become even more complex when bisexuality is defined in terms of sexual behavior, potential behavior, or willingness to engage in certain sexual behaviors. Several of lesbians' arguments lead to the conclusion that the woman who engages in both lesbian and heterosexual behavior is the political equivalent of the heterosexual, or at best, that she is less feminist than the woman who engages in only lesbian behavior but perhaps slightly more feminist than the complete heterosexual. For example, the arguments that lesbianism

is an implicit protest against patriarchy, that the lesbian lifestyle embod-
ies the feminist ideal of independence from men and provides self-
knowledge and self-esteem, and that all feminists should at least be
political lesbians if not sexual lesbians all characterize the behavioral
bisexual as a feminist failure. The argument that lesbians have greater
insight and resources to offer the feminist movement leads to the conclusion that bisexuals are, in fact, even more of a political liability than
heterosexual women are because bisexuals do not merely give their
energy to men instead of women; they take women's energy and give it
to men. This is compounded by the fact that women who continue to
relate to men forego the opportunity to demonstrate that lesbianism is a
choice and thereby collude with heterosexist interpretations of lesbianism.

Bisexual behavior is also problematic for the notion of lesbian ethnicity because, just as bisexual attraction threatens the clarity of the
defining characteristic of lesbian ethnicity, bisexual behavior provides
visible evidence that the boundaries between lesbians (the oppressed
group) and heterosexuals (the oppressor) are neither clear nor fixed.
Allies cannot be clearly distinguished from enemies and allies sometimes
become enemies and vice versa. Under such circumstances, the struggle
for liberation is very difficult.

In contrast, a few of lesbians' arguments have positive implications
for bisexuality defined in terms of behavior. The feminists who argue for
every woman's right to a self-defined sexuality, the sex positivists, and
those who argue that sexual relations with women are no more important than nonsexual ones or that heterosexual relations do not preclude feminism, have no difficulty accepting the woman who behaves
bisexually as a feminist on a par with the lesbian.

Perhaps the most interesting implication for behavioral bisexuality
follows from the argument that lesbianism should be defined in terms of
relationships with women instead of in terms of the absence of relationships with men. Although this argument succeeds in defining lesbianism
in positive terms, it simultaneously defines bisexuality out of existence
by classifying any woman who engages in lesbian behavior as a lesbian,
regardless of whether or not she also engages in heterosexual behavior.
It is ironic that creating a positive definition of lesbianism necessarily
defines bisexuality in the most negative terms possible—as nonexistent.

Other interesting implications follow from the argument that the goal of gay liberation is the elimination of gender, and the argument that all women are inherently bisexual and therefore potentially lesbian. If the elimination of gender is the goal of gay liberation, then the ideal world of the future would be a bisexual world in which people love each other regardless of gender. Behavioral bisexuality, though it would not be recognized as such in that world, would be the norm. Cultural feminists whose own position is heavily grounded in the notion of gender, of course, strongly oppose this vision of the ideal future world and consider bisexuality a threatening, not a welcome, prospect. The argument that all women are inherently bisexual developed to support the argument that all women could and should become lesbians. Within this context, behavioral bisexuality—as are bisexual desire and bisexual identity—is understandable, although it misses the point, which is to realize the lesbian aspect of one's potential. But if arguments that heterosexual behavior is antifeminist are rejected, then the concept of universal inherent bisexuality leads us back to the conclusion that the ideal world of the future is a bisexual world and that feminists should struggle to create this world—an outcome that is far afield from the intentions of the lesbian feminists who proposed the idea that all women are inherently bisexual.

In summary, arguments that were used to construct lesbianism as a political issue have a variety of implications for the political meaning of bisexuality. These arguments all contributed to the formation of a pluralistic lesbian ideology which, despite its internal contradictions and disagreements, is at least sufficient to provide individual lesbians with a feeling that they belong to a group that can provide them with an identity. But the arguments arrived at that point via such different routes that when they are applied to a different subject—bisexuality—their differences emerge in full force. Because of these differences, lesbians disagree about what bisexuality is, and because they cannot agree on what it is, they cannot agree on its political meaning nor on how they should react to it. Is it a feeling of attraction, an identity, a lifestyle, or does it even exist at all? Are bisexuals allies, enemies, followers, hindrances, or neutral observers? Should lesbians welcome them, convert them, pity them, or shun them? Lesbians cannot agree on what bisexuality is because they do not agree on what lesbianism is. By necessity, lesbians have learned to overlook their disagreements about the nature of lesbianism in order to get on with the important business of living as lesbians, but when they discuss bisexuality they are forced to reexamine their own old issues. The disagreements lesbians have with each other about bisexuality that I explored in chapter 4—does bisexuality exist, what is bisexuality, what are bisexuals like, how should lesbians feel about and relate to bisexuals—arise out of their own disagreements with each other about themselves.

Amid all of these differences, however, the one implication that follows consistently from almost all of lesbians' arguments is the implication that bisexuality per se, regardless of how it is defined, has no politics. In some cases, this conclusion is reached because bisexuality is considered the political equivalent of heterosexuality or the political equivalent of lesbianism. In other cases, it is reached because bisexuality is considered politically irrelevant or nonexistent. In other words, lesbian politics have been constructed at the expense of the possibility of a bisexual politics. In the late 1980s and early 1990s, bisexuals set themselves the task of politicizing bisexuality, just as lesbians embarked on the politicization of lesbianism in the early 1970s. Because lesbian politics rest heavily on the denial of bisexual politics, bisexuals' efforts to create a bisexual politics are necessarily threatening to the still fragile process of lesbian politicization, a topic I will explore in chapter 8. But first, I turn to the topic of bisexuals' own attitudes toward bisexuality.

BISEXUAL WOMEN'S VOICES: WHAT DO BISEXUAL WOMEN THINK ABOUT BISEXUALITY AND THE ROLE OF BISEXUALS IN SEXUAL POLITICS?

In chapters 4, 5, and 6 I explored lesbians' attitudes toward bisexuality and bisexual women and showed how the controversy about bisexuality among lesbians reflects lesbians' historically rooted disagreements about whom they are as lesbians. In this chapter and the next, I turn my attention to bisexual women and the effects of lesbians' attitudes on them. As marginal members of the lesbian community, bisexual women are exposed to lesbians' various attitudes and beliefs about bisexuality. Although these attitudes and beliefs are varied, negative attitudes are more widespread and have greater symbolic presence in the lesbian community than positive ones; therefore, these are the attitudes that bisexuals are most likely to encounter. How do bisexual women respond to these attitudes? Do they agree with lesbians about the nature of their differences? Do they share lesbians' desires to maintain some distance in social and political situations? Or, do they reject these attitudes and spend their energy refuting lesbians' beliefs about bisexuality? Or, perhaps, do they ignore lesbians' attitudes altogether, opting to participate in the lesbian community insofar as they can benefit from it without either assimilating or rebelling against the attitudes that dominate that community? What do bisexual women think of themselves? To find out, we must listen to bisexual women's voices. [1]

Bisexual respondents were asked the same question that was asked of lesbian respondents, "What is your opinion of bisexuality?" Their spontaneous answers to this question reveal their conceptions of the issues surrounding bisexuality, as well as their positions on these issues. To a large extent, the issues raised by bisexual women are similar to those raised by lesbians. Their opinions on these issues are sometimes dramatically different from lesbians' opinions, but sometimes they are surprisingly similar.

DOES BISEXUALITY EXIST?

It would be tautological to say that women who identify themselves as bisexual believe that bisexuality exists—or would it? Most bisexual respondents do believe that bisexuality exists, but a few have reservations. Emily, for example, has some doubt about whether true bisexuality exists. She wrote, "Sometimes I wonder if this is a cop-out for someone who can't admit/accept being gay—but I also wonder if it isn't possible to be truly attracted to both men and women." Five other bisexual women also expressed some skepticism or argued that some people who claim to be bisexual are not really bisexual. The remaining thirty-six indicated either implicitly or explicitly that they do indeed believe that bisexuality exists.

The bisexual women who stated clearly that they do believe that bisexuality exists did so in very different terms than their lesbian counterparts. Whereas lesbians typically referred to bisexuality as a legitimate or valid form of sexuality, or stated simply "it exists," not a single bisexual respondent used the words "legitimate" or "valid," and only one used the word "exist"—and this bisexual respondent used the word in the context of describing lesbians' attitudes toward bisexuals. Instead, bisexual women described bisexuality as "natural," a word choice used to indicate bisexual existence by only 2% of lesbians as compared to 11% of bisexual respondents. For example, one stated simply, "I think it's healthy and natural." Several other bisexual respondents did not use the word "natural" itself, but argued that most or all people would be bisexual if not for socialization, or that bisexuality is a healthy form of sexuality, thereby implying that it is natural.

These different word choices reveal that lesbians and bisexual women appeal to different sources of authority when making claims for bisexual existence. Lesbians who described bisexuality as "legitimate" asserted the existence of bisexuality on the basis of its symbolic acceptability, whereas bisexuals who described bisexuality as "natural" based their claims on an appeal to an essence that is intrinsically valuable by virtue of its truth. Both lesbian and bisexual respondents were defending bisexuality from unstated attacks on its existence—if these women did not perceive attacks on the existence of bisexuality, there would have been no reason for them to assert its existence—but the nature of the attack is perceived differently by lesbian and bisexual women, thus requiring different defenses.

Lesbian women are involved in the discourse of the lesbian community in which attacks on bisexuality tend to revolve around the accusation that bisexuality is a political cop-out. In such an atmosphere, assertions of the naturalness of bisexuality would fail to hit their mark, since nature is not the issue. Even if bisexuality were judged to be natural, it would still be vulnerable to the charge that it is bad politics and the argument that individuals should subvert their "natural" bisexual impulses to the demands of politics in a patriarchal and heterosexist society. This is, in fact, what many lesbians themselves have done, as shown in chapter 4. Thus, to defend bisexuality, lesbian women must assert its symbolic legitimacy, i.e., not the fact of its existence but its right to exist.

Bisexual women, on the other hand, apparently feel little need to defend bisexuality against the lesbian community's attacks on its right to exist. Instead, bisexual women look to their own experience as evidence of the existence of bisexuality. They experience their own bisexuality as essence and build their bisexual identity on this experience. Hence, it stands to reason that they would call on this essence when supporting their assertion of bisexual existence, and that they would not feel the need to seek political sanction to demonstrate the legitimate existence of something that they already *know* exists.

Thirty-two percent of bisexual respondents made extreme claims for bisexual existence, asserting that most or all people are really bisexual or that bisexuality is much more common than it appears to be. Faced with the reality that few people actually identify themselves as bisexual or appear to be bisexual, these bisexual women typically posited the existence of a common bisexual potential that is often not actualized, or asserted that most people are in fact bisexual but refuse to acknowledge this fact to themselves and others.

If there is a common bisexual potential, how do bisexuals conceptualize this potential and how do they believe it is transformed into heterosexual or lesbian identities and behaviors? Patty described the bisexual potential as a "capacity to be sexual with both sexes," and Colleen "agree[s] with Freud—people are born 'polymorphous perverse.' " In other words, "people are born without a sexual orientation and are subsequently socialized mainly into heterosexuality."

Whereas Colleen argued that the transformation from polymorphous perversity to heterosexual predominance is accomplished by means of socialization, other bisexual respondents believe that heterosexuality and lesbianism result from individuals' lack of awareness of the full range of their sexual feelings, or from denial of these feelings. For example, Rosa argued that bisexuality would be more common if people would only allow themselves to experience all their feelings. She wrote, "It should be the preferred lifestyle of the majority of people who, eventually, come to understand both their masculine and feminine needs and natures." In this view, lesbianism and heterosexuality are lifestyles adopted by default or through ignorance.

In contrast, 5 bisexual respondents believe that individuals "choose" to "go one way or the other," to "lead a (lesbian) lifestyle," or to "commit" themselves to one lifestyle based on the sex of their current romantic partner. In other words, individuals might *be* bisexual or potentially bisexual, but they choose to *live* as either homosexuals or heterosexuals. Karolynn explained that this choice is based not on personal preferences, but on the politics of sexuality that make maintaining a bisexual identity in this society difficult,

> *That is probably what the majority of people potentially are but that, it's easier to deal with the politics, rules and roles of either choosing to live a straight life or a gay life, at least for longer blocks of time. (Karolynn)*

Tracy disagrees that the forces that pressure individuals to choose to live either a homosexual or heterosexual life are social. She believes that the necessity for a "choice" stems from the inherent conflicts present in bisexuality itself:

> *As a bisexual woman, I feel it is more difficult to live with than being straight or gay—leads to more confusion early in life when a person is personally establishing what their sexual identity is. Also, creates conflicts in relationships and is a distraction to be attracted to both sexes. I chose to lead a lesbian lifestyle . . . (Tracy)*

No matter what the explanation for the transformation of bisexual potential into lesbian or heterosexual identity and behavior, the result is a collective illusion that bisexuality is much less common than it really is. As Camille put it, bisexuality is "the norm" even though "the rest of the world both gay and straight doesn't admit it," but that's "their problem."

How do bisexual respondents who made extreme assertions of bisexual existence compare to lesbian respondents who made similar assertions about the universality or ubiquity of bisexuality? First of all, they are more numerous; whereas one out of three bisexual women believes that most or all people are bisexual, only one out of seven lesbians expressed the same idea.[2] The content of the opinions of bisexual and lesbian women who made this claim, however, are remarkably similar. Both bisexuals and lesbians explained the apparent scarcity of bisexuality by distinguishing between bisexual potential and heterosexual or lesbian identities and behaviors, providing many of the same explanations for the transformation from the one to the other. Members of both groups argued variously that individuals are socialized into heterosexuality, unaware of their own bisexuality, or pressured to commit themselves to either homosexuality or heterosexuality for social or political reasons. The only notable difference in the explanations offered by bisexual and lesbian respondents is that a number of lesbian respondents referred to an "ideal society" in which bisexuality would be more common or more politically acceptable. One bisexual woman suggested that someday in the future bisexuality might be more common, but not a single bisexual woman mentioned the concept of an ideal society. Instead, bisexual women focused on pointing out the aspects of our contemporary society that discourage bisexuality.

It is not surprising that bisexual women are more likely than lesbians to assert that most or all people are bisexual. On a practical level, bisexual women like any minority have an interest in maximizing their numbers, whereas lesbians have a converse interest in maximizing their own numbers—two processes that necessarily occur at each other's expense, given current concepts of sexuality. Ideologically, it is also advantageous to bisexuals to maximize the importance of bisexuality as an issue by emphasizing its prevalence. But the actual process by which individual bisexual women and lesbians arrive at their respective opinions probably has little to do with political self-preservation or promotion. It is probably a result of much subtler perceptual processes. As demonstrated in a separate study of lesbian and bisexual women's perceptions of the sexual orientations of hypothetical targets (Rust-Rodríguez 1989), bisexual women are more likely to perceive others as bisexual whereas lesbians are more likely to perceive others as lesbian. In other words, both lesbians and bisexual women tend to perceive other women as having the same sexual orientation as they themselves do. There are several possible reasons for this phenomenon, including a tendency to perceive sameness between the self and others, a tendency to fill information gaps with desirable rather than undesirable information, and the possibility that lesbian-identified and bisexual-identified women have different definitions of bisexuality. Whatever the explanation, the fact remains that bisexual women do in fact tend to perceive bisexuality where lesbians perceive lesbianism. The bisexual population thus appears to be larger to bisexual women than to lesbian women. In other words, bisexual women are more likely than lesbians to believe that most or all people are bisexual because that is in fact what they find to be the case on the basis of their own observations.

It is also not surprising that bisexual respondents, unlike lesbians, did not describe hypothetical ideal societies in which bisexuality would be more common. As I showed in chapter 6, lesbians belong to a historical tradition in which heterosexuality—especially heterosexual behavior—is anti-feminist. In order to reconcile the early gay liberationist goal of the elimination of gender with the lesbian feminism moral imperative to be a lesbian, lesbians constructed the concept of a post-revolutionary utopia in which people would be able to relate to each other without regard to gender, but which had not yet arrived. The concept of the ideal society is, therefore, an important element in lesbian feminist ideology. Bisexuals, on the other hand, believe that bisexuality exists in the current society and they find it acceptable here and now;

they have no need to hypothesize an ideal society in which such would be the case. In other words, they have no motivation to adopt the concept of an ideal society as part of their political ideologies and, according to the findings of this study, they have not done so.

WHAT IS BISEXUALITY? OR, WHY IS EVERYONE STANDING UP?

There are probably as many definitions of bisexuality among bisexual women as there are bisexual women; there is clearly no consensus either on what bisexuality is, or on who is bisexual. Some bisexuals define bisexuality in terms of actual sexual behavior or as a potential for actual sexual behavior, whereas others define it in terms of emotional or sexual feelings of attraction. Many define it as a gender blind form of sexuality. But no matter which criterion is used, bisexual women are faced with the same question that confronts lesbians—in a world in which people do not conform to ideal types, where do we draw the line between bisexuality and lesbianism? Bisexual respondents' comments in response to the question, "What is your opinion of bisexuality?" suggest that bisexuals favor different definitions and generally define bisexuality more broadly than lesbians do. Nevertheless, many of the comments made by bisexuals bear a striking resemblance to the comments made by lesbians.

Many bisexual respondents described bisexuality as a potential or as an essential quality that many people possess, but that only some people express through actual feelings of attraction or sexual behavior. According to this definition, people can *be*—and *are*—bisexual without ever experiencing an attraction to one sex or the other and without ever having sexual relations with one sex or the other. In contrast to lesbian respondents, most of whom define a bisexual as a person who feels attracted to or has sexual relations with both sexes, very few bisexual women define bisexuals as people who necessarily have these actual emotional and physical experiences. The definition of bisexuality as a potential or essential quality is a broader definition that defines a much larger proportion of the population as bisexual than do definitions that depend upon actual experiences. It is this definition of bisexuality that underlies the belief in universal or almost universal bisexuality discussed above, and that accounts for the differences in lesbians' and bisexuals' estimates of the prevalence of bisexuality.

But some bisexual women do define bisexuality in terms of actual sexual behavior or sexual attraction. Comments made by these bisexual women are very similar to the comments made by lesbians. Compare, for example, the following quotes from a bisexual woman and a lesbian who both define bisexuality in terms of a desire for both homosex and heterosex,

> *Someone who is comfortable in relating to either sex in a sexual manner. (Corinne, Bisexual)*

> *Man or woman who likes both sexes and likes to engage in sexual intimacy with them. (Liz, lesbian)*

and this pair of quotes from respondents who define as bisexual only those people who have actually acted on their desires for both homosex and heterosex:

> *Someone who is attracted to both (sexes) and pursues it farther at some point. (Adrienne, Bisexual)*

> *Attraction to and physically and emotionally "acting" out the sexual preference simultaneously or at separate times. (Vashti, lesbian)*

Or, consider this pair of quotes from a bisexual woman, who calls herself bisexual because she is attracted to both women and men even though she lives a lesbian lifestyle, and a lesbian, who would agree that she is bisexual:

> *I feel that most people are bisexual to some degree whether they admit it to themselves or others or not . . . . I chose to lead a lesbian lifestyle . . . as my emotional attachments are closer to women. (Tracy, Bisexual)*

> *I define sexuality as on a continuum from attraction to same sex to opposite sex. However, society defines two cultures/gay and straight. Bisexuals (those who feel both attractions) usually choose one group for validation and support. (Riannon, lesbian)*

Both Tracy and Riannon conceptualize sexuality as a continuum of attractions in which people are more or less attracted to the same or the other sex, or, as Tracy put it, more or less bisexual. Both also refer to people who are attracted to both women and men as bisexual, even if they are more attracted to one sex or the other and even if they are sexually active with only one sex. In other words, their definitions of bisexuality are nearly identical.

Some bisexual respondents bypass the issue of "degrees" of attraction to women and men by defining bisexuality as a humanistic, gender-blind way of relating to others. They see bisexuality as a way of loving the person, not their sex, or of being nondiscriminatory in their attractions to others. For example, Ludwiça wrote, "I feel as if I'm open to respond to the person, not just the gender." This way of conceptualizing bisexuality places bisexuality at the forefront of liberal thinking; it is an equal opportunity way of loving others. Evelyn draws a clear distinction between homosexuals and heterosexuals, who discriminate against people of one sex or the other, and bisexuals, who do not discriminate. To her, being bisexual means "I do not exclude who I choose to love, emotionally and/or sexually, by virtue of the person's sex."

Not surprisingly, this definition of bisexuality—and its implications regarding the moral superiority of bisexuality as a way of relating to others—is much more popular among bisexual respondents than among lesbian respondents. As noted in chapter 4, only 8% of lesbians described bisexuality as gender blind; in contrast, 28% of bisexual women described bisexuality as gender blind.[3] Although the number of bisexual women involved is too small to draw definitive conclusions, the percentage difference is great enough to suggest that there is a real difference in the way bisexuals and lesbians tend to view bisexuality.

But the relative popularity of the definition of bisexuality as gender blind among bisexuals as compared to lesbians should not be allowed to overshadow the fact that most bisexuals do not define bisexuality as gender blind. Most bisexual women ascribe to a basically dichotomous conceptualization of sexuality, in which bisexuality is a derivative form of sexuality composed of a combination of homosexuality and heterosexuality. This is true of bisexual women who define bisexuality in terms of actual attractions or behaviors as well as those who believe in a universal or nearly universal bisexual potential or essence. The former revealed their hybridized conception of bisexuality by referring to bisexuals as people who are attracted to *both* women and men, or who have sexual relations with *both* women and men. Recall, for example, Liz, who defined a bisexual as a person "who likes both sexes," and Rosa, who argued that bisexuality "should be the preferred lifestyle of the majority of people who, eventually, come to understand both their masculine and feminine needs and natures." Similarly, Shannon believes that "most, but certainly not all, people are bisexual to some degree, possibly because of genetic makeup, i.e., presence of male and female hormones in people." Rosa and Shannon not only conceptualize bisexuality as a hybrid sexuality, they also believe that it stems from a masculine/feminine duality inherent in most or all people, either in the form of hybridized gender in the case of Rosa or in the form of hybridized biological sex in the case of Shannon.

The latter typically described bisexuality as a potential to go "either way," as if the bisexual potential were a combination of homosexual and heterosexual potential, either or both of which might be realized at any given point in a person's life:

> I believe that most people are inherently bisexual and that loving relationships with both sexes lead to freer emotional expression. At the same time, I also believe that it is virtually impossible to have deep, loving relationships with more than one person at a time (of any sex) and that at any point in time a bisexual must make a commitment to one or the other sexual orientation depending on the person they are with. (Roberta, Bisexual)

Roberta's choice of words—"a commitment to one or the other *sexual orientation*"—is revealing. For Roberta, making a monogamous commitment to a particular person is synonymous to making a commitment to *be* either heterosexual or lesbian; one's relationship becomes one's essence. People might have a bisexual potential, but their sexual orientation depends on the gender of the person to whom they are currently committed. In contrast, Cheryl defines the potential itself as bisexuality; people who are bisexual are bisexual regardless of the gender of the person to whom they currently happen to be committed:

> I define bisexuality as the ability to be deeply involved emotionally and sexually with both men and women. This doesn't preclude being in a monogamous relationship. More people are probably bisexual than homosexual. (Cheryl, Bisexual)

Despite their disagreement over the question of whether bisexuality is a potential or an expression of that potential, Roberta and Cheryl both conceptualize bisexuality as a hybrid form of sexuality. They share this conceptualization with 65% of the bisexual women in this study.

BISEXUALS' IMAGES AND FEELINGS
ABOUT THEMSELVES

How do bisexuals perceive themselves as a group? How do they feel
about themselves? Within the lesbian community, they are portrayed as
traitors, cowards, and opportunists. Most lesbians prefer to avoid them
as friends and refuse to date them. How do bisexuals respond to these
accusations and rejections? At the very least, one might expect that
bisexual women would use the question "What is your opinion of
bisexuality?" as an opportunity to defend themselves against some of
the charges made against them by lesbians. In fact, bisexuals had surprisingly little to say about their images and feelings about bisexuality—
despite the fact that this is exactly what the question asked for. Most
lesbians raised these issues; one in two bisexuals did not. Bisexuals'
silence suggests strongly that bisexuals have little to say on these topics,
i.e., they have few images of bisexuality and no strong feelings about
bisexuals as a group.

Positive Images

Among the 22 bisexuals who did paint images of bisexuality in answer
to the question, "What is your opinion of bisexuality?" positive images
are more common than negative images. Eight bisexual women described bisexuality simply as "natural" or "healthy." For example, Lisa
thinks "that bisexuality indicates a 'healthy' awareness of oneself . . .
An integration of personality." Eight other bisexual women described
bisexuality as a more "open" form of sexuality. For example, Marilyn
described bisexuality as "an openness to possibilities, to potentials," and
Gloria feels that bisexuality is "an ideal state of being—open to all
encounters and developments." Shirley and Muriel argued that bisexuality "gives the widest possible options," and Dana described bisexuality
as "a greater expansion into loving the being of a person and not only
the sex of the person." Similarly, Jameelah believes that it is a "more
universal way of thinking about/being sexual(ly oriented)," Cathy said
that being bisexual "makes me feel accepting, freer," and Michelle finds
bisexuality "liberating." Healthiness/naturalness and openness were the

only two positive images of bisexuality mentioned by more than one bisexual respondent.

Unflattering and Existentially Invalidating Images

Although negative images are less common among bisexual respondents than positive images, they are more varied and detailed. In fact, most of the many unflattering and existentially invalidating images of bisexuality found to be prevalent among lesbians were echoed by at least one bisexual respondent.[4] The most commonly mentioned was "confusion." The 5 bisexuals who mentioned confusion made comments similar to the comments made by lesbians. For example, lesbian respondent Naomi believes that people who think they are bisexual are really just confused,

> I don't believe it exists. People who believe they are bisexuals are in a state of confusion. (Naomi)

and bisexual respondent Evelyn agrees that this is true of some bisexuals, although she allows that bisexuality does exist and that some people are truly bisexual, not confused:

> I think some women consider themselves bisexual who really aren't, but have confusion and problems ... I endorse it if it is honest. (Evelyn)

Lesbian respondent Yvette sees a different relationship between bisexuality and confusion. She sees confusion as an inherent aspect of bisexuality; in other words, she believes not that people call themselves bisexual because they are confused, but that bisexual people must be confused because they are bisexual. To her, bisexuality "seems like it would be a confusing life." This image of bisexuality was echoed by bisexual respondents Cathy, Harriet, and Tracy, who said that they find it confusing themselves, at least sometimes. Many lesbians believe that this confusion stems from the internal struggle that occurs between bisexuals' homosexual and heterosexual feelings, and bisexual respondent Sylvia agreed. She feels that being bisexual "causes a great struggle of emotions within."

Bisexual respondent Gloria reflected lesbians' accusations that bisexuals have difficulty making commitments to other people. She feels that "unfortunately, [bisexuality] can be used not to make a commitment." Similarly, Charlotte agrees with the many lesbians who believe that bisexuals are promiscuous or, at least, nonmonogamous; she wrote, "it is impossible to be a practicing bisexual and retain fidelity to your partners." Although Charlotte seems to avoid the charge that bisexuals per se are infidelitous by using the modifier "practicing," in truth she is implicating all bisexuals. By "practicing bisexual," Charlotte means someone who is sexually involved with a man and a woman at the same time. For her, as for most other bisexual women and most lesbians, bisexuality is a combination of homosexuality and heterosexuality. The expression of bisexuality therefore necessarily means that one has more than one lover; whereas heterosexuals and lesbians can express their sexualities in a monogamous context, bisexuals cannot express their sexuality and simultaneously be monogamous.

Finally, two bisexual women echoed lesbians' charge that bisexual women "cop out" by refusing to acknowledge their lesbianism in order to avoid stigma. Again, their comments sound just like the comments made by lesbians. For example, one of the two bisexual women wrote that bisexuality is "okay as long as that's where you really are—and you're not just avoiding homosexuality," a comment that is very similar to the comments made by lesbians like Nel, "Some people hide behind this label because it's more acceptable than being gay."

The fact that only two bisexual respondents referred to bisexuality as a way to avoid the stigma of lesbianism in answer to the question "What is your opinion of bisexuality?" does not accurately reflect the prevalence of this attitude among bisexual women. Bisexual respondents' answers to closed-ended questions that asked specifically about this issue indicate that this image is fairly popular among bisexual women. Half (51%) of bisexual women agreed with the statement "Society makes it difficult to be a lesbian, so some women claim to be bisexual when they are really lesbians who are afraid to admit it" (table 7.1). Although this is a substantial percentage, by itself it does not indicate that bisexuals perceive bisexual identity to be more likely than any other identity to be a façade. When bisexuals were asked to respond to a similar statement about lesbians, "Some lesbians really are somewhat attracted to men, but they are afraid to express these feelings because other lesbians would not approve of them," three-quarters (73%) agreed; in other words, bisexuals were more likely to state that lesbians deny their bisexuality than that bisexuals deny their lesbianism. So far, it appears that bisexuals evaluate themselves favorably in comparison to lesbians. But the arithmetic difference between individual bisexual respondents' answers to these questions reveals that, on an individual basis, one in four bisexual women believes that denial is more common among women who say they are bisexual than among women who say they are lesbian (figure 7.1). In other words, one in four bisexual respondents is more suspicious of other women's bisexual identities than of other women's lesbian identities. Although this is a minority, it is a substantial minority, especially when we consider that the attitude being measured calls into question the legitimacy of bisexual identity. The point merits emphasis; one in four women who *call themselves bisexual* accords *less* legitimacy to bisexual identity than she does to lesbian identity.

Findings pertaining to the belief that bisexuality is a transitional identity through which some women pass before they come out as lesbians are even more dramatic. Even though no bisexual respondents characterized bisexual identity as transitional in answer to the question "What is your opinion of bisexuality?" their answers to closed-ended questions confirm that many do think of it as such. Three quarters of bisexual women agreed that a "few" or "less than half" of "Women who say they are bisexual will eventually realize that they are lesbians" (table 7.2). On the basis of this figure alone it would seem that bisexuals merely acknowledge the possibility that some bisexual women will come out as lesbians while minimizing the proportion of bisexual women who will do so. But subtracting bisexuals' responses to that statement from their responses to the statement, "Some women who claim to be lesbians will eventually find out that they actually are bisexual, or straight," reveals that 44% of bisexual respondents believe that lesbians are even less likely to come out as bisexual or straight than bisexuals are to come out as lesbians (figure 7.2). In other words, two out of five bisexual respondents believe that bisexual identity is more likely to be transitional than lesbian identity or, conversely, that lesbian identity is more likely to be a "mature" identity representing one's final destination in the process of coming out. Again, 44% is a minority—the other 56% of bisexuals apparently do not believe that bisexual identity is more likely to be transitional—but when we consider that these bisexual-identified women believe that women who call themselves bisexual generally have less insight and knowledge of their own sexuality than women who call themselves lesbians, this 44% minority seems very large indeed. Apparently, despite the fact that no bisexual respondents spontaneously described bisexuality as a transitional identity, almost half of them see it as such.

Amid all of the bisexuals who echoed the negative images of bisexuality expressed by lesbians, only one bisexual specifically disagreed with any of these negative images; Cheryl pointed out that bisexuality does not preclude nonmonogamy. The facts that bisexual women expressed so many of the same unflattering and existentially invalidating attitudes about bisexuality that lesbians did and that only one bisexual raised her voice in protest suggests that many bisexual women have accepted lesbians' views of bisexuality.

Political Images

Very few bisexual women wrote about bisexuality in political terms, either positively or negatively. Unlike lesbians, no bisexual women ranted about heterosexual privilege, described bisexuals as political fence-sitters or opportunists, or accused bisexuals of lacking political commitment to sexual liberation. One bisexual woman described bisexuality as apolitical, in contrast to lesbianism, which implies a political commitment to women:

> although I consider myself "bisexual," I feel that (given the power relations between men/women and straights/gays/lesbians) bisexuality is an "easy apolitical out" for many people. (Colleen)

The fact that most bisexual women did not even discuss bisexuality in political terms suggests that Colleen is not alone in perceiving bisexuality as apolitical. Apparently, the majority of bisexual women do not perceive bisexuality as a political lifestyle, or bisexual identity as a political identity.

Bisexual respondents' answers to closed-ended questions confirm that most of them perceive bisexuals as less political and less politically worthy than lesbians. When bisexuals were asked to agree or disagree with the statements, "Bisexuals are not as committed to other women as lesbians are; they are more likely to desert their female friends," and "It can be dangerous for lesbians to trust bisexuals too much, because when

the going really gets rough, they are not as likely to stick around and
fight it out," the majority of bisexual respondents disagreed with each
statement (figure 7.3). This is not surprising; both of these statements
make explicit comparisons between bisexual and lesbian women that are
clearly unflattering to bisexuals. What is surprising is that a sizable
minority of bisexuals actually *agreed* with each statement; one out of
nine agreed that bisexuals are less committed than lesbians, and one out
of four agreed that lesbians can't trust bisexuals to stick around when
the going gets rough. In both cases, the extent and the strength of
bisexuals' agreement does not match that found among lesbians, but
the fact that any agreement was found among bisexuals at all is very
telling.

Even more revealing is the fact that a few bisexual women's attempts
to defend themselves against the charge of disloyalty actually demonstrate the depth to which they have internalized doubts about their
political worthiness. For example, Adrienne defines a bisexual woman
as "[s]omeone who identifies with women spiritually, collectively, emotionally, physically, etc. but still maintains a relationship with a man
or pursues them." This defense of bisexual women's political loyalty
incorporates the premise of the accusation that bisexuals lack loyalty by
implying that it is the lesbian component of bisexuality, not bisexuality
per se, that is the source of bisexuals' political worthiness.

If so many bisexual women are willing to agree with statements that
clearly denigrate bisexuals' political loyalties in direct comparison to
lesbians, how many bisexuals have more subtle negative political attitudes about bisexuals as a group? In addition to the statements that
made direct comparisons between bisexuals and lesbians, bisexuals were
asked to respond to paired statements that made indirect comparisons
between bisexual and lesbian women. Bisexuals' responses to these statements show that, when asked to describe bisexual and lesbian women
separately, an even larger proportion of bisexual women described bisexuals as less political and less politically worthy than lesbians.

For example, when asked how easy or difficult it is for bisexual
women to pass as heterosexual, 64% said it was slightly to very easy,
but when they were asked how easy or difficult it is for lesbians to pass,
only 32% said it was easy (table 7.3). Taking the difference between
respondents' answers to these questions reveals that *three-quarters*
(73%) of bisexual women believe that it is easier for bisexuals to pass

than for lesbians to pass (figure 7.4). When asked to estimate the percentages of bisexual and of lesbian women who would want to pass (table 7.4), 54% gave higher estimates for bisexuals than for lesbians (figure 7.5). In other words, most bisexual women believe that bisexuals are more able and willing to pass as heterosexual than lesbians are. In both cases, these figures are only 10% less than the comparable figures for lesbians; despite the fact that these beliefs are politically detrimental to bisexual women vis-à-vis lesbians, bisexual women are nearly as likely to hold them as lesbians are.

If bisexuals agree with lesbians that they are more able and willing to pass as heterosexual, do they also agree that they are better able to avoid heterosexist prejudice and discrimination than lesbians are? Yes, many do. When asked to rate the degree of prejudice experienced by bisexuals and by lesbians, half of bisexual respondents rated the two groups equally (table 7.5, figure 7.6). But the other 47% said that lesbians experience more prejudice than bisexuals. Similarly, 57% rated discrimination against bisexuals and discrimination against lesbians as equal in severity, but 40% said that lesbians experience more discrimination than bisexuals. In other words, nearly half of bisexual respondents believe that they are less oppressed than lesbians; a belief they share with 80% of lesbian respondents.

Bisexual respondents were also asked whom they believe is responsible for the oppression of women, lesbians, and bisexuals. Fifty percent replied that the forces that oppress bisexuals are identical to either the forces that oppress lesbians or the forces that oppress women; they saw no difference between their experiences of oppression as bisexuals and the experiences of either women in general or lesbians. Among the other 50%, a few said that bisexuals' oppression is less intense but qualitatively identical to lesbians' oppression, and several said that bisexuals' oppression is identical to lesbians' except that bisexuals are also oppressed by lesbians and heterosexuals who do not understand bisexuality and pressure bisexuals to choose a side. Complaints about the treatment of bisexuals by both gays/lesbians and heterosexuals also arose in 7 bisexuals' answers to the question "What is your opinion of bisexuality?" For example, Cathy said, "at times I feel judged by both sides," and Evelyn said, "I get really tired of people telling me I don't exist." Except for this last point, bisexuals' comments about the forces that oppress them indicate that bisexuals generally do not perceive themselves as being oppressed as bisexuals per se. Instead, they perceive themselves as being oppressed for their gender or their "lesbianism." But the few bisexuals who mentioned lack of understanding or pressure from lesbians/gays and heterosexuals have identified a uniquely bisexual form of oppression and in so doing they have begun to perceive themselves as oppressed for their *bisexuality*.

The fact that some bisexuals identified a uniquely bisexual form of oppression is an indication that a political view of bisexuality is beginning to develop among some bisexuals. Also, the fact that several bisexuals perceived lesbians as oppressors suggests that they are beginning to see a qualitative difference between their interests as bisexuals and the interests of lesbians. The first step toward politicization of a minority group is the recognition of collective oppression and a collective oppressor. Although none of the seven bisexual women who complained spontaneously about lesbians' lack of acceptance put their complaints in political terms, they had taken the first step toward the politicization of their bisexual identities by recognizing both a form of collective bisexual oppression and a collective oppressor.

But four other bisexual women did describe bisexuality in rudimentary political terms. For example, Jameelah commented that bisexuality is "a difficult position to take politically," and Michelle described bisexuality as "politically incorrect." Neither of these women explained what they meant by "politically," but their use of the word suggests that they have begun to think of their bisexuality in political terms, if only because straights' and gays' motivations for rejecting bisexuals are political and not because bisexuality per se is political. Finally, one bisexual woman wrote about bisexuality in unmistakably political terms by locating the source of bisexual oppression in social structural power dynamics and thereby providing the only truly political characterization of bisexuality found among the nearly four dozen bisexual-identified women in this study:

> *It's the norm, but white male culture forces our thinking into either/or patterns. I believe most people are truly bisexual, but it's hard to express it when everyone expects you to choose one sex or the other. (Beverly)*

Social and Political Preferences—Images Translate into Feelings

Lesbians' negative and apolitical images of bisexual women translate into a preference to avoid bisexual women socially and politically. If bisexual women generally share lesbians' images of bisexuality, do they also share lesbians' preference to associate with lesbians instead of bisexual women? Again, the answer is yes; a surprising number of bisexual-identified women prefer to associate with lesbians instead of other bisexuals.

No bisexual women expressed an aversion to associating with other bisexual women in answer to the question "What is your opinion of bisexuality?" but when they were asked closed-ended questions about their social and political preferences about one-quarter consistently expressed a preference for lesbians over other bisexual women (figures 7.7, 7.8). On average, bisexuals' preferences are neither as strong nor as pervasive as lesbians' preferences, but the fact that such a large percentage of bisexual women prefer lesbians at all is remarkable. Like lesbians, bisexuals' social preferences are strongest in the most intimate social situation of all—dating. Fully one-third of bisexual women said that they would prefer to date a lesbian than to date another bisexual woman. In fact, one in five bisexual women placed themselves at the extreme end of the preference scale, thereby describing their aversion to dating other bisexual women in the strongest terms possible. Another third do not care whether their dates are lesbian or bisexual, and the last third prefer to date bisexual women. Bisexuals are only slightly less likely to care whether their friends are lesbian or bisexual. One out of two bisexuals would be equally likely to make friends with another woman regardless of whether she were lesbian or bisexual, but 29% prefer to have lesbian friends. Previous researchers have found that in the laboratory people can be induced to prefer members of their own groups by simply naming the groups and placing people in them, even if the groups are fictitious and the assignments random or based on trivial characteristics (e.g., Allen and Wilder 1975; Billig and Tajfel 1973). In light of the ease with which researchers can create in-group preferences in the laboratory, the significance of the finding that some bisexual women prefer bisexuals over lesbians pales in comparison to the finding that so many bisexuals prefer to associate with lesbians, not bisexual women. Unfortunately, it might be difficult for bisexual women to find lesbians to date or befriend, given most lesbians' strong antipathy toward associating with bisexual women.

In large group situations, bisexuals' preferences shift slightly toward other bisexual women. Two out of five bisexuals said that they are more comfortable among bisexuals than among lesbians and that they would prefer to belong to a bisexual discussion group than to a lesbian discussion group, and the majority of the other three-fifths expressed no preference either way. Conceivably, this is because bisexuals fear lesbians' disapproval more in larger groups. In intimate situations, social bonds are close and presumably each person in a dyad belongs to the dyad out of choice; any lesbian who would knowingly date or be friends with a bisexual woman has apparently chosen to do so. In larger groups, however, each individual does not necessarily approve of every other group member; hence, in larger groups a bisexual woman is more likely to encounter lesbians who would not choose to associate with bisexuals. Moreover, when a bisexual is in an intimate relationship with one lesbian, each woman has an equal opportunity to contribute to their collective understanding of the relationship. In a larger group dominated by lesbians, the bisexual woman might feel outnumbered and unable to offset the general anti-bisexual atmosphere.

Bisexuals' preferences in political situations resemble their preferences in social situations. Approximately one in two bisexuals would trust other bisexuals in positions of political leadership at least as much as she would trust lesbians. But one in four would rather work with a lesbian than with a bisexual on a gay rights campaign, and one in four would rather be represented by a lesbian than a bisexual lobbyist. The only political situation in which bisexuals were more likely to express a greater degree of trust toward bisexual women (42%) than toward lesbians (13%) was giving a speech to a local citizen's group about alternative lifestyles. Perhaps, because the question about the speech asked respondents whom they would prefer to replace them personally— as opposed to representing them as members of a larger interest group— they thought it appropriate to choose someone similar to themselves. Or perhaps, under the assumption that the local citizen's group would be predominantly heterosexual, bisexual women might feel that a bisexual speaker would be able to relate to the audience better than a lesbian.

The Impact of Bisexual Women's Personal Politics and Experiences on Their Attitudes toward Bisexuality

Race, Education, Class, and Other Demographic Differences

There is no evidence that bisexual women of different races, classes, income levels, or education levels have different definitions of bisexuality or different thoughts and feelings about bisexuality. Given the relatively small number of bisexual women in this study, this finding is only tentative; however, there is no indication that a larger sample of bisexual women would have produced different results.

There is some evidence, however, of generational differences in bisexual women's attitudes. Women who have been out as bisexuals for longer periods of time are more likely to agree with lesbians that lesbians shouldn't trust bisexual women. No bisexual women who came out as bisexual less than three years prior to the study agreed that bisexuals are untrustworthy, whereas 29% of those who had been out as bisexual for three or more years and 40% of those who had been out as bisexual for eleven or more years agreed with this sentiment ($r = .31$, $p = .05$). It is fairly unlikely that bisexual women actually become more receptive to lesbians' negative opinions about bisexuals the longer they have been out as bisexuals; a more plausible explanation for this finding is that women who came out as bisexual during the heyday of lesbian feminism in the 1970s were more thoroughly exposed to negative opinions about bisexuality than bisexuals who have come out more recently after the advent of queer politics.

Political Differences: Do Political Bisexuals Speak for Anyone?

There are few political sentiments among bisexuals at all, let alone any that are related to their attitudes toward bisexuality. When they were asked to list the social and political issues about which they were concerned, bisexuals demonstrated more interest in general women's and gay issues than in issues pertaining specifically to their own orientation.

Seventy-seven percent listed women's or feminist issues and 49% listed gay issues, but only five respondents mentioned lesbian issues and none mentioned bisexual issues. Asked how strong a sense of belonging they feel toward women as a group, most (60%) expressed a very strong sense of belonging, whereas only 14% reported a comparable sense of belonging toward bisexuals as a group. Bisexuals' feelings of belonging contrast sharply with lesbians', who reported feeling more strongly attached to lesbians in particular (41%) than to women in general (30%). Bisexuals make less distinction between lesbians' political interests and bisexuals' political interests than lesbians do; 71% of bisexuals feel that lesbians' and bisexuals' interests are the "same" or "slightly different," compared to 43% of lesbians. Again, the findings indicate that bisexual women derive their politics from their status as women or by equating their interests with lesbian interests, not from their status as bisexuals. Given the lack of political concern about bisexuality among bisexuals, it is not surprising that these largely nonexistent political attitudes are unrelated to bisexuals' attitudes about bisexuality.

Personal Experiences

The bisexual women who participated in this study have had a variety of different personal experiences. Every one has had at least one heterosexual relationship, 40% have been married to a man, 40% have been involved in nonmarital heterosexual relationships that they described as "serious," and the other 20% have been involved in more casual relationships with men. At the time of the study, 42% were involved in relationships with men and 53% were involved in relationships with women, ranging from dating to marriages and unions. One-quarter have children. Most (84%) have identified themselves as lesbians at some time in their lives; 64% have switched between lesbian and bisexual identities two or more times. Their feelings of attraction range from 10% to 80% heterosexual—none are exclusively attracted to only one sex. The majority (64%) are predominantly attracted to women, and only 16% described themselves as equally attracted to both sexes.

I showed in chapter 5 that lesbians' attitudes toward bisexual women are related to their experiences of their own sexuality. In particular, lesbians who have previously identified themselves as bisexual or who feel attracted to men are less adamant about avoiding association with bisexual women than are lesbians whose past and current experiences are more "purely" lesbian. One might expect that bisexual women's feelings about associating with lesbians would similarly reflect their own personal experiences with heterosexuality, lesbian identity, and feelings of sexual attraction. For example, one might expect that bisexual women who have a history of lesbian identification would be more inclined to associate with lesbians than bisexual women who have never considered themselves lesbians would, either because they feel a kinship to a community of women with whom they once shared an identity or because they adopted lesbians' biases while they were lesbians themselves.

The findings of this study indicate that no aspects of bisexuals' identity histories or past heterosexual experiences are related to their feelings about bisexual women vis-à-vis lesbians.[5] However, bisexuals' *current* heterosexual relationships and feelings are related to their social and political preferences. In other words, the degree to which bisexual women trust each other and want to socialize with each other depends on the genders of the people to whom they are currently attracted or with whom they are currently romantically involved.

The stronger a bisexual woman's feelings of heterosexual attraction are, the less she is willing to associate with lesbians and the more she prefers to associate with other bisexual women instead (figure 7.9). In intimate social situations, bisexuals' preferences mirror their feelings of attraction; on average, those whose feelings are predominantly heterosexual prefer to date and make friends with bisexuals, those who are equally attracted toward women and men do not care whether their dates and friends are lesbian or bisexual, and those whose feelings are predominantly homosexual prefer to date and make friends with lesbians. In larger group situations, those whose feelings are as little as 30% heterosexual are more comfortable among bisexuals than lesbians, but those with only 10 to 20% heterosexual feelings still prefer to be among lesbians.[6] Presumably, bisexual women with strong heterosexual feelings prefer to associate with other bisexual women because they would not be able to express or discuss their heterosexual (or *bi*sexual) feelings as easily with lesbians, who might dismiss them as remnants of heterosexual socialization. Other bisexual women would be more likely to validate all of their sexual desires because they share the experience of being attracted to both women and men. But if other bisexuals share both their attractions to women and their attractions to men, why then would any bisexuals—even those whose feelings are predominantly homosexual—prefer to associate with lesbians?

The relationship between the gender of bisexuals' current romantic partners and their social and political preferences raises the same question because bisexual women who are in relationships with other women prefer to associate with lesbians, whereas bisexual women who are in relationships with men prefer to associate with bisexuals (figure 7.10). This is true in a variety of social and political contexts, though bisexuals' preferences are stronger in some contexts than others. For example, bisexual women who are involved with women are, on average, just as comfortable among lesbians as they are among bisexual women, but if their relationship is serious they prefer to discuss it with lesbians.[7] In contrast, bisexual women who are not involved with women are more comfortable and more willing to discuss their romantic lives with bisexual women than with lesbians, especially if they are dating or involved with a man. Those who are involved with both women and men simultaneously prefer to discuss their romantic lives with other bisexuals.[8] Bisexuals' preferences for friends follow a similar pattern. Bisexual women who are involved with women prefer to have lesbian rather than bisexual friends—even if they are simultaneously involved with men— whereas those who are involved with men only prefer to have bisexual friends.

Bisexuals' dating preferences do not show as marked a relationship to the genders of their partners as their preferences in less intimate social situations do; although the pattern is similar, it is not statistically significant. This might be because the question about dating was prefaced with the contingency phrase, "If you were not involved in a relationship now, ... " Therefore, respondents who are in relationships would have imagined what their preferences would be if they were single; i.e., in the absence of their current partner. It is, therefore, not surprising to find that the gender of their partners is more weakly related to the preferences bisexuals expressed in answer to this question than to the preferences they expressed in answer to other questions.

Bisexuals' political preferences show the same pattern as their social preferences. On average, bisexuals who are in serious relationships with women prefer to work with lesbians and be represented by lesbian lobbyists in the struggle for "gay rights." Those who are involved with both women and men simultaneously, whose relationships with women are only casual, or who are not romantically involved with anyone would be equally happy to trust their political fate to a bisexual woman as to a lesbian. Only those who are involved exclusively with men have more political confidence in bisexual women than in lesbians. When the situation in question is giving a speech to a local citizen's group, however, bisexuals' political confidence in each other increases. Unlike rights campaigning or lobbying, giving a speech is not an overtly political situation, and I hypothesized above that bisexuals are more willing to trust their peers in this situation either because the speaker being replaced (the respondent herself) is bisexual anyway, or because they reason that a largely heterosexual audience would be able to relate better to a bisexual speaker than to a lesbian speaker. Bisexuals who are involved with women partners only are, on average, just as willing to send a lesbian as another bisexual woman in their place, but bisexuals who are not involved with anyone, who are involved with men only, or who are involved with both women and men simultaneously prefer to be replaced by another bisexual.

Political trust is often based on the perception of a shared oppression. Given the relationship between bisexuals' political preferences and the genders of their current romantic partners, it is not surprising that bisexuals' perceptions of the severity of prejudice against bisexuals also depend on whether they are in relationships with women or with men (figure 7.11). Bisexuals who are involved with both women and men believe that lesbians experience substantially more prejudice than bisexual women do, whereas bisexuals who are involved exclusively with men or not involved with anyone believe that bisexuals experience almost as much prejudice as lesbians.

These findings suggest that bisexuals' perceptions of their social needs and political interests flow out of the nature of their current relationships.[9] If they are involved with women, then they perceive their social needs and political interests as being more like lesbians' than like bisexuals'. This might appear reasonable on the surface, since a bisexual woman who is involved with another woman shares the social and legal problems of lesbians. But, everything else equal, this fact would justify an *equal* willingness to associate with lesbians or with bisexuals; it does not explain a *preference for lesbians*. Apparently, everything else is not equal. Bisexuals who are in relationships with women, even though they continue to call themselves bisexual, obviously feel they have more in common with lesbians on the basis of their relationship status than they have in common with bisexuals on the basis of their sexual orientation or sexual identity. Bisexual identity can withstand changes in one's relationships; a woman can call herself bisexual whether she is involved with a woman, a man, both women and men, or no one at all. But this bisexual identity does not form a bond with other bisexuals that is strong enough to withstand the same changes in relationships. The bisexual women who participated in this study apparently do not feel a sense of social connection or political trust with other bisexuals on the basis of shared bisexual identity. They do not perceive themselves as having social needs or political interests that stem from their bisexuality and that are capable of surviving changes in their romantic involvements; that is, they do not perceive themselves as having *bisexual* social needs or political interests.

SUMMARY

The two most striking findings about bisexual women's attitudes about bisexuality are the extent to which they resemble lesbians' attitudes and the extent to which they reflect an apolitical view of bisexuality in which bisexuals lack unique political interests. Bisexual women, as marginal members of the lesbian community, are exposed to lesbians' attitudes and have apparently adopted many of them as their own in spite of their unflattering nature. Given this fact, it would be easy to blame lesbians for oppressing bisexual women. We have to keep in mind, however, that the lesbian ideologies that give negative definitions and political meanings to bisexuality are ideologies that arose out of lesbians' own attempts to give positive definitions and political meanings to lesbianism. Lesbians, as well as bisexuals, live in a culture in which sexuality is conceptualized dichotomously, and lesbian ideologies developed to speak to lesbians' needs within that culture. These lesbian ideologies have had oppressive consequences for bisexuals, but the heterosexist ideologies they challenge are no less oppressive to bisexuals. The fact that this book is concerned with lesbians' attitudes toward bisexuals, and not with the possibly more antagonistic attitudes of the larger heterosexist society, reflects not lesbians' greater blame in the oppression of bisexuals, but their closer cultural relationship with bisexuals and their greater potential as political allies.

The resemblance between bisexuals' and lesbians' attitudes about bisexuality is evident in bisexuals' images of bisexuality and feelings about other bisexuals as well as their definitions of bisexuality. For example, a substantial minority of bisexuals expressed the same variety of detailed negative images of bisexuality as lesbians did in answer to the question "What is your opinion of bisexuality?" The fact that negative attitudes exist at all among bisexuals is remarkable and shows the extent to which bisexual women's images of themselves have been shaped by lesbian feminist discourse. Moreover, the minority of bisexuals who spontaneously expressed these negative attitudes might in fact represent a much larger proportion of bisexual respondents who hold these attitudes but did not happen to express them; findings from a few closed-ended questions suggest that particular negative attitudes are in fact much more widespread among bisexuals than their spontaneous comments indicate, and there is no reason not to expect that the same is true of other negative attitudes. Also striking is the fact that among those bisexuals who did not express the same negative attitudes as lesbians, few bothered to attempt to refute lesbians' negative images of bisexuality. Positive images of bisexuality are actually more common than negative ones among bisexuals, but they are much less varied and refined, suggesting that they represent only the beginnings of the development of a more positive view of bisexuality among bisexuals.

Bisexuals' negative images of bisexuality are reflected in their feelings about associating with other bisexuals. A substantial proportion of bisexual women actually prefer to associate with lesbians instead of other bisexual women in social situations, and have greater political trust in lesbians than they do in other bisexual women. Given the ease with which in-group preferences are induced among strangers in the laboratory, this finding points to the depth of bisexuals' self-denigration. Many believe, as lesbians do, that they and other bisexuals are less faithful as lovers, less desirable as friends, and less trustworthy as compatriots in the battle for sexual liberation. The value bisexuals place on their social and political relationships with other bisexuals reflects the value they place on themselves, which is almost as low as the value given them by the majority of lesbians, who shun them.

Bisexuals' definitions of bisexuality also closely resemble lesbians'. The majority of bisexual women, like the majority of lesbians, define bisexuality in terms of behaviors or attractions and conceptualize bisexuality as a hybrid combination of homosexuality and heterosexuality. This does not negate the fact that bisexuals are more likely than lesbians to define bisexuality as gender blindness, but the fact remains that even among bisexuals this is a minority position. Bisexual women are also more likely than lesbians to make extreme claims about bisexual existence, but again this is a minority position even among bisexuals and those who took it gave many of the same explanations lesbians did for the transformation of bisexual potential into heterosexual and lesbian realities.

Perhaps the most surprising findings are that some bisexual women actually doubt whether bisexuality exists at all, and that several bisexual women are more skeptical of women who call themselves bisexual than they are of women who call themselves lesbian. Given the fact that they call themselves bisexual, these attitudes have serious consequences for their own self-images and reflect the powerful influence lesbian arguments—and dichotomous constructions of sexuality in general—have had on bisexual women. The bisexual women who did assert the existence of bisexuality did so on the basis of their experience of a bisexual essence; an argument that undoubtedly reflects the basis for bisexuals' belief that bisexuality exists, but that fails to respond effectively to lesbians' charge that bisexuality is politically illegitimate.

Like lesbians, bisexuals generally view bisexuality as apolitical. Insofar as bisexuals perceive themselves as having political interests, they perceive these interests as stemming from their gender or their "lesbianism," not their bisexuality per se. Many believe that bisexuals are less politically trustworthy, most believe that bisexuals are more willing and able to pass as heterosexual, and about half believe that bisexuals experience less prejudice and discrimination than lesbians. In contrast to lesbians, who feel themselves more politically aligned with other lesbians in particular than with gays or women in general, bisexuals feel strongly aligned with women and make little distinction between lesbians' interests and their own interests as bisexuals. Bisexuals' lack of alignment with other bisexuals shows up in the fact that their preferences for social and political association are based not on their bisexual identity, but on the gender of their current romantic partners; if they are involved with a woman they prefer to associate with lesbians, and if they are involved with a man they prefer to associate with bisexuals. In short, the bisexual women in this study generally lack both a sense of commitment to bisexuals as a group and a sense of a uniquely bisexual politics.

There are, however, some seeds of a bisexual politics to be found in bisexuals' comments. For example, the claim that bisexuality is universal or ubiquitous has political implications because it effectively maximizes both the number of bisexual women and the importance of the issue of bisexuality to the population at large. Even if bisexuals make this claim for the simple reason that that is how they see the world based on their definition of bisexuality rather than for political purposes, the political implications remain. Another basis for a bisexual politics lies in the concept of bisexuality as a gender-blind form of sexuality. This concept defines bisexuality as qualitatively different from homosexuality and heterosexuality; not as a derivative form of sexuality, but as a form of sexuality in its own right. This definition provides the basis for an independent political analysis of bisexuality (Rust 1992a), and, with its implication that bisexuality is a morally superior form of sexuality because it is nondiscriminatory, it also provides the basis for a positive and political image of bisexuality. Finally, a few bisexuals indicated that they feel oppressed by both lesbians/gays and heterosexuals, thus identifying a uniquely bisexual form of oppression and an oppressor. Since the current study was done in the mid-1980s, these seeds have borne some fruit. In the last chapter, I will bring us up to date by examining the political arguments bisexuals made in the late 1980s and early 1990s, and the impact of these claims on lesbian politics.

8

ANOTHER REVOLUTION ON THE POLITICAL WHEEL: THE POLITICIZATION OF BISEXUALITY

Since the study described in this book was done in the mid 1980s, bisexuals have made great strides in the process of building a political movement of their own. In the space of a few years, a few isolated bisexual support groups and local resource centers—similar in purpose to the homophile groups of the 1950s that predated gay liberation— have been replaced by an international network of groups ranging from support groups to publishing collectives, archives, and political action groups. Bisexual political activists, once nearly nonexistent, now communicate with each other via electronic mail and conference calls, meet each other at national and international conferences, and elect delegates to represent different geographic regions in a national bisexual organization. In other words, bisexuals have rapidly built the structures and institutions that provide the supporting framework for a political movement. Needless to say, during these few years of rapid structural growth, there has been a great deal of heated discussion about what the ideology of this movement should be. Although, structurally, the bisexual movement already resembles an advanced political movement—largely because many bisexual activists are experienced veterans of the left, feminist, and lesbian movements who know how to build the framework of a movement—the ideological debates reflect the movement's infancy.

The ideological problems that bisexuals face are strikingly similar to the ideological problems lesbians in the feminist movement faced in the early 1970s. Like lesbians, the most important task facing bisexuals is politicizing an apolitical sexual identity, so that that identity can provide the basis for political claims-making. But the political arena in which bisexuals are faced with this task differs from the political arena in which lesbians politicized lesbianism in some important ways. When lesbians began to politicize lesbian identity, sexuality was considered a private, not a political, matter. Therefore, lesbians' first steps in the politicization of lesbianism were the politicization of sexuality and the simultaneous desexualization of lesbianism. They gave to lesbianism a politics that served lesbian interests and that constructed lesbians on one hand and heterosexual (feminists) on the other hand as sexual interest groups. Two decades later, bisexuals are faced with a political arena in which sexuality has already been politicized and these two interest groups have already found their voices and staked out their territories. Bisexuals' task, then, is to reconstruct the political arena. Bisexuals have to give new political meanings to sexuality that serve their interests as bisexuals, and they have to introduce themselves as an interest group with a voice.

The fact that bisexuals face a context in which sexuality is already politicized is reflected in the greater complexity of the political discourse within which bisexuals must make their voice heard. In the 1970s, lesbians struggled to legitimate themselves within two dominant political traditions, the feminist and the ethnic political traditions. Each tradition offered its own language of political legitimation; feminism offered a language of legitimation based on personal experience and choice whereas ethnic politics offered a language of legitimation based on essential being. To politicize lesbianism, lesbians developed their own political language, the language of lesbian feminism. Today, lesbian feminism—or, more broadly speaking, sexual identity politics—is a third established political tradition, and bisexuals must somehow make their voices heard not only in the languages of feminism and ethnicity, but in the language of sexual identity politics.

In many ways, the arguments bisexuals are using to politicize bisexuality resemble the arguments lesbians used to politicize lesbianism. However, because the context in which bisexuals face this task is different from the context lesbians faced in the 1970s, their arguments must be adapted to their own unique circumstances. Both the similarities and the differences can be illustrated by examining the current debate among bisexuals about the ideological underpinnings of the bisexual movement. The beginnings of this debate were found among the bisexual women who participated in the study described in this book; since then, the debate has exploded on the pages of bisexual publications and the computer screens of bisexual activists. Chapter 1 examined the treatment of bisexuality by the lesbian press; this chapter will bring us full circle by exploring the newly emerging bisexual press.

THE BISEXUAL PRESS: FORUM FOR THE DISCUSSION OF BISEXUAL IDENTITY, COMMUNITY, AND IDEOLOGY

In the late 1980s and early 1990s, dozens of bisexual organizations began publishing newsletters, and one organization, the Bay Area Bisexual Network (BABN), began publishing a magazine called *Anything That Moves: Beyond the Myths of Bisexuality*. The number and technical sophistication of bisexual publications is still substantially less than that offered by the lesbian and gay press, but these publications already constitute an identifiable bisexual press that provides a forum for the discussion of bisexual political ideology and a vehicle for the creation of a bisexual identity, community, and politic.

Until recently, however, page space in bisexual newsletters was not devoted to ideological discussion. Instead, newsletters focused primarily on items pertaining to the structure of the bisexual movement. Common items included calendars of events, reports about conferences, notes from business meetings, fund raising issues, descriptions of groups' organizational structures, appeals for volunteers to help with organizational tasks, calls for papers to be submitted to forthcoming bisexual anthologies and other publications, and announcements of the results of elections in local and national bisexual groups, of the formation of new groups and publications, and of the times and places of upcoming meetings and social events. This emphasis on structural matters was especially characteristic of the late 1980s and the very early 1990s, as illustrated by two newsletters, *Bi Women* and *North Bi Northwest*. For example, the May 1987 issue of *Bi Women* published a one-and-a-half-page long list of bisexual organizations in the U.S. and Europe and the minutes of two coordinating committee meetings that focused on structural items, such as office space, managing the telephone, and financial issues. In January 1989, *Bi Women* encouraged its readers to become involved in a planned U.S.-Canadian [North American] Bisexual Network (named the North American Multicultural Bisexual Network at its inception, the organization was later renamed BiNet USA). The two-column article described the structure of the organization and the networking responsibilities of its delegates in detail but made no mention of the purpose or goals of the organization; readers unfamiliar with the organization were left to infer its purpose from its name and/or structure.[1] In September 1991, *North Bi Northwest* printed a report of the second annual conference of BiNet USA.[2] The report focused on explaining the name change and enumerated the proposed projects of the organization, including the establishment of a newsletter and the appointment of a task force to find a location for the following year's conference. Again, ideological issues were largely absent from the report. During these years, most of the newsletter page space that was not devoted to structural issues was filled with news reports about events of interest to the entire lesbian, gay, and bisexual community, book and movie reviews, poetry, and original fiction, including erotica.

Early in the 1990s, bisexual newsletters began paying more attention to ideological issues. In November 1991, *Bi Women* reported on two bisexual community meetings that had been held in Boston. This time, the report discussed the issues that arose and explicitly stated that bisexuals need to develop a sense of themselves as bisexuals and talk about the goals of the bisexual movement.[3] In May 1993, *North Bi Northwest* printed a report on the first Northwest regional BiNet USA conference, which differed substantially from its 1991 report on the national BiNet conference.[4] The 1993 report described the topics of the workshops at the conference, information that reflected the issues organizers and attendees considered important. In March 1994, *North*

Bi Northwest reported the formation of a new local bisexual group, describing the group's goals instead of its organizational structure.[5]

Among the ideological issues facing bisexuals are the questions "Who are we?" and "What do we stand for?" The first question is important because a concept of what it means to be bisexual would enhance bisexuals' sense of identity as individuals and as a community. Also, in the ethnic political tradition, constructing themselves as a definable group would legitimate bisexuals' political demands. But amid the general lack of attention paid to bisexual ideology in bisexual publications, the question of definition seems to have been intentionally avoided rather than simply overlooked. When the question is raised, the answer is usually that bisexuals come in "all shapes, sizes, and colors,"[6] and that bisexuality therefore defies definition. For example, Beth Reba Weise observed that "every city, every group, has its own identity" and that these identities range from "sex-positive/sex-radical groups to vanilla feminist groups, married bi men's support groups to Queer Nation activist groups, strongly non-gay identified to queerer than queer."[7] Kathleen Bennett wrote, "The only thing that bisexual couples have in common among themselves is the fact that every coupling is a unique and individual situation,"[8] and Deborah Anapol discussed polyfidelity and reminded readers that not all bisexual partnerships are two-person "couples."[9] In other words, bisexuals are a diverse group with no single quality in common.

A few authors have made isolated attempts to propose definitions. In general, these definitions are broad in an effort to encompass bisexual diversity, and they reflect ideological concerns about self-determination and gender that I will discuss later. For example, Paul Smith argued that "[h]ow we self-identify is all the justification we need" to be considered "really" bisexual.[10] Although this definition has met little to no resistance in the printed bisexual media, some bisexual activists privately express concerns about even this libertarian definition. Other authors offer their own definitions of bisexuality, usually emphasizing that they are personal definitions that might not work for everyone or in every situation. For example, during an interview with *Newsweek*, Robyn Ochs defined bisexuality as "the *potential* for being sexually and/or romantically involved with members of either gender," hoping to dispel stereotypes of bisexuals as promiscuous.[11] Finally, some authors have attempted to identify "types" of bisexuals,[12] but these typologies are usually offered with the intention of demonstrating the variety of ways to be bisexual rather than nailing down definitions.

Bisexuals are not unaware of the advantages of developing a definition of bisexuality that might form the basis for an ethnic bisexual identity. For example, Sharon Gonsalves wrote that "[l]abels are important for members of oppressed groups. They create an in-group and out-group, a minority culture from which we derive strength." [13] Naomi Tucker also pointed out that labels facilitate visibility and provide support (1991). But, nevertheless, Gonsalves, Tucker, and other bisexual activists shy away from specifying the substance of what those labels should mean and warn that labels can be limiting.

Besides resisting the question of definition, bisexual activists generally spend little effort constructing a historical sense of "who we are" as bisexuals. Occasionally, there are attempts to identify bisexuals in history; for example, the September 1991 issue of *North Bi Northwest* included a list of "[p]eople who had relations with both sexes." But by and large, bisexuals are constructing a history not by reclaiming bisexuality in the past, but by documenting the activities of the contemporary bisexual movement. For example, *Anything That Moves #4* published a detailed account of the history of the struggle to get "bi" included in the title of the 1993 March on Washington, and *BiNet Newsletter* 1(1), published in August 1991, documented the founding and development of BiNet USA. Bisexual conferences are often videotaped as a way of recording history. This emphasis on the contemporary is not accidental. Amanda Udis-Kessler warned bisexuals not to make the same mistake lesbians and gays did by attempting to reconstruct history in order to create a heritage for themselves. [14] She pointed out that doing so would involve identifying as bisexual people who had not identified themselves as bisexual, thus violating individuals' rights to self-definition and trivializing the specific historical circumstances that had led to the development of a bisexual identity in contemporary society.

Compared to the question of what bisexuality is, the question of what bisexuals stand for receives a great deal of attention in the bisexual press and, although there are controversial issues, has produced some basic ideological groundwork. Three dominant themes have emerged that apparently enjoy widespread acceptance as tenets of the bisexual politic. The first theme is the emphasis on diversity. Of course, one aspect of this diversity is the very sexual diversity that renders a definition of bisexuality problematic—not only differences in relationship status and views of bisexuality, but also differences in sexual practices. But bisexuals also encourage each other to celebrate other types of diversity, particularly racial/ethnic and cultural diversity. Bennett described diversity as "one of the major rallying cries of the bisexual movement,"[15] and Autumn Courtney wrote about her realization that "all oppressions are linked together."[16] Courtney's comment implies that this linkage is one reason for taking diversity seriously, but ideological justifications or explanations given for the celebration of diversity are rare. Instead, the importance of acknowledging diversity is usually taken as self-evident and the emphasis on diversity is found throughout bisexual organizing and writing; it is not ghettoized as a "special issue."

The celebration of sexual diversity is reflected in the pervasiveness of sex-positive or sex-radical philosophies which eschew political constraints on sexuality in favor of sexual open-mindedness. For example, BiNet USA held a focus group on sex positivism to ensure that BiNet represents the interests of a variety of people, including sex workers and sadomasochists as well as celibates.[17] *Anything That Moves* published an issue called "The Joy of Bi Sex," and *North Bi Northwest* also devoted an issue to the discussion and celebration of sex. Not all bisexuals ascribe to sex positivism, but for those who don't it exists as a philosophy to be reckoned with. For example, Erica Avery recounted an incident in which a woman at a workshop on sex positivism at a BiNet conference asked "What is sex positivism?" and was soundly rebuked; apparently, she was expected not only to be familiar with the philosophy, but supportive of it.[18]

Attention to racial/ethnic diversity is also fairly pervasive. Bisexual organizations typically include references to race and other social differences in their statements of purpose. The Bay Area Bisexual Network describes itself as "supporting the rights of all women and men to develop as whole beings without oppression because of age, race, religion, color, class or different abilities" in addition to differences of "sexual preference, gender, gender preference, and/or responsible consensual sexual behavior practices."[19] Issue #2 of the magazine published by BABN, *Anything That Moves,* was devoted to the topic of community, including a discussion of the diversity of that community. The issue included articles by Peggy Krouskoff about being an Arab-American bisexual woman, and by Thyme S. Siegel on anti-Jewish oppression. The Seattle Bisexual Women's Network (SBWN) held a workshop on racism for itself because White members wanted to learn how to make SBWN a "more inviting and safe place for women of color."[20] A few months later, Emily Susan Manning, a European-American woman, suggested that the low turn-out of Women of Color might be due to SBWN's primary focus on gender—a consequence of its feminist ideology—which tends to exclude issues important to Women of Color.[21] Some organizations describe or name themselves as "multicultural"; the removal of this term when NAMBN changed its name to BiNet USA was very controversial.[22] Despite the change in name, the organization reaffirmed its commitment to multiculturalism, and the Fall 1991 issue of *BiNet Newsletter,* the newsletter of BiNet USA, included an article entitled "Tips for organizers: Multi-cultural/multi-ethnic outreach" by Cianna Stewart, which was later reprinted in *North Bi Northwest,* the newsletter of SBWN.[23]

A commonly expressed sentiment is that the bisexual community derives strength, and perhaps even unity, from its diversity.[24] But even more ideologically promising is the idea that the bisexual community derives its uniqueness and its political nature from its diversity. Smith suggested that an appreciation of the strength in diversity could be "the unique contribution of the bisexual community to other communities," i.e., that which the bisexual community is in a unique position to develop and offer.[25] Elias Farajajé-Jones also sees a special relationship between bisexuality and multiculturalism; he argued that both are "rooted in challenging monodimensional structures of thinking and acting (monoculturalism and monosexuality)."[26] In other words, the very diversity that prevents bisexuals from identifying their common characteristic and thereby defining themselves as a political group in the ethnic tradition nevertheless provides bisexuals with an ideological purpose; the diversity itself becomes the basis for the political meaning of bisexuality.

Farajajé-Jones's comment also illustrates the second ideological theme that has emerged from discussions in the bisexual press. This theme is the conceptualization of bisexuality as a challenge to traditional Western thinking, particularly categorical thinking, and the argument that the political goal of bisexuals should be to break down dichotomous classification systems. This includes not only the dichotomous conceptualization of sexuality in which people are divided into homosexuals and heterosexuals, but also dichotomous gender in which people are classified as either women or men. [27]

In keeping with the ideological emphasis on diversity, the argument that bisexuality challenges categorical thinking usually begins with the assertion that there is unlimited variation and fluidity in human sexual desires and behaviors. Often, this point is supported by scientific research, particularly the Kinsey reports, and sometimes, it borders on pure essentialism. [28] This unlimited sexual variety is forced into a certain number of categories constructed by society—namely, homosexuality and heterosexuality—thus limiting people's sexual expression and abridging their right to sexual self-determination. Bisexuals, by refusing to classify their sexuality as either homosexual or heterosexual and by refusing to limit their sexual expressions to the patterns sanctioned by society, present a challenge to these restrictive categories and in so doing strike a blow for sexual liberation and sexual self-determination. [29] For example, Ellen Brenner wrote that her self "steadfastly refuses to fit in any of the boxes society has created," and Betty Aubut said in an interview that she identifies politically as a bisexual because, to her, bisexual means "opposing restrictive categories." [30] Raven Gildea wrote that when bisexuals refuse to "fit into one of two mutually exclusive categories," they "challenge the either/or thinking on which Western civilization is based." [31] Bisexuality can be co-opted into the sexual dichotomy if it is conceptualized as a hybrid form of sexuality. Smith rejected the concept of bisexuality as "half-homosexual and half-heterosexual" precisely to preserve bisexuals' status as outsiders to the homosexual and heterosexual categories. [32] By existing outside the categories homosexual and heterosexual, bisexuals challenge the existence of those categories and further the "real goal of the bi movement," which is "to widen the options" because "people should be free to love whomever they choose in whatever manner that works best for them." [33]

Bisexuality is a challenge to categorical thinking about sexuality not only because it does not fit into either of the two existing categories, but because it is itself difficult to define in categorical terms. If bisexuals had a common characteristic by which they could be defined and distinguished from homosexuals and heterosexuals, bisexuality could be constructed as a third category, thereby preserving categorical thought if not dichotomous sexuality. But we have already seen that bisexuals are in no hurry to develop a simple definition of bisexuality by which they could reconstruct themselves as a group in the ethnic tradition. In addition to celebrating the diversity of the bisexual community, many bisexuals feel that the concept of bisexuality itself should "embrace fluidity, subtle shading, ambiguity, wide variance, and flexibility in sexual experience and response." [34] Such a concept is difficult to express in categorical language. Other individuals recognize that labels lead to categorization and therefore reject labels; Tucker "refuse[s] to limit myself by squeezing my sexuality into a one-word definition" (1991:245). Lucy Friedland and Liz A. Highleyman (1991) acknowledge that categories are useful tools but caution that they are not ends in themselves and must be open to change when they become limiting. Thus, bisexuality and bisexuals resist being co-opted into categorical thinking and in doing so, remain a challenge to dichotomous sexuality. Again, the very diversity of the bisexual community that makes it difficult for bisexuals to agree on a definition of bisexuality provides bisexuals with a political purpose and an ideological position.

Some bisexuals embrace the concept of a sexual continuum as an alternative to the dichotomous model of sexuality. The continuum model represents the viewpoint that sexuality is not categorical; that is, that there is variety in human sexuality and that there are no clear dividing lines amid this variety. It also has the advantage of permitting the modeling of sexual fluidity, which can be expressed in terms of movement along the continuum. On this continuum, bisexuality exists between homosexuality and heterosexuality, and connects them. As such, bisexuality is a "bridge" between homosexuality and heterosexuality, and promises to serve as the mediator in the sexual identity wars. [35] As attractive as this concept might be, Avery asserted that the concept of a continuum—on which people are generally assumed to "progress" from heterosexuality to "full-fledged queerness"—merely reflects the split between homosexuality and heterosexuality that bisexuals should be challenging. [36] Responding to Avery, Pat Cattolico suggested that the continuum should have asexuality ("that is, not at all sexual") and sexuality ("that is, what we today call bisexual") as its endpoints, with monosexuality "somewhere in the middle." [37] Ideally, however, both women preferred to simply acknowledge that all people are "just sexual beings," thus rejecting all methods of modeling sexual variation.

If bisexuality challenges dichotomous sexuality, it also challenges the dichotomous distinction between women and men. Different authors have offered slightly different explanations of how bisexuality subverts gender. Smith perceives bisexuals as in "revolt against gender-based roles" because bisexuals do not conform to gender roles in "deciding with whom we have sex."[38] In other words, for a bisexual, choice of sexual partners is not an aspect of one's own gender role. Karin Baker and Helen Harrison argued that "[b]isexuality works to subvert the gender system and everything it upholds because it is not based on gender. In addition, bisexual identity and struggle lend themselves in a special way to exploring the possibility that women and men are 'more alike than different,' and that variations in human character bear no intrinsic connection to biological sex."[39] In other words, bisexuality diminishes the importance and the size of the difference between women and men. Tucker agreed with Baker and Harrison that "[s]ome of us are bisexual because we do not pay much attention to the gender of our attractions," but she argued that other people are bisexual because "we do see tremendous gender differences and want to experience them all." No matter what the mechanism—whether by disentangling erotic choice from gender role, by reducing the importance of partner gender in erotic choice, by minimizing gender differences, or by adding the option "both" to "either/or" gendered thinking—all of these theorists agree that bisexuality contributes to the breakdown of dichotomous gender.

Furthermore, as gender dichotomies break down, hierarchies based on gender—for example, male domination and compulsory heterosexuality—will weaken. There is, therefore, an intimate connection between bisexuality and both women's and lesbian/gay liberation. Some bisexuals hope that the bisexual movement will exceed the accomplishments of the feminist and lesbian/gay movements. For example, Sarah Listerud hopes that bisexuals can penetrate the "heterosexual hegemony" farther than lesbians and gays have been able to do, by creating spaces within heterosexual society where it is OK to be queer.[40] As Gildea put it, "The bisexual movement has the potential to take queer liberation to new heights."[41] With regard to feminism, Ellen Barnett argued that "[b]isexuals are also in the best position to make a real difference in the way men and women relate to each other. We have to learn how to create and maintain truly equitable relationships with our partners regardless of their gender." She conceded that "there are bisexuals who are not feminists as there are feminists that are not bi or lesbian," but her argument establishes bisexuality itself as not only feminist, but more feminist than lesbianism.[42] Other bisexuals make the more modest claim that "a politicized bisexual movement can play a significant role in the struggle to end women's oppression and for lesbian and gay liberation"[43] and caution against the temptation of thinking that bisexuality is a superior form of sexuality,[44] a trap that would thwart the liberatory goals of the bisexual movement as it did the lesbian movement.

It should be noted that a decline in the significance of gender does not imply the elimination of gender; although some activists privately advocate the erasure of gender differences, this viewpoint is expressed only rarely in bisexual publications. On the contrary, the viewpoint expressed most often is that gender differences should be appreciated and celebrated, as any other form of diversity should be celebrated. Androgyny is a gender variation that, like any other gender variation, should be enjoyed; it is not an ideal toward which all bisexuals should strive.[45] What needs to be eliminated is not gender, but oppression based on gender. That is, gender should not be prescribed on the basis of biological sex, it should not dictate one's opportunities or choices in life, and it need not be a determining factor in the choice of sexual partners. Gender should be liberating, not limiting.

To facilitate the decline of the significance of gender, some bisexuals define bisexuality as a form of sexuality independent of gender, or assert that they fall in love with the "person," not the "gender." For example, Weise wrote that she and her friends fall in love with the person first; the fact that that person is either male or female has social and political consequences for the relationship that follows but is irrelevant to the process of falling in love.[46] BABN's statement of purpose reinforces the insignificance of gender: "We support relationships among people *regardless* of gender" (italics mine).[47] Other bisexuals do not see gender as completely irrelevant, but assert that—unlike homosexuals and heterosexuals—gender is not a determinative factor in their choice of partners.[48]

To emphasize the distinction between bisexuals, for whom gender might be an irrelevant or relatively unimportant factor in choosing partners, and homosexuals and heterosexuals who practice gender exclusivity, some bisexuals refer to homosexuals and heterosexuals as "monosexuals." This terminology has the effect of creating a unifying definition of bisexuality by constructing bisexuals as people whose common characteristic is their refusal to practice gender exclusivity. As such, it is a definition that has the potential to create an ethnic bisexual identity. But, as I mentioned earlier, some bisexual activists warn against constructing bisexuals as a minority group in the ethnic political tradition. To do so would reproduce the type of dichotomous thinking that is gradually becoming the antithesis of bisexual ideology, and it would impose on lesbians and gay men a construction of themselves that is not of their own choosing, thereby violating their right to self-definition.

If bisexuality poses a challenge to dichotomous gender, then it follows that one might adopt a bisexual identity as a way to protest dichotomous gender and the oppressions that are based on gender. In other words, bisexuality can be seen not only as consistent with the political goal of dismantling gender, but as a means toward that goal. Lenore Norrgard reported that this is already happening. She wrote, "Some bisexuals feel very strongly that they have made a philosophical or even a political choice: they believe that everyone can and should be capable of loving both genders both emotionally and sexually, and favor neither over the other in any way." She underscored the political nature of this choice by asserting that although for some people this choice is "directly supported by their own personal experience," others find that their philosophy "doesn't work out for them in practice." [49] In other words, they identify as bisexual for political, not personal reasons. Kaplan is among those whose bisexual identity is at least in part a political, rather than a sexual, statement; her bisexual identity is her way of saying "*no* to a world where gender determines my desire and my behavior." [50] Here lies the beginnings of a "political bisexuality" analogous to the "political lesbianism" of the 1970s. Tucker warned bisexuals not to follow lesbians too far on this path, because "we must be careful not to make the mistakes of some of our lesbian sisters who profess sexual acceptance" but whose efforts to validate lesbianism led them to "invalidate bisexuality as an orientation" (1991:246). Bisexuals must keep their sights on the goal of promoting sexual self-definition for everyone.

The third ideological theme developing in the bisexual press pertains to the form of bisexual oppression and the appropriate responses to this oppression. Any political movement needs to be motivated by an understanding of that which it seeks to change; in the case of liberation movements, this means an understanding of the nature and source of the oppression that prevents liberty. One of the forms of bisexual oppression that bisexuals have identified is a general misunderstanding of bisexuality. This misunderstanding is often described in terms of "myths" about bisexuality.[51] In the absence of a clear sense of what does constitute bisexuality, it might seem difficult to identify any beliefs about bisexuality as "myths," but there is in fact considerable agreement among bisexuals in this area. Most of this agreement revolves not around the stance that particular beliefs about bisexuality are untrue, but around the position that they are overgeneralizations.

For example, one frequently mentioned myth is that bisexuals are not monogamous. The name of the magazine *Anything That Moves* is controversial because, critics say, it promotes this myth. Authors who mention the nonmonogamy myth in order to challenge it are usually careful to say that it is untrue not because all bisexuals are monogamous, but because not all bisexuals are nonmonogamous. For example, after describing her own varied sexual history, Bettykay told readers not to generalize from her behavior to all bisexuals because, regarding promiscuity, "some are, and some aren't."[52] Here, the issue of diversity arises; some bisexuals are monogamous, some are duogamous, some are polyfidelitous, and some are not fidelitous. What is offensive about the image of bisexuals as nonmonogamous is the assumption that nonmonogamy is by definition or by fact necessarily a characteristic shared by all bisexuals. Authors who dispute the "myth of nonmonogamy" are also usually careful to distance themselves from any implication that nonmonogamy is undesirable, thus conforming to the tenet that bisexuals should celebrate diversity. A notable exception to this position is taken by Robin Margolis, whose BiCentrist Alliance (BCA) does not welcome members who are interested in "unconventional" sexual practices such as threesomes, heavy S & M, or swinging.[53]

Another myth frequently discussed by authors in bisexual publications is the image of bisexuals as AIDS carriers. Bisexuality came to popular and scientific attention in the mid 1980s largely because heterosexuals and epidemiologists began to fear that bisexuals would be the gateway through which AIDS would spread from the gay population to the heterosexual population. Ironically, the ensuing condemnation of bisexuality helped create bisexuality as a recognizable form of sexuality and is in large part responsible for the rapid growth of the bisexual movement in the late 1980s.[54] But now that this movement is taking shape, one of its goals is to counteract the negative publicity. As part of this effort, bisexual newsletters monitor coverage of bisexuality in the mainstream media, where bisexuality is almost invariably presented in the context of AIDS. For example, the July 13, 1987, issue of *Newsweek* included the article "Bisexuals and AIDS," and the September 1987 issue of *Bi Women* printed two letters that were written by bisexuals in response to that article. In keeping with the bisexual tenet of acknowledging diversity, both letters pointed out that some bisexuals are, indeed, irresponsible in their sexual behavior. But both letters also pointed out that most bisexuals are practicing safer sex and, along with gays and lesbians, are taking the lead in educating others about AIDS.

Perhaps the most oppressive myth identified in the bisexual press is the myth that bisexuality does not exist, a myth that results from the dichotomization of sexuality. The myth of nonexistence is a circumstance that few oppressed groups have had to confront; because of it, before bisexuals can claim to be oppressed and begin to protest this oppression, they must prove their own existence. Thus, Smith felt the need to assert, after pointing out that gays and lesbians regard bisexuals as confused, that "[w]e are 'really' bisexual."[55] The fact that such an assertion needed to be made in a publication by and for bisexuals is as telling as the statement itself; apparently bisexuals, as well as non-bisexuals, need to have the existence of bisexuality affirmed. On a more positive note, Brenner pointed out that "since we supposedly didn't exist, nobody has made up any rules for us and we can make up our own rules."[56] In other words, not existing gives bisexuals a great deal of freedom.

If bisexuals are oppressed by myths, then what should bisexuals' response to this oppression be? The primary, and perhaps the only, strategy suggested so far in the bisexual press is visibility. By appearing. on talk shows and operating speakers' bureaus, bisexuals can provide non-bisexuals with examples of monogamous and duogamous bisexuals, thereby disproving the nonmonogamy myth.[57] By writing letters to mainstream publications that portray bisexuals as AIDS risks, bisexuals can present themselves as responsible people who practice safer sex and educate others about AIDS. By coming out as bisexual, bisexuals disprove the myth that bisexuality does not exist.[58] To help bisexuals make themselves visible, ads in bisexual publications encourage bisexual readers to buy bisexual buttons and t-shirts. To give bisexuals an opportunity to be visible, BiNet USA—whose statement of purpose lists the facilitation of "bisexual visibility" as one of its primary goals—declared Valentine's Day, 1992, to be the First Bisexual Visibility Day. This event was repeated in 1993 and 1994 with kiss-ins and other demonstrations.

In addition to general myths about bisexuality, bisexuals also perceive themselves as being oppressed by lesbians and gay men. Like AIDS, the hostility bisexuals experience in lesbian/gay communities is one of the factors that motivated bisexuals to turn their attention toward forming a bisexual movement. [59] In the bisexual press, discussion of the lack of acceptance bisexuals find in the lesbian and gay communities often arises in connection with news events, such as controversies over the nominal and actual inclusion of bisexuals in Lesbian and Gay Pride Marches. For example, Holly L. Danyliw wrote to *Bi Women* to express her surprise at being heckled by lesbian onlookers as she marched with a bisexual sign in the Boston Pride march. [60] In August/September 1991, *North Bi Northwest* devoted several pages to stories about "Encounters with lesbians" that explored the topic of bisexual-lesbian relations. Some bisexuals attempt to explain lesbians' hostility as "misdirected anger" borne of their own oppression, or fear of their own bisexuality. [61] The latter idea is expressed in the acronym "BLAS," which stands for "Bisexual Label Avoidance Syndrome." Bisexuals respond to lesbians' and gays' intolerance by criticizing their political narrow-mindedness, which stands in stark contrast to the celebration of diversity that characterizes the developing bisexual politic. In 1991, a guerrilla street theater group parodied rigid lesbian/gay exclusivity by administering the "Acme Bi Detector" test to passersby in the Castro district of San Francisco. [62]

The lesbian/gay community is not presented as uniformly hostile to bisexuals, however. Stories about pleasant encounters and bisexual inclusion in lesbian/gay events are as numerous as negative reports. There is also acknowledgment that increasing bisexual visibility is successfully changing lesbians' and gays' attitudes. In 1989, Gonsalves recounted an incident in which a lesbian stood up for bisexual inclusion, and noted that such acceptance had been lacking only five years earlier when she came out as bisexual after identifying herself as a lesbian. [63] Ganapati Durgahdas made a similar observation about growing acceptance in the gay men's community in 1992. [64]

The bisexual press keeps tabs on the treatment of bisexuality in the lesbian/gay press. In the Spring of 1991, *Anything That Moves* reviewed *Outweek*'s article "The Bisexual Revolution." It described the article as

"well-balanced," in contrast to the "bi-bashing article" more characteristic of the lesbian/gay press.[65] In 1992, Carol A. Queen criticized *Out/
Look* magazine for its treatment of bisexuality in the cover story "What
do bisexuals want?" and for suppressing the issue of bisexuality at the
annual Out/Write '92 conference that occurred shortly after the article
appeared.[66] In November 1992, *North Bi Northwest*'s own cover story
was a reprint of the follow-up article that *Out/Look* published after
"What do bisexuals want?"

Bisexuals are divided over how to respond to lesbian/gay hostility.
Some feel that they are being excluded from a movement that represents
their interests as much as it represents lesbian/gay interests. This sentiment is summarized in the slogan, "Bi liberation is gay liberation." In
other words, bisexuals "share the same issues with gays and lesbians in
the content (sic) of the dominant heterosexist culture."[67] Kaahumanu
argued that right-wing defenders of heterosexism lump all non-hetero-
sexuals together as queers; for example, Amendment 2 in Colorado
listed "bisexuals" along with lesbians and gays as undesirables.[68] Bisexuals are not "half-homosexuals" whose suffering is thereby diminished;
when bisexuals are oppressed, they are oppressed in the same ways and
as much as lesbians/gays. "As bisexuals, we do not get half-bashed or
only partly discriminated against, we don't lose half our children or half
our jobs."[69] In other words, bisexual oppression is gay oppression, and
bisexuals rightfully belong to the same movement as lesbians and gays.

Bisexuals who take the position that bi liberation is gay liberation
argue that bisexuals should be part of the lesbian/gay movement, and
that lesbians/gays should acknowledge the place of bisexuals in that
movement by adding the "b-word" to lesbian/gay organizations and
events. Some lesbians/gays respond to this demand by chastising bisexuals for trying to reap the benefits of gay liberation now that the real
lesbians and gay men have done all the hard work. But bisexuals respond
that they have been in the so-called lesbian/gay movement all along. As
Smith put it, "It isn't as though we just showed up on the scene and are
the 'Me Too Generation' of queer liberation. Bisexuals have been there
all along and in significant numbers."[70] Bisexuals have been invisible
because they "have not publicly identified themselves as bisexuals for
fear of the community's rejection,"[71] but they are no longer willing to
stay in the closet. Other lesbians/gays respond to bisexuals' demands
for nominal inclusion by arguing that "lesbian/gay" already includes

bisexuals; after all, "bi liberation is gay liberation." Robyn Ochs and Pam Ellis responded to this by analogizing the position of bisexuals in the early 1990s to the position of lesbians in the early gay movement, or to the position of women in a sexist society; i.e., "bisexual" is included in "lesbian/gay" the same way "lesbian" is included in "gay," or "she" is included in the generic "he."[72]

A great deal of page space in bisexual publications is devoted to monitoring the inclusion of bisexuality in lesbian/gay events and organizations. For example, in July 1989, *Bi Women* reported that bisexuals were included in the title of the 1989 Annual Pride March in Northampton; in July 1990, *Bi Women* reported that the word "bisexual" had once again been removed from the name of the Northampton March.[73] Similar sporadic inclusion occurred at the annual Lesbian, (Bisexual) & Gay Studies Conference, a history documented in *North Bi Northwest,* which also analyzed the degree to which bisexuality was included in the content of the conference.[74] In 1990, *North Bi Northwest* proudly reported that bisexual speakers had been invited to address the members of P-FLAG (Parents and Friends of Lesbians and Gays) and, while there, had helped to dispel several myths about bisexuality. In 1992, Seattle became the first major city in the U.S. to include the word "bisexual" in the name of its pride march.[75] In 1993, after a long lobbying effort,[76] bisexuals celebrated the inclusion of bisexuals in the name of the third March on Washington (MOW). This celebration was slightly dampened, however, by the fact that the word included in the name was "bi," not "bisexual," which bisexuals took as an attempt to desexualize both bisexuality and the March.

Not all bisexuals agree that the bisexual movement should be part of the lesbian/gay movement. Robin Margolis of the BiCentrist Alliance, for example, rejects the "LesBiGay" model of bisexual organizing because she argues that bisexual culture is diluted when bisexuals are included among lesbians and gays. Bisexuals have different interests than lesbians/gays do, and therefore bisexuals need to organize their own separate movement. This is a minority view, however; other bisexual activists tend to reject the BiCentrist position as divisive and separatist.

Another issue on which bisexuals disagree is the relationship between women and men. In a movement dedicated to reducing the significance of gender, one might expect that women and men would engage in mutual cooperation. But complete cooperation is prevented by several factors, most notably the fact that gender is still a very real phenomenon. Women and men have been socialized differently, and attempts to create a truly non-gendered movement are often frustrated by this reality. For example, some bisexual women complain that in mixed-gender bisexual groups they encounter men whose interest lies in finding women for sexual partners. Bisexual women, who are sexually socialized as women, motivated in part by the antipathy toward bisexuality of lesbian feminism, and trained in political ideology by feminism, are less interested in finding sexual partners and more interested in developing a bisexual community and discussing ideological issues. In cities where separate organizations are founded for bisexual women and men, the men's groups often fold while the women's groups continue meeting and publishing newsletters. Many cities have bisexual women's groups and mixed-gender groups, but no bisexual men's groups. Some bisexual activists attribute the greater stability of bisexual women's groups to women's greater political training as veterans of feminism; others attribute it to gender socialization that prevents men from expressing their feelings and performing facilitating tasks in group discussions. In contrast to most political movements, which are led by men, in the bisexual movement women activists tend to outnumber men activists.

Relations between the genders are not only problematic in mixed gender settings. The issue also arises in bisexual women's groups. For example, *Bi Women* is published by a bisexual women's group, the Boston Bisexual Women's Network (BBWN). In September 1987, *Bi Women* announced that it was considering adopting a more liberal policy that would make it easier for men to subscribe and invited readers to comment. Several readers' comments were published in March 1988, most of which favored allowing men to subscribe but restricting their contributions. The editors continued to solicit readers' comments, and finally, in July 1989, the editors announced that 63% of readers had voted to allow men on the mailing list. In November 1991, Stephanie Berger reported that attendees at a bisexual community meeting in Boston had generally agreed that there needed to be more communication between the bisexual women's and the bisexual men's networks in Boston;[77] less than two years later, the Boston Bisexual Men's Network folded.

Transgender issues are also problematic in the bisexual movement, particularly in some bisexual women's groups. In the bisexual movement as a whole, transgendered individuals are celebrated not only as an aspect of the diversity of the bisexual community, but because, like bisexuals, they do not fit neatly into dichotomous categories. Jim Frazin wrote that "the construction and deconstruction of gender" is a subject of mutual interest to bisexuals and transsexuals who are, therefore, natural allies.[78] Tucker argued that the bisexual movement should include transgender politics on its agenda "because we as a bisexual movement are visionary in our need and desire to break down dichotomies, creating a powerful and diverse body of queers to smash the heterosexual monolith."[79] At BiNet USA's Third Annual Meeting, the organization adopted a statement that the organization would "acknowledge and support transgender bisexuals in the organization itself and the broader bisexual community."[80]

But many bisexual women's groups are actively feminist, and as such, they attempt to combine feminism with bisexual ideology. The cultural feminists who defined feminism during the 1980s—the decade during which many bisexual women's groups were formed—were generally hostile toward transgenderists, whom they perceived as male intruders in women's space. Bisexual women must, therefore, reconcile feminist distrust of transgenderists with the bisexual celebration of gender diversity. This issue arose for the Seattle Bisexual Women's Network, which publishes *North Bi Northwest*. In January 1991, SBWN held a meeting to "resolve the question of whether male-to-female transsexuals would be welcome as full members in the group," but the issue proved to be too controversial for consensus. Ironically, the report of this meeting in *North Bi Northwest* was placed directly above an article that reported that the Ingersoll Gender Center, a center for transgendered individuals, had invited bisexuals to come speak to them so that they could further understand bisexuality. An article by Lenore Norrgard in the same issue of *North Bi Northwest* argued against including transsexuals because "[m]ale-to-female transsexuals are not women" and if they are admitted, "we will no longer be a women's group."[81] In May 1991, after a year of "heated"[82] debate, *North Bi Northwest* reported a provisional policy of partial membership for transsexuals; if they had been living full-time for at least a year as women, they would be allowed to attend large meetings and mixed-gender meetings, but not the Newcomers Group and social gatherings defined as "women-born-women only." One year later, discussion was reopened and, in May 1994, transgender and transsexual women who had been living as women for one year were welcomed without further restrictions. [83]

In summary, ideological discourse in the bisexual press has intensified in recent years, and some themes have emerged. In general, bisexual ideology celebrates diversity and challenges categorical thinking, particularly the dichotomous construction of gender and sexuality. By challenging dichotomous gender and sexuality, the bisexual movement undermines sexism and heterosexism and aligns itself with feminism and lesbian/gay liberation. Bisexuals struggle to convince others of their feminism and their gayness; to do so, they must reconcile feminism with the celebration of gender diversity and gain recognition as part of the lesbian/gay movement. Among the bisexual movement's goals are the education of others to dispel myths about bisexuality and sexual liberation for everyone; it aims to achieve these goals primarily through visibility. Bisexual activists generally decline to establish a single definition for bisexuality and spend little energy on constructing a bisexual history; to do so would construct a bisexual ethnicity, thereby undermining the celebration of diversity and the challenge to traditional categorical thinking.

DÉJÀ VU?

Many of the arguments that bisexuals are using to politicize bisexuality are very similar to arguments that lesbians used in the 1970s to politicize lesbianism. But there are also some important differences between the two movements, because the political arena in which bisexuals are struggling for recognition is substantially different from the one lesbians faced two decades ago. To a large extent, therefore, the bisexual movement is another revolution on the same political wheel, but perhaps the bisexual movement is also a revolution, period. To understand both possibilities, we have to look at the similarities and the differences between the lesbian movement of the early 1970s and the bisexual movement of the early 1990s.

The bisexual movement's roots in the lesbian/gay movement are analogous to the lesbian movement's roots in the feminist and gay movements. Contemporary bisexual activists concentrate much of their energy on building a home within the lesbian/gay movement by arguing that "bi liberation is gay liberation" and demanding that lesbian/gay organizations and events nominally and actually include bisexuals. Similarly, early lesbian feminists initially struggled to find a home within the feminist and gay movements. Like early lesbian feminists who argued that lesbians had been in the feminist movement all along but remained hidden because of feminists' homophobia, bisexuals argue that bisexuals have been in the lesbian/gay movement all along but remained hidden because of biphobia.

Lesbian feminists eventually lost patience with the homophobia of feminists and the sexism of gay men, and established an independent lesbian feminist movement. Among bisexuals, the vision of an independent bisexual movement is a minority opinion; the separatist BiCentrist Alliance is considered outside the mainstream of bisexual political thought. But at the same time, despite most activists' insistence that bisexuals rightfully belong in the lesbian/gay movement, they are building the structure of a separate bisexual movement complete with a national bisexual network and international conferences. Moreover, ideology is beginning to follow suit; most of the bisexual women who participated in my study in 1986 saw their interests as flowing from their genders and their "gayness," not from their bisexuality, whereas the bisexual activists whose opinions appeared in bisexual publications of the late 1980s and early 1990s identified unique bisexual interests. Whether the LesBiGay model of political organizing will continue to dominate bisexual political strategy, or whether bisexual ideology will continue to develop in an independent direction to be followed eventually by a shift in political strategy as occurred in the lesbian movement, remains to be seen.

One strategy used by both lesbians and bisexuals to politicize themselves is to present their movements as challenges to established ways of thinking. Lesbian feminists argued that heterosexuality is a political institution that upholds patriarchy and that lesbianism, as an alternative to heterosexuality, is therefore political and feminist. Early lesbian feminists also argued that lesbianism is feminist because it challenges gender—specifically, the male definition of feminine gender that defines a "real woman" as a female who has sex with men. Contrary to the feeling of feminists at the time that lesbians were marginal constituents of the feminist movement and that the movement should focus on the needs of "women," not "lesbians," lesbians argued that they were the quintessential women and that the movement should not only address lesbians' needs but recognize lesbians as the true feminists. Thus, lesbianism was initially constructed as a challenge to gender. But once "woman" was reconstructed to include "lesbian," lesbians became part of the prevailing gender structure. In effect, lesbianism was co-opted into gender and ceased to be a challenge to it. Furthermore, the rise of cultural feminism reified rather than challenged gender, maximized rather than minimized the differences between women and men, and created a concept of lesbianism that was dependent on the preservation of gender.

Similarly, bisexual activists argue that categorical Western thinking is oppressive because it limits people's options, and that bisexuality is political because it challenges categorical thinking. Specifically, bisexuality is a challenge to dichotomous thinking about both gender and sexuality. Because bisexuality challenges these dichotomies, it undermines oppression based on them, i.e., sexism and heterosexism. Therefore, if lesbianism is political and feminist, bisexuality is political, feminist, and queer. If lesbianism undermines the heteropatriarchy, bisexuality undermines not only the heteropatriarchy but the fundamental structure of Western thought.

Given lesbians' initial challenge to gender, one might expect bisexuals' efforts to break down gender to be well received among lesbians. But because of the change in the relationship of lesbianism to gender that occurred with the reconstruction of womanhood and the rise of cultural lesbian feminism, bisexuals' contemporary challenge to gender is also a threat to lesbianism. Lesbianism is now part of the gender establishment that bisexuals seek to break down. Bisexuals' challenge to gender is no less than a challenge to the very existence of lesbianism, because of the dependence of lesbianism on gender for definition. Instead of being allies in the struggle against gender, because of the course taken by lesbian feminism in the two decades before the inception of the bisexual movement, lesbians and bisexuals have emerged with contrary political goals in reference to gender.

Bisexuality's challenge to dichotomous sexuality poses a threat to lesbianism that is even more direct. Lesbians contributed to the construction of dichotomous sexuality, primarily through their efforts to construct lesbians as an ethnic group. To become an ethnic group, lesbians had to distinguish themselves from non-lesbians and create the appearance of clear and fixed boundaries between themselves as the oppressed and heterosexuals as the oppressor. Lesbians are now part of the society that is based on dichotomous ways of thinking. If bisexuals are a threat to sexual dichotomy, they are a threat to lesbians.

This threat is multiple. At the very least, bisexuals are a material threat to lesbians because as the new category "bisexual" becomes available as an alternative to the homosexual/heterosexual dichotomy, some women who would otherwise have placed themselves in the lesbian category will place themselves in the new bisexual category. Lesbians will therefore lose numbers. However, the real threat is not to the size of the lesbian population, but to the ethnicity of lesbianism. By challenging and ultimately destroying the sexual dichotomy, bisexuals threaten to undermine the clarity of the distinction between lesbians and heterosexuals. If some people are bisexual—particularly if that bisexuality is conceptualized in hybrid terms—then the distinction between homosexuality and heterosexuality is not clear at all. If some people are both homosexual and heterosexual, then lesbians cannot be clearly distinguished from heterosexuals. If lesbians cannot be clearly distinguished from heterosexuals, then how can they claim to be oppressed by heterosexuals, and how can they struggle to win their liberation from heterosexuals? If the sexual dichotomy is destroyed, lesbians are deprived of their ethnicity, and of the strategies for liberation that flow from ethnicity.

If bisexuals were to construct themselves as an ethnic group, then the threat to lesbianism would be alleviated. The sexual dichotomy would be replaced by a sexual trichotomy, and the clarity of the category "lesbian" could be restored. But bisexuals show little indication that they will take this path, at least not in the near future. One might argue that the bisexual movement is simply too young to have yet constructed itself as an ethnic movement, but the lack of attention bisexuals are giving to the question of defining bisexuality stands in sharp contrast to the lively debates that occurred among lesbians on this issue in the early 1970s. The prevailing message in the bisexual press is that bisexuals should avoid establishing a single definition of bisexuality based on identifiable common characteristics, and little effort is being made to create bisexual ancestors or a bisexual heritage. Bisexuals are not constructing themselves as an ethnic group, precisely because they wish to remain a challenge to dichotomous gender and dichotomous sexuality. In so doing, they are not only refusing to place themselves into the ethnic political tradition; they are threatening to remove all of sexual identity politics from the realm of ethnic political discourse, thereby destroying other sexual minorities' abilities to utilize the language of ethnic politics to make their political claims.

Another strategy lesbian feminists used to politicize lesbianism was the desexualization of lesbianism. Because they were struggling to find a political voice in a period when sexuality was not recognized as political, to present themselves as political they had to distance themselves from sexuality. The rise of cultural feminism facilitated this effort by recalling the ideal of asexual womanly purity. But lesbians' efforts to politicize lesbianism contributed to the development of a sexual politics, and lesbians' efforts to desexualize lesbianism was one impetus for the rise of sex positivism. When bisexual activists appeared in the arena, sexuality was already politicized and sex positivism was in full swing. Because sex positivism is consistent with the bisexual emphasis on diversity, it was easily incorporated into the developing bisexual ideology, and because sexuality was politicized, this move was not antithetical to the process of bisexual politicization. Because of the historical period in which the bisexual movement has emerged, bisexuals can present themselves as both sexual and political; they can and do celebrate sexuality while simultaneously demanding recognition of their political voice.

Although they have largely escaped the desexualizing influence of lesbian feminism, bisexuals, especially bisexual women, cannot ignore the relationship that lesbian feminism constructed between lesbianism and feminism. In chapter 6, we saw how lesbian feminists first constructed lesbianism as consistent with feminism, and then argued that lesbians are the best feminists because they are independent of men and have the vision and resources to create women's space. According to this analysis, bisexual women collaborate with the enemy (men) and are, in some senses, even more detrimental to the feminist movement than heterosexual women are. Contemporary bisexual activists, having claimed that bisexuality is feminist, have to reconstruct the relationship between feminism and sexuality to support their claim. Among the specific problems they face are how to build a mixed-gender movement that is feminist, and whether to welcome transgenderists to women's space within that movement. Building a feminist mixed-gender movement means challenging the argument that feminism depends on women's space and refuting the charge that by associating with men bisexuals are collaborating with the enemy. Welcoming transgenderists requires that bisexual women reject the reification of gender that took place with the growth of cultural feminism. Neither task will be easy, but their importance to bisexual women is evident in the number of authors who have addressed the task of constructing a feminist bisexuality. [84]

Another difference between the lesbian and bisexual movements that is attributable to the different contexts in which they developed lies in their willingness to universalize their identities and interests. Many early lesbian feminists declared that "all women are lesbians." This claim served to present the lesbian movement as a movement for all women, and was based either on a concept of universal bisexuality, on arguments about the artificiality of culturally imposed heterosexuality, or on the redefinition of lesbianism as a form of feminist resistance. The concept of a universal bisexuality seems ready-made for a bisexual movement that might also want to emphasize its broad applicability and large constituency, but surprisingly, this idea has not been picked up enthusiastically by activists writing in the bisexual press. It was expressed by many of the bisexual women who took part in my study in 1986, but the fact that it does not appear consistently in the bisexual press suggests that the bisexual women in my study encountered the idea within lesbian feminism and found it personally gratifying. As such, it was evidence of the influence lesbian ideology had on them, not evidence of the beginnings of a bisexual ideology. Instead of proclaiming "everyone is bisexual," activists warn each other to respect the self-identities of those who choose not to identify as bisexual. The fact that bisexuals advocate respect for others' self-identities reflects the fact that the bisexual movement is developing in a context in which sexuality has already been politicized and lesbians and gay men have already constituted themselves as interest groups and invested heavily in their identities. As Tucker pointed out, "If we claim self-definition for ourselves, then we must accord that right to others" (1991:246). In the early 1970s, lesbians did not have to take into account other already established identity-based sexual minorities.

This does not imply that lesbian feminists did not also consider self-identity important. They did, but for very different reasons than bisexuals. At the height of lesbian feminism, identity was considered a political statement, or a means toward an end. Women should, therefore, identify themselves as lesbians for political reasons regardless of what they thought they "really" were sexually. In contrast, bisexuals consider self-identity important because self-determination is important; bisexual identity is not an identity to be adopted for political reasons, but because that is how one wishes to define oneself for whatever reason, and others should respect that self-definition. This might be partially due to the early stage of the bisexual movement; after all, early lesbian feminists also advocated the right of women to sexual self-determination. As bisexual ideology develops and bisexuality acquires specific political meanings, it is quite possible that individuals will begin to adopt bisexual identity for political reasons. In fact, it appears that some individuals already have; Rachel Kaplan is a case in point. Kaplan does not claim that she calls herself bisexual for solely political reasons; i.e., she does not suggest that bisexual identity is imposed or self-imposed on individuals who don't feel they are "really" bisexual. However, individuals like her might represent the beginning of a new breed of "political bisexuals" analogous to "political lesbians."

Finally, the role of race and ethnicity within the lesbian and bisexual movements differs, largely because of the different historical time periods in which the two movements developed. Lesbian feminism began, and remained, primarily a white movement. Lesbians who felt that the movement should pay attention to racial and ethnic issues shouldered the burden of calling other lesbians' attention to the problem and constructing elaborate arguments about the relationships among oppressions in order to convince them of the importance of the issue. Considerable debate occurred over the exact relationships among different oppressions; for example, do all oppressions arise from the same root, or is one oppression fundamental? If one is fundamental, is it classism, racism, or sexism? Contemporary bisexual activists not only inherit these arguments,[85] but have come forth in a historical period in which the celebration of racial/ethnic diversity and efforts to eliminate racial/ethnic oppression need no justification. Therefore, they do not spend a great deal of energy asserting that the bisexual movement should be multicultural. From its inception, bisexuals declared the movement to be multicultural; the work that remains is the work of making sure that it is in fact multicultural.

In summary, bisexuals, like lesbians, are faced with the task of politicizing a sexual identity, but bisexuals live in a very different political world than early lesbian feminists did. Not only have politics in general changed in the intervening two decades, but the lesbian/gay movement itself has created an entirely new political tradition. As a result of the lesbian/gay movement, sexuality has been politicized, and lesbians and gays are established political interest groups. To establish their own political voice, bisexuals must insert themselves into an ongoing discourse of sexual identity politics. In a very real sense, the lesbian/gay movement created bisexuals as an oppressed group by creating a discourse in which lesbians/gays and heterosexuals, but not bisexuals, were defined into political existence. Thus, the lesbian/gay movement not only altered the political arena by creating a new political tradition; it also created the need for a bisexual movement.

To politicize bisexual identity, bisexuals are using some of the same arguments and strategies that lesbians used to politicize lesbian identity. Just as lesbians initially challenged traditional gender and recognized that the demise of gender would render their own sexual identities meaningless, bisexuals are presenting bisexuality as a challenge to dichotomous gender and dichotomous sexuality. In so doing, both movements challenge established ways of thinking and promise to contribute to the breakdown of oppression based on gender and sexuality. For this reason, both movements envision themselves as sexual liberation movements, and both consider themselves feminist movements.

But beyond these similarities, there are differences that reflect the different political contexts of the two movements. For example, to politicize lesbianism, lesbians had to desexualize it, whereas contemporary bisexuals can claim both their sexuality and their political voice because the sex-positive movement and the politicization of sexuality have made it possible to have both. Lesbians constructed a relationship between lesbianism and feminism that established lesbians as the best feminists and bisexuals as traitors; bisexuals must now reconstruct that relationship to support their claim that the bisexual movement is a feminist movement. Lesbian feminists initially valued sexual self-determination for women, but after developing a clear political ideology they began to see lesbian identity as an identity every woman can and should adopt.

Contemporary bisexual activists advocate respect for individuals' sexual self-definitions, but they avoid the argument that all people can and should become bisexual-identified because they, unlike early lesbian feminists, face a political arena in which others already have political sexual self-identities that demand respect. Finally, lesbian feminists spent considerable energy discussing the relationships between sexism, heterosexism, racism, and classism to demonstrate the importance of taking race and class into account. Bisexuals take the importance of multiculturalism for granted, because lesbian feminism has already made the necessary connections and because society in general is more cognizant of the pervasive importance of race, class, ability, etc., and the need to actively struggle against all forms of oppression.

Because bisexuals are attempting to assert themselves in an ongoing political discourse in which lesbians have a considerable stake, bisexuals pose a challenge to lesbians. Lesbians have become invested in a gender-based definition of lesbianism. Bisexuals, by challenging both dichotomous gender and dichotomous sexuality, challenge the very existence of lesbianism. By refusing to construct themselves as an ethnic group, bisexuals undermine lesbian ethnicity and threaten the tenuous legitimacy all sexual identity-based minorities have gained in the realm of ethnic political discourse. Defined out of existence by lesbian feminism, bisexuals now threaten the existence of lesbianism and the future of the lesbian movement as we know it.

THE FUTURE OF SEXUAL IDENTITY POLITICS

Both the lesbian and the bisexual movements are part of a historical dialectic process in which each political cycle sets the stage for the next. The feminist and gay movements set the stage for the lesbian movement by providing a context for the politicization of lesbians and eventually the establishment of a separate movement. Likewise, lesbian feminism and gay liberation set the stage for the emergence of a bisexual movement by reifying the concept of dichotomous sexuality and thereby politicizing bisexuals, who are currently in the process of establishing a movement. As lesbian feminism matured, it became independent of its feminist and gay parent movements, passed through the stage of ideological coalescence followed by ideological rigidity, and eventually lost sight of its original goals. The contemporary bisexual movement is a younger movement that is still seeking a home in the lesbian/gay movement and has not yet had time to develop and solidify an ideology.

What remains to be seen is whether bisexuals will follow the trajectory of the lesbian movement. Will the bisexual movement, like the lesbian movement, become independent of its political parents, or will it continue to seek a home in the lesbian/gay movement? Will it develop a party line that will then solidify into a new form of political correctness and ideological hegemony? Will it lose track of its focus on diversity and its goal of breaking down limiting gender and sexual categories, allowing itself to be co-opted into the gender system and constructed as a new sexual category? Or, will it keep sight of its current goals and remain a movement for sexual self-determination and liberation? If it does, it might prove to be the final revolution on the wheel of sexual identity politics.

• Appendix A: Figures •

262

Figure 3.1: SEXUAL SELF-IDENTITY

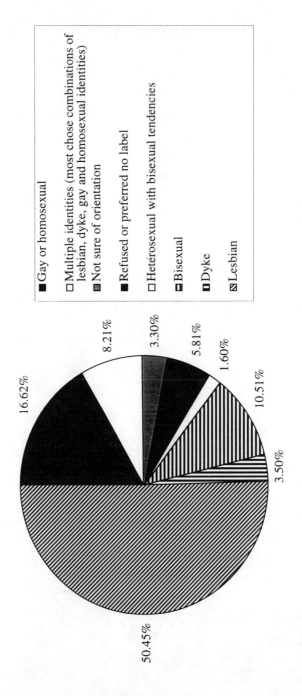

- Gay or homosexual
- Multiple identities (most chose combinations of lesbian, dyke, gay and homosexual identities)
- Not sure of orientation
- Refused or preferred no label
- Heterosexual with bisexual tendencies
- Bisexual
- Dyke
- Lesbian

16.62%

8.21%

3.30%

5.81%

1.60%

10.51%

3.50%

50.45%

Figure 3.2: EMPLOYMENT STATUS

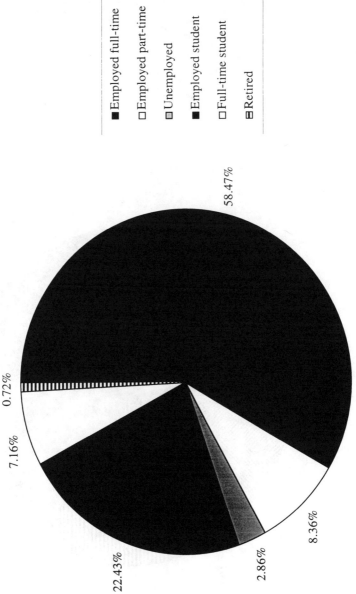

- ■ Employed full-time
- □ Employed part-time
- ▣ Unemployed
- ■ Employed student
- □ Full-time student
- ▦ Retired

58.47%

0.72%

7.16%

22.43%

2.86%

8.36%

Figure 3.3: INCOME

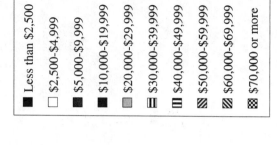

Less than $2,500
$2,500-$4,999
$5,000-$9,999
$10,000-$19,999
$20,000-$29,999
$30,000-$39,999
$40,000-$49,999
$50,000-$59,999
$60,000-$69,999
$70,000 or more

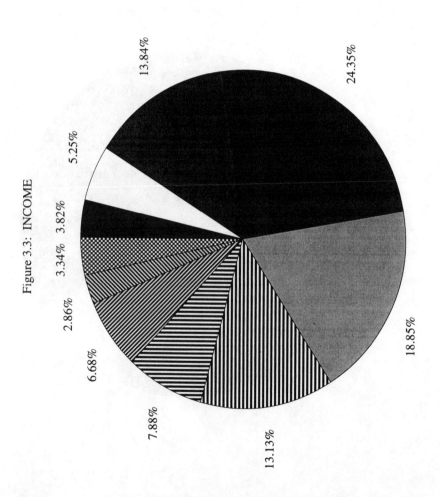

13.84%

24.35%

5.25%

3.82%

3.34%

2.86%

18.85%

6.68%

7.88%

13.13%

Figure 3.4: AGE DISTRIBUTION OF PARTICIPANTS, AND PREVALENCE OF LESBIAN AND
BISEXUAL IDENTITIES AMONG PARTICIPANTS IN DIFFERENT AGE RANGES

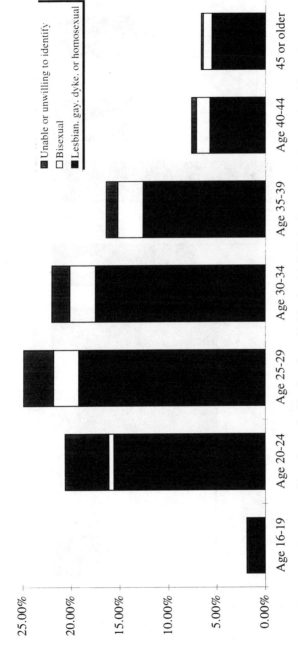

Note: Percentages are percentages of the entire sample. Therefore, the total height of each individual column represents the proportion of the sample in that age range.
Significance: The differences in sexual self-identification between participants in different age ranges are significant, chi-square = 23, df = 12, p = .03. Conversely, the average ages of participants with different sexual self-identities are significantly different, F (2,419) = 7.548, p = .0006.

Figure 3.5: HISTORY OF HETEROSEXUAL RELATIONSHIPS BY SEXUAL SELF-IDENTITY

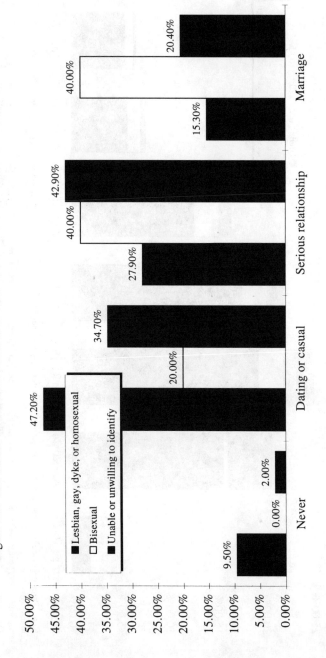

Significance: The differences in heterosexual history between participants with different sexual self-identities are significant, chi-square = 32, df = 6, p = .0001.

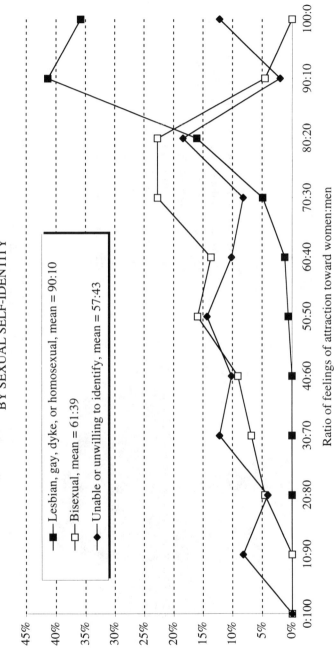

Figure 3.6: FEELINGS OF SEXUAL ATTRACTION TOWARD WOMEN AND MEN
BY SEXUAL SELF-IDENTITY

Legend:
■ Lesbian, gay, dyke, or homosexual, mean = 90:10
□ Bisexual, mean = 61:39
◆ Unable or unwilling to identify, mean = 57:43

y-axis: 45%, 40%, 35%, 30%, 25%, 20%, 15%, 10%, 5%, 0%

x-axis: 0:100, 10:90, 20:80, 30:70, 40:60, 50:50, 60:40, 70:30, 80:20, 90:10, 100:0

Ratio of feelings of attraction toward women:men

Significance: F = 187.22, df = (2, 414), p = .0001.

Figure 4.1: LESBIANS' SPONTANEOUSLY MENTIONED BELIEFS ABOUT
WHETHER BISEXUALITY EXISTS

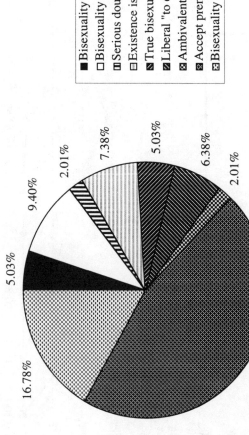

- ■ Bisexuality does not exist (explicit statement)
- □ Bisexuality does not exist (strong implication)
- ⊞ Serious doubt, but reserving judgment
- ▤ Existence is unlikely, but possible
- ▨ True bisexuality exists, but is rare
- ▧ Liberal "to each her own"
- ▨ Ambivalent feelings
- ▩ Accept premise that bisexuality exists
- ⊠ Bisexuality does exist (explicit statement)

Note: Lesbians who believe that everyone, or almost everyone, is potentially bisexual are not indicated in this chart because this belief is often combined with a belief in the actual nonexistence of bisexuality. The 16% of lesbians who believe in a universal bisexual potential are scattered throughout the categories indicated on the chart.

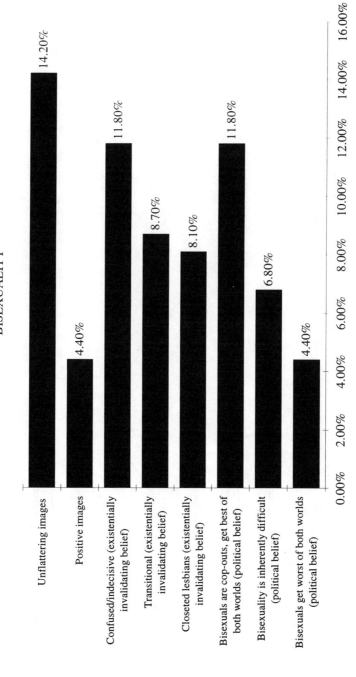

Figure 4.2: FREQUENCY OF LESBIANS' SPONTANEOUSLY MENTIONED IMAGES OF BISEXUALITY

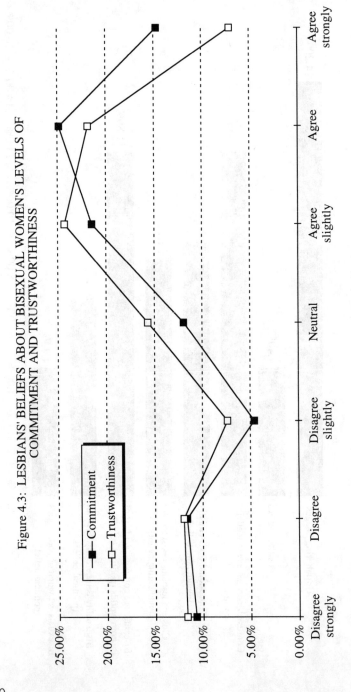

Figure 4.3: LESBIANS' BELIEFS ABOUT BISEXUAL WOMEN'S LEVELS OF COMMITMENT AND TRUSTWORTHINESS

Figure 4.4: LESBIANS' PERCEPTIONS OF THE RELATIVE DEGREE OF
PREJUDICE AND DISCRIMINATION EXPERIENCED BY
BISEXUAL WOMEN AND LESBIANS

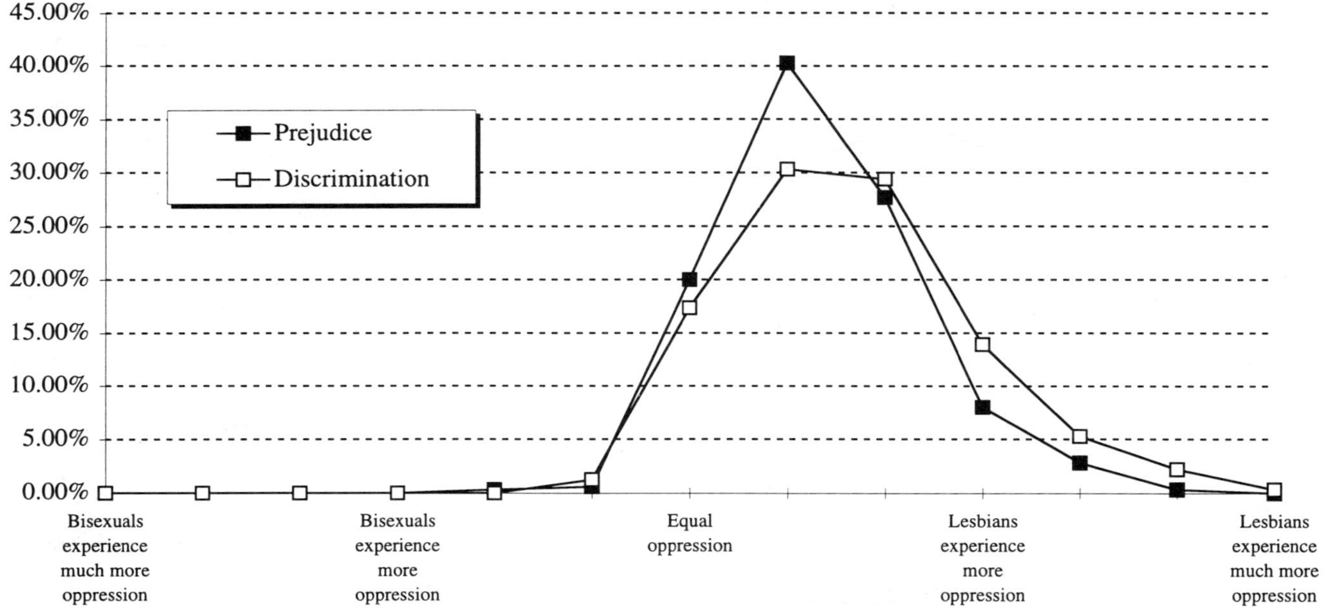

271

Figure 4.5: LESBIANS' PREFERENCES FOR ASSOCIATING SOCIALLY WITH BISEXUALS OR WITH OTHER LESBIANS

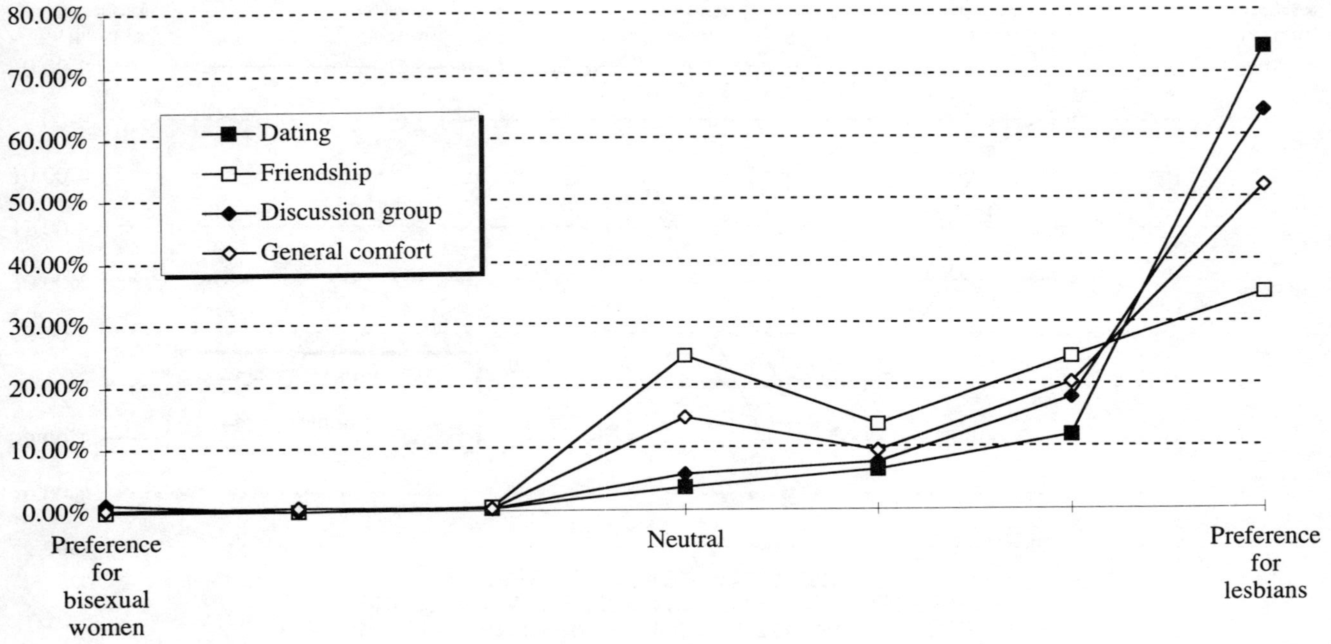

Figure 4.6: LESBIANS' PREFERENCES FOR ASSOCIATING POLITICALLY WITH BISEXUALS OR WITH OTHER LESBIANS

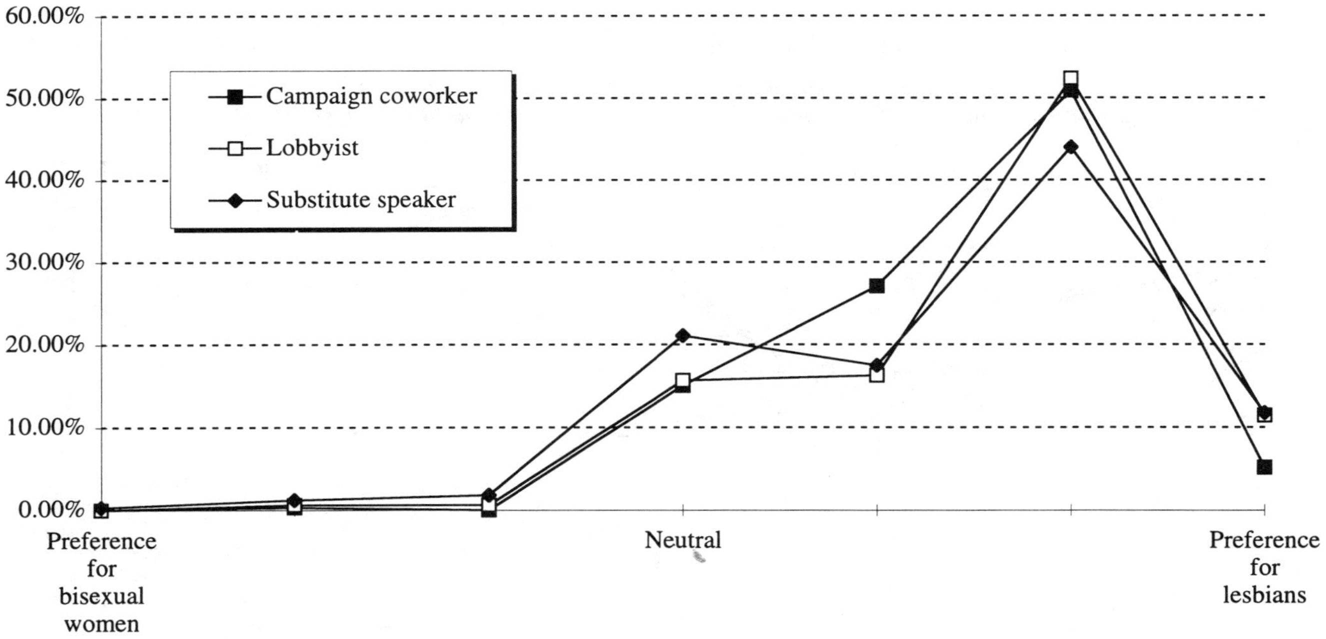

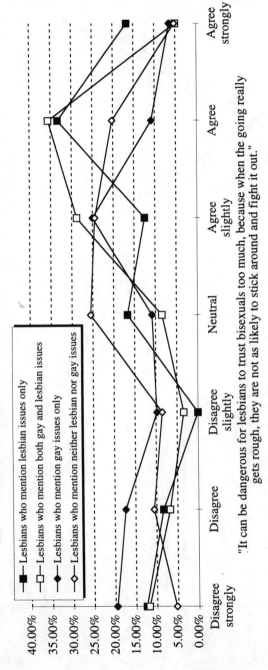

Figure 5.1: DIFFERENCES IN BELIEFS ABOUT BISEXUALITY AMONG LESBIANS WHO ARE CONCERNED ABOUT LESBIAN ISSUES EXCLUSIVELY AND LESBIANS WHO ARE CONCERNED ABOUT GAY ISSUES GENERALLY OR WHO ARE NOT CONCERNED AT ALL

"It can be dangerous for lesbians to trust bisexuals too much, because when the going really gets rough, they are not as likely to stick around and fight it out."

Note: The four categories shown in this figure were recombined into two categories, respectively representing lesbians who mention lesbian issues and lesbians who do not, to yield the percentages given in the text.

Significance: Chi-square = 42.55, df = 18, p = .0009; F = 5.24, df = (3, 265), p = .002. The chi-square significance test is given in addition to the F-test because, strictly speaking, the agree-disagree scale is an ordinal, not an interval, scale.

This figure is continued on the next page.

Figure 5.1 (cont'd): DIFFERENCES IN BELIEFS ABOUT BISEXUALITY AMONG LESBIANS WHO ARE CONCERNED ABOUT LESBIAN ISSUES EXCLUSIVELY AND LESBIANS WHO ARE CONCERNED ABOUT GAY ISSUES GENERALLY OR WHO ARE NOT CONCERNED AT ALL

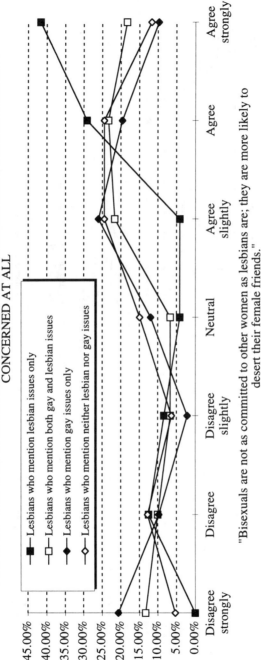

"Bisexuals are not as committed to other women as lesbians are; they are more likely to desert their female friends."

Note: These four categories shown in this figure were recombined into two categories, respectively representing lesbians who mention lesbian issues and lesbians who do not, to yield the percentages given in the text.

Significance: Chi-square = 38.03, df = 18, p = .004; F = 3.72, df = (3, 266), p = .01. The chi-square significance test is given in addition to the F-test because, strictly speaking, the agree-disagree scale is an ordinal, not an interval, scale.

275

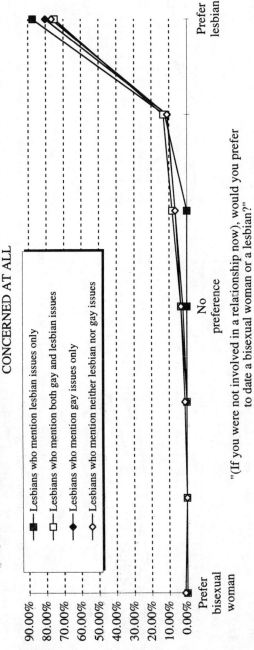

Figure 5.2: DIFFERENCES IN FEELINGS TOWARD BISEXUALS AMONG LESBIANS WHO ARE CONCERNED ABOUT LESBIAN ISSUES EXCLUSIVELY AND LESBIANS WHO ARE CONCERNED ABOUT GAY ISSUES GENERALLY OR WHO ARE NOT CONCERNED AT ALL

— ■ — Lesbians who mention lesbian issues only
— □ — Lesbians who mention both gay and lesbian issues
— ◆ — Lesbians who mention gay issues only
— ◇ — Lesbians who mention neither lesbian nor gay issues

"(If you were not involved in a relationship now), would you prefer to date a bisexual woman or a lesbian?"

Note: Findings for the question about discussion group preferences are not presented because they are very similar to the findings for the question about general comfort, and findings for the question about the substitute speaker are not presented because they are very similar to the findings for the question about the lobbyist.

Significance: Chi-square = 7.39, df = 15, n.s.; F = 1.23, df = (3, 261), n.s. The chi-square significance test is given in addition to the F-test because, strictly speaking, the preference scale is an ordinal, not an interval, scale.

This figure is continued on the next page.

276

Figure 5.2 (cont'd): DIFFERENCES IN FEELINGS TOWARD BISEXUALS AMONG
LESBIANS WHO ARE CONCERNED ABOUT LESBIAN ISSUES EXCLUSIVELY AND
LESBIANS WHO ARE CONCERNED ABOUT GAY ISSUES GENERALLY OR WHO ARE NOT
CONCERNED AT ALL

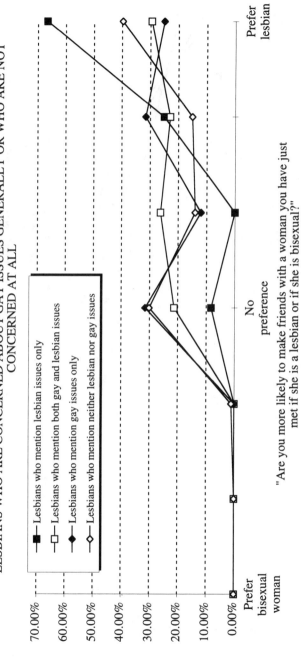

"Are you more likely to make friends with a woman you have just
met if she is a lesbian or if she is bisexual?"

Significance: Chi-square = 32.38, df = 12, p = .001; F = 4.58, df = (3, 266), p = .004. The chi-square significance test is given in addition to the F-test because, strictly speaking, the preference scale is an ordinal, not an interval, scale.

This figure is continued on the next page.

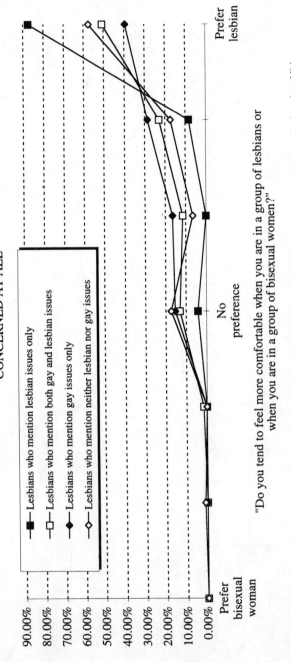

Figure 5.2 (cont'd): DIFFERENCES IN FEELINGS TOWARD BISEXUALS AMONG LESBIANS WHO ARE CONCERNED ABOUT LESBIAN ISSUES EXCLUSIVELY AND LESBIANS WHO ARE CONCERNED ABOUT GAY ISSUES GENERALLY OR WHO ARE NOT CONCERNED AT ALL

Legend:
- ■ Lesbians who mention lesbian issues only
- □ Lesbians who mention both gay and lesbian issues
- ◆ Lesbians who mention gay issues only
- ◇ Lesbians who mention neither lesbian nor gay issues

"Do you tend to feel more comfortable when you are in a group of lesbians or when you are in a group of bisexual women?"

Significance: Chi-square = 28.60, df = 15, p = .02; F = 3.80, df = (3, 264), p = .01. The chi-square significance test is given in addition to the F-test because, strictly speaking, the preference scale is an ordinal, not an interval, scale.

This figure is continued on the next page.

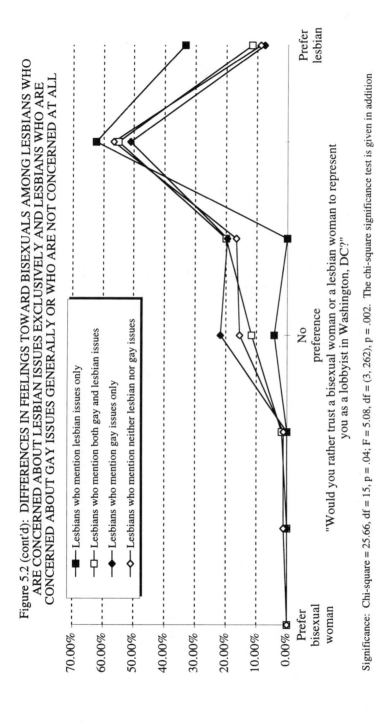

Figure 5.2 (cont'd): DIFFERENCES IN FEELINGS TOWARD BISEXUALS AMONG LESBIANS WHO ARE CONCERNED ABOUT LESBIAN ISSUES EXCLUSIVELY AND LESBIANS WHO ARE CONCERNED ABOUT GAY ISSUES GENERALLY OR WHO ARE NOT CONCERNED AT ALL

Legend:
- Lesbians who mention lesbian issues only
- Lesbians who mention both gay and lesbian issues
- Lesbians who mention gay issues only
- Lesbians who mention neither lesbian nor gay issues

X-axis: Prefer bisexual woman / No preference / Prefer lesbian

Y-axis: 0.00%, 10.00%, 20.00%, 30.00%, 40.00%, 50.00%, 60.00%, 70.00%

"Would you rather trust a bisexual woman or a lesbian woman to represent you as a lobbyist in Washington, DC?"

Significance: Chi-square = 25.66, df = 15, p = .04; F = 5.08, df = (3, 262), p = .002. The chi-square significance test is given in addition to the F-test because, strictly speaking, the preference scale is an ordinal, not an interval, scale.

This figure is continued on the next page.

279

Figure 5.2 (cont'd): DIFFERENCES IN FEELINGS TOWARD BISEXUALS AMONG LESBIANS WHO ARE CONCERNED ABOUT LESBIAN ISSUES EXCLUSIVELY AND LESBIANS WHO ARE CONCERNED ABOUT GAY ISSUES GENERALLY OR WHO ARE NOT CONCERNED AT ALL

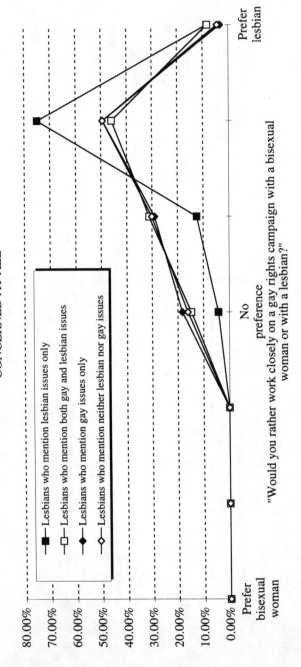

"Would you rather work closely on a gay rights campaign with a bisexual woman or with a lesbian?"

Significance: Chi-square = 10.38, df = 9, n.s.; F = 2.53, df = (3, 267), p = .06. The chi-square significance test is given in addition to the F-test because, strictly speaking, the preference scale is an ordinal, not an interval, scale.

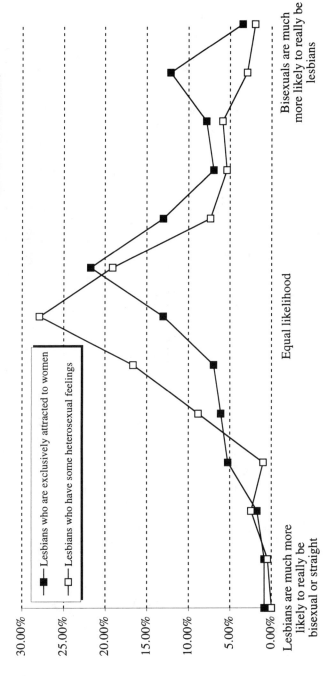

Figure 5.3: EXCLUSIVITY OF LESBIANS' SEXUAL ATTRACTION TOWARD WOMEN AND BELIEFS ABOUT THE RELATIVE AUTHENTICITY OF BISEXUAL AND LESBIAN IDENTITIES

— ■ — Lesbians who are exclusively attracted to women

— □ — Lesbians who have some heterosexual feelings

Lesbians are much more likely to really be bisexual or straight

Equal likelihood

Bisexuals are much more likely to really be lesbians

Significance: Chi-square = 34.77, df = 12, p = .0005; F = 9.07, df = (1, 317), p = .003. The chi-square significance test is given in addition to the F-test because, strictly speaking, the likelihood scale is an ordinal, not an interval, scale.

281

Figure 5.4: EXCLUSIVITY OF LESBIANS' SEXUAL ATTRACTION TOWARD WOMEN AND BELIEFS
ABOUT BISEXUAL WOMEN'S TRUSTWORTHINESS COMPARED TO LESBIANS

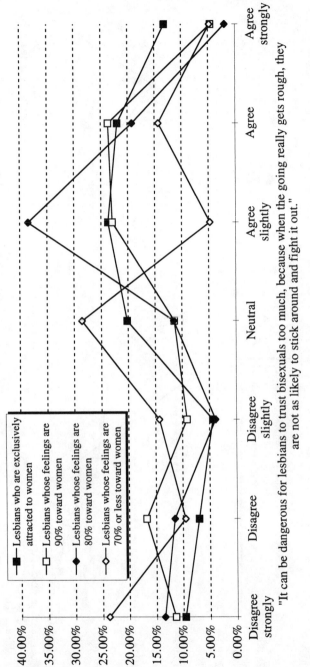

"It can be dangerous for lesbians to trust bisexuals too much, because when the going really gets rough, they
are not as likely to stick around and fight it out."

Significance: Chi-square = 35.78, df = 18, p = .008; F = 3.31, df = (3, 314), p = .02. The chi-square significance test is given in addition to the
F-test because, strictly speaking, the agree-disagree scale is an ordinal, not an interval, scale.

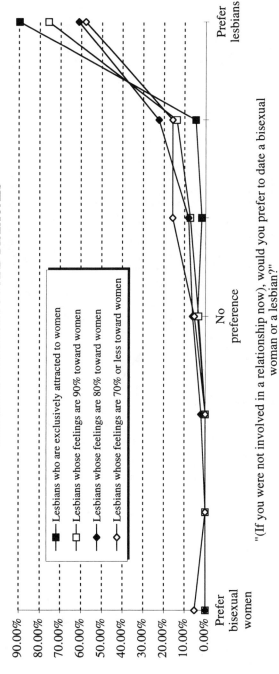

Figure 5.5: EXCLUSIVITY OF LESBIANS' SEXUAL ATTRACTION TOWARD WOMEN AND LESBIANS' FEELINGS TOWARD BISEXUALS

Legend:
- Lesbians who are exclusively attracted to women
- Lesbians whose feelings are 90% toward women
- Lesbians whose feelings are 80% toward women
- Lesbians whose feelings are 70% or less toward women

Y-axis: 90.00%, 80.00%, 70.00%, 60.00%, 50.00%, 40.00%, 30.00%, 20.00%, 10.00%, 0.00%

X-axis: Prefer bisexual women — No preference — Prefer lesbians

"(If you were not involved in a relationship now), would you prefer to date a bisexual woman or a lesbian?"

Note: Findings for the question about the gay rights campaign and the substitute speaker are not presented because they are similar to the findings for the question about the lobbyist. The substitute speaker findings are statistically insignificant.

Significance: Chi-square = 42.25, df = 15, p = .0002; $F = 7.28$, df = (3, 309), p = .0001. The chi-square significance test is given in addition to the F-test because, strictly speaking, the preference scale is an ordinal, not an interval, scale.

Note: This figure is continued on the next page.

283

Figure 5.5 (cont'd): EXCLUSIVITY OF LESBIANS' SEXUAL ATTRACTION TOWARD WOMEN AND LESBIANS' FEELINGS TOWARD BISEXUALS

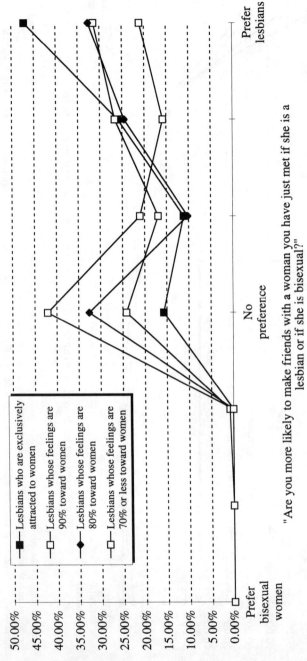

"Are you more likely to make friends with a woman you have just met if she is a lesbian or if she is bisexual?"

Significance: Chi-square = 17.76, df = 12, p = n.s.; F = 4.35, df = (3, 314), p = .005. The chi-square significance test is given in addition to the F-test because, strictly speaking, the preference scale is an ordinal, not an interval, scale.

Note: This figure is continued on the next page.

Figure 5.5 (cont'd): EXCLUSIVITY OF LESBIANS' SEXUAL ATTRACTION TOWARD WOMEN AND LESBIANS' FEELINGS TOWARD BISEXUALS

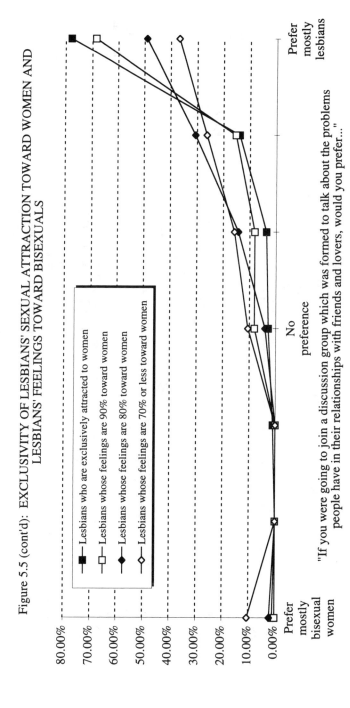

Significance: Chi-square = 39.47, df = 15, p = .0005; F = 6.10, df = (3, 309), p = .0005. The chi-square significance test is given in addition to the F-test because, strictly speaking, the preference scale is an ordinal, not an interval, scale.

"If you were going to join a discussion group which was formed to talk about the problems people have in their relationships with friends and lovers, would you prefer..."

Note: This figure is continued on the next page.

285

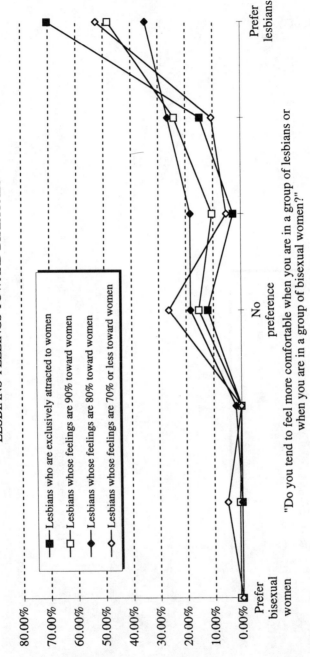

Figure 5.5 (cont'd): EXCLUSIVITY OF LESBIANS' SEXUAL ATTRACTION TOWARD WOMEN AND LESBIANS' FEELINGS TOWARD BISEXUALS

Legend:
■ Lesbians who are exclusively attracted to women
□ Lesbians whose feelings are 90% toward women
◆ Lesbians whose feelings are 80% toward women
◇ Lesbians whose feelings are 70% or less toward women

"Do you tend to feel more comfortable when you are in a group of lesbians or when you are in a group of bisexual women?"

Significance: Chi-square = 40.33, df = 18. p = .002; F = 4.84, df = (3, 312), p = .003. The chi-square significance test is given in addition to the F-test because, strictly speaking, the preference scale is an ordinal, not an interval, scale.

Note: This figure is continued on the next page.

Figure 5.5 (cont'd): EXCLUSIVITY OF LESBIANS' SEXUAL ATTRACTION TOWARD WOMEN AND
LESBIANS' FEELINGS TOWARD BISEXUALS

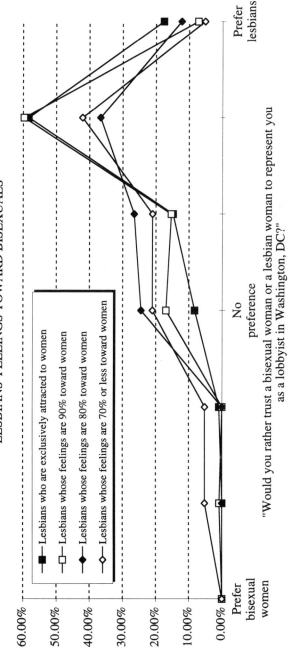

"Would you rather trust a bisexual woman or a lesbian woman to represent you
as a lobbyist in Washington, DC?"

Legend:
■ Lesbians who are exclusively attracted to women
□ Lesbians whose feelings are 90% toward women
◆ Lesbians whose feelings are 80% toward women
◇ Lesbians whose feelings are 70% or less toward women

Significance: Chi-square = 34.64, df = 15, p = .003; F = 4.93, df = (3, 311), p = .002. The chi-square significance test is given in addition to the F-test because, strictly speaking, the preference scale is an ordinal, not an interval, scale.

287

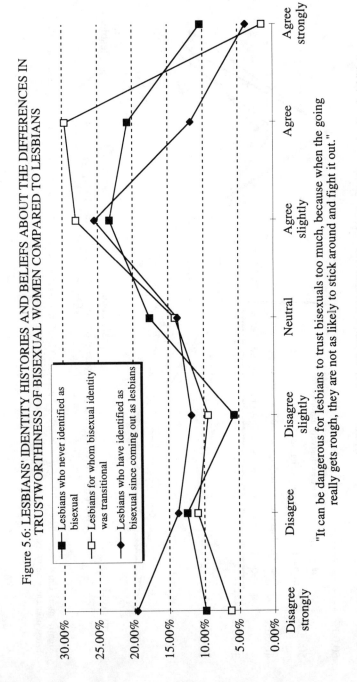

Figure 5.6: LESBIANS' IDENTITY HISTORIES AND BELIEFS ABOUT THE DIFFERENCES IN TRUSTWORTHINESS OF BISEXUAL WOMEN COMPARED TO LESBIANS

Legend:
- Lesbians who never identified as bisexual
- Lesbians for whom bisexual identity was transitional
- Lesbians who have identified as bisexual since coming out as lesbians

"It can be dangerous for lesbians to trust bisexuals too much, because when the going really gets rough, they are not as likely to stick around and fight it out."

Significance: Chi-square = 19.10, df = 12, p = .09; F = 3.75, df = (2, 305), p = .025. The chi-square significance test is given in addition to the F-test because, strictly speaking, the agree–disagree scale is an ordinal, not an interval, scale.

288

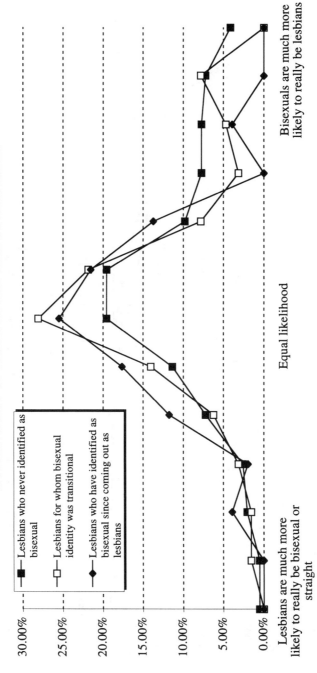

Figure 5.7: LESBIANS' IDENTITY HISTORIES AND BELIEFS ABOUT THE RELATIVE AUTHENTICITY OF BISEXUAL AND LESBIAN IDENTITIES

Significance: Chi-square = 23.45, df = 24, n.s.; F = 4.71, df = (2, 306), p =.01. The chi-square significance test is given in addition to the F-test because, strictly speaking, the likelihood scale is an ordinal, not an interval, scale.

289

290

Figure 5.8: LESBIANS' IDENTITY HISTORIES AND FEELINGS ABOUT BISEXUAL WOMEN

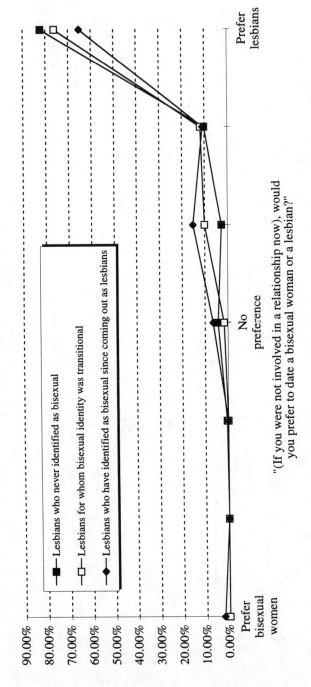

"(If you were not involved in a relationship now), would you prefer to date a bisexual woman or a lesbian?"

Significance: Chi-square = 20.17, df = 10, p = .03; F = 4.70, df = (2, 288), p = .01. The chi-square significance test is given in addition to the F-test because, strictly speaking, the preference scale is an ordinal, not an interval, scale.

Note: This figure is continued on the next page.

Figure 5.8 (cont'd): LESBIANS' IDENTITY HISTORIES AND FEELINGS ABOUT BISEXUAL WOMEN

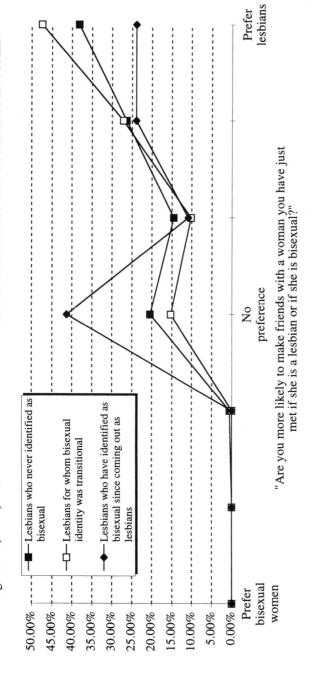

Significance: Chi-square = 14.22, df = 8, p = .08; F = 5.69, df = (2, 288), p = .004. The chi-square significance test is given in addition to the F-test because, strictly speaking, the preference scale is an ordinal, not an interval, scale.

Note: This figure is continued on the next page.

Figure 5.8 (cont'd): LESBIANS' IDENTITY HISTORIES AND FEELINGS ABOUT BISEXUAL WOMEN

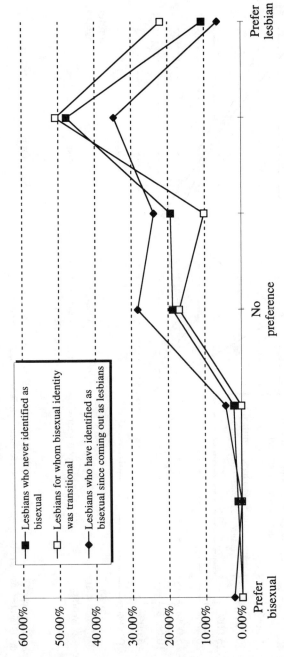

"If you were going to make a speech to a local citizens' group about alternatives to traditional heterosexual relationships . . . would you rather trust a bisexual woman or a lesbian to go in your place?"

Significance: Chi-square = 21.67, df = 12, p = .04; F = 6.59, df = (2, 288), p = .002. The chi-square significance test is given in addition to the F-test because, strictly speaking, the preference scale is an ordinal, not an interval, scale.

Figure 7.1: COMPARISON BETWEEN BISEXUAL WOMEN'S AND LESBIANS' BELIEFS ABOUT THE RELATIVE AUTHENTICITY OF BISEXUAL AND LESBIAN IDENTITIES

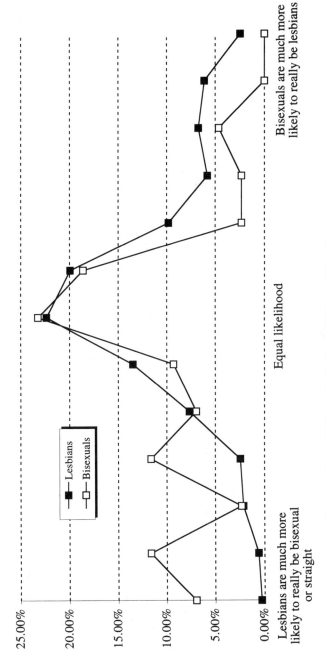

Significance: Chi-square = 56.74, df = 12, p = .0001; F = 27.25, df = (1, 367), p = .0001. The chi-square significance test is given in addition to the F-test because, strictly speaking, the likelihood scale is an ordinal, not an interval, scale.

Figure 7.2: COMPARISON BETWEEN BISEXUAL WOMEN'S AND LESBIANS' BELIEFS ABOUT THE
RELATIVE LIKELIHOOD THAT BISEXUAL WOMEN'S AND LESBIANS' IDENTITIES ARE
TRANSITIONAL

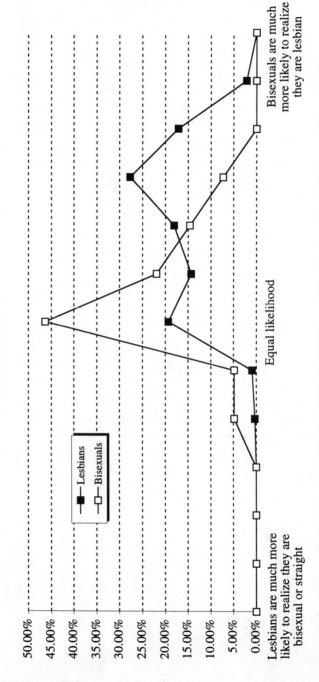

Significance: Chi-square = 40.62, df = 7, p = .0001; F = 40.27, df = (1, 360), p = .0001.   The chi-square significance test is given in addition to
the F-test because, strictly speaking, the likelihood scale is an ordinal, not an interval, scale.

Figure 7.3: BISEXUAL WOMEN'S BELIEFS ABOUT BISEXUAL WOMEN'S LEVELS OF
COMMITMENT AND TRUSTWORTHINESS COMPARED TO LESBIANS

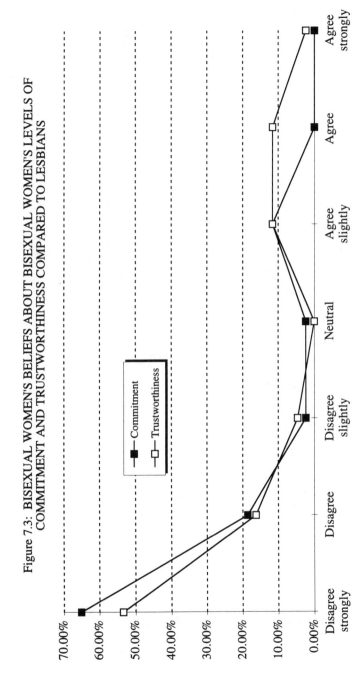

Significance: Compared to lesbians (see fig. 4.3), bisexuals' responses to both measures are significantly different at p = .0001.

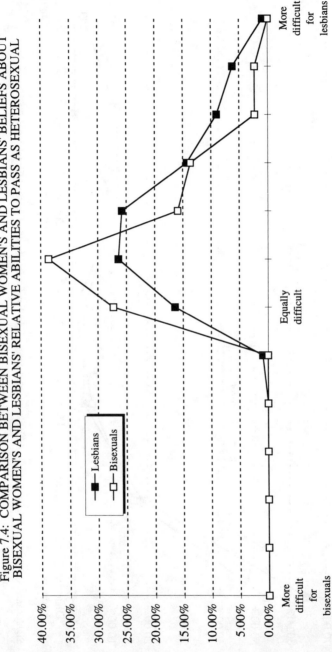

Figure 7.4: COMPARISON BETWEEN BISEXUAL WOMEN'S AND LESBIANS' BELIEFS ABOUT BISEXUAL WOMEN'S AND LESBIANS' RELATIVE ABILITIES TO PASS AS HETEROSEXUAL

Significance: Chi-square = 10.18, df = 7, n.s.; F = 6.70, df = (1, 364), p = .01. The chi-square significance test is given in addition to the F-test because, strictly speaking, the ease of passing scale is an ordinal, not an interval, scale.

296

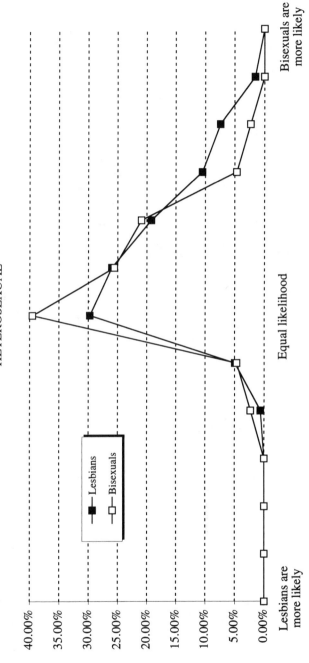

Figure 7.5: COMPARISON BETWEEN BISEXUAL WOMEN'S AND LESBIANS' BELIEFS ABOUT THE RELATIVE LIKELIHOOD THAT BISEXUAL WOMEN AND LESBIANS DESIRE TO PASS AS HETEROSEXUAL

Significance: Chi-square = 6.05, df = 7, n.s.; F = 4.11, df = (1, 364), p = .04. The chi-square significance test is given in addition to the F-test because, strictly speaking, the likelihood scale is an ordinal, not an interval, scale.

Figure 7.6: BISEXUAL WOMEN'S PERCEPTIONS OF THE RELATIVE DEGREE OF PREJUDICE AND DISCRIMINATION EXPERIENCED BY BISEXUAL WOMEN AND LESBIANS

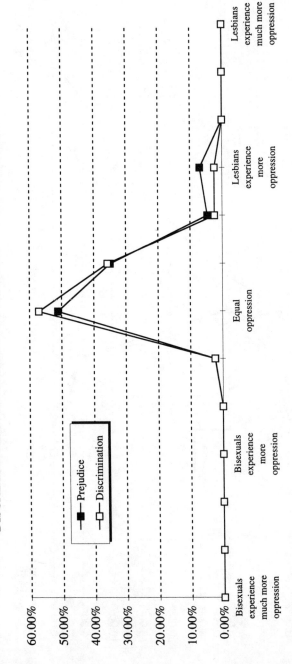

Significance, perceptions of prejudice compared to lesbians' (see fig. 4.4): Chi-square = 26.81, df = 7, p = .0004; F = 17.25, df = (1, 366), p = .0001.
Significance, perceptions of discrimination compared to lesbians' (see fig. 4.4): Chi-square = 45.08, df = 7, p = .0001; F = 35.77, df = (1, 363), p = .0001.
The chi-square significance test is given in addition to the F-test because, strictly speaking, the prejudice and discrimination perception scales are ordinal, not interval, scales.

298

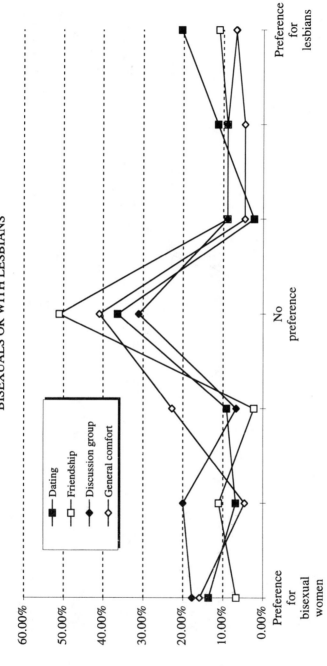

Figure 7.7: BISEXUAL WOMEN'S PREFERENCES FOR ASSOCIATING SOCIALLY WITH OTHER BISEXUALS OR WITH LESBIANS

Significance: All comparisons to lesbians (see fig. 4.5) are significant at p = .0001.

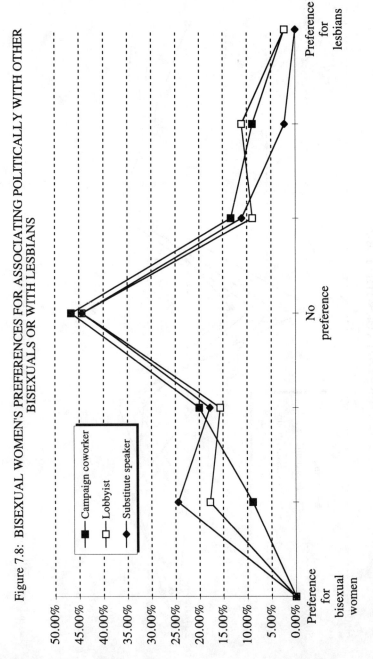

Figure 7.8: BISEXUAL WOMEN'S PREFERENCES FOR ASSOCIATING POLITICALLY WITH OTHER BISEXUALS OR WITH LESBIANS

Significance: All comparisons to lesbians (see fig. 4.6) are significant at p = .0001.

Figure 7.9: STRENGTH OF BISEXUAL WOMEN'S HETEROSEXUAL FEELINGS AND THEIR
FEELINGS TOWARD OTHER BISEXUAL WOMEN

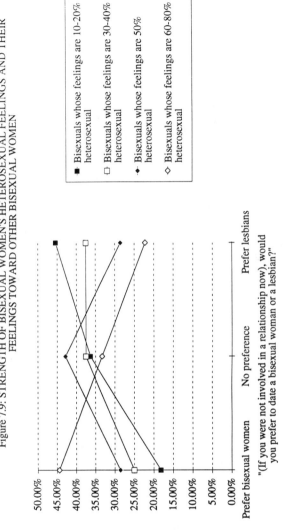

■ Bisexuals whose feelings are 10-20% heterosexual

□ Bisexuals whose feelings are 30-40% heterosexual

♦ Bisexuals whose feelings are 50% heterosexual

◇ Bisexuals whose feelings are 60-80% heterosexual

"(If you were not involved in a relationship now), would you prefer to date a bisexual woman or a lesbian?"

Significance: F = 1.03, df = (3, 39), n.s.

Note: This figure is continued on the next page.

301

Figure 7.9 (cont'd): STRENGTH OF BISEXUAL WOMEN'S HETEROSEXUAL FEELINGS AND THEIR FEELINGS TOWARD OTHER BISEXUAL WOMEN

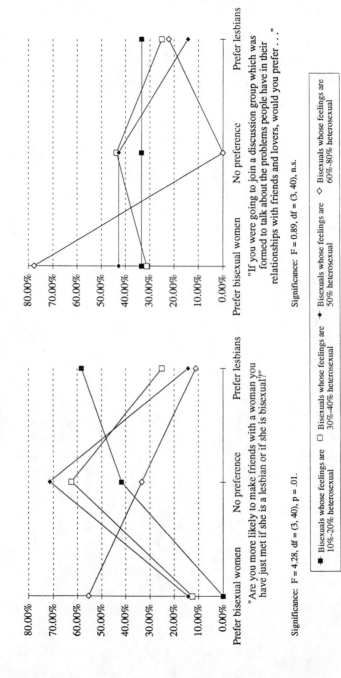

Significance: F = 4.28, df = (3, 40), p = .01.

"Are you more likely to make friends with a woman you have just met if she is a lesbian or if she is bisexual?"

Significance: F = 0.89, df = (3, 40), n.s.

"If you were going to join a discussion group which was formed to talk about the problems people have in their relationships with friends and lovers, would you prefer . . . "

Note: This figure is continued on the next page.

302

Figure 7.9 (cont'd): STRENGTH OF BISEXUAL WOMEN'S HETEROSEXUAL FEELINGS AND
THEIR FEELINGS TOWARD OTHER BISEXUAL WOMEN

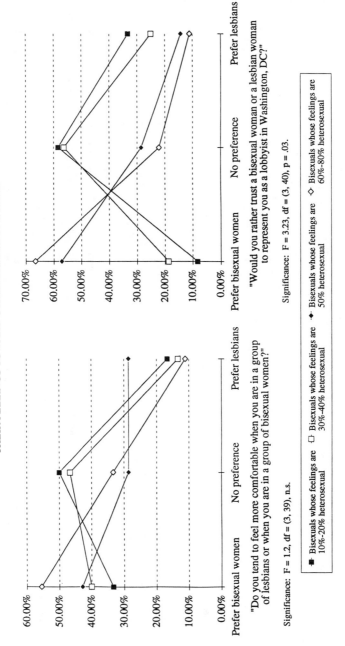

"Do you tend to feel more comfortable when you are in a group
of lesbians or when you are in a group of bisexual women?"

Significance: F = 1.2, df = (3, 39), n.s.

"Would you rather trust a bisexual woman or a lesbian woman
to represent you as a lobbyist in Washington, DC?"

Significance: F = 3.23, df = (3, 40), p = .03.

■ Bisexuals whose feelings are □ Bisexuals whose feelings are ◆ Bisexuals whose feelings are ◇ Bisexuals whose feelings are
10%-20% heterosexual   30%-40% heterosexual   50% heterosexual   60%-80% heterosexual

303

Figure 7.10: GENDER OF BISEXUAL WOMEN'S CURRENT PARTNERS AND THEIR FEELINGS
TOWARD OTHER BISEXUAL WOMEN

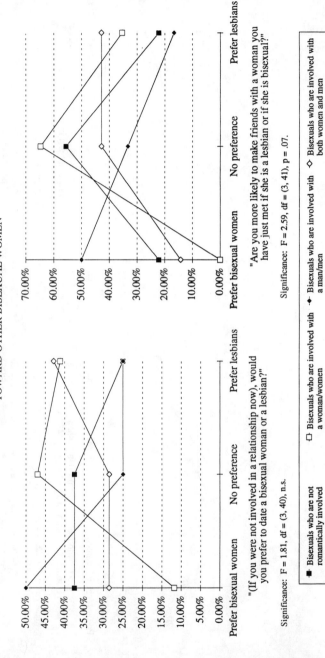

"(If you were not involved in a relationship now), would
you prefer to date a bisexual woman or a lesbian?"

Significance: F = 1.81, df = (3, 40), n.s.

"Are you more likely to make friends with a woman you
have just met if she is a lesbian or if she is bisexual?"

Significance: F = 2.59, df = (3, 41), p = .07.

■ Bisexuals who are not
   romantically involved

□ Bisexuals who are involved with
   a woman/women

◆ Bisexuals who are involved with
   a man/men

◇ Bisexuals who are involved with
   both women and men

Note: This figure is continued on the next page.

Figure 7.10 (cont'd): GENDER OF BISEXUAL WOMEN'S CURRENT PARTNERS AND THEIR
FEELINGS TOWARD OTHER BISEXUAL WOMEN

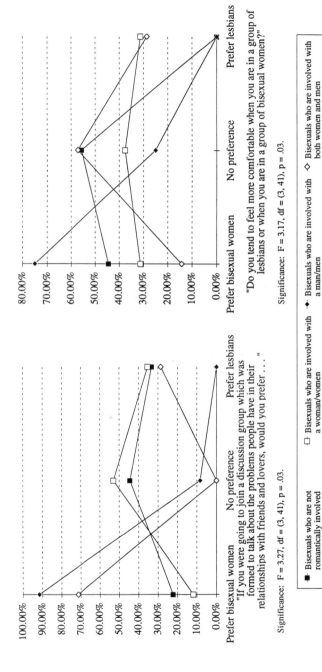

"If you were going to join a discussion group which was
formed to talk about the problems people have in their
relationships with friends and lovers, would you prefer . . . "

Significance: F = 3.27, df = (3, 41), p = .03.

"Do you tend to feel more comfortable when you are in a group of
lesbians or when you are in a group of bisexual women?"

Significance: F = 3.17, df = (3, 41), p = .03.

■ Bisexuals who are not   □ Bisexuals who are involved with   ◆ Bisexuals who are involved with   ◇ Bisexuals who are involved with
  romantically involved   a woman/women   a man/men   both women and men

Note: This figure is continued on the next page.

305

Figure 7.10 (cont'd): GENDER OF BISEXUAL WOMEN'S CURRENT PARTNERS AND THEIR
FEELINGS TOWARD OTHER BISEXUAL WOMEN

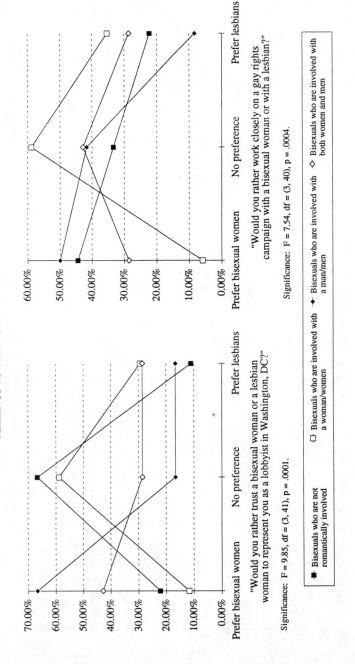

"Would you rather trust a bisexual woman or a lesbian
woman to represent you as a lobbyist in Washington, DC?"

Significance: F = 9.85, df = (3, 41), p = .0001.

"Would you rather work closely on a gay rights
campaign with a bisexual woman or with a lesbian?"

Significance: F = 7.54, df = (3, 40), p = .0004.

■ Bisexuals who are not
romantically involved

□ Bisexuals who are involved with
a woman/women

♦ Bisexuals who are involved with
a man/men

◇ Bisexuals who are involved with
both women and men

Figure 7.11: GENDER OF BISEXUAL WOMEN'S CURRENT PARTNERS AND THEIR PERCEPTIONS OF THE RELATIVE DEGREE OF PREJUDICE EXPERIENCED BY BISEXUAL WOMEN AND LESBIANS

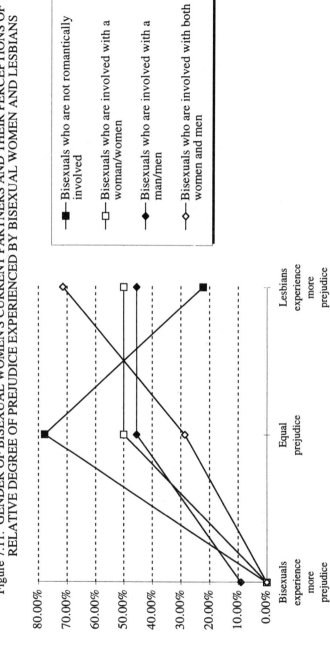

Significance: $F = 3.24$, df $= (3, 39)$, p $= .03$.

• APPENDIX B: TABLES •

Table 4.1
LESBIANS' BELIEFS ABOUT THE PROPORTIONS OF BISEXUAL WOMEN AND LESBIANS WHOSE IDENTITIES ARE TRANSITIONAL

What proportion of women who say they are bisexual do you think will eventually realize that they are lesbian?

	None	Few/ some	Under half	Half	Over half	Most	All	Total
%	0.31%	17.59%	14.82%	18.52%	30.25%	18.52%	0.0%	100%
(n)	(1)	(57)	(48)	(60)	(98)	(60)	(0)	(324)

What proportion of women who say they are lesbians do you believe will eventually realize that they are actually bisexual or straight?

	None	Few/ some	Under half	Half	Over half	Most	All	Total
%	6.17%	85.8%	6.48%	0.62%	0.62%	0.31%	0.0%	100%
(n)	(20)	(278)	(21)	(2)	(2)	(1)	(0)	(324)

Note: See fig. 7.2 for a graph of lesbians' beliefs about the relative likelihood that bisexual women's and lesbians' identities are transitional, obtained by subtracting individual lesbians' answers to these two questions.

Table 4.2
LESBIANS' BELIEFS ABOUT THE AUTHENTICITY OF BISEXUAL AND LESBIAN IDENTITIES

"Society makes it difficult to be a lesbian, so some women claim to be bisexual when they are really lesbians who are afraid to admit it." How strongly do you agree or disagree with this statement?

	Disagree strongly	Disagree	Disagree slightly	Neutral	Agree slightly	Agree	Agree strongly	Total
%	3.38%	5.83%	2.76%	4.91%	26.69%	32.21%	24.23%	100%
(n)	(11)	(19)	(9)	(16)	(87)	(105)	(79)	(326)

"Some lesbians really are somewhat attracted to men, but they are afraid to express these feelings because other lesbians would not approve of them." How strongly do you agree or disagree with this statement?

	Disagree strongly	Disagree	Disagree slightly	Neutral	Agree slightly	Agree	Agree strongly	Total
%	12.54%	8.26%	4.89%	5.81%	28.75%	28.75%	11.01%	100%
(n)	(41)	(27)	(16)	(19)	(94)	(94)	(36)	(327)

Note: See fig. 7.1 for a graph of lesbians' beliefs about the relative authenticity of bisexual and lesbian identities, obtained by subtracting individual lesbians' answers to these two questions.

Table 4.3
LESBIANS' BELIEFS ABOUT BISEXUAL WOMEN'S AND LESBIANS'
ABILITIES TO PASS AS HETEROSEXUAL

In general, if a bisexual woman *wanted* to pretend that she was straight, how easy or difficult do you think pretending to be straight would be?

	Very difficult	Relatively difficult	Somewhat difficult	Neither	Somewhat easy	Relatively easy	Very easy	Total
%	1.23%	2.46%	17.85%	7.08%	15.08%	29.23%	27.08%	100%
(n)	(4)	(8)	(58)	(23)	(49)	(95)	(88)	(325)

In general, if a lesbian/gay woman *wanted* to pretend that she was straight... do you think this would be easy or difficult for her to do?

	Very difficult	Relatively difficult	Somewhat difficult	Neither	Somewhat easy	Relatively easy	Very easy	Total
%	3.7%	13.58%	14.2%	5.56%	25.0%	20.99%	16.98%	100%
(n)	(12)	(44)	(46)	(18)	(81)	(68)	(55)	(324)

Note: See fig. 7.4 for a graph of lesbians' beliefs about bisexual women's and lesbians' relative abilities to pass as heterosexual, obtained by subtracting individual lesbians' answers to these two questions.

Table 4.4
LESBIANS' BELIEFS ABOUT BISEXUAL WOMEN'S AND LESBIANS'
DESIRES TO PASS AS HETEROSEXUAL

Imagine that it is *very easy* for all bisexuals to pretend that they are heterosexual. What proportion of bisexual women do you think *would want* to pretend they're heterosexual?

	None	Few/ some	Under half	Half	Over half	Most	All	Total
%	2.78%	10.19%	11.73%	14.20%	18.83%	38.27%	4.01%	100%
(n)	(9)	(33)	(38)	(46)	(61)	(124)	(13)	(324)

Imagine that it is *very easy* for all lesbians/gay women to pretend that they are heterosexual. What proportion of lesbians/gay women do you believe *would want* to pretend they're heterosexual?

	None	Few/ some	Under half	Half	Over half	Most	All	Total
%	6.15%	26.77%	21.54%	21.54%	16.0%	8.0%	0.0%	100%
(n)	(20)	(87)	(70)	(70)	(52)	(26)	(0)	(325)

Note: See fig. 7.5 for a graph of lesbians' beliefs about the relative likelihood that bisexual women and lesbians desire to pass as heterosexual, obtained by subtracting individual lesbians' answers to these two questions.

Table 4.5
LESBIANS' BELIEFS ABOUT THE DEGREES OF PREJUDICE AND DISCRIMINATION
EXPERIENCED BY BISEXUAL WOMEN AND LESBIANS

How much prejudice do you feel there is in the general U.S. population against bisexual women?

	None	Almost none	A bit	Some	Quite a bit	Very great deal	More than any other group	Total
%	0.62%	3.08%	6.77%	35.39%	34.46%	19.69%	0.0%	100%
(n)	(2)	(10)	(22)	(115)	(112)	(64)	(0)	(325)

How much prejudice do you feel there is in the general U.S. population against lesbians/gay women?

								Total
%	0.0%	0.30%	0.30%	1.82%	16.11%	70.52%	10.94%	100%
(n)	(0)	(1)	(1)	(6)	(53)	(232)	(36)	(329)

How much discrimination do you feel there is in the general U.S. population against bisexual women?

								Total
%	1.54%	10.49%	12.96%	35.49%	24.69%	14.20%	0.62%	100%
(n)	(5)	(34)	(42)	(115)	(80)	(46)	(2)	(324)

How much discrimination do you feel there is in the general U.S. population against lesbians/gay women?

								Total
%	0.0%	0.0%	0.92%	5.51%	16.82%	65.44%	11.32%	100%
(n)	(0)	(0)	(3)	(18)	(55)	(214)	(37)	(327)

Table 5.1
EXCLUSIVITY OF LESBIANS' SEXUAL ATTRACTION TOWARD WOMEN AND
BELIEFS ABOUT THE AUTHENTICITY OF BISEXUAL AND LESBIAN IDENTITIES

"Society makes it difficult to be a lesbian, so some women claim to be bisexual when they are really lesbians who are afraid to admit it." How strongly do you agree or disagree with this statement?

	Disagree strongly	Disagree	Disagree slightly	Neutral	Agree slightly	Agree	Agree strongly	Total
Lesbians who are exclusively attracted to women	6.96% (8)	6.96% (8)	3.48% (4)	3.48% (4)	21.74% (25)	28.7% (33)	28.7% (33)	100% (115)
Lesbians who have some heterosexual feelings	1.47% (3)	5.39% (11)	2.45% (5)	5.88% (12)	28.43% (58)	35.29% (72)	21.08% (43)	100% (204)

Significance: Chi-square = 11.87, df = 6, p = .06; F = 0.96, df = (1, 317), n.s.

"Some lesbians really are somewhat attracted to men, but they are afraid to express these feelings because other lesbians would not approve of them." How strongly do you agree or disagree with this statement?

	Disagree strongly	Disagree	Disagree slightly	Neutral	Agree slightly	Agree	Agree strongly	Total
Lesbians who are exclusively attracted to women	22.61% (26)	9.57% (11)	3.48% (4)	8.7% (10)	30.43% (35)	19.13% (22)	6.09% (7)	100% (115)
Lesbians who have some heterosexual feelings	6.86% (14)	7.84% (16)	5.88% (12)	4.41% (9)	27.45% (56)	33.82% (69)	13.73% (28)	100% (204)

Significance: Chi-square = 27.62, df = 6, p = .0001; F = 20.69, df = (1, 317), p = .0001. The chi-square significance test is given in addition to the F-test because, strictly speaking, the agree-disagree scale is an ordinal, not an interval, scale.

Table 5.2
LESBIANS' IDENTITY HISTORIES AND BELIEFS ABOUT THE AUTHENTICITY
OF BISEXUAL AND LESBIAN IDENTITIES

"Society makes it difficult to be a lesbian, so some women claim to be bisexual when they are really lesbians who are afraid to admit it." How strongly do you agree or disagree with this statement?

	Disagree strongly	Disagree	Disagree slightly	Neutral	Agree slightly	Agree	Agree strongly	Total
Lesbians who never identified as bisexual	4.12% (8)	5.15% (10)	3.09% (6)	5.15% (10)	27.84% (54)	29.38% (57)	25.26% (49)	100% (194)
Lesbians for whom bisexual identity was transitional	3.12% (2)	7.81% (5)	3.12% (2)	3.12% (2)	21.88% (14)	37.5% (24)	23.44% (15)	100% (64)
Lesbians who identified as bisexual since coming out lesbian	1.96% (1)	7.84% (4)	1.96% (1)	7.84% (4)	25.49% (13)	27.45% (14)	27.45% (14)	100% (51)

Significance: Chi-square = 4.92, df = 12, n.s.; F = .009, df = (2, 306), n.s.

"Some lesbians really are somewhat attracted to men, but they are afraid to express these feelings because other lesbians would not approve of them." How strongly do you agree or disagree with this statement?

	Disagree strongly	Disagree	Disagree slightly	Neutral	Agree slightly	Agree	Agree strongly	Total
Lesbians who never identified as bisexual	17.53% (34)	8.25% (16)	4.64% (9)	6.7% (13)	29.9% (58)	25.26% (49)	7.73% (15)	100% (194)
Lesbians for whom bisexual identity was transitional	7.81% (5)	9.38% (6)	4.69% (3)	6.25% (4)	26.56% (17)	31.25% (20)	14.06% (9)	100% (64)
Lesbians who identified as bisexual since coming out lesbian	0.0% (0)	5.88% (3)	5.88% (3)	3.92% (2)	29.41% (15)	39.22% (20)	15.69% (8)	100% (51)

Significance: Chi-square = 19.02, df = 12, p = .09; F = 7.61, df = (2, 306), p = .0006. The chi-square significance test is given in addition to the F-test because, strictly speaking, the agree-disagree scale is an ordinal, not an interval, scale.

Table 7.1
BISEXUALS' BELIEFS ABOUT THE AUTHENTICITY OF
BISEXUAL AND LESBIAN IDENTITIES

"Society makes it difficult to be a lesbian, so some women claim to be bisexual when they are really lesbians who are afraid to admit it." How strongly do you agree or disagree with this statement?[a]

	Disagree strongly	Disagree	Disagree slightly	Neutral	Agree slightly	Agree	Agree strongly	Total
%	16.28%	16.28%	6.98%	9.3%	23.26%	13.95%	13.95%	100%
(n)	(7)	(7)	(3)	(4)	(10)	(6)	(6)	(43)

"Some lesbians really are somewhat attracted to men, but they are afraid to express these feelings because other lesbians would not approve of them." How strongly do you agree or disagree with this statement?[b]

	Disagree strongly	Disagree	Disagree slightly	Neutral	Agree slightly	Agree	Agree strongly	Total
%	4.55%	9.09%	2.27%	11.36%	13.64%	29.55%	29.55%	100%
(n)	(2)	(4)	(1)	(5)	(6)	(13)	(13)	(44)

Significance, compared to lesbians (see table 4.2):
a. Chi-square = 28.41, df = 6, p = .0001; F = 26.55, df = (1, 367), p = .0001.
b. Chi-square = 17.98, df = 6, p = .006; F = 4.92, df = (1, 369), p = .03.
The chi-square significance test is given in addition to the F-test because, strictly speaking, the agree-disagree scale is an ordinal, not an interval, scale.

Table 7.2

BISEXUALS' BELIEFS ABOUT THE PROPORTIONS OF BISEXUAL WOMEN AND
LESBIANS WHOSE IDENTITIES ARE TRANSITIONAL

What proportion of women who say they are bisexual do you think will eventually realize
that they are lesbian?[c]

	None	Few/ some	Under half	Half	Over half	Most	All	Total
%	0.0%	41.46%	31.71%	12.2%	14.63%	0.0%	0.0%	100%
(n)	(0)	(17)	(13)	(5)	(6)	(0)	(0)	(41)

What proportion of women who say they are lesbians do you believe will eventually realize
that they are actually bisexual or straight?[d]

	None	Few/ some	Under half	Half	Over half	Most	All	Total
%	0.0%	73.81%	16.67%	4.76%	4.76%	0.0%	0.0%	100%
(n)	(0)	(31)	(7)	(2)	(2)	(0)	(0)	(42)

Significance, compared to lesbians (see table 4.1):
c. Chi square = 28.09, df − 5, p = .0001; F = 27.09, df = (1, 363), p = .0001.
d. Chi-square = 20.09, df = 5, p = .001; F = 16.04, df = (1, 364), p = .0001.
The chi-square significance test is given in addition to the F-test because, strictly speaking, the
agree-disagree scale is an ordinal, not an interval, scale.

Table 7.3

BISEXUAL WOMEN'S BELIEFS ABOUT BISEXUAL WOMEN'S AND LESBIANS'
ABILITIES TO PASS AS HETEROSEXUAL

In general, if a bisexual woman *wanted* to pretend that she was straight, how easy or difficult do you think pretending to be straight would be?[e]

	Very difficult	Relatively difficult	Somewhat difficult	Neither	Somewhat easy	Relatively easy	Very easy	Total
%	2.27%	6.82%	25.0%	2.27%	22.73%	27.27%	13.64%	100%
(n)	(1)	(3)	(11)	(1)	(10)	(12)	(6)	(44)

In general, if a lesbian/gay woman *wanted* to pretend that she was straight . . . do you think this would be easy or difficult for her to do?[f]

	Very difficult	Relatively difficult	Somewhat difficult	Neither	Somewhat easy	Relatively easy	Very easy	Total
%	11.36%	27.27%	22.73%	6.82%	13.64%	15.91%	2.27%	100%
(n)	(5)	(12)	(10)	(3)	(6)	(7)	(1)	(44)

Significance, compared to lesbians (see table 4.3):
e. Chi-square = 9.43, df = 6, n.s.; F = 4.71, df = (1, 367), p = .03.
f. Chi-square = 2.03, df = 6, n.s.; F = 0.05, df = (1, 366), n.s.
The chi-square significance test is given in addition to the F-test because, strictly speaking, the agree-disagree scale is an ordinal, not an interval, scale.

Table 7.4

BISEXUAL WOMEN'S BELIEFS ABOUT BISEXUAL WOMEN'S AND LESBIANS'
DESIRES TO PASS AS HETEROSEXUAL

Imagine that it is *very easy* for all bisexuals to pretend that they are heterosexual. What proportion of bisexual women do you think *would want* to pretend they're heterosexual?[g]

	None	Few/ some	Under half	Half	Over half	Most	All	Total
%	4.65%	18.6%	9.3%	23.26%	34.88%	9.3%	0.0%	100%
(n)	(2)	(8)	(4)	(10)	(15)	(4)	(0)	(43)

Imagine that it is *very easy* for all lesbians/gay women to pretend that they are heterosexual. What proportion of lesbians/gay women do you believe *would want* to pretend they're heterosexual?[h]

	None	Few/ some	Under half	Half	Over half	Most	All	Total
%	13.95%	18.6%	25.58%	25.58%	16.28%	0.0%	0.0%	100%
(n)	(6)	(8)	(11)	(11)	(7)	(0)	(0)	(43)

Significance, compared to lesbians (see table 4.4):
g. Chi-square = 20.68, df = 6, p = .002; F = 8.77, df = (1, 365), p = .003.
h. Chi-square = 8.26, df = 5, n.s.; F = 1.43, df = (1, 366), n.s.
The chi-square significance test is given in addition to the F-test because, strictly speaking, the agree-disagree scale is an ordinal, not an interval, scale.

Table 7.5
BISEXUAL WOMEN'S BELIEFS ABOUT THE DEGREES OF PREJUDICE AND
DISCRIMINATION EXPERIENCED BY BISEXUAL WOMEN AND LESBIANS

How much prejudice do you feel there is in the general U.S. population against bisexual women?[i]

	None	Almost none	A bit	Some	Quite a bit	Very great deal	More than any other group	Total
%	0.0%	2.33%	6.98%	13.95%	32.56%	41.86%	2.33%	100%
(n)	(0)	(1)	(3)	(6)	(14)	(18)	(1)	(43)

How much prejudice do you feel there is in the general U.S. population against lesbians/gay women?[k]

%	0.0%	0.0%	0.0%	4.44%	22.22%	68.89%	4.44%	100%
(n)	(0)	(0)	(0)	(2)	(10)	(31)	(2)	(45)

How much discrimination do you feel there is in the general U.S. population against bisexual women?[m]

%	0.0%	0.0%	4.76%	21.43%	28.57%	42.86%	2.38%	100%
(n)	(0)	(0)	(2)	(9)	(12)	(18)	(1)	(42)

How much discrimination do you feel there is in the general U.S. population against lesbians/gay women?[n]

%	0.0%	0.0%	0.0%	15.56%	17.78%	57.78%	8.89%	100%
(n)	(0)	(0)	(0)	(7)	(8)	(26)	(4)	(45)

Significance, compared to lesbians (see table 4.5):
i. Chi-square = 21.62, df = 6, p = .001; F = 10.02, df = (1, 366), p = .002.
k. n.s.
m. Chi-square = 28.41, df = 6, p = .0001; F = 25.49, df = (1, 364), p = .0001.
n. n.s.
The chi-square significance test is given in addition to the F-test because, strictly speaking, the agree-disagree scale is an ordinal, not an interval, scale.

319

• Notes •

1. This organization has since been renamed the "Bisexual Network of the USA" or "BiNet USA."

CHAPTER 1

1. I also collected articles and letters about bisexuality from almost two dozen other national and local lesbian and gay magazines, newspapers, and newsletters, including *Lesbian Connection, Outweek, QW, Genre, Deneuve, Lavender Reader, Gaybook Magazine, Lesbian and Gay Socialist, Open Hands, Lesbian Ethics, The Lavender Network, Rites, Gay Community News, Bay Windows, The Village Voice, San Francisco Bay Times, The Washington Blade, New York Native, Seattle Gay News, The Gay News-Telegraph, The Guardian, The Empty Closet, Pink Triangle,* and *Outlines.* Because of space limitations, I cannot describe the treatment of bisexuality in all these publications. In general, the publications described represent the range and variety of treatments of bisexuality found in lesbian and gay publications.
2. Subscription and other circulation information was obtained from Karen Troshynski-Thomas and Deborah M. Burek, eds., *The Gale Directory of Publications and Broadcast Media* (Detroit, MI: Gale Research, Inc., 1994).
3. Debra Chasnoff (outgoing executive editor), *Out/Look* (Fall 1990).
4. *10 Percent,* no. 6.
5. *10 Percent,* no. 5.
6. *10 Percent,* no. 2.
7. Readers' genders and biological sexes are assumed on the basis of their first names and any pertinent references made in their letters to the editor. In many cases, these assumptions were confirmed with independent information.
8. Lee, *The Advocate,* no. 375.
9. Letters by Kurka, Harrell, and Griffis, *The Advocate,* no. 453.
10. Young, *The Advocate,* no. 412.
11. Goodkin, *The Advocate,* no. 412.
12. *The Advocate,* no. 523 (April 1989).
13. *The Advocate,* no. 564.

14. *The Advocate*, no. 578.
15. Kevin Koffler, "A New Sandra Bernhard?" *The Advocate*, no. 554.
16. Louis Chunovic, "The World Turns for Dack Rambo," *The Advocate*, no. 595.
17. Richard Laermer, "Nona Hendryx, Both Sides Now," *The Advocate*, no. 596.
18. With the exception of a brief clash between two readers following the Rambo article. (Chrysler, *The Advocate*, no. 598, and Neville, *The Advocate*, no. 601).
19. *Out/Look*, no. 7 (Winter 1990).
20. Letters from Shaw, Zylan, Mennis, Sadowski in *Out/Look*, no. 8 (Spring 1990).
21. Letters from Ochs, Tingwald, Higgins, anonymous, Conforti, Pearlman, "S.C." in *Out/Look*, no. 9 (Summer 1990).
22. Stone, *Out/Look*, no. 10 (Fall 1990).
23. *10 Percent*, no. 2.
24. Marcus, *10 Percent*, no. 5.
25. *Lesbian Contradiction*, no. 2 (Spring 1983).
26. Fay, *Lesbian Contradiction*, no. 6 (Spring 1984).
27. Paz, *Lesbian Contradiction*, no. 21 (Winter 1988); Sugars, *Lesbian Contradiction*, no. 26 (Spring 1989); Dwinell, *Lesbian Contradiction*, no. 27 (Summer 1989).
28. Pekarsky, *Lesbian Contradiction*, no. 25 (Winter 1989).
29. *Lesbian Contradiction*, no. 25 (Winter 1989).
30. Letters by Dashu, Murphy, Louise, *Lesbian Contradiction*, no. 28 (Fall 1989).
31. Murphy and Weiss, *Lesbian Contradiction*, no. 17 (Winter 1987).
32. Brt, *Lesbian Contradiction*, no. 18 (Spring 1987).
33. Anonymous, *Lesbian Contradiction*, no. 18 (Spring 1987).
34. Dajenya, "Sisterhood crosses gender preference lines," *Lesbian Contradiction*, no. 29 (Winter 1990). Marilyn Murphy, "The Gay-Straight Split Revisited," *Lesbian Contradiction*, no. 28 (Fall 1989).
35. Jane Litwoman, "Some thoughts on bisexuality," *Lesbian Contradiction*, no. 29 (Winter 1990).
36. Alena Smith, "Heads or Tails," *Lesbian Contradiction*, no. 44 (Fall 1993).

CHAPTER 2

1. Although Benkert, who wrote under the pseudonym "Kertbeny," coined the word "homosexual" in 1869, historians debate the origins of the concept of a type of person who is sexually oriented toward members of her or his own sex. The concept is at least a few years older; Ulrichs named the "Uranian," later "urning," in 1864, and Trumbach (1977) argued that the 18th-century concept of the "sodomite" as a man who has a preference for members of his own sex was also an essentialist concept akin to the modern concept of the "homosexual." See also Bullough (1990).

2. The debate between essentialism and constructionism is not the same as the debate over whether sexual orientation is a result of biology, socialization, or choice. Even if our desires have a biological basis, constructionists would argue that we give meaning to these desires in a cultural context. Conversely, even if we become lesbian/gay or heterosexual as a result of life experiences, this does not mean that our lesbianism/gayness or heterosexuality cannot be essential. For discussion of essentialism and/or constructionism as applied to sexuality, see Boswell (1990), Caplan (1987), Epstein (1987), Foucault (1978), Hart (1984), Kitzinger (1987), Richardson (1983/84), Rust (1993a), Trumbach (1977), and Weeks (1986).

3. Other authors have written comprehensive and detailed accounts of the history of sexology. See, for example, Irvine (1990), Kitzinger (1987), and Weeks (1981, 1986).

4. The dichotomous model of sexuality has been discussed in detail by Ross (1984). Several authors have traced the historical origins and development of this model, including Bullough and Bullough (1977), DeCecco and Shively (1983/84), Foucault (1979), Hoffman (1983/84), Paul (1985), and Richardson (1983/84). In her own review of the literature, Richardson cites the historical treatments of McIntosh (1968), Plummer (1975, 1981a, 1981b), and Weeks (1981, 1982).

5. The Kinsey et al. data are the source of the oft-quoted figure, "ten percent of the population is gay." The ten-percent figure was not reported in the original 1948 and 1953 volumes; it resulted from a later calculation. People who use the ten-percent figure should keep in mind that Kinsey et al. studied erotic experiences and responsiveness, not identity. Many people engage in homosexual sex without considering themselves homosexual. The ten-percent figure is often used to impress heterosexuals with the size of the gay constituency, but in truth the figure tells us nothing about the percentage of people who consider themselves gay, nor about the percentage of people who are politically aligned with the gay movement.

6. Sex Life of the American Woman and the Kinsey Report, edited by Albert Ellis, was listed under "lesbianism" in 1954; otherwise, "lesbianism" did not appear in the Sociological Abstracts as a separate heading until 1968.

7. These figures refer to articles listed under the indicated headings only; there were additional articles during these years whose abstracts included the words "homosexual" or "lesbian" but which were not listed under these headings.

8. For example, this suggestion was made by Blumstein and Schwartz (1977b), Kaplan and Rogers (1984), Money (1987), Ross (1984), and Zinik (1985).

CHAPTER 3

1. More accurately, representative sampling methods guarantee that each member of a population has a *known* chance of being selected. For many reasons, researchers sometimes choose to give certain members of a population a greater chance of being selected than others.

2. The self-administered questionnaire was based on the results of preliminary pilot and pre-test studies. I began the research with a pilot study of nine unstructured face-to-face interviews with self-identified lesbian and bisexual women. The purpose of the pilot study was to find out what issues were important to lesbian and bisexual women and what the ranges of opinion on these issues were. A rough draft of the questionnaire in partially self-administered form was written based on these interviews, and the questionnaire was pre-tested during face-to-face interviews with 26 more women. The questionnaire was then converted to an entirely self-administered instrument and pre-tested on a new sample of 10 women. Six trained lesbian and bisexual female interviewers and I conducted the interviews during the first pre-test, and comments from these interviewers and from the women who participated in the second pre-test were solicited and used to revise the questionnaire once more.

3. In social psychology, "self-identity" is the way a person perceives herself. Presented identity is the way she presents herself to others, and perceived identity is how others perceive her. Many of us think of ourselves one way, but sometimes present ourselves differently to different people depending on how comfortable we are with them and how much we want to reveal about our sexuality. For the purpose of this study, it was important to know how women perceived *themselves*, without the filters they might use for other people. If I had asked simply, "Are you a lesbian, or bisexual, or ... " I might have gotten answers that reflected presented or perceived identity, rather than self-identity.

4. In other publications based on this study, I have included as lesbians some respondents who initially hesitated to identify themselves as lesbians, but did so when asked a second time. Hence, the sample size varies slightly from that reported elsewhere.

5. Table 32 "Resident population by race, 1990," in *Statistical Abstract of the United States 1993*, produced by the U.S. Department of Commerce Bureau of the Census.

6. Respondents' feelings of sexual attraction were measured by asking respondents to place themselves on a single 11–point scale ranging from "100% sexually attracted to women/0% attracted to men" through "0% attracted to women/100% attracted to men." The use of a single bipolar scale was not meant to imply that homosexual and heterosexual feelings are opposite or contrary experiences, nor that gender is the sole criterion of sexual attraction, nor that respondents do not differ on other dimensions of sexual feeling, such as libido strength. Ideally, gender-directed sexual feelings should be measured with separate scales representing homosexual and heterosexual feelings as suggested by Shively and DeCecco (1977), and by separate scales representing past, present, and ideal feelings as suggested by Klein, Sepekoff, and Wolf (1985). However, I was primarily interested in participants' feelings at the time of the survey, and given constraints on questionnaire length, I judged the single scale sufficient for the purposes of the current research. This

compromise was made with respect to the measurement of sexual feelings only; participants' past and present sexual and romantic behaviors were assessed more extensively.

7. One might expect that women with more "radical" lesbian identities (e.g., Dyke or Lesbian as opposed to Gay or Homosexual) would be more exclusive in their attractions to women. This was not the case; there were no differences in the degree of heterosexual attraction expressed by Lesbians, Dykes, Gay women, and Homosexual women.

8. Many lesbians who had never identified themselves as bisexual had wondered if they were bisexual. For a detailed discussion of the identity histories and coming out experiences of the lesbian and bisexual women in this study, including the ages at which they experienced various milestone events, see Rust (1993a).

CHAPTER 4

1. Throughout this book, all respondents' names are pseudonyms. When a respondent is quoted more than once, the same pseudonym is used each time.

2. Lesbians who defined bisexuality in terms of feelings were 20% more likely than lesbians who defined it in terms of behavior to answer the question "What is your opinion about bisexuality?" by stating explicitly that bisexuality exists.

3. Because the magnitudes of the increments in this seven-point scale are neither known nor quantifiable, subtracting one score from the other produces a rough estimate of the degree of difference perceived, not an exact measure of this degree.

CHAPTER 5

1. Because respondents' definitions of bisexuality and conceptualizations of sexuality were inferred from their answers to the question "What is your opinion of bisexuality?" and inference was not possible in all cases, the number of Lesbians of Color on which these findings are based is only 15. The finding that there are no racial differences is, therefore, suggestive at best. Findings about the prevalence of different conceptions of sexuality among lesbians are not presented because of space limitations. The interested reader is referred to Rust (1992a).

2. In addition to comparing the attitudes of lesbians of different chronological ages, I compared the attitudes of lesbians who came out during different historical periods, regardless of their age at the time they came out. No differences in attitudes were found. This finding suggests that lesbians' attitudes reflect the historical circumstances that existed at the time most of their age peers came out, rather than the historical circumstances that existed at the time they themselves came out. This might be explained by the fact that most women, when they begin to come out, seek lesbians of their own age

for support. They therefore learn the attitudes and definitions that are pertinent to lesbians of their own age cohort, even though the historical circumstances that were originally responsible for the formation of these attitudes
and definitions have since changed, and even though younger lesbians coming
out at the same time might be learning very different attitudes and definitions.
3. There is no evidence that the difference in beliefs about the existence of
   bisexuality stems from a difference in the way lesbians with varying degrees
   of heterosexual attraction define bisexuality. Lesbians with varying degrees
   of heterosexual attraction are equally likely to define bisexuality in terms of
   attractions as opposed to behaviors.

CHAPTER 6

1. The phrase "Pink and Blue Herring" combines two subcultural symbols.
   "Pink and blue" refers to the colors in a popular "bisexual pride" button
   that displays overlapping pink and blue triangles. The area of overlap is
   lavender, the color that symbolizes the "Lesbian and Gay" movement.
   "Herring" is taken from "lavender herring," a term that was applied to the
   lesbian issue within the feminist movement in 1970 to indicate that it was a
   trivial issue that would distract feminists from the real issues (Radicalesbians 1970). Marotta (1981:236n) attributed the phrase "lavender herring"
   to Susan Brownmiller, who referred to lesbians as "a lavender *herring*,
   perhaps, but surely no clear and present danger" in "Sisterhood is Powerful!" *New York Times Magazine*, March 15, 1970, p. 140.
2. This story, which assumes the perspective of lesbians within the feminist
   movement, is told in greater detail by many authors including Abbott and
   Love (1971, 1972), Adam (1987), Brown (1976), Dixon (1988), Goodman
   et al. (1983), and Penelope (1984/1991). See also Weitz (1984), who uses
   the Daughters of Bilitis publication *The Ladder* to tell the story of the
   growth of lesbian feminism from a different perspective.
3. I use the term "Black" instead of "African-American" here because it is the
   term these activists chose to use themselves, and because it reflects the
   politics of the time period. The term is not synonymous with African-
   American, either politically or demographically.
4. These works include Adam (1987), Cant and Hemmings (1988), Echols
   (1984), Faderman (1991), Goodman et al. (1983), King (1986), and Marotta (1981). In this chapter, I use the term "lesbian feminism" broadly to
   refer to all these strains of thought collectively, i.e., to identify any ideology
   that includes both lesbian and feminist elements, or any feminist argument
   made on behalf of or by lesbians. This is similar to the post-mid-1970s
   meaning of the term as described by Hess et al. (1981/1991).
5. The group adopted the name Radicalesbians after the presentation of "The
   Woman-Identified Woman" (Abbott and Love 1972) but the paper is usually attributed to the Radicalesbians and sometimes erroneously to Rita
   Mae Brown individually.

6. See also Abbott and Love (1971).
7. See also Goodman et al. (1983).
8. See also Berson's 1972 essay articulating The Furies' ideology. For an articulation of the Leeds Revolutionary Feminist Group's position, see their essay "Political lesbianism: The case against heterosexuality" in *Love Your Enemy?* In this essay, they wrote "The heterosexual couple is the basic unit of the political structure of male supremacy. In it each individual woman comes under the control of an individual man" (Leeds 1979/1981:6). A more recent statement of the argument that heterosexuality is a political institution is Rich's "Compulsory heterosexuality and lesbian existence" (1980/1983). Compare to Jones' analysis of marriage as an institution that oppresses and divides women (1970) and Millett's analysis of the politics of "patriarchal marriage" (1970).
9. Lillian Faderman, who characterized lesbian feminists as hoping that they will change the social structure through having personal relationships with women (1981), observed that the seeds of this idea appeared in *The Ladder* before the advent of modern lesbian feminism. Commenting on Betty Friedan's *The Feminine Mystique,* an author in *The Ladder* wrote that the book suggested that lesbianism permits "an escape from being cast into a social stereotype which degrades their individuality and limits their activity to the point where it may begin to make an impact on the world outside the home" (Faderman 1981:381, quoted from a "Review of *The Feminine Mystique,*" in *The Ladder,* vol. 7, no. 6, p. 9, March 1963).
10. Quoted in Adam (1987:89).
11. Atkinson's own attitudes illustrate this change. In a speech given in February 1969, Atkinson said, "The lesbian solution to the problem of women is to evade it, that is, to opt for an apolitical solution. Feminism is, of course, a political position" (1969/1974:25).
12. Elsa Gidlow, "Lesbianism as a liberating force," *Heresies: A Feminist Publication on Art and Politics,* vol. 1, no. 2, pp. 94–95 (May 1977), quoted in Faderman (1981:385).
13. Faderman found this argument in *The Ladder* as early as 1965. She quoted a letter from pp. 25–26 of *The Ladder,* vol. 9, no. 9 (June 1965), in which a reader commented that many women would "like to find the kind of emotional satisfaction that is possible only on a sustained basis between equal partners" but that "[i]n today's world this kind of life is open only to the lesbian" (1981:381). Johnston (1973) and Abbott and Love (1971) also characterized lesbian relationships as egalitarian.
14. Lois Hart, remarks made on WBAI radio program "Womankind," quoted by Marotta (1981:233–234) who cites pp. 350–351 of a transcript of the program that appears in Leslie B. Tanner, *Voices from Women's Liberation* (New York: New American Library, 1970), pp. 349–361.
15. "Readers respond," *The Ladder,* no. 13, p. 43 (April–May 1969), quoted in Marotta (1981:233). See also Weitz (1984) for documentation of the emergence of feminist and lesbian feminist ideas in *The Ladder.*

16. Shelley's invitation to lesbians to be proud of their lesbianism should be compared to the sentiment expressed by the staff of *Purple September,* who wrote, "since we ourselves reject the straight norm we are able to experience our lesbianism as a (relative) given that integrates our feminism with our personal experience" (1975:83). In this sentence, the authors manage to pat themselves on the back for the feminism of their lifestyle without asserting that they chose this lifestyle. They do this by congratulating themselves for rejecting the straight norm, not for choosing lesbianism. Their rejection of the straight norm allows them to appreciate the compatibility of their lesbian lifestyle, which they did not choose, with their feminism.

17. Frye cited Hoagland as a source of the idea that the category lesbian does not exist in phallocratic conceptual schemes. Hoagland had argued that the lesbian exists outside a reality that does not include her, and that she is therefore free from the constraints of this reality and has "access to knowledge which is inaccessible to those whose existence *is* countenanced by the system" (Hoagland 1978, cited by Frye 1983c:152–153).

18. See also Marotta (1981) and Faderman for a discussion of the process by which lesbianism "came to be regarded as the quintessence of feminism" (1991:206).

19. The success of this transformation is demonstrated by a quote from a heterosexual woman approximately one decade later. Apparently oblivious to the debates that occurred in the early 1970s over the feminist privatization of lesbianism, Angela Hamblin wrote that heterosexual feminists have to "grapple with male definitions, male assumptions and male power in one of the most intimate areas of our lives" and that "over the past decade an increasing number of feminist women have been involved in transforming the basis upon which we are prepared to share our sexuality with men. It has been, for the most part, a very private struggle which, despite the support which many individual women have given each other, has not as yet been validated by the women's liberation movement as a whole." She felt that heterosexual feminists were "thrown back into defining our relationships with men as belonging to the 'personal' sphere of our lives, cut off from our 'political' concerns," exactly the same complaint voiced by lesbians a decade earlier (1983:105).

20. On this point, the Leeds Revolutionary Feminist Group and the Gorgons agreed with The Furies. The Leeds group wrote that women in heterosexual couples help support male supremacy by strengthening its foundation, and analogized heterosexual feminists to resistors in Nazi-occupied Europe who blow up bridges in the daytime and then repair them at night (1979/1981). In other words, heterosexual feminists undermine their own feminist work. The Gorgons argued that heterosexual women "collaborate with patriarchy by putting time and energy into men" (1978/1991:395). Alice, Gordon, Debbie, and Mary, whose essay appeared in the same lesbian separatist anthology as the Gorgons', were less condemnatory but equally exclusive of heterosexual women: "While we do not see straight women as our oppres-

sors or as our enemy, their interests are often opposite to ours, and, as the agents of men, their behavior is sometimes oppressive to us. Therefore, our primary work and group associations will be with other lesbians" (1973/1991a:33).

The Leeds group also agreed with Solomon that heterosexual women drain lesbians' feminist energy by diverting it to needs created by their heterosexual relationships.

21. The transformation of the meaning of the phrase "the personal is political" is explored by Echols (1984), who points out that the phrase's original descriptive meaning evolved into a prescriptive meaning. In fact, the phrase underwent many transformations. The arguments presented in this chapter alone illustrate the following meanings: The personal reflects the political status quo (with the implication that the personal should be examined to provide insight into the political); the personal serves the political status quo; one can make personal choices in response to or protest against the political status quo; one's personal life influences one's personal politics or determines the limits of one's understanding of the political status quo; the personal is a personal political statement; personal choices can influence the political status quo; one's personal choices reveal or reflect one's personal politics; one should make personal choices that are consistent with one's personal politics; personal life and personal politics are indistinguishable; personal life and personal politics are unrelated. The transformation of the relationship between the personal and the political is partially illustrated by the history of the phrase, "Feminism is the theory, lesbianism is the practice," recounted by King (1986).

22. Compare Dixon's opinion that lesbianism and feminism are synonymous by definition to the opinion expressed by Shelley, who perceived a causal relationship in which Lesbianism allowed or encouraged a woman to become feminist, "I have met many, many feminists who were not Lesbians—but I have never met a Lesbian who was not a feminist .... Lesbians, because they are not afraid of being abandoned by men, are less reluctant to express hostility toward the male class" (1969/1970:345–6).

23. Similarly, Mary Daly (1978) distinguished between "lesbians," who are woman-identified, and "gay women," who relate to women sexually but are male-identified and collaborate with gay men.

24. These include letters written to the Leeds feminists themselves, to *Wires*, the internal national newsletter of the women's liberation movement in which the "Political lesbianism" essay had been published originally, and to Onlywomen Press, which published *Love Your Enemy?*, as well as statements from the members of Onlywomen Press.

25. See also Koedt (1971/1973) and Ferguson (1981), neither of whom were responding directly to the Leeds' "Political lesbianism" paper, for more extensive arguments criticizing the idea that women can undermine male supremacy simply by having sex with women instead of men. For example, pointing out that it is a personal solution to a political problem, Koedt

argued that the moral imperative to be a lesbian was a perversion of the phrase "the personal is political" and that advocating exclusive heterosexuality is antithetical to the lesbian and gay movement's original argument that with whom one sleeps does not matter.

26. Political lesbianism met with the approval of many lesbian feminists outside the Leeds Revolutionary Feminist Group. For example, Atkinson wrote, "There are women in the Movement who engage in sexual relations with other women, but who are married to men; these women are not lesbians in the political sense. These women claim the right to private lives; they are collaborators. There are other women who have never had sexual relations with other women, but who have made and live a total commitment to this Movement; these women are lesbians in the political sense" (1972/1973:12). Emphasizing the importance of politics over sexual behavior, she declared at the opening of the new headquarters of DOB-New York that "I'm enormously less interested in whom you sleep with than I am in with whom you're prepared to die" (quoted in Marotta 1981:262). Julia Penelope agreed with Atkinson that real allies were defined by their political, not their sexual, loyalties, but argued that "[u]nfortunately, we frequently choose *what* we're willing to die for on the basis of *who* we sleep with, and that's the 'grain of truth' that makes the reduction to 'sexual preference' sound plausible" (Penelope 1984/1991:527).

27. The woman was an interviewee quoted on p. 140 of Angela Stewart-Park and Jules Cassidy, *We're Here: Conversations with Lesbian Women* (London: Quartet Books, 1977).

28. Echols tied the reconciliation between heterosexual and lesbian feminists to the rise of cultural feminism, which packaged female separatism in a form that could appeal to a broader (read: heterosexual) audience. She also pointed out that the reconciliation was superficial because heterosexual women's feminism was still perceived as inferior. Heterosexual women were no longer perceived as traitors, but in exchange they had been given the role of victim (Echols 1984).

29. As early as 1972, Abbott and Love described "Lesbians' " wariness of "Political Lesbians." See Gay Revolution Party Women's Caucus (1971/1972) for a discussion of feminist realesbians' moral and political concerns about politicalesbianism. The Caucus argued that politicalesbians should become realesbians by having sex with women but that politicalesbians who seek sex with realesbians lay a "male trip" on realesbians by sexually objectifying them. Therefore, politicalesbians should bring each other out. Snitow, Stansell, and Thompson (1983) discussed the fact that the advent of the desexualized, or political, lesbian seemed to erase the differences between heterosexual and lesbian feminists, but that in reality it merely suppressed rather than eliminated the tensions that existed between them.

30. The members of the Gutter Dyke Collective found "celibate straight women" burdensome even when they did acknowledge the difficulties real lesbians had to face. In their experience, heterosexual women who chose to

be celibate for feminist reasons and accepted "the fact that true feminism should ultimately lead to lesbianism" (1973/1991:28) tended to view real lesbians as more perfect than themselves. This imposed the burden of responsibility on the lesbian and allowed celibate heterosexual women to use lesbians as confessors for the purpose of unburdening themselves of their own failings as feminists.

31. This process has been constructed by historians of lesbianism as a process of "desexualization," but Rich offered an alternative construction. She argued that lesbians were discovering "the erotic in female terms: as that which is unconfined to any single part of the body or solely to the body itself, as an energy not only diffuse but, as Audre Lorde has described it, omnipresent" (Rich 1980/1983:193, citing Lorde 1979). In other words, it is not a process of desexualization, but a process of the demasculinization of sexuality. See Richardson (1992) for a critique of the language of "sex" as male-defined and an analysis of the 1970s "desexualization" of the lesbian within feminist discourse and of the "resexualization" of the lesbian in the 1980s.

32. See Vicinus (1992) for a discussion of the problems of constructing lesbian history based on modern concepts of the lesbian. See Ferguson (1981) for a critique of efforts to create a transhistorical definition of lesbianism as ignoring the historical specificity of modern lesbian consciousness.

33. Vicinus (1982:147–148) cites Cook (1977:48) as the source of the quote, "Women who love women, who choose women to nurture and support and to create a living environment in which to work creatively and independently are lesbians."

34. Strong women in history could also be claimed as lesbian ancestors even in spite of evidence of heterosexual behavior, which could always be explained away as the result of the social constraints of the time or dismissed as irrelevant to the definition of lesbianism. An example of this is Rich (1980/1983), who refers to the "double life" of ancestral lesbians, by which she means the fact that they (also) had heterosexual relationships.

A more recent example of the reconstruction of women to create lesbian ancestors via the dismissal of contrary evidence is the story of Kate Millet. An article in *Time* magazine on Dec. 8, 1970, reported statements Millet had made regarding her own sexuality. In subsequent retellings of the story, Millett is sometimes reported as having revealed her bisexuality, and othertimes reported as having revealed her lesbianism. See Abbott and Love (1972) for an account of the actual events.

35. "Gene Damon" also claimed spinsters as the ancestors of the modern lesbian. She argued that "In this same male-oriented society, with its double standards waving proudly in every arena, we still 'accept' the erroneous premise that there are millions of women who have no sexual interests in life. These are the women who make up our vast sea of lifelong spinsters whose outward mannerisms and behavior quite rightly lead to the erroneous assumption that they are 'sexless' beings. Most of the leaders of the DOB

agree that countless hundreds of thousands of women who can never conform to Kinsey statistics, are still, whether expressed or not, Lesbians.
We are also quick to agree that most of these women, faced with this
announcement, would die of shock on the spot" (1970:337). In other
words, these spinsters are the ancestors of the modern Lesbian even though
they might never have had lesbian sex, and even though they would have
been shocked at the thought. Their apparent sexlessness was a result of the
male-oriented society in which they lived; they were, regardless of the lack
of evidence, "really" lesbians. Here, "Damon" is arguing that to be an
ancestor of the modern lesbian, a woman need not only not have had
lesbian sex; she also need not even be aware of her feelings for women. The
lesbian is an essential, historical creature who existed even though she did
not know she existed; the task for the modern lesbian is merely to look
back at history to find her. "Gene Damon" is an alias of Barbara Grier
(Weitz 1984).

36. For additional discussion of nineteenth-century romantic friendships and
their construction as the predecessors of modern lesbian relationships, see
Smith-Rosenberg (1975) and Jeffreys (1985).

37. It was this "fundamental departure" from original lesbian feminist princi-
ples that motivated Alice Echols to distinguish the new philosophy by
renaming it "cultural feminism" (Echols 1984). The transformation of radical feminism into cultural feminism is illustrated in the personal story of
Liza Cowan. In an essay written in 1978, she explained that "[w]hen I first
became a feminist, I rejected the notion that there was any basic difference
between men and women" (1978/1991:223). But later, she came to believe
that the notion of "humanism" kept men in control and that men were
responsible for the creation of pollution, racism, and other evils that had
developed during their domination.

38. See Echols (1983, 1984) for a discussion of the transformation of feminist
thinking about gender with the rise of cultural feminism and the differences
between radical feminism and cultural feminism, particularly the differences
in the ways in which radical feminists and cultural feminists thought about
sexuality and the relationship between sexual liberation and women's liberation.

39. See also Katz (1983) for a discussion of the use of the concept of innate
differences between men and women by feminists of the early 1900s.

40. See Faderman (1991) for a discussion of the conflict between lesbian cultural feminists and lesbian sex radicals. See Richardson (1992) for documentation of the growth of lesbian sex culture.

41. The contrast between pleasure and danger is taken from the title of the
book *Pleasure and Danger: Exploring Female Sexuality,* Carole S. Vance,
ed. (New York: William Morrow and Company, 1984).

42. For other discussions of the role of gender in various feminist, lesbian, and
gay ideologies, see Adam (1987), Echols (1984), Evans (1993), Faderman
(1991), and Seidman (1993).

43. Shelley wrote, "Maybe after the revolution, people will be able to love each other regardless of skin color, ethnic origin, occupation, or type of genitals. But if that's going to happen, it will only happen because we make it happen—starting right now" (1969/1970:348).

44. Some theorists, including Johnston and Brown who are cited in the text, did not refer to a "bisexual potential" per se, but rather to a homosexual or lesbian potential that exists in all women, including those whose behavior is heterosexual. Their arguments were similar to those of lesbians who did posit a bisexual potential. For example, Abbott and Love invoked Simone de Beauvoir to argue that "all women are naturally homosexual" (Abbott and Love 1971:609, quoting from Simone de Beauvoir, *The Second Sex*, New York: Bantam Books, 1961: 382).

45. This idea was put forth very early in the formation of lesbian feminist ideology by the Radicalesbians, who wrote in the first paragraph of "The Woman-Identified Woman" that the lesbian "may not be fully conscious of the political implications of what for her began as personal necessity, but on some level she has not been able to accept the limitations and oppression laid on her by the most basic role of her society—the female role" (1970:49).

46. Statement made on "Womankind," quoted in Marotta (1981:233).

47. Marotta described the Redstockings and The Feminists as cultural radicals, and the New York Radical Women and WITCH as interested in a combination of revolutionary and radical ideologies (1981). WITCH and the Redstockings were offshoots of New York Radical Women, and The Feminists was an offshoot of NOW.

48. As noted by Marotta (1981) and Adam (1987), the consciousness raising group is a strategy that was borrowed by feminists from the New Left movement. The cultural radical perspective of the New Left viewed oppression as the result of cultural sexism, racism, classism, etc., rather than a simple consequence of prejudice and discrimination. The solution, therefore, was to transform the culture itself. Consciousness raising groups were the technique used to develop visions of the new nonracist, nonsexist, nonclassist culture. But despite the radical origins of the consciousness raising group, the consequence of its use in the feminist movement was the development of women's culture that transformed women into an ethnic group and ultimately permitted feminists to avail themselves of nationalistic strategies.

49. Weitz (1984), in her examination of etiological views expressed in *The Ladder*, suggests that lesbians accepted the medical model in which lesbianism was seen as a process of development, not a choice, because they could thereby construct themselves as victims deserving toleration instead of evil people deserving condemnation. The argument that essentialism is consistent with the interests of sexual minorities is also supported by the fact that, unlike the lesbian feminist movement and despite the strides made in pride and autonomy in the 1980s and 1990s, the contemporary gay men's movement retains a primarily essentialist ideology. Contemporary

essentialist views among gay men cannot be attributed to internalized heterosexism; 1990s gay ideology clearly reflects the experiences and interests of gay men themselves. The reaction to research on the biological correlates of sexual orientation, for example, LeVay's (1991) study of the hypothalamus and more recent genetic studies, clearly demonstrates that the gay movement has an interest in promoting the opinion that sexual orientation is biologically determined. See Adam (1987) and Epstein (1987) for a discussion of gay ethnicity and the fact that the gay movement borrowed concepts and strategies from racial and ethnic political movements. For a discussion of the essentialism of "gay women" versus the lesbian feminist argument that lesbianism is chosen, see also Faderman (1991).

50. Faderman provided evidence that lesbian and gay activists consciously borrowed ethnic political tactics. For example, she reported that articles in *The Ladder* in the mid to late 1960s compared lesbians to other oppressed minorities, and that the Homophile League explicitly advocated copying the tactics used by other protesting minorities (1991). Also, Abbott and Love observed in 1971 that lesbians were emulating the tactics of women's liberation, which in turn had emulated Black liberation. "Gene Damon" noted that lesbians' efforts to construct themselves as an ethnic group were not welcomed by traditional ethnic minorities, and described some of the differences between lesbians and traditional ethnic minorities: "We have an unusual minority position. Some of the 'true' ethnic minorities resent our considering ourselves a minority. For example, we do not share a common racial or a common religious background, nor, indeed, any common background except our one difference: we prefer our own sex, sexually and in every other way" (1970:335–336).

51. Statement made on "Womankind," quoted by Marotta (1981:233).

52. The quote is from Marotta (1981:259), who reported that Kennedy made this argument to DOB-New York at its August, 1970 membership meetings.

53. Johnston also saw sexism as the most basic form of oppression. She focused in particular on the relationship of sexism to heterosexism, arguing that prejudice against gay men is based on prejudice against women because gay men are perceived as being like women. Sexism is, therefore, the direct parent of heterosexism, and the lesbian, as the figure who unites these two forms of oppression, is the "key figure in the social revolution to end the sexual caste system" (1973:183).

54. See also Alice et al. (1973/1991a,b).

55. Although Brown argued that sexism is the most basic form of oppression, she and Shelley felt that actively fighting racism and classism is just as important as fighting sexism and heterosexism. They criticized more moderate lesbian activists for focussing exclusively on sexism and heterosexism, and for incorporating middle class values into their goals and strategies. See, for example, Adam (1987) and Marotta (1981).

56. Some lesbian feminist theorists discussed the implications of their own arguments for bisexuality. Usually these discussions were brief (e.g., Abbott

and Love 1972; Brown 1972/1975), but the interested reader can find fairly detailed discussions in Alice et al. (1973/1991a:38n2), the C.L.I.T. Collective's "C.L.I.T. Statement No. 2" (1974/1991), Goodman et al. (1983), Johnston (1973), and Ulmschneider (1973/1975).

57. As the Leeds Revolutionary Feminist Group put it, "the value of calling yourself a political lesbian is to state that you are not sexually available to men" (1981:68).

58. By this logic, the celibate non-lesbian, on the other hand, is politically acceptable because she refuses to relate to men, even though she does not relate to women. This position was expressed by the lesbian separatist Gutter Dyke Collective, which wrote in 1973, "women who consider themselves celibate, not lesbian, fighting for a loving female world and recognizing that there is no reconciliation with men, are our allies" (1973/1991:28–29). The operative condition here is "no reconciliation;" The Gutter Dyke Collective was not sanctioning women who would abstain from relations with men simply as a means toward an end, after which they would return to men. They were welcoming women who, like lesbians, had forsworn relations with men forever. Alice et al. also expressed their willingness to form alliances with non-lesbian "feminist separatists" (1973/1991a:37). Not all lesbian separatists who placed the emphasis on a refusal of relations with men welcomed non-lesbian celibates, however, a position that was acknowledged by The Gutter Dyke Collective even as they argued its untenability in light of the fact that many lesbians are themselves often celibate and that therefore the difference between the non-lesbian celibate and the lesbian was of no political import.

59. Myron and Bunch wrote "Some new bonds are beginning to emerge between lesbians and single women. We share a common economic and psychological reality: we are solely responsible for our lives—all of our lifetime. . . . We must provide for ourselves . . . This economic and psychological reality develops more strength and spirit in individual women" (1975:13).

60. This position is also described by Faderman (1991), who presents it as the lesbian feminist position on bisexuality.

61. See Koedt (1971/1973) for an articulation of this position.

62. Compare my interpretation of the implications of Rich's lesbian continuum for bisexuals to Kaplan's (1992).

63. Atkinson (1972/1973:12), quoted earlier in this chapter.

64. Other authors have also constructed bisexuality as a threat to lesbian and gay ethnicity. See, for example, Seidman (1993) and Udis-Kessler (1990).

CHAPTER 7

1. Although a total of 59 respondents classified themselves as bisexual, only 40 of these women did so unhesitatingly and unqualifiedly and also provided an answer to the question "What is your opinion of bisexuality?" The quotes in

this chapter are all drawn from these latter 40 women, and all percentages
are calculated on a base that includes only these 40 women.

2. These numbers represent fifteen bisexual respondents or 37.5% of bisexual
respondents, and forty-seven lesbian respondents or 15.2% of lesbian respondents.

3. This 28% is based on the 25 bisexual women who provided implicit or
explicit definitions of bisexuality in their answers to the question "What is
your opinion of bisexuality?"

4. The negative images that were *not* spontaneously mentioned by any bisexual
respondents are: Bisexuals are in a transition phase to lesbianism; bisexuals
spread diseases to lesbians; bisexuals are oversexed; bisexuals are merely
experimenting with lesbian sexuality; and bisexuals are unaware of or undecided about (as opposed to confused about) their sexuality. Except for the
first, all of these images were fairly rare among lesbians, so their complete
absence among bisexual respondents—who are much fewer in number than
lesbian respondents—might be a matter of chance, and does not negate the
statement that most of lesbians' negative attitudes about bisexuals were
echoed by bisexuals themselves.

5. Some patterns were found, although they were not consistent or significant
enough to report in the text, they are reported in this footnote in the interest
of completeness.

   Bisexuals who identified themselves as lesbians in the past—particularly
if they switched back and forth between bisexual and lesbian identities two
or more times—tend to agree more strongly that some bisexuals are really
lesbians than bisexuals who never identified themselves as lesbians do. This
makes sense; those who previously identified themselves as lesbians are more
likely to have associated with lesbians and thereby adopted lesbians' belief
that women who call themselves bisexual are really lesbians who are afraid
to admit it. However, this is the only belief that is significantly correlated
with bisexuals' identity histories, and it is therefore probably a false positive.

   Bisexuals who never identified themselves as lesbians show consistently
stronger social preferences for bisexual women over lesbians than bisexuals
with a history of lesbian identification, and bisexuals who switched identities
two or more times show no preference for bisexuals at all. The largest
difference is in the context of dating; bisexuals who never identified themselves as lesbian are more likely to prefer to date bisexual women (60% of
those with a preference), whereas bisexuals who identified themselves as
lesbian in the past are more likely to prefer to date lesbians (57% of those
with a preference). None of these relationships are statistically significant,
but this might be due to the small number of bisexuals who have never
identified themselves as lesbian (n = 7). In a larger sample, this pattern might
achieve statistical significance.

6. There was one bisexual woman who was a notable exception to this pattern;
she described herself as 80% attracted to men, but unlike other bisexuals
with predominantly heterosexual feelings, she reported that she strongly

preferred to associate with lesbians. She came out as a lesbian in the mid 1970s and retains a strong political identification with lesbians, saying that she expects whatever happens to lesbians to affect her "a lot," whereas whatever happens to bisexuals will affect her "just a little." If this one woman is excluded from the bisexual subsample, correlations between bisexuals' feelings of heterosexual attraction and the four measures of social preference range from r = .347 to r = .553, with p-values ranging from .01 to .0001, indicating a moderately strong and significant correlation between the strength of bisexual women's heterosexual feelings and their preferences for associating with other bisexual women.

7. Findings regarding the impact of the seriousness of bisexuals' relationships with women and with men on their preferences for association are not presented because few are statistically significant. The relationship mentioned in the text is significant, with p = .03.

8. This specific finding is not statistically significant; all others reported in the text are.

9. Keep in mind that these findings are based on cross-sectional data; neither actual changes in respondents' relationship statuses nor the effects of such changes on bisexuals' social and political preferences have been observed. There might well be some individuals in the study whose social and political preferences would not change if their relationship statuses changed. However, the fact that individuals with different relationship statuses have different social and political preferences suggests that, in the aggregate, bisexuals' preferences are based on their current relationship status rather than their bisexual identity.

CHAPTER 8

1. Lucy Friedland, "A giant leap for bi-kind: The U.S.-Canadian [North American] Bisexual Network," *Bi Women*, vol. 6, no. 6, pp. 1, 3, 5 (December 1988/January 1989).

2. No byline, "Bi Net: Bisexual network out and loud!" *North Bi Northwest*, vol. 4, no. 4, pp. 1, 13 (August/September 1991).

3. Stephanie Berger, "Thinking about community: What do we want?" *Bi Women*, vol. 9, no. 5, pp. 1, 6, 7 (October/November 1991).

4. ben e factory, "Bi's are out and loud at first northwest regional conference," *North Bi Northwest*, vol. 6, no. 2, pp. 1, 8 (April/May 1993).

5. Kathleen O'Bryan, "South Sound Binet signs on," *North Bi Northwest*, vol. 7, no. 1 (February/March 1994).

6. Kathleen O'Bryan, "South Sound Binet signs on," *North Bi Northwest*, vol. 7, no. 1, p. 3 (February/March 1994).

7. Beth Reba Weise, "The bisexual community: Viable reality or revolutionary pipe dream?" *Anything That Moves*, no. 2, p. 20 (Spring 1991).

8. Kathleen Bennett, "The sweet bi and bi: Male-female couples in the bisexual

world," *North Bi Northwest*, vol. 4, no. 5, p. 13 (October/November 1991).

9. Deborah M. Anapol, "The future of the family and fate of our children," *Anything That Moves*, no. 4, pp. 38–40.

10. Paul Smith, "Locating the bi movement within the civil right (*sic*) struggle," *North Bi Northwest*, vol. 3, no. 5, p. 10 (October/November 1990).

11. *Bi Women*, vol. 5, no. 4, p. 9 (August/September 1987).

12. For example, the March 1987 issue of *Bi Women* (vol. 5, no. 1, p. 8) reprinted an article entitled "Paths to integration" by Roger from *Bi and Large*, newsletter of the Seattle Bisexual Support Network, vol. 4, which distinguished between "proportional bisexuality," "physical-attraction-based bisexuality," "gender or political-centered bisexuality," and three other types of bisexuality. At the end of the list, the author emphasized that the purpose of the list was descriptive, not definitive, and that the types described were ideal, not real: "This non-exhaustive listing is set down to aid our ever-growing awareness of the varied ways we can positively integrate our sexuality with the rest of our lives. Do you find elements of more than one of these ways in yourself?"

13. Sharon Gonsalves, "On bisexuals in the lesbian community," *Bi Women*, vol. 7, no. 4, p. 4 (August/September 1989).

14. Amanda Udis-Kessler, "Whose culture is it anyway? On reclaiming famous bisexuals," *North Bi Northwest*, vol. 3, no. 6, pp. 3–4 (December 1990/ January 1991).

15. Kathleen E. Bennett, "Parade name change: Reality or rhetoric," *North Bi Northwest*, vol. 5, no. 3 (June 1992).

16. Autumn Courtney, "The only thing constant . . . is change," *Anything That Moves*, no. 4, p. 31 (1992). Laura M. Perez and Victor Raymond also assert that the struggle for sexual freedom is inherently linked to the struggles against "sexism, racism, classism, ableism, ageism and all other isms" ("Bisexuals included in the March on Washington," *Bi Women*, vol. 11, no. 1, p. 6 (February/March 1993).

17. This focus group met at the 1992 BiNet Annual Meeting, the notes of which are reported in *BiNet News*, December 15, 1992.

18. Erica Avery, "Big group and big fun at BiNet National Conference," *North Bi Northwest*, vol. 6, no. 3 (June/July 1993).

19. This statement appears on the inside cover of each issue of *Anything That Moves*.

20. Lucy Gibson, "Racism workshop," *North Bi Northwest*, vol. 3, no. 6, p. 7 (December 1990/January 1991).

21. Emily Susan Manning, "On racism and on anti-sexism," *North Bi Northwest*, vol. 4, no. 2, pp. 4, 5, 13, 15 (April/May 1991).

22. The reasons given both for and against the name change reflect the organizations' general concern about diversity. Supporters of the change argued that including "multicultural" in the name of the organization implied that it was not also interested in nonracial/ethnic forms of diversity. Elias Farajajé-

Jones, who did not perceive "multiculturalism" in solely racial/ethnic terms, argued that eliminating "multicultural" from the name was an example of the powerful making decisions that reflect their own reality. (See Elias Farajajé-Jones, "Multikulti feminist bis no more?" *Anything That Moves*, no. 5, pp. 18–19, 1993.) The issue was extremely controversial, and deadlocked the 1993 national BiNet USA meeting.

23. Cianna Stewart, "Multicultural organizing and outreach," *North Bi Northwest*, vol. 5, no. 1, pp. 9, 18, and "Tips for organizers," *North Bi Northwest*, vol. 5, no. 1, p. 17 (February 1992).
24. For example, in her keynote address to the Fifth Annual East Coast Bisexual Network Conference on Bisexuality, Lani Kaahumanu identified diversity as the source of bisexuals' strength. Excerpts of this speech were printed in *Bi Women*, vol. 7, no. 3, pp. 1, 4, 7 (June/July 1989). The full title of the conference was "The Fifth Annual East Coast Bisexual Network Conference on Bisexuality: Culture, Community, Coalition-Building." Kaahumanu also expressed this same sentiment in Lani Kaahumanu, "March on Washington," *BiNet Newsletter*, vol. 1, no. 3, p. 1 (February 1992).
25. Paul Smith, "The straight poop: A political opinion column," *Anything That Moves*, no. 2, p. 5 (Spring, 1991).
26. Elias Farajajé-Jones, "Multikulti feminist bis no more?" *Anything That Moves*, no. 5, p. 19 (1993).
27. For detailed theoretical discussions of the challenge posed by bisexuality to dichotomous thinking, and to oppressions based on dichotomous thinking, see Bennett (1992), Friedland and Highleyman (1991), and Rust (1992a).
28. For example, Rachel Kaplan rejected all social categories, even those created by people attempting to challenge the traditional dichotomy, by arguing that "[t]he problem with all sexual politics is its reliance on language to create reality when the only real truth about sexuality is in the body." ("Another coming out manifesto disguised as a letter to my mother," *North Bi Northwest*, vol. 3, no. 5, p. 3, October/November 1990.)
29. An example of this argument is Natalie Bacon's "Who am I?" originally printed in *Bi-Lines*, November 1986, and later reprinted in *Bi Women*, vol. 5, no. 1 (February/March 1987).
30. The Ellen Brenner quote is from "The article I have been threatening to write ever since I joined the network, or My life as a lesbian-identified bisexual fag hag," *Bi Women*, vol. 7, no. 3, p. 1 (June/July 1989). The Betty Aubut statement is quoted by Robyn Ochs in "Bi of the month: Betty Aubut," *Bi Women*, vol. 5, no. 2, p. 2 (April/May 1987). Other bisexuals have described the type of thinking challenged by bisexuality as "binary thinking" or "either/or thinking." Lenore Norrgard uses the term "binary computer-think" ("What is 'bisexual'? Am I? Are you?" *North Bi Northwest*, vol. 4, no. 6, p. 16 (December 1991/January 1992), and Erica Avery refers to "split thinking" ("SBWN: The personal and the political," *North Bi Northwest*, vol. 5, no. 6, p. 1 (December/January 1993).

31. Raven Gildea, "Pride: The challenge of working for change," *North Bi Northwest*, vol. 5, no. 4, p. 1 (August/September 1992).

32. Paul Smith, "The straight poop: A political opinion column. Are we a movement yet?" *Anything That Moves*, no. 4, p. 11 (1992). Sara Liebe attempted to provide an alternative to the half-gay, half-straight concept of bisexuality by analogizing bisexuals and sassafras trees. Through a fictional character, she said that "[p]eople don't criticize a sassafras tree for inconsistency" because it has three different leaf shapes; instead, people consider all three leaf shapes to be "three manifestations of [the sassafras's] treeness." In other words, everything bisexuals do they do as bisexuals, not as heterosexuals or homosexuals depending on the gender of their partners (Sara Liebe, "The three leaves of the sassafras," *North Bi Northwest*, vol. 3, no. 5, p. 6 (October/November 1990).

33. Ellen Barnett, "Which came first, the bisexual or the feminist?" *North Bi Northwest*, vol. 4, no. 6, p. 8 (December 1991/January 1992).

34. Erica Avery, "SBWN: The personal and the political," *North Bi Northwest*, vol. 5, no. 6, p. 1 (December/January 1993). For an extensive discussion of the ways in which bisexuality defies categorization because it encompasses diversity and change, see Gibian (1992).

35. The idea that bisexuality can serve as a bridge between heterosexuals and lesbians/gays is expressed by Marcia Deihl and Betty Aubut, although neither woman links this idea to the concept of a sexual continuum (Marcia Deihl, Letter to *Gay Community News* reprinted in *Bi Women*, vol. 8, no. 3, pp. 7–8 (June/July 1990); Aubut is quoted in Robyn Ochs, "Bi of the month: Betty Aubut," *Bi Women*, vol. 5, no. 2, p. 2 (April/May 1987).

36. Erica Avery, "SBWN: The personal and the political," *North Bi Northwest*, vol. 5, no. 6, p. 1 (December/January 1993).

37. Pat Cattolico, "Opinion: Reader responds to personal/political," *North Bi Northwest*, vol. 6, no. 1, p. 6 (February/March 1993).

38. Paul Smith, "The straight poop: A political opinion column," *Anything That Moves*, no. 3, p. 5 (Summer 1991).

39. Karin Baker and Helen Harrison, Letter, *Bi Women*, vol. 8, no. 3, p. 5 (June/July 1990). See also Baker (1992).

40. Beth Reba Weise describes Listerud's philosophy in "The bisexual community: Viable reality or revolutionary pipe dream?" *Anything That Moves*, no. 2, pp. 22–23 (Spring 1991).

41. Raven Gildea, "Pride: The challenge of working for change," *North Bi Northwest*, vol. 5, no. 4, p. 1 (August/September 1992).

42. Ellen Barnett, "Which came first, the bisexual or the feminist?" *North Bi Northwest*, vol. 4, no. 6, p. 8 (December 1991/January 1992).

43. Karin Baker, Letter, *BiWomen*, vol. 8, no. 3, p. 6 (June/July 1990).

44. See, for example, Shuster (1991).

45. Paul Talbert's article "Dancing for the androgynous god" is rare in its mention of androgyny. Talbert does not hold androgyny up as an ideal because it is genderless per se, however; instead, he values it because it represents the overthrow of imbalanced "gender roles and gender power"

341

(*North Bi Northwest*, vol. 6, no. 6, pp. 9, 11, December/January 1993). Liz Highleyman contrasted the opinion of a European bisexual theorist who felt that androgynous bisexuality is the ideal of the future with the views of most American bisexual activists whom she characterized as thinking "of bisexuality as part of a continuum of valid options," rather than a superior form of sexuality (Liz Highleyman, "First International Bisexual Conference," *North Bi Northwest*, vol. 5, no. 1, p. 5, February 1992).

46. Beth Reba Weise, "Small losses and greater betrayals," *Bi Women*, vol. 8, no. 3, p. 9 (June/July 1990).

47. This statement of purpose is printed on the inside front cover of every issue of *Anything That Moves*.

48. For example, this idea is expressed by "Robin," who is described by Kathleen Bennett in "The sweet bi and bi: Male-female couples in the bisexual world," *North Bi Northwest*, vol. 4, no. 5, p. 12 (October/November 1991).

49. Lenore Norrgard, "What is 'bisexual?' Am I? Are you?" *North Bi Northwest*, vol. 4, no. 6, p. 16 (December 1991/January 1992).

50. Rachel Kaplan, "Another coming out manifesto disguised as a letter to my mother," *North Bi Northwest*, vol. 3, no. 5, p. 3 (October/November 1990).

51. Lists of these myths and responses to them appear frequently in the bisexual press. See, for example, Sumpter (1991). Shuster identifies the persistence of myths about bisexuality as one of the "remaining challenges" of the bisexual movement (1991:267).

52. Bettykay, "Politically and socially bi," *North Bi Northwest*, vol. 3, no. 6, p. 10 (December 1990/January 1991). The fear that others will generalize from some individuals' active sex lives to all bisexuals has kept other bisexuals from writing about their sexual experiences; two years after Bettykay's article, Alison noted that little has been written about group sex because bisexuals are hesitant to use precious bisexual page space to reinforce stereotypes (Alison, "Group sex: Some thoughts and experiences," *North Bi Northwest*, vol. 6, no. 2, p. 9, April/May 1993). A lengthier example of the "some are, some aren't" argument is provided by Norrgard (1991), who notes that some bisexuals are quick to assure others that bisexuals can be monogamous. She identifies this as a half truth and encourages bisexuals to acknowledge the diversity of the bisexual community, instead of defending bisexuality by buying into the cultural valuation of monogamy.

53. See Beth Reba Weise, "The bisexual community: Viable reality or revolutionary pipe dream?" *Anything That Moves*, no. 2, p. 23 (Spring 1991), or the newsletter *Bisexual Centrist*, published by the BiCentrist Alliance.

54. See Autumn Courtney, "The only thing constant . . . is change," *Anything That Moves*, no. 4, p. 30 (1992), for a brief discussion of the effect of public opinion on bisexuals during the early years of the AIDS crisis.

55. Paul Smith, "Locating the bi movement within the civil right struggle," *North Bi Northwest*, vol. 3, no. 5, p. 10 (October/November 1990).

56. Ellen Brenner, "The article I have been threatening to write ever since I

joined the network, or My life as a lesbian-identified bisexual fag hag," *Bi Women*, vol. 7, no. 3, p. 6 (June/July 1989).

57. For example, in November 1990, *North Bi Northwest* reported that two bisexual people had spoken to a P-FLAG meeting; in February 1992, the same newsletter reported the appearance of bisexual activists on the *Sonya Live* show; and, in May 1993, it reported that bisexuals had appeared on *Donahue*. Talk shows looking for bisexual guests often contact the best-known bisexual activists, who in turn publicize the request via electronic mail and other media.

58. Lani Kaahumanu made this point in her keynote address to the Fifth Annual East Coast Bisexual Network Conference on Bisexuality. See *Bi Women*, vol. 7, no. 3, p. 4 (June/July 1989).

59. See, for example, Amanda Udis-Kessler, "Culture and community: Thoughts on lesbian-bisexual relations," *North Bi Northwest*, vol. 4, no. 1, pp. 3–4 (February/March 1991).

60. Holly L. Danyliw, Letter to BBWN, *Bi Women*, vol. 9, no. 5, p. 4 (October/November 1991).

61. The first point is from a letter written by Ingrid Sell, *Bi Women*, vol. 8, no. 3, p. 6 (June/July 1990). The second point is suggested by Lani Kaahumanu, who interpreted her own previous biphobia to her suppressed bisexual feelings in her keynote address to the Fifth Annual East Coast Bisexual Network Conference on Bisexuality.

62. See Gary North and Karla Rossi, "Bi visibility in gay community takes 'dramatic' turn," *Anything That Moves*, no. 2, pp. 14–15 (Spring 1991).

63. Sharon Gonsalves, "On bisexuals in the lesbian community," *Bi Women*, vol. 7, no. 4, p. 1 (August/September 1989).

64. Reported by Loraine Hutchins, "A movement on the rise," *Anything That Moves*, no. 4, p. 26 (1992).

65. Gary North and Karla Rossi, "Bi visibility in gay community takes 'dramatic' turn," *Anything That Moves*, no. 2, pp. 14–15 (Spring 1991).

66. Carol A. Queen, "Out/Write '92 and Out/Look Magazine do it again— Bisexuals are Out/Raged," *Anything That Moves*, no. 4, pp. 14–15 (1992).

67. Paul Smith, "The straight poop: A political opinion column. Are we a movement yet?" *Anything That Moves*, no. 4, p. 11 (1992).

68. Statement made in Lani Kaahumanu's speech at the March on Washington in 1993. Reprinted in *Anything That Moves*, no. 5, pp. 16, 36 (1993).

69. This particular quote is taken from Laura M. Perez and Victor Raymond, "Bisexuals included in the March on Washington," *Anything That Moves*, no. 5, p. 15 (1993). This way of expressing the ludicrousness of the idea that bisexuals are half oppressed because they are only half-homosexual is, however, very common. Its first copyrighted appearance might be Robyn Ochs' "Gay Liberation is our liberation," p. 2, in Geller (1990), an altered version of "Gay liberation is our liberation" published in *Bi Women*, vol. 5, no. 4, p. 4 (August/September 1987).

70. Paul Smith, "The straight poop: A political opinion column," *Anything That Moves*, no. 2, p. 5 (Spring 1991).

71. Michele Moore, "Notes from all over," *Bi Women,* vol. 6, no. 1, p. 2 (February/March 1988).
72. Robyn Ochs and Pam Ellis, "The 4th annual lesbian, bisexual and gay studies conference: A call for papers and a call for action," *North Bi Northwest,* vol. 4, no. 1, p. 13 (February/March 1991).
73. The history of the Northampton controversy was also reported in *Anything That Moves,* no. 2 (Spring 1991).
74. Robyn Ochs and Pam Ellis, "The 4th annual lesbian, bisexual and gay studies conference: A call for papers and a call for action," *North Bi Northwest,* vol. 4, no. 1, pp. 1, 12, 13 (February/March 1991). See also Rebecca Kaplan and Annie Senghas, " . . . and bisexual (?) conference," *North Bi Northwest,* vol. 5, no. 1, pp. 4, 7 (February 1992).
75. Reported in *North Bi Northwest,* vol. 5, no. 2, p. 4 (April/May 1992).
76. A detailed account of the history behind bi inclusion in MOW 93 can be found in Lani Kaahumanu, "It's official! The 1993 March on Washington for Lesbian, Gay and Bi (yes!) Equal Rights and Liberation: April 25," *Anything That Moves,* no. 4, pp. 22–25 (1992).
77. Stephanie Berger, "Thinking about community: What do we want?" *Bi Women,* vol. 9, no. 5, p. 7 (October/November 1991).
78. Jim Frazin, "Kate Bornstein: On gender and belonging," *Anything That Moves,* no. 3, p. 21 (Summer 1991).
79. Naomi Tucker, "The natural next step: Including transgender in our movement," *Anything That Moves,* no. 4, p. 37 (1992).
80. *BiNet News,* December 15, 1992, p. 9.
81. Lenore Norrgard, "Are we still a women's group?" *North Bi Northwest,* vol. 4, no. 1, p. 7 (February/March 1991).
82. Beth Reba Weise, "Final decision on transsexuals in SBWN," *North Bi Northwest,* vol. 4, no. 2, p. 6 (April/May 1991).
83. Anabelle P., "Another final decision: Transsexuals in SBWN," *North Bi Northwest,* vol. 7, no. 2, p. 14 (April/May 1994).
84. Among the authors who have addressed the subject of feminist bisexuality or who have written in response to lesbian feminism are Dajenya (1991), Elliot (1991), and Schneider (1991). *Closer to Home: Bisexuality and Feminism* edited by Weise (1992) is entirely devoted to the subject of feminist bisexuality.
85. An example of this is a quote from Weise, in which she suggested that "[p]erhaps in some ways we are in a unique position to challenge yet another patriarchal ideology by being multi-cultural, multi-racial, multi-gendered, multi-experienced, multi-sexual." Weise provided no explanation of what being multi-everything has to do with challenging patriarchy. She did not have to, because she expected her audience to be cognizant of the connections between oppressions that feminism forged (Beth Reba Weise, "The bisexual community: Viable reality or revolutionary pipe dream?" *Anything That Moves,* no. 2, p. 21, Spring 1991).

• Bibliography •

Abbott, Sidney, & Barbara Love. 1971. "Is women's liberation a lesbian plot?" In *Woman in Sexist Society: Studies in Power and Powerlessness,* edited by Vivian Gornick & Barbara K. Moran, 601–621. New York: Basic Books.

———. 1972. *Sappho Was a Right-on Woman: A Liberated View of Lesbianism.* New York: Stein and Day.

Adam, Barry D. 1987. *The Rise of a Gay and Lesbian Movement.* Boston: Twayne Publishers.

Alice, Gordon, Debbie, & Mary. 1973/1991a. "Separatism." In *For Lesbians Only: A Separatist Anthology,* edited by Hoagland & Penelope, 31–40. London: Radical Feminist Lesbian Publishers, 1991. (Originally published in *Lesbian Separatism: An Amazon Analysis,* July 1973, Seattle.)

———. 1973/1991b. "Problems of our movement." In *For Lesbians Only: A Separatist Anthology,* edited by Hoagland & Penelope, 379–394. London: Radical Feminist Lesbian Publishers, 1991. (Originally published in *Lesbian Separatism: An Amazon Analysis,* July 1973, Seattle.)

Allen, Vernon L., & David A. Wilder. 1975. "Categorization, belief similarity, and intergroup discrimination." *Journal of Personality and Social Psychology,* 32, no. 6, 971–977.

Atkinson, Ti-Grace. 1969/1974. "Juniata I: The sacrificial lambs." In *Amazon Odyssey,* edited by Ti-Grace Atkinson, 25–40. New York: Links Books, 1974. (Originally given as a speech at Juniata College on February 20, 1969.)

———. 1970/1974. "Lesbianism and feminism: Justice for women as 'unnatural'." In *Amazon Odyssey,* edited by Ti-Grace Atkinson, 131–134. New York: Links Books, 1974. (Originally written at the request of the *New York Times* Op–Ed Page on Dec. 21, 1970, but never published by them.)

———. 1972/1973. "Lesbianism and feminism." In *Amazon Expedition: A Lesbian Feminist Anthology,* edited by Phyllis Birkby, Bertha Harris, Jill Johnston, Esther Newton, & Jane O'Wyatt, 11–14. Albion, CA: Times Change Press, 1973. (Originally published in 1972 in the *Village Voice.*)

Baker, Karin. 1992. "Bisexual feminist politics: Because bisexuality is not enough." In *Closer to Home: Bisexuality & Feminism,* edited by Elizabeth Reba Weise, 255–267. Seattle, WA: The Seal Press.

Beal, Frances M. 1970. "Double jeopardy: To be black and female." In *Sisterhood is Powerful: An Anthology of Writings from the Women's Liberation Movement,* edited by Robin Morgan, 382–396. New York: Random House.

Bell, Allan P., & Martin S. Weinberg. 1978. *Homosexualities: A Study of Diversity Among Men and Women.* New York: Simon and Schuster.

Bennett, Kathleen. 1992. "Feminist bisexuality: A both/and option for an either/or world." In *Closer to Home: Bisexuality & Feminism,* edited by Elizabeth Reba Weise, 205–231. Seattle, WA: The Seal Press.

Berson, Ginny. 1972/1991. "The Furies." In *For Lesbians Only: A Separatist Anthology,* edited by Hoagland & Penelope, 24–27. London: Radical Feminist Lesbian Publishers, 1991. (Originally published in *The Furies,* no. 1, January 1972, and in *Lesbianism and the Women's Movement,* ed. Nancy Myron & Charlotte Bunch. Baltimore: Diana Press, 1975.)

Billig, Michael, & Henri Tajfel. 1973. "Social categorization and similarity in intergroup behavior." *European Journal of Social Psychology,* 3, no. 1, 27–52.

Birmingham Revolutionary Feminist Group, anonymous member. 1981. "Letter." In *Love Your Enemy? The Debate between Heterosexual Feminism and Political Lesbianism,* 33–35. London: Onlywomen Press Ltd. (First published in Birmingham women's liberation newsletter and *Wires 94.*)

Blumstein, Philip W., & Pepper Schwartz. 1974. "Lesbianism and bisexuality." In *Sexual Deviance and Sexual Deviants,* edited by Erich Goode and R. Troiden, 278–295. New York: William Morrow.

———. 1976a. "Bisexuality in men." *Urban Life,* 5, no. 3 (October), 339–358.

———. 1976b. "Bisexuality in women." *Archives of Sexual Behavior,* vol. 5, 171–181.

———. 1977a. "Bisexual women." In *The Social Psychology of Sex,* edited by J. P. Wiseman, 154–162. New York: Harper and Row.

———. 1977b. "Bisexuality: Some social psychological issues." *Journal of Social Issues,* 33, no. 2, 30–45.

Boswell, John. 1990. "Concepts, experience, and sexuality." In *Forms of Desire: Sexual Orientation and the Social Constructionist Controversy,* edited by Edward Stein, 133–173. New York: Garland Publications.

Brierley, Harry. 1984. "Gender identity and sexual behavior." In *The Psychology of Sexual Diversity,* edited by Kevin Howells. New York: Basil Blackwell.

Brown, Rita Mae. 1972/1975. "The shape of things to come." In *Lesbianism and the Women's Movement,* edited by Nancy Myron & Charlotte Bunch, 69–77. Baltimore, MD: Diana Press, 1975. (First written on behalf of The Furies and published in 1972 in *Women: A Journal of Liberation,* vol. 2, no. 4, 44–46.)

———. 1976a. "Coitus interruptus." In *A Plain Brown Rapper,* 29–34. Oakland, CA: Diana Press.

——— 1976b. "Say it isn't so." In *A Plain Brown Rapper,* 47–51. Oakland, CA: Diana Press.

———. 1976c. "Hanoi to Hoboken: A round trip ticket." In *A Plain Brown Rapper,* 63–71. Oakland, CA: Diana Press.

———. 1976d. "Living with other women." In *A Plain Brown Rapper,* 73–77. Oakland, CA: Diana Press.

———. 1976e. "Take a lesbian to lunch." In *A Plain Brown Rapper*, 79–95. Oakland, CA: Diana Press.

———. 1976f. "Roxanne Dunbar." In *A Plain Brown Rapper*, 119–128. Oakland, CA: Diana Press.

———. 1976g. "The Good Fairy." In *A Plain Brown Rapper*, 181–191. Oakland, CA: Diana Press.

Bullough, Vern. 1990. "The Kinsey Scale in historical perspective." In *Homosexuality/Heterosexuality: Concepts of Sexual Orientation*, edited by David P. McWhirter, Stephanie A. Sanders, & June Machover Reinisch, 3–14. New York: Oxford University Press.

Bullough, Vern, & Bonnie Bullough. 1977. *Sin, Sickness, and Sanity: A History of Sexual Attitudes.* New York: New American Library.

Bunch, Charlotte. 1972/1975. "Lesbians in revolt." In *Lesbianism and the Women's Movement*, edited by Nancy Myron and Charlotte Bunch, 29–37. Baltimore, MD: Diana Press, 1975. (First published in *The Furies*, January 1972.)

Cant, Bob, & Susan Hemmings, eds. 1988. *Radical Records: Thirty Years of Lesbian and Gay History, 1957–1987.* New York: Routledge.

Caplan, Pat. 1987. *The Cultural Construction of Sexuality.* New York: Tavistock Publications.

Carpenter, Val. 1988. "Amnesia and antagonism: Anti-lesbianism in the youth service." In *Radical Records: Thirty Years of Lesbian and Gay History, 1957–1987*, edited by Bob Cant & Susan Hemmings, 169–180. New York: Routledge.

C.L.I.T. Collective. 1974/1991. "C.L.I.T. statement #2." In *For Lesbians Only: A Separatist Anthology*, edited by Hoagland & Penelope, 357–367. London: Radical Feminist Lesbian Publishers, 1991. (Originally published in *off our backs*, 1974.)

Cloutte, Penny. 1981. "Letter." In *Love Your Enemy? The Debate between Heterosexual Feminism and Political Lesbianism*, 14–16. London: Onlywomen Press Ltd. (First published in *Wires 84.*)

Cook, Blanche Wiesen. 1977. "Female support networks and political activism: Lillian Wald, Crystal Eastman, Emma Goldman." *Chrysalis*, no. 3 (Autumn).

Cowan, Liza. 1978/1991. "Separatist symposium." In *For Lesbians Only: A Separatist Anthology*, ed. Hoagland & Penelope, 220–234. London: Radical Feminist Lesbian Publishers, 1991. (Originally published in *Dyke, A Quarterly*, no. 6 (Summer 1978), Tomato Publications.)

Dajenya. 1991. "Sisterhood crosses gender preference lines." In *Bi Any Other Name: Bisexual People Speak Out*, edited by Loraine Hutchins & Lani Kaahumanu, 247–251. Boston: Alyson Publications, Inc.

Daly, Mary. 1978. *Gyn/Ecology.* Boston: Beacon.

Damon, Gene. 1970. "The least of these: The minority whose screams haven't yet been heard." In *Sisterhood Is Powerful: An Anthology of Writings from the Women's Liberation Movement*, edited by Robin Morgan, 333–343. New York: Random House.

DeCecco, John P., & Michael G. Shively. 1983/84. "From sexual identity to sexual relationships: A contextual shift." *Journal of Homosexuality*, vol. 9, no. 2/3 (Winter 1983/Spring 1984), 1–26.

Diamond, Milton. 1993. "Homosexuality and bisexuality in different populations." *Archives of Sexual Behavior*, vol. 22, no. 4, 291–310.

Dixon, Janet. 1988. "Separatism: A look back at anger." In *Radical Records: Thirty Years of Lesbian and Gay History, 1957–1987*, edited by Bob Cant & Susan Hemmings, 69–84. New York: Routledge.

Echols, Alice. 1983. "The new feminism of Yin and Yang." In *Powers of Desire: The Politics of Sexuality*, edited by Ann Snitow, Cristine Stansell, & Sharon Thompson, 439–459. New York: Monthly Review Press.

———. 1984. "The taming of the id: Feminist sexual politics, 1968–1983." In *Pleasure and Danger: Exploring Female Sexuality*, edited by Carole S. Vance, 50–72. London: Routledge.

Elliot, Beth. 1991. "Bisexuality: The best thing that ever happened to lesbian-feminism?" In *Bi Any Other Name: Bisexual People Speak Out*, edited by Loraine Hutchins & Lani Kaahumanu, 324–328. Boston: Alyson Publications.

Ellis, Albert. 1954. *Sex Life of the American Woman and the Kinsey Report.* New York: Greenberg Publishers,

Epstein, Steven. 1987. "Gay politics, ethnic identity: The limits of social constructionism." *Socialist Review*, vol. 17, no. 2, 10–54.

Evans, David T. 1993. *Sexual Citizenship: The Material Construction of Sexualities*. New York: Routledge.

Faderman, Lillian. 1981. *Surpassing the Love of Men: Romantic Friendship and Love between Women from the Renaissance to the Present*. New York: William Morrow and Company.

———. 1991. *Odd Girls and Twilight Lovers: A History of Lesbian Life in Twentieth-Century America*. New York: Columbia University Press.

Feldman, M. P., & M. J. MacCulloch. 1971. *Homosexual Behavior: Therapy and Assessment*. Oxford: Pergamon.

Feldman, Philip. 1984. "The homosexual preference." In *The Psychology of Sexual Diversity*, edited by Kevin Howells. New York: Basil Blackwell.

Ferguson, Ann. 1981. "Patriarchy, sexual identity, and the sexual revolution." Published as part of Ann Ferguson, Jacquelyn N. Zita, & Kathryn Pyne Addelson. "On 'Compulsory heterosexuality and lesbian existence': Defining the issues." *Signs*, vol. 7, no. 1, 158–199.

Foucault, Michel. 1978. *The History of Sexuality: An Introduction. Volume I.* New York: Vintage Books.

———. 1979. *The History of Sexuality*. New York: Vintage Books.

Freimuth, Marilyn J., & Gail A. Hornstein. 1982. "A critical examination of the concept of gender." *Sex Roles*, vol. 8, no. 5, 515–532.

Friedland, Lucy, & Liz A. Highleyman. 1991. "The fine art of labeling: The convergence of anarchism, feminism, and bisexuality." In *Bi Any Other Name: Bisexual People Speak Out*, edited by Loraine Hutchins & Lani Kaahumanu, 285–298. Boston: Alyson Publications.

Frye, Marilyn. 1977/1983a. "Some reflections on separatism and power." First presented at a meeting of the Society for Women in Philosophy, Eastern Division, in December of 1977. First published in *Sinister Wisdom* 6, Summer 1978. Page citations in the current text are from pp. 95–109 in Marilyn Frye. 1983. *The Politics of Reality: Essays in Feminist Theory.* Trumansburg, NY: The Crossing Press.

———. 1983b. "Lesbian feminism and the gay rights movement: Another view of male supremacy, another separatism." In *The Politics of Reality: Essays in Feminist Theory,* 128–151. Trumansburg, NY: The Crossing Press.

———. 1983c. "To be and be seen: The politics of reality." In *The Politics of Reality: Essays in Feminist Theory,* 152–174. Trumansburg, NY: The Crossing Press. (Earlier version published under the title "To be and be seen: Metaphysical misogyny" in *Sinister Wisdom,* vol. 17, 57–70 (no date on publication).)

Gay Liberation Front Women. 1971/1972. "Lesbians and the ultimate liberation of women." In *Out of the Closets: Voices of Gay Liberation,* edited by Karla Jay & Allen Young, 201–203. New York: Douglas/Links, 1972. (Originally published as a mimeographed leaflet, under the title "GLF Women" in *Come Out!* vol. 1, no. 7, Dec. 1970–Jan. 1971.)

Gay Revolution Party Women's Caucus. 1971/1972. "Realesbians and politicalesbians." In *Out of the Closets: Voices of Gay Liberation,* edited by Karla Jay & Allen Young, 177–181. New York: Douglas/Links, 1972. (Originally published as "Realesbians, politicalesbians, and the women's liberation movement" in *Ecstasy,* June 1971.)

Gibian, Ruth. 1992. "Refusing certainty: Toward a bisexuality of wholeness." In *Closer to Home: Bisexuality & Feminism,* edited by Elizabeth Reba Weise, 3–16. Seattle, WA: The Seal Press.

Goodman, Gerre, George Lakey, Judy Lashof, & Erika Thorne. 1983. *No Turning Back: Lesbian and Gay Liberation for the '80s.* Philadelphia: New Society Publishers.

Gorgons. 1978/1991. "Response by the Gorgons." In *For Lesbians Only: A Separatist Anthology,* edited by Hoagland & Penelope, 394–398. London: Radical Feminist Lesbian Publishers, 1991. (Originally published in *Dyke, A Quarterly,* no. 6 (Summer 1978), Tomato Publications.)

Grimsditch, Dianne. 1981. "Letter." In *Love Your Enemy? The Debate between Heterosexual Feminism and Political Lesbianism,* 19–20. London: Onlywomen Press Ltd. (First published in *Wires 86.*)

Gregory, Debby. 1981. "Letter." In *Love Your Enemy? The Debate between Heterosexual Feminism and Political Lesbianism,* 40–44. London: Onlywomen Press Ltd.

Gutter Dyke Collective. 1973/1991. "Over the walls." In *For Lesbians Only: A Separatist Anthology,* edited by Hoagland & Penelope, 27–31. London: Radical Feminist Lesbian Publishers, 1991. (Originally published in *Dykes and Gorgons,* May/June 1973.)

Hamblin, Angela. 1983. "Is a feminist heterosexuality possible?" In *Sex and

Love: New Thoughts on Old Contradictions, edited by Sue Cartledge &
Joanna Ryan, 105–123. London: Women's Press.

Hart, John. 1984. "Therapeutic implications of viewing sexual identity in terms
of essentialist and constructionist theories." *Journal of Homosexuality,* vol. 9,
no. 4 (Summer), 39–51.

Heron, Gilly. 1981. In *Love Your Enemy? The Debate between Heterosexual
Feminism and Political Lesbianism,* 17–18. London: Onlywomen Press Ltd.
(First published in the *Brighton & Hove Women's Liberation Newsletter,*
February 1980.)

Hess, Katharine, Jean Langford, & Kathy Ross. 1981/1991. "Comparative separatism." In *For Lesbians Only: A Separatist Anthology,* edited by Hoagland
and Penelope, 125–132. London: Radical Feminist Lesbian Publishers, 1991.
(Originally published in 1981 in *Feminismo Primero: Un Ensayo Sobre Sepa-
ratismo Lesbiano/Feminism First: An Essay on Lesbian Separatism.* Trans. by
Helen Weber & Fabiola Rodríguez. Seattle, WA: Tsunami Press.)

Hoagland, Sarah. 1978. "Lesbian epistemology." Paper presented at Midwestern
Division of the Society for Women in Philosophy.

Hoffman, Richard J. 1983/84. "Vices, gods and virtues: Cosmology as mediating
factor in attitudes toward male homosexuality." *Journal of Homosexuality,*
vol. 9, no. 2/3, 27–44.

Hollibaugh, Amber, & Cherríe Moraga. 1981/1983. "What we're rollin around
in bed with: Sexual silences in feminism." In *Powers of Desire: The Politics of
Sexuality,* edited by Ann Snitow, Christine Stansell, & Sharon Thompson,
394–405. New York: Monthly Review Press, 1983. (First published in *Heresies,* no. 12 in 1981.)

Hooker, Evelyn. 1957. "The adjustment of the male overt homosexual." *Journal
of Projective Techniques,* vol. 21, 18–31.

———. 1958. "Male homosexuality in the Rorschach." *Journal of Projective
Techniques,* vol. 22, 33–54.

Hunt, Morton. 1974. *Sexual Behavior in the 1970's.* Chicago: Playboy Press.

Hutchins, Loraine, & Lani Kaahumanu, eds. 1991. *Bi Any Other Name: Bisexual People Speak Out.* Boston: Alyson Publications.

Irvine, Janice M. 1990. *Disorders of Desire: Sex and Gender in Modern American Sexology.* Philadelphia: Temple University Press.

Janus, Samuel S., & Cynthia L. Janus. 1993. *The Janus Report on Sexual
Behavior.* New York: John Wiley & Sons.

Jeffreys, Sheila. 1985. *The Spinster and Her Enemies: Feminism and Sexuality
1880–1930.* London: Zed Press.

Johnston, Jill. 1973. *Lesbian Nation: The Feminist Solution.* New York: Simon
and Schuster.

Johnson, Anne M., Jane Wadsworth, Kaye Wellings, & Julia Field. 1994. *Sexual
Attitudes and Lifestyles.* London: Blackwell Scientific Publications.

Jones, Beverly. 1970. "The dynamics of marriage and motherhood." In *Sisterhood is Powerful: An Anthology of Writings from the Women's Liberation
Movement,* edited by Robin Morgan, 49–66. New York: Random House.

Jones, Justine. 1981. "Why I liked screwing? Or, is heterosexual enjoyment based on sexual violence?" In *Love Your Enemy? The Debate between Heterosexual Feminism and Political Lesbianism,* 21–24. London: Onlywomen Press Ltd. (Paper first presented at Leeds Conference on Sexual Violence Against Women, November, 1981.)

Kaplan, Gisela T., & Lesley J. Rogers. 1984. "Breaking out of the dominant paradigm: A new look at sexual attraction." *Journal of Homosexuality,* vol. 10, no. 3/4, 71–75.

Kaplan, Rebecca. 1992. "Compulsory heterosexuality and the bisexual existence: Toward a bisexual feminist understanding of heterosexism." In *Closer to Home: Bisexuality & Feminism,* edited by Elizabeth Reba Weise, 269–280. Seattle, WA: The Seal Press.

Katz, Jonathan Ned. 1983. *Gay/Lesbian Almanac: A New Documentary.* New York: Harper & Row.

Kertbeny, K. M. 1969a. *Das Gemeinschadliche des Section 143 des Preuszichen Strafgesetzbuches vom 14 April 1851 und daher seine notwendige Tilgung als Section 152 im Entwurfe eines Strafgesetzbuches für den Norddeutschen Bund.* [The public nuisance section (Section 143) of the Prussian Penal Code from 14 April, 1851 and its necessary succession as Section 152 in the draft of a Penal code for the Confederation of North German states]. Leipzig: Serbe.

———. 1969b. *Section 142 des Preuszichen Strafgesetzbuches vom 14 April 1851 und seine Aufrechterhaltung als Section 152 im Entwurfe eines Strafgesetzbuches für den Norddeutschen Bund.* [Section 142 of the Prussian Penal code of April 14, 1851, and its continuation as Section 152 in the draft of a penal code for the Confederation of North German states]. Leipzig: Serbe. (Reprinted in 1905 by Magnus Hirschfeld in *Jahrbuch für sexuelle Zwischenstufen,* 6, 3–66.)

King, Katie. 1986. "The situation of lesbianism as feminism's magical sign: Contests for meaning and the U.S. women's movement, 1968–1972." *Communication,* vol. 9, no. 1 (Fall), 65–91.

Kinsey, Alfred C., Wardell B. Pomeroy, & Clyde E. Martin. 1948. *Sexual Behavior in the Human Male.* Philadelphia: W. B. Saunders.

Kinsey, Alfred C., Wardell B. Pomeroy, Clyde E. Martin, & Paul H. Gebhard. 1953. *Sexual Behavior in the Human Female.* Philadelphia: W. B. Saunders.

Kitzinger, Celia. 1987. *The Social Construction of Lesbianism.* Beverly Hills, CA: Sage.

Klein, Fred/Fritz. 1978. *The Bisexual Option: A Concept of One Hundred Percent Intimacy.* New York: Arbor House.

Klein, Fritz, Barry Sepekoff, & Timothy J. Wolf. 1985. "Sexual orientation: A multi-variable dynamic process." *Journal of Homosexuality,* vol. 11, no. 1/2, 35–49.

Koedt, Anne. 1971/1973. "Lesbianism and feminism." In *Radical Feminism,* edited by Anne Koedt, Ellen Levine, & Anita Rapone, 246–258. New York: Quadrangle Books, 1973. (Originally copyrighted by Anne Koedt and published in *Notes from the Third Year,* 1971.)

Laumann, Edward O., John H. Gagnon, Robert T. Michael, & Stuart Michaels. 1994. *The Social Organization of Sexuality: Sexual Practices in the United States*. Chicago: The University of Chicago Press.

Laws, Sophie. 1981. "Letter." In *Love Your Enemy? The Debate between Heterosexual Feminism and Political Lesbianism*, 12–13. London: Onlywomen Press Ltd. (First published in *Wires 83*.)

Leeds Revolutionary Feminist Group. 1979/1981. "Political lesbianism: The case against heterosexuality." In *Love Your Enemy? The Debate between Heterosexual Feminism and Political Lesbianism*, 5–10. London: Onlywomen Press Ltd., 1981. (First presented at a conference in September 1979, later published in *Wires 81*.)

———. 1981. "Afterwords from Leeds Revolutionary Feminists." In *Love Your Enemy? The Debate between Heterosexual Feminism and Political Lesbianism*, 66–68. London: Onlywomen Press Ltd.

LeVay, Simon. 1991. "A difference in hypothalamic structure between heterosexual and homosexual men." *Science*, vol. 253, no. 5023, 1034–1037.

Lewis, Sasha Gregory. 1979. *Sunday's Women: A Report on Lesbian Life Today*. Boston: Beacon Press.

Lorde, Audre. 1979. *Uses of the Erotic: The Erotic as Power*. Out & Out Books Pamphlet No. 3. New York: Out & Out Books.

———. 1983. "There is no hierarchy of oppressions." *Interracial Books For Children Bulletin*, vol. 14, no. 3/4, 9.

———. 1988/1990. "I am your sister: Black women organizing across sexualities." In *A Burst of Light*. Ithaca, NY: Firebrand Books. (Page citations in the current text are from pp. 321–325 in Gloria Anzaldúa, ed. 1990. *Making Face, Making Soul: Haciendo Caras*. San Francisco, CA: Aunt Lute Foundation Books.)

MacDonald, A.P. 1983. "A little bit of lavender goes a long way: A critique of research on sexual orientation." *Journal of Sex Research*, vol. 9, no. 1 (February), 94–100.

MacDonald Jr., A. P. 1981. "Bisexuality: Some comments on research and theory." *Journal of Homosexuality*, vol. 6, no. 3 (Spring), 21–35.

Maniscalco, Pauline. 1981. In *Love Your Enemy? The Debate between Heterosexual Feminism and Political Lesbianism*, 31–32. London: Onlywomen Press Ltd. (Written in June 1980, and first published in *Wires 92*.)

Marotta, Toby. 1981. *The Politics of Homosexuality*. Boston: Houghton Mifflin Company.

McIntosh, Mary. 1968. "The homosexual role." *Social Problems*, vol. 16.

Millett, Kate. 1970. *Sexual Politics*. London: Virago.

Money, John. 1987. "Sin, sickness, or status? Homosexual gender identity and psychoneuroendocrinology." *American Psychologist*, vol. 42, no. 4 (April), 384–399.

Myron, Nancy, & Charlotte Bunch. 1975. "Introduction." In *Lesbianism and the Women's Movement*, edited by Nancy Myron & Charlotte Bunch, 9–13. Baltimore, MD: Diana Press.

Norrgard, Lenore. 1991. "Can bisexuals be monogamous?" In *Bi Any Other*

Name: Bisexual People Speak Out, edited by Loraine Hutchins & Lani Kaahumanu, 281–284. Boston: Alyson Publications.

Packwood, Marlene. 1981. "Letter in response to Leeds Revolutionary Feminist Group's 'Political lesbianism' paper." Published as pp. 26–29 in *Love Your Enemy? The Debate between Heterosexual Feminism and Political Lesbianism.* London: Onlywomen Press Ltd.

Paul, Jay P. 1985. "Bisexuality: Reassessing our paradigms of sexuality." *Journal of Homosexuality,* vol. 11, no. 1/2 (Spring), 21–34.

Penelope, Julia. 1984/1991. "The mystery of lesbians." In *For Lesbians Only: A Separatist Anthology,* edited by Hoagland & Penelope, 506–547. London: Radical Feminist Lesbian Publishers, 1991. (Originally published in *Lesbian Ethics,* vol. 1, no. 1–3, 1984–1985.)

Pettitt, Ann. 1981. "Letter." In *Love Your Enemy? The Debate between Heterosexual Feminism and Political Lesbianism,* 14. London: Onlywomen Press Ltd. (First published in *Wires 83.*)

Pitman, Joy. 1981. "Letter." In *Love Your Enemy? The Debate between Heterosexual Feminism and Political Lesbianism,* 44–45. London: Onlywomen Press Ltd.

Plummer, Kenneth. 1975. *Sexual Stigma: An Interactionist Account.* Boston: Routledge and Kegan Paul.

———. 1981a. "Going gay: Identities, life cycles and lifestyles in the male gay world." In *The Theory and Practice of Homosexuality,* edited by Diane Richardson & John Hart. London: Routledge and Kegan Paul.

———. 1981b. "Homosexual categories: Some research problems in the labeling perspective of homosexuality." In *The Making of the Modern Homosexual,* edited by Kenneth Plummer. London: Hutchinson.

Purple September Staff, The. 1975. "The normative status of heterosexuality." In *Lesbianism and the Women's Movement,* edited by Nancy Myron & Charlotte Bunch, 79–83. Baltimore, MD: Diana Press.

Radicalesbians. 1970. "The woman-identified woman." Originally distributed at the Second Congress to Unite Women in 1970. Later published in 1972 in *The Ladder,* vol. 14, 6–8, and then reprinted in numerous publications. (Page citations in the current text are from pp. 49–55 in *Come Out! Selections from the Radical Gay Liberation Newspaper.* 1970. New York: Times Change Press.)

Reid, Coletta. 1975. "Coming out in the women's movement." In *Lesbianism and the Women's Movement,* edited by Nancy Myron & Charlotte Bunch, 91–103. Baltimore, MD: Diana Press.

Rich, Adrienne. 1980/1983. "Compulsory heterosexuality and lesbian existence." First published in *Signs: Journal of Women in Culture and Society,* vol. 5, no. 4. (Page citations in the current text are from pp. 177–205 in Ann Snitow, Christine Stansell, & Sharon Thompson, eds. 1983. *Powers of Desire: The Politics of Sexuality.* New York: Monthly Review Press.)

Richardson, Diane. 1983/84. "The dilemma of essentiality in homosexual theory." *Journal of Homosexuality,* vol. 9, no. 2/3 (Winter/Spring), 79–90.

———. 1992. "Constructing lesbian sexualities." In *Modern Homosexualities: Fragments of Lesbian and Gay Experience*, edited by Ken Plummer, 187–199. New York: Routledge.

Rickford, Frankie. 1981. "Letter." In *Love Your Enemy? The Debate between Heterosexual Feminism and Political Lesbianism*, 11–12. London: Onlywomen Press Ltd. (First published in *Wires 82*.)

Rogers, Susan M., & Charles R. Turner. 1991. "Male-male sexual contact in the U.S.A: Findings from five sample surveys, 1970–1990." *Journal of Sex Research*, vol. 28, no. 4, 491–519.

Ross, Michael W. 1984. "Beyond the biological model: New directions in bisexual and homosexual research." *Journal of Homosexuality*, vol. 10, no. 3/4, 63–70.

Ross, Michael W., & Jay P. Paul. 1992. "Beyond gender: The basis of sexual attraction in bisexual men and women." *Psychological Reports*, vol. 71, no. 3, 1283–1290.

Rust, Paula C. 1992a. "Who are we and where do we go from here?" In *Closer to Home: Bisexuality & Feminism*, edited by Elizabeth Reba Weise, 281–310. Seattle, WA: The Seal Press.

———. 1992b. "The politics of sexual identity: Sexual attraction and behavior among lesbian and bisexual women." *Social Problems*, vol. 39, no. 4, 366–386.

———. 1993a. " 'Coming out' in the age of social constructionism: Sexual identity formation among lesbian and bisexual women." *Gender & Society*, 7, no. 1, 50–77.

———. 1993b. "Neutralizing the political threat of the marginal woman: Lesbians' beliefs about bisexual women." *Journal of Sex Research*, vol. 30, no. 3, 214–228.

Rust-Rodríguez, Paula. 1989. *When Does the Unity of a "Common Oppression" Break Down? Reciprocal Attitudes between Lesbian and Bisexual Women*. Ph.D. Dissertation. University of Michigan. Ann Arbor, MI: University Microfilms International.

Schneider, Ann. 1991. "Guilt politics." In *Bi Any Other Name: Bisexual People Speak Out*, edited by Loraine Hutchins & Lani Kaahumanu, 275–278. Boston: Alyson Publications.

Seidman, Steven. 1993. "Identity and politics in a 'postmodern' gay culture: Some historical and conceptual notes." In *Fear of a Queer Planet: Queer Politics and Social Theory*, edited by Michael Warner, 105–142. Minneapolis: University of Minnesota Press.

Shelley, Martha. 1969/1970. "Notes of a radical lesbian." In *Sisterhood Is Powerful: An Anthology of Writings from the Women's Liberation Movement*, edited by Robin Morgan, 343–348. New York: Random House. (Earlier version published in 1969 in *Come Out: A Liberation Forum for the Gay Community*.)

Shively, Michael G., & John P. DeCecco. 1977. "Components of sexual identity." *Journal of Homosexuality*, vol. 3, no. 1, 41–48.

Shuster, Rebecca. 1991. "Beyond defense: Considering next steps for bisexual liberation." In *Bi Any Other Name: Bisexual People Speak Out,* edited by Loraine Hutchins & Lani Kaahumanu, 266–274. Boston: Alyson Publications.

Smith, Barbara. 1983. "Homophobia: Why bring it up?" *Interracial Books For Children Bulletin,* vol. 14, no. 3/4, 7–8.

Smith, Tom W. 1991. "Adult sexual behavior in 1989: Number of partners, frequency of intercourse and risk of AIDS." *Family Planning Perspectives,* vol. 23, no. 3, 102–107.

Smith-Rosenberg, Carroll. 1975. "The female world of love and ritual: Relations between women in 19th century America." *Signs,* vol. 1, no. 1, 1–29.

Snitow, Ann, Christine Stansell, & Sharon Thompson, eds. 1983. *Powers of Desire: The Politics of Sexuality.* New York: Monthly Review Press.

Solomon, Barbara. 1972/1975. "Taking the bullshit by the horns." In *Lesbianism and the Women's Movement,* edited by Nancy Myron & Charlotte Bunch, 39–47. Baltimore, MD: Diana Press, 1975. (First published in *The Furies,* March–April, 1972.)

Stein, Edward. 1990. *Forms of Desire: Sexual Orientation and the Social Constructionist Controversy.* New York: Garland.

Stone, Alexandra. 1981. "Statement." In *Love Your Enemy? The Debate between Heterosexual Feminism and Political Lesbianism,* 61. London: Onlywomen Press Ltd.

Sumpter, Sharon Forman. 1991. "Myths/realities of bisexuality." In *Bi Any Other Name: Bisexual People Speak Out,*" edited by Loraine Hutchins & Lani Kaahumanu, 12–13. Boston: Alyson Publications.

Trumbach, Randolph. 1977. "London's sodomites: Homosexual behavior and western culture in the 18th century." *Journal of Social History,* vol. 11, no. 1, 1–33.

———. 1990. "Review essay: Is there a modern sexual culture in the West; or, Did England never change between 1500 and 1900?" *Journal of the History of Sexuality,* vol. 1, no. 2, 296–309.

Tucker, Naomi. 1991. "What's in a name?" In *Bi Any Other Name: Bisexual People Speak Out,* edited by Loraine Hutchins & Lani Kaahumanu, 244–246. Boston: Alyson Publications.

Udis-Kessler, Amanda. 1990. "Bisexuality in an essentialist world." In *Bisexuality: A Reader and Sourcebook,* edited by Thomas Geller, 51–63. Ojai, CA: Times Change Press.

Ulmschneider, Loretta. 1973/1975. "Bisexuality." In *Lesbianism and the Women's Movement,* edited by Nancy Myron & Charlotte Bunch, 85–88. Baltimore, MD: Diana Press. (First published in *The Furies,* March–April 1973.)

Ulrichs, K. H. 1864. *"Vindex." Social-Juristische Studien über mannmännliche Geschlechtsliebe.* [Socio-legal studies on male-male sexual love]. Leipzig: Matthes.

———. 1865. *"Formatrix." Anthropologische Studien über urnische Liebe.* [Anthropological studies in homosexual love]. Leipzig: Matthes.

Vicinus, Martha. 1982. "Sexuality and power: A review of current work in the history of sexuality." *Feminist Studies*, vol. 8 (Spring), 133–156.

———. 1992. " 'They wonder to which sex I belong': The historical roots of the modern lesbian identity." *Feminist Studies*, vol 18., no. 3, 467–497.

Walby, Sylvia. 1990. *Theorizing Patriarchy*. Cambridge, MA: Basil Blackwell.

Warner, Michael. 1993. *Fear of a Queer Planet: Queer Politics and Social Theory*. Minneapolis: University of Minnesota Press.

Weeks, Jeffrey. 1981. "Discourse, desire and sexual deviance: Some problems in a history of homosexuality." In *The Making of the Modern Homosexual*, edited by K. Plummer. London: Hutchinson.

———. 1982. *Sex Politics and Society: The Regulation of Sexuality Since 1800*. London: Longman.

———. 1986. *Sexuality*. New York: Tavistock Publications.

Weise, Elizabeth Reba, ed. 1992. *Closer to Home: Bisexuality & Feminism*. Seattle, WA: The Seal Press.

Weitz, Rose. 1984. "From accommodation to rebellion: The politicization of lesbianism." In *Women-Identified Women*, edited by Trudy Darty & Sandee Potter, 233–248. Palo Alto, CA: Mayfield Publishing Co.

Wilkie, Liz. 1981. "Letter in response to Leeds Revolutionary Feminist Group's 'Political lesbianism' paper." Published as pp. 29–31 in *Love Your Enemy? The Debate between Heterosexual Feminism and Political Lesbianism*. London: Onlywomen Press Ltd. (First published in *Wires 92*.)

Wilson, Anna. 1981. "Statement." In *Love Your Enemy? The Debate between Heterosexual Feminism and Political Lesbianism*, 60–61. London: Onlywomen Press Ltd.

Wittig, Monique. 1981/1991. "One is not born a woman." In *For Lesbians Only: A Separatist Anthology*, edited by Hoagland & Penelope, 439–448. London: Radical Feminist Lesbian Publishers. (Originally published in *Feminist Issues*, vol. 1, no. 2, Winter 1981.)

Wolff, Charlotte. 1971. *Love Between Women*. New York: Harper and Row.

Wood, Jessica. 1981. "Letter to Onlywomen Press in response to Leeds Revolutionary Feminist Group's 'Political lesbianism' paper," written February, 1981. Published as pp. 51–54 in *Love Your Enemy? The Debate between Heterosexual Feminism and Political Lesbianism*. London: Onlywomen Press Ltd.

Wright, Janet. 1981. "Letter." In *Love Your Enemy? The Debate between Heterosexual Feminism and Political Lesbianism*, 32–33. London: Onlywomen Press Ltd. (First published in *Wires 93*.)

Zinik, Gary. 1985. "Identity conflict or adaptive flexibility? Bisexuality reconsidered." *Journal of Homosexuality*, vol. 11, no. 1/2, 7–19.

• SUBJECT INDEX •

Acquired Immune Deficiency Syndrome (AIDS), 19, 25–26, 31, 78, 243–244, 245

Advocate, The, 9, 10, 11, 12–15, 16, 18, 19, 21, 22, 321 nn. 8–13, 322 nn. 14–19

Age, 38, 103, 325–326 n. 2; of sample and survey staff, 5, 37, 40, 42–43, 45; diversity of in lesbian communities, 7, 8; age-ism, 71, 236, 338 n. 16; attitudes of lesbians of varying, 105–107, 111, 325 n. 2; attitudes of bisexuals of varying, 221

Amendment 2, Colorado, 246

Androgyny, 159, 241, 340 n. 45

Anything That Moves: Beyond the Myths of Bisexuality, 232, 235, 236, 243, 245, 337 n. 7, 338 nn. 9, 16, 339 nn. 22, 25, 26, 340 nn. 32, 38, 40, 341 nn. 47, 53, 54, 342 n. 62, 64–70, 343 nn. 73, 76, 78, 79, 85

Attractions, sexual or romantic: to same sex, 29, 54, 132, 166; to other sex, 28; monosexual, 16; to women and men, or bisexual, 12, 14, 16, 21, 28, 29, 32, 53–54, 60, 62–64, 69, 70–71, 79, 96, 112, 185, 195, 202, 205, 207–209, 228; to all genders, 240; regardless of gender, 209, 240, 242; same-sex versus other-sex, 29, 48–49, 212; bisexual compared to monosexual, 33; use in defining sexual orientation, or as related to sexual identity, 27–28, 32, 35, 43, 58, 104, 112, 194, 199, 204, 207, 325 n. 2; to women as the defining characteristic of lesbianism, 152, 158, 184, 194; as

irrelevant to sexual orientation, 68, 167, 184–185, 188, 189; as a consequence of political convictions, 140, 150–151, 190; as essential, 28; as constructed, 27–28, 323 n. 2; fluidity of, 31, 238; to men among lesbians, 17, 20, 21, 23; distribution among women in current study, 43–44, 222, 324 n. 6, 325 n. 7; to men among lesbians in current study, 44, 111; lesbians' beliefs about, 114–115, 118; political meaning ascribed to bisexual attraction by lesbians, 186–187, 190, 195–196, 198, 199; as related to lesbians' attitudes about bisexuality, 113–117, 120–122, 222–224, 326 n. 3; bisexuals' beliefs about, 213; as related to bisexuals' attitudes about bisexuality, 223. *See also* Lesbianism, desexualization of; Sex positivism

Bay Area Bisexual Network (BABN), 232, 236, 241

Bernhard, Sandra, 15

Bi Any Other Name: Bisexual People Speak Out, 2, 15

BiCentrist Alliance (BCA), 243, 247, 251

BiNet Newsletter, 235, 237

BiNet USA, 233, 235, 236, 237, 244, 249, 321 n. 1. *See also* North American Multicultural Bisexual Network

Biphobia, 251, 342 n. 61. *See also* Images of bisexuals

BiPOL, 1

Birmingham Revolutionary Feminist Group, 151–152, 158

357

358 SUBJECT INDEX

Bisexual: political movement, 1–2, 4, 15,
18, 22, 23, 230–232, 240–243, 245,
247–259; politics, 5, 15, 18, 19, 22, 23,
184–200, 215–218, 221–222, 225–226,
229, 230–259; inclusion in the lesbian/
gay movement, 15, 18, 19, 22, 23, 245–
247, 251, 259; identity, or identification
as, 5, 12, 16, 18, 35, 41–42, 44–45, 50,
65–68, 79–84, 85, 94, 98, 102, 185,
186, 188, 189, 190, 192, 194, 196–197,
203–204, 206, 213–215, 218, 226, 228,
232, 234, 235, 240, 242, 256, 257–258;
Label Avoidance Syndrome (BLAS),
245; bisexual identity among lesbians,
111–113, 117–122, 222, 325 n. 8; men,
14, 248. See also Bisexuals; Images of
bisexuals
Bisexual conferences: First International,
1; Third International, 2; BiPOL, 1
Bisexual Information and Counseling
Service, 14
Bisexuality: incidence, 29, 31; question of
the existence of, 1, 13, 14, 15, 29, 34,
47–57, 62, 71, 79, 83, 95, 102, 103–
104, 105, 106, 108–109, 112–113, 116,
184, 189, 190, 192, 193, 195, 198, 200,
202–207, 212, 228, 258, 325 n. 2,
326 n. 3; universal potential for, 33, 53–
57, 60, 70, 165–166, 192–193, 199,
203–206, 208, 210, 229, 255, 333 n.
44; definition of, or construction of the
meaning of, 4, 14, 47, 48–49, 51, 57–
71, 77, 94, 104, 112, 121, 184–200,
206, 207–210, 227, 228, 229, 234–235,
238, 241, 244, 250, 253, 336 n. 3;
desexualization of, 247, 254; definition
in terms of gender blindness, 22, 69–70,
71, 79, 199, 207, 209, 211, 228, 229,
240, 241; political, 242, 256
Bisexuals: as an ethnic group, 234–235,
239, 242, 250, 253–254, 258
Bisexual Visibility Day, 245
Bi Women, 233, 244, 245, 247, 248,
337 n. 1, 338 nn. 11–13, 16, 339 nn.
24, 29, 30, 340 nn. 35, 39, 43, 341 n.
46, 342 nn. 58, 60, 61, 63, 69, 343 nn.
71, 77
Black civil rights movement, 125, 144,
154, 171, 173

Bornstein, Kate, 19
Boston Bisexual Men's Network (BBMN),
248
Boston Bisexual Women's Network
(BBWN), 248
Bright, Susie, 157

Caucus, The, 136
Centers for Disease Control (CDC), 25, 31
Class, 38; of sample, 5, 37, 42, 45;
diversity of in lesbian communities, 7, 8;
classism, or oppression based on class,
137, 179–181, 236, 256, 258, 333 n.
48, 334 n. 55, 338 n. 16; attitudes of
lesbians of varying, 105, 111, 121;
attitudes of bisexuals of varying, 221;
women as a class, 149, 156, 164–165,
170, 175, 329 n. 22
Closer to Home: Bisexuality & Feminism,
2
Coming out, 13, 30, 44–45, 50, 66, 105–
107, 111, 113, 117–119, 120, 122, 125,
151, 221, 244, 245, 269, 325 n. 8. See
also Images of bisexuals, bisexuality as a
transitional phase
Congress to Unite Women, 153, 182
Continuum: lesbian, 168, 193, 335 n. 62;
feminist, 146; asexual-bisexual, 239

Daughters of Bilitis, 3, 29, 136, 178,
326 n. 2, 330 n. 26, 331 n. 35, 334 n.
52
Desire, sexual. See Attractions, sexual

Essence: essentialism versus social
constructionism, 27–28, 323 n. 2;
sexuality as, 4, 35, 167, 210, 238,
322 n. 1; lesbian, 169, 170, 194, 332 n.
35; bisexual, 95, 192, 203, 207, 209,
228; heterosexual as distinct from
homosexual, 33; lesbian women as
distinct from heterosexual women, 165;
whether identity should reflect sexual,
67–68; importance in ethnic political
tradition, 162–163, 231; lesbianism as
an ethnic, 171–182, 333 n. 49; gender
as, or essential womanhood, 127, 155–
156, 159–162, 191, 332 n. 39
Essentialism. See Essence

• AUTHOR INDEX •